D1002149

ARCHAEOLOGY

GARLAND REFERENCE LIBRARY
OF SOCIAL SCIENCE
(VOL. 54)

ARCHAEOLOGY
A Bibliographical Guide to the Basic Literature

Robert F. Heizer
Thomas R. Hester
Carol Graves

GARLAND PUBLISHING, INC. • NEW YORK & LONDON
1980

© 1980 Carol Graves; The Robert F. Heizer Estate;
and Thomas R. Hester
All rights reserved

Library of Congress Cataloging in Publication Data

Heizer, Robert Fleming, 1915–
   Archaeology, a bibliographical guide to the basic
literature.

   (Garland reference library of social science ;
v. 54)
   Includes index.
   1. Archaeology—Bibliography. I. Hester,
Thomas R., 1946–   joint author. II. Graves,
Carol, joint author. III. Title.
Z5131.H44   [CC165]   016.9301   77-83376
ISBN 0-8240-9826-9

Printed on acid-free, 250-year-life paper
Manufactured in the United States of America

822939

CONTENTS

PREFACE

Robert F. Heizer began plans for this bibliography in 1968. In February, 1969, he received a grant for the preparation of a "basic bibliography of archaeology" from the Wenner-Gren Foundation for Anthropological Research (New York; Grant No. 2336). Work was then initiated, and in 1971, Professor Heizer invited me to participate in the effort. The review and compilation of thousands of references continued until 1979, at which time the bibliography was assembled in manuscript. Professor Heizer died on July 18 of that year, following a long and valiant struggle with cancer. In late 1979, I asked Carol Graves to assist me in the completion of the bibliography. Her work has been instrumental in the culmination of this lengthy project.

Despite its title, this bibliography does not pretend to be complete, and we did not begin the project with the intention of listing every item that has ever been published within the discipline. Rather, our emphasis has been on those publications which are important reference and research aids. In some cases, our own research interests over the past decade are reflected in lengthier listings in some categories than in others. In addition, the bibliography is slanted toward New World and English-language publications, although we have made an effort to include reasonable coverage of the Old World, Africa, and Asia. We are certain to have missed or omitted important references; such omissions are unintentional.

Our goal in the preparation of this bibliography has been to assemble a guide to basic sources in the vast literature of archaeology. For beginning students or amateur archaeologists, there is a staggering body of literature to be confronted, and we hope we have selected those references which will lead them to further research in their areas of interest. There is also a rapidly growing involvement in archaeology among the general public, and we hope that this bibliography will be consulted as a reference volume in public libraries.

We believe that the bibliography will have the greatest value for professional archaeologists, for both teaching and research purposes. Anyone who has taught a college-level archaeology course knows the frequency with which students request lists of references for a particular subject area, especially when they are preparing term papers. This bibliography can show students where to start looking. Inter-library loan facilities can be used to obtain references not available in one's own campus library.

Archaeologists carrying out research projects can use the bibliography as an initial source for locating major publications relevant to their studies. In cultural resource management projects, lead time for project development is usually short, and so is the time allotted for report preparation. Perhaps the bibliography will be of assistance in this area by serving to pinpoint previously published data on certain topics.

The portions of this bibliography related to lithic technology, experiments, and petrographic studies were previously published (1) by Hester and Heizer as Addison-Wesley Module in Anthropology, No. 29 (1973); (2) by J.A. Graham, Heizer, and Hester, "A Bibliography of Replicative Experiments in Archaeology," and T.R. Hester, "Lithic Technology: An Introductory Bibliography" (Archaeological Research Facility, University of California, Berkeley, 1973); and (3) by Heizer and Graham, "Replicative Experiments in Archaeology," Studia Ethnographica et Folkloristica in Honorem Bela Gunda (Debrecen, Hungary, 1971). Because of the detailed nature of these publications, some of the references listed in them have not been included here. On the other hand, many sources published since 1973 have been added in those categories.

We are grateful to the Wenner-Gren Foundation and to its Director for Research, Dr. Lita Osmundsen, for supporting this work.

We would like to acknowledge the assistance of Susan Terauds, Elizabeth Jo Goode, Frieda Barefield, and Mary Lou Ellis for their help at various stages in the preparation of the bibliography. Our thanks are also extended to staff members at the Archaeological Research Facility, University of California,

Berkeley, and the Center for Archaeological Research, The University of Texas at San Antonio. Elizabeth G. Frkuska of the Center and Arnold Gutierrez (undergraduate student in Business Data Systems at The University of Texas at San Antonio) helped to prepare the index, and we extend our gratitude for their efforts in this arduous task.

The encouragement, cooperation, and patience offered by Garland Publishing, particularly by Ralph Carlson and Lawrence Davidow, are also gratefully acknowledged.

Thomas R. Hester
San Antonio, Texas
May 23, 1980

ARCHAEOLOGY

I. NATURE AND PURPOSE OF ARCHAEOLOGY

ADAMS, R. McC.

1 1968 Archeological Research Strategies: Past and Present.
        Science 160:1187-1192.

ANGEL, J.L.

2 1953 Classical Archaeology and the Anthropological Approach.
        In G.E. Mylonas and D. Raymond, eds., Studies Presented to
        David Moor Robinson:1224-1231. Washington University
        Press, St. Louis, Mo.

BRAIDWOOD, R.J.

3 1960 Archeologists and What They Do. Watts, New York.

CHILDE, V.G.

4 1933 Is Prehistory Practical? Antiquity 7:410-418.

5 1956 Piecing Together the Past. Praeger, New York.

6 1971 Progress and Archaeology. Greenwood Press, Westport, Conn.

CLARK, J.G.D.

7 1953 Archaeological Theories and Interpretations. In A.L.
        Kroeber, ed., Anthropology Today:343-360. University of
        Chicago Press, Chicago.

8 1954 The Study of Prehistory. Cambridge University Press, New
        York.

9 1970 Aspects of Prehistory. University of California Press,
        Berkeley.

10 1977 World Prehistory: In New Perspective, 3rd ed. Cambridge
        University Press, New York.

CLEATOR, P.E.

11 1957 The Past in Pieces: An Archaeological Appraisement. Allen
        & Unwin, London.

COPLEY, G.J.

12 1958 Going into the Past. Puffin Books P 5117, Harmondsworth,
        England.

DEETZ, J.

13 1967 Invitation to Archaeology. Natural History Press, Garden
        City, N.Y.

EHRICH, R.W.

14   1954   Anthropology in a Liberal-Arts Curriculum.   Journal for
            Higher Education 25:357-362.

FAGAN, B.M.

15   1978   Archaeology: A Brief Introduction.   Little, Brown and
            Company, Boston.

GOODWIN, A.J.H.

16   1946   The Terminology of Prehistory.   South African Archaeological
            Bulletin 1(4):91-100.

GORENSTEIN, S.

17   1965   Introduction to Archaeology.   Basic Books, New York.

GRIMES, W.G.

18   1954   The Scientific Bias of Archaeology.   The Advancement of
            Science 1(10):343-346.   London.

HAMMOND, A.L.

19   1974   The New Archaeology: Toward a Social Science.   Science 172
            (3988):1119-1120.

HAWKES, C.

20   1954   Archeological Theory and Method: Some Suggestions from the
            Old World.   American Anthropologist 56:155-168.

HESTER, T.R., R.F. HEIZER, and J.A. GRAHAM

21   1975   Field Methods in Archaeology.   6th ed.   Mayfield Publishing
            Co., Palo Alto, Cal.

HOLE, F., and R.F. HEIZER

22   1973   An Introduction to Prehistoric Archeology.   3rd ed.   Holt,
            Rinehart and Winston, New York.

ISAAC, G.L.

23   1972   Whither Archaeology?   Antiquity 65:123-129.

JENNINGS, J.D.

24   1973   The Social Uses of Archaeology.   Addison-Wesley Module in
            Anthropology 41.

McGIMSEY, C.R., III.

25   1972   Public Archeology.   Seminar Press, New York.

MacNEISH, R.S.

26   1978   The Science of Archaeology?   Duxbury Press, North Scituate,
            Mass.

MAGNUSSON, M.

27 1973 Introducing Archaeology. Henry Z. Walck, Inc., New York.

NEUSTUPNÝ, E.

28 1971 Whither Archaeology? Antiquity 64:34-39.

NICKERSON, G.S.

29 1972 The Implication of a Self-Fulfilling Prophecy in American Archaeology. American Antiquity 37(4):551-553.

PIGGOTT, S.

30 1959 Approach to Archeology. Harvard University Press, Cambridge, Mass.

PYDDOKE, E.

31 1964 What is Archaeology? Roy Publishers, New York.

RANDALL-MacIVER, D.

32 1933 Archaeology as a Science. Antiquity 7:5-20.

REDMAN, C.L., ed.

33 1973 Research and Theory in Current Archeology. John Wiley and Sons, New York.

ROE, D.

34 1972 Prehistory: An Introduction. University of California Press, Berkeley.

ROUSE, I.

35 1953 The Strategy of Culture History. In A.L. Kroeber, ed., Anthropology Today:57-76. University of Chicago Press, Chicago.

36 1972 Introduction to Prehistory: A Systematic Approach. McGraw-Hill, New York.

SHEPHERD, W.

37 1966 Archaeology. Signet, New American Library, New York.

SUMMERS, R.

38 1967 On the Interpretation of Archaeological Data. South Africa Journal of Science 3(8):343-345.

TALLGREN, A.M.

39 1937 The Method of Prehistoric Archaeology. Antiquity 11(42): 152-161.

TAYLOR, W.W.

40 1948 A Study of Archeology. American Anthropological Association, Memoir 69.

THOMAS, D.H.

41 1974 Predicting the Past: An Introduction to Anthropological
           Archaeology. Holt, Rinehart and Winston, New York.

TRIGGER, B.G.

42 1968 Beyond History: The Methods of Prehistory. Holt, Rinehart
           and Winston, New York.

43 1978 Time and Traditions: Essays in Archaeological Interpretation.
           Columbia University Press, New York.

WHEELER, R.E.M.

44 1950 What Matters in Archaeology? Antiquity 24:122-130.

45 1954 Archaeology from the Earth. Penguin Books, Harmondsworth,
           England.

WILLEY, G.R., and P. PHILLIPS

46 1958 Method and Theory in American Archaeology. University of
           Chicago Press, Chicago.

WILSON, D.

47 1975 The New Archaeology. Alfred A. Knopf, New York.

WILSON, J.A.

48 1942 Archaeology as a Tool in Humanistic and Social Studies.
           Journal of Near Eastern Studies 1:3-9.

WOOLLEY, L.

49 1958 History Unearthed. Ernest Benn, London.

50 1960 Digging Up the Past. 2nd ed. Pelican Books A4, Baltimore.

II. HISTORY OF ARCHAEOLOGY

BALLESTEROS GABROIS, M.

51 1960 Spanische archäologische Forschungen in Amerika im 18. Jahrhundert (Spanish Archaeological Investigations in America in the 18th Century). Tribus, Veroffentlichungen des Linden-Museums 9:185–190. Stuttgart.

BRATTON, F.G.

52 1972 A History of Egyptian Archaeology. Apollo Edition, Thomas Y. Crowell, New York.

BREUIL, H.

53 1941 The Discovery of the Antiquity of Man. Royal Anthropological Institute of Great Britain and Ireland, London.

CASSON, S.

54 1939 The Discovery of Man: The Story of the Inquiry into Human Origins. Harper and Bros., New York.

CERAM, C.W.

55 1958 The March of Archaeology. Alfred A. Knopf, New York.

CHILDE, V.G.

56 1944 The Future of Archaeology. Man 44:18–19.

57 1944 Historical Analysis of Archaeological Method (a Review of G. Daniel's The Three Ages). Nature 153:206–207.

CRAWFORD, O.G.S.

58 1932 The Dialectical Process in the History of Science. The Sociological Review 24:165–173. London.

59 1951 Archaeological History: A Review. Antiquity 25(97):9–12.

DANIEL, G.E.

60 1943 The Three Ages. Cambridge University Press, Cambridge, England.

61 1950 A Hundred Years of Archaeology. Macmillan, London.

62 1954 The Background to Antiquarianism and Archaeology. Archaeological Newsletter 5:1–4. London.

63 1959 The Idea of Man's Antiquity. Scientific American 201: 167–176.

64   1962   The Idea of Prehistory. Watts, London.

65   1966   Man Discovers His Past. Gerald Duckworth, London.

66   1967   The Origins and Growth of Archaeology. Penguin Books A885,
            Harmondsworth, England.

67   1971   The Origins and Growth of Archaeology. Apollo Edition,
            Thomas Y. Crowell, New York.

68   1975   A Hundred and Fifty Years of Archaeology. Gerald Duckworth,
            London.

DAUX, G.

69   1948   Les Étapes de l'Archéologie. Presses Universitaires de
            France, Paris.

De PAOR, L.

70   1967   Archaeology: An Illustrated Introduction. Penguin Books,
            Baltimore.

DEUEL, L.

71   1961   The Treasures of Time. Avon Books No. N-105, New York.

72   1967   Conquistadors Without Swords. St. Martin's Press, New
            York.

EYDOUX, H.P.

73   1968   History of Archaeological Discoveries. Leisure Arts Ltd.,
            London.

FAGAN, B.M.

74   1976   The Rape of the Nile: Tomb Robbers, Tourists, and
            Archaeologists in Egypt. Scribner's, New York.

FINEGAN, J.

75   1979   Archaeological History of the Ancient Middle East. Westview
            Press, Boulder, Colo.

FITTING, J.E., ed.

76   1973   The Development of North American Archaeology. Anchor
            Press, Doubleday, New York.

GATHERCOLE, P.

77   1971   Patterns in Prehistory: An Examination of the Later Thinking
            of V. Gordon Childe. World Archaeology 3(2):225-232.

GREENE, J.C.

78   1959   The Death of Adam. Iowa State University Press, Ames.

GRIFFIN, J.B.

79   1959   The Pursuit of Archeology in the United States. American
            Anthropologist 61:379-388.

GRIFFITHS, J.G.

80 1956 Archaeology and Hesiod's Five Ages. Journal of the History
          of Ideas 17:109-119.

HALLOWELL, A.I.

81 1960 The Beginnings of Anthropology in America. In F. de Laguna,
          ed., Selected Papers from the American Anthropologist 1888-
          1920:1-90. Harpers, New York.

HARRIS, M.

82 1968 The Rise of Anthropological Theory: A History of Theories
          of Culture. Thomas Y. Crowell, New York.

HEIZER, R.F.

83 1962 The Background of Thomsen's Three Age System. Technology
          and Culture 3:259-266.

84 1969 Man's Discovery of His Past. Peek, Palo Alto, Cal.

HODGSON, J.

85 1822 On the Study of Antiquities. Archaeologia Aeliana 1:ix-xix.

KENDRICK, T.D.

86 1950 British Antiquity. Methuen and Co., London.

KLINDT-JENSEN, O.

87 1975 A History of Scandinavian Archaeology. Thames and Hudson,
          London.

LYNCH, B.D., and T.F. LYNCH

88 1968 The Beginnings of a Scientific Approach to Prehistoric
          Archaeology in 17th and 18th Century Britain. Southwestern
          Journal of Anthropology 24:33-65.

MARSDEN, B.M.

89 1974 The Early Barrow-Diggers. Noyes Press, Park Ridge, N.J.

NELSON, N.C.

90 1937 Prehistoric Archaeology, Past, Present and Future. Science
          85:81-89.

PALLOTTINO, M.

91 1968 The Meaning of Archaeology. Thames and Hudson, London.

PEAKE, H.J.E.

92 1940 The Study of Prehistoric Times. Journal of the Royal
          Anthropological Institute 70:103-146. London.

PEET, T.E.

93 1943 The Great Tomb-Robberies of the Twentieth Egyptian Dynasty.
          Clarendon Press, Oxford.

PIGGOTT, S.

94   1937   Prehistory and the Romantic Movement.   Antiquity 11(41):31-38

95   1950   William Stukely, an Eighteenth-Century Antiquary.   Clarendon Press, Oxford.

96   1976   Ruins in a Landscape, Essays in Antiquarianism.   University Press, Edinburgh.

ROSS, J.B.

97   1938   A Study of Twelfth Century Interest in the Antiquities of Rome.   Medieval and Historiographical Essays in Honor of James Westfall Thompson:302-321.   University of Chicago Press, Chicago.

SCHUYLER, R.L.

98   1971   The History of American Archaeology: An Examination of Procedure.   American Antiquity 36(4):383-409.

SHORR, P.

99   1935   The Genesis of Prehistorical Research.   Isis 23:425-443.

SILVERBERG, R.

100   1964   Great Adventures in Archaeology.   Dial Press, New York.

SMITH, A.H.

101   1916   Lord Elgin and His Collection.   Journal of Hellenic Studies 36:163-372.

STIRLING, M.W.

102   1968   Early History of the Olmec Problem.   In Dumbarton Oaks Conference on the Olmec:1-8.   Dumbarton Oaks, Washington, D.C.

TAYLOR, W.W.

103   1954   Southwestern Archeology: Its History and Theory.   American Anthropologist 56:461-570.

TOULMIN, S., and J. GOODFIELD

104   1965   The Discovery of Time.   Harper and Row, New York.

TRIGGER, B.G.

105   1968   Major Concepts of Archaeology in Historical Perspective.   Man 3(4):527-541.

WACE, A.J.B.

106   1949   The Greeks and Romans as Archaeologists.   Société Royale d'Archéologie d'Alexandrie, Bulletin 38.

WATERS, H.B.

107   1934   The English Antiquaries of Sixteenth, Seventeenth and Eighteenth Centuries.   E. Walters, London.

WAUCHOPE, R.

108 1965 They Found Buried Cities. University of Chicago Press, Chicago.

WHEELER, M. (R.E.M.)

109 1957 A Book of Archaeology: Seventeen Stories of Discovery. Cassell, London.

110 1959 A Second Book of Archaeology. Cassell, London.

WILKINS, J.

111 1961 Worsaae and British Antiquities. Antiquity 35(139):214-220.

WILLEY, G.R.

112 1968 One Hundred Years of American Archaeology. In J.O. Brew, ed., One Hundred Years of Anthropology:29-56. Harvard University Press, Cambridge, Mass.

WILLEY, G.R., ed.

113 1974 Archaeological Researches in Retrospect. Winthrop Publishers, Inc., Cambridge, Mass.

WILLEY, G.R., and J.A. SABLOFF

114 1974 A History of American Archaeology. W.H. Freeman, San Francisco.

WILMSEN, E.N.

115 1965 An Outline of Early Man Studies in the United States. American Antiquity 31:172-192.

WILSON, T.

116 1899 The Beginnings of the Science of Prehistoric Anthropology. Proceedings, American Association for the Advancement of Science 48:309-353. Washington, D.C.

WORTHAM, J.D.

117 1971 The Genesis of British Egyptology, 1549-1906. University of Oklahoma Press, Norman.

III. THE WORK OF THE ARCHAEOLOGIST

A. APPROACHES TO PREHISTORY

BINFORD, L.R.

118 1962 Archaeology as Anthropology. American Antiquity 28:217-225.

BROTHWELL, D.R.

119 1962 The Scientific Revolution in Archaeology. Discovery 23: 22-27.

CALDWELL, J.R.

120 1959 The New American Archaeology. Science 129:303-307.

CHENHALL, R.G.

121 1971 Positivism and the Collection of Data. American Antiquity 36(3):372-373.

CLARK, J.G.D.

122 1953 The Economic Approach to Prehistory. Proceedings, British Academy 39:215-238.

123 1959 Perspectives in Prehistory. Proceedings, Prehistoric Society 25:1-14.

CLARKE, D.

124 1973 Archaeology: The Loss of Innocence. Antiquity 47(185):6-18.

DEETZ, J.F.

125 1970 Archeology as a Social Science. Bulletin of the American Anthropological Association 3:115-125.

EISENBERG, L.

126 1971 Anthropological Archaeology: Ethnography or Ethnology. Plains Anthropologist 16(54), Pt. 1:298-301.

FITTING, J.E.

127 1969 Whither Archaeology? A Review of Some Recent Literature. Michigan Archaeologist 15(4):113-120.

FLANNERY, K.

128 1972 The Cultural Evolution of Civilizations. Annual Review of Ecology and Systematics 3:399-426.

HARISS, J.C.

129 1971 Explanations in Prehistory. Proceedings, Prehistoric
           Society 37(1):38-55.

HIGHAM, C.F.W.

130 1969 Towards an Economic Prehistory of Europe. Current Anthro-
           pology 10(2-3):139-150.

HOGARTH, A.C.

131 1972 Common Sense in Archaeology. Antiquity 46:301-303.

KROEBER, A.L.

132 1931 Historical Reconstruction of Culture Growths and Organic
           Evolution. American Anthropologist 33:149-156.

McBURNEY, C.B.M.

133 1950 The Geographical Study of the Older Palaeolithic Stages
           in Europe. Proceedings, Prehistoric Society 16:163-183.

MARTIN, P.S.

134 1971 The Revolution in American Archaeology. American Antiquity
           36(1):1-8.

MEIRING, A.J.D.

135 1958 The Importance of a Biological Approach to Archaeology.
           South African Journal of Science 56(6):135-142.

PIGGOTT, S.

136 1965 Approach to Archaeology. McGraw-Hill Book Co., New York.

RENFREW, C.

137 1970 New Configurations in Old World Archaeology. World
           Archaeology 2:199-211.

ROUSE, I.

138 1965 The Place of "Peoples" in Prehistoric Research. Journal,
           Royal Anthropological Institute of Great Britain and
           Ireland 95(1-2):1-15.

SABLOFF, J.A., et al.

139 1973 Recent Developments in Archaeology. Annals of The
           American Academy of Political and Social Science 408:
           103-118.

SCHIFFER, M.B., ed.

140 1978- Advances in Archaeological Method and Theory, Vols. 1 and 2.
     1979 Academic Press, New York.

SCHWARTZ, D.W.

141 1968 An Overview and Initial Analysis of a Conceptual Inventory

of American Archaeology. Proceedings, 8th International Congress of Anthropological and Ethnological Sciences 3: 172-174.

STEWARD, J.H., and F.M. SETZLER

142 1938 Function and Configuration in Archaeology. American Antiquity 4:4-10.

STRONG, D.E., ed.

143 1973 Archaeological Theory and Practice. Academic Press, New York.

SUMMERS, R.

144 1967 Penelope: Or the Future of the African Archaeology. South African Journal of Science 63(4):125-130.

TRIGGER, B.G.

145 1978 Time and Traditions: Essays in Archaeological Interpretation. Columbia University Press, New York.

WATSON, P.J., S.A. LeBLANC, and C.L. REDMAN

146 1971 Explanation in Archeology. Columbia University Press, New York and London.

WELLS, L.H.

147 1962 A Prehistorian's Approach to Prehistory. In B.D. Malan and H.B.S. Cooke, eds., The Contribution of C. van Riet Lowe to Prehistory in Southern Africa. South African Archaeological Bulletin (Supplement) 17(65):82.

WHEELER, R.E.M.

148 1950 What Matters in Archaeology? Antiquity 24(95):122-130.

1. Models of Prehistoric Cultural Development and Change:
Evolution, Migration, and Invasion

ADAMS, R.M.

149 1956 Some Hypotheses on the Development of Early Civilizations. American Antiquity 21:227-232.

150 1966 The Evolution of Urban Society. Weidenfeld and Nicolson, London.

ADAMS, W.Y.

151 1968 Invasion, Diffusion, Evolution? Antiquity 42:194-215.

BOHMERS, A.

152 1964 Evolution and Archaeology I; Introduction. Palaeohistoria 10:1-2.

153 1964 Evolution and Archaeology II; Evolution, Revolution, and
           Epitomization. Palaeohistoria 10:3-14.

BRAIDWOOD, R.J.

154 1960 Levels in Prehistory: A Model for the Consideration of the
           Evidence. In S. Tax, ed., Evolution After Darwin:143-151.
           University of Chicago Press, Chicago.

CHANEY, R.P.

155 1972 Scientific Inquiry and Models of Socio-Cultural Data
           Patterning: An Epilogue. In D.L. Clarke, ed., Models in
           Archaeology:991-1032. Methuen and Co., London.

CHILDE, V.G.

156 1936 Man Makes Himself. Watts, London.

157 1944 Archaeological Ages as Technological Stages. Journal,
           Royal Anthropological Institute of Great Britain and
           Ireland 74, Pts. 1 and 2:7-24.

158 1951 Social Evolution. Watts, London.

CLARK, J.G.D.

159 1966 The Invasion Hypothesis in British Prehistory. Antiquity
           40:172-189.

CLARKE, D.L.

160 1972 Models and Paradigms in Contemporary Archaeology. In D.L.
           Clarke, ed., Models in Archaeology:1-60. Methuen and Co.,
           London.

DANIEL, G.E.

161 1941 The Dual Nature of the Megalithic Colonisation of
           Prehistoric Europe. Proceedings, Prehistoric Society
           7:1-49.

162 1971 From Worsaae to Childe: The Models of Prehistory.
           Proceedings, Prehistoric Society 37, Pt. 2:140-153.

DAUNCEY, K.D.M.

163 1942 The Strategy of Anglo-Saxon Invasion. Antiquity 16(61):
           51-63.

DIXON, R.B.

164 1928 The Building of Cultures. Scribner's, New York.

GLADWIN, H.S.

165 1931 Independent Invention versus Diffusion. American Antiquity
           3:156-160.

GROUBE, L.M.

166 1967 Models in Prehistory: A Consideration of the New Zealand

Evidence. Archaeology and Physical Anthropology in Oceania 2(1):1-27.

HAMMOND, N.

167 1971 Diffusion and Invention: An Example from Field Archaeology. Man 6:295-296.

HILL, J.N.

168 1972 The Methodological Debate in Contemporary Archaeology: A Model. In D.L. Clarke, ed., Models in Archaeology: 61-108. Methuen and Co., London.

KATZ, E., and M.L. LEVIN

169 1963 Traditions of Research in the Diffusion of Innovation. American Sociological Review 28:237-252.

KROEBER, A.L.

170 1944 Configurations of Culture Growth. University of California Press, Berkeley.

McKERN, W.C.

171 1939 The Midwestern Taxonomic Method as an Aid to Archaeological Culture Study. American Antiquity 4:301-313.

MEGGERS, B., ed.

172 1959 Evolution and Anthropology: A Centennial Appraisal. Anthropological Society of Washington, Washington, D.C.

MORGAN, L.H.

173 1875 Ethnical Periods. Proceedings, American Association for the Advancement of Science 24:266-274.

NUNLEY, P.

174 1971 Archaeological Interpretation and the Particularistic Model: The Coahuiltecan Case. Plains Anthropologist 16(54), Pt. 1:302-310.

PIGGOTT, S.

175 1960 Prehistory and Evolutionary Theory. In S. Tax., ed., Evolution After Darwin:85-98. University of Chicago Press, Chicago.

PITT-RIVERS, A.L.F.

176 1906 The Evolution of Culture and Other Essays. J.L. Myres, ed. Clarendon Press, Oxford.

RENFREW, C., ed.

177 1973 The Explanation of Culture Change: Models in Prehistory. Gerald Duckworth and Co. Ltd., London.

RILEY, C.L., J.C. KELLEY, C.W. PENNINGTON, and R.L. RANDS

178 1971 Man Across the Sea, Problems of Pre-Columbian Contact.
           University of Texas Press, Austin.

ROCK, J.T.

179 1974 The Use of Social Models in Archaeological Interpretation.
           Kiva 40(1-2):81-92.

ROUSE, I.

180 1957 Culture Area and Co-Tradition. Southwestern Journal of
           Anthropology 13:123-133.

181 1964 Archeological Approach to Cultural Evolution. In W.
           Goodenough, ed., Exploration in Cultural Anthropology:
           455-468. McGraw-Hill, New York.

ROWE, J.H.

182 1966 Diffusionism and Archaeology. American Antiquity 31:
           334-337.

SCHIFFER, M.B.

183 1976 Behavioral Archeology. Academic Press, New York.

SMITH, P.E.L.

184 1968 Explanation in Archeology. In S. Binford and L. Binford,
           eds., New Perspectives in Archeology:33-40. Aldine Pub-
           lishing Co., Chicago.

SOUTH, S.

185 1955 Evolutionary Theory in Archaeology. Southern Indian
           Studies 7:10-32. Chapel Hill, N.C.

STEWARD, J.H.

186 1955 Theory of Cultural Change. University of Illinois Press,
           Urbana.

187 1967 Cultural Evolution Today. Christian Century 84:203-207.

STOLTMAN, J.B.

188 1978 Temporal Models in Prehistory: An Example from Eastern
           North America. Current Anthropology 19(4):703-746.

WATSON, P.J., S.A. LeBLANC, and C.L. REDMAN

189 1974 The Covering Law Model in Archaeology: Practical Uses and
           Formal Interpretations. World Archaeology 6(2):125-132.

WHEELER, M. (R.E.M.)

190 1952 Archaeology and the Transmission of Ideas. Antiquity
           26(104):180-192.

WHITE, L.A.

191 1947 Evolutionary Stages, Progress, and the Evaluation of
           Cultures. Southwestern Journal of Anthropology 3:165-192.

192 1957 Evolution and Diffusion. Antiquity 124:214-218.

            2. The Processual Approach in Archaeology

BINFORD, L.R.

193 1963 "Red Ocher" Caches from the Michigan Area: A Possible
           Case of Cultural Drift. Southwestern Journal of
           Anthropology 19(1):89-108.

194 1965 Archaeological Systematics and the Study of Culture
           Process. American Antiquity 31(2), Pt. 1:203-210.

195 1968 Some Comments on Historical versus Processual Archaeology.
           Southwestern Journal of Anthropology 24(3):267-275.

196 1977 For Theory Building in Archaeology. Academic Press, New
           York.

BOULDING, K.

197 1956 General Systems Theory--The Skeleton of Science. Management
           Science 2:197-208.

BRAIDWOOD, R.J., and G. WILLEY

198 1962 Courses Toward Urban Life. Viking Fund Publications in
           Anthropology 32.

CALDWELL, J.R.

199 1958 Trend and Tradition in the Prehistory of the Eastern
           United States. Memoirs of the American Anthropological
           Association 88.

CHILDE, V.G.

200 1965 Man Makes Himself. Watts, London.

COLLINS, M.B.

201 1975 Sources of Bias in Processual Data: An Appraisal. In J.W.
           Mueller, ed., Sampling in Archaeology:26-32. University
           of Arizona Press, Tucson.

DETHLEFSEN, E., and J. DEETZ

202 1966 Death's Heads, Cherubs and Willow Trees: Experimental
           Archaeology in Colonial Cemeteries. American Antiquity
           31:502-510.

DORWIN, J.T.

203 1971 The Bowen Site: An Archaeological Study of Culture Process
           in the Late Prehistory of Central Indiana. Indiana Histori-
           cal Society, Prehistory Research Series 4(4). Indianapolis.

DRIVER, H.E.

204 1962 The Contribution of A.L. Kroeber to Culture Area Theory
           and Practice. Indiana University Publications in Anthro-
           pology and Linguistics Memoir 18.

FLANNERY, K.V.

205 1967 Culture History vs. Culture Process: A Debate in American
           Archaeology. Scientific American 217(2):119-122.

206 1968 Archeological Systems Theory and Early Mesoamerica. In
           B. Meggers, ed., Anthropological Archeology in the
           Americas:67-87. Anthropological Society of Washington.

207 1972 The Cultural Evolution of Civilizations. Annual Review
           of Ecology and Systematics 3:399-426.

FRITZ, J.M., and F.T. PLOG

208 1970 The Nature of Archaeological Explanation. American
           Antiquity 35(4):405-412.

GIBBON, G.E.

209 1972 Cultural Dynamics and the Development of the Oneota
           Life-Way in Wisconsin. American Antiquity 37(2):166-185.

HILL, J.N., ed.

210 1977 Explanation of Prehistoric Change. University of New
           Mexico Press, Albuquerque.

KELLEY, J.C.

211 1952 Factors Involved in the Abandonment of Certain Peripheral
           Southwestern Settlements. American Anthropologist 54:
           356-387.

KLEJN, L.S.

212 1977 A Panorama of Theoretical Archaeology. Current Anthro-
           pology 18(1):1-42.

KRAUSE, R.A., and R.M. THORNE

213 1971 Toward a Theory of Archaeological Things. Plains Anthro-
           pologist 16:245-257.

KROEBER, A.L.

214 1962 A Roster of Civilizations and Culture. Viking Fund
           Publications in Anthropology 33.

215 1963 Cultural and Natural Areas of Native North America.
           4th printing. University of California Press, Berkeley.

KUSHNER, G.

216 1970 A Consideration of Some Processual Designs for Archaeology
           as Anthropology. American Antiquity 35(2):125-132.

MARTIN, P.S., J.B. RINALDO, E. BLUHM, H.C. CUTLER, and R. GRANGE

217   1952   Mogollon Cultural Continuity and Change: The Stratigraphic
             Analysis of Tularosa and Cordova Caves. Fieldiana
             Anthropology 40. Chicago Natural History Museum, Chicago.

MORGAN, C.G.

218   1973   Archaeology and Explanation. World Archaeology 4(3):
             259-276.

MUNRO, R.

219   1897   Prehistoric Problems. W. Blackwood & Sons, London.

PLOG, F.T.

220   1974   The Study of Prehistoric Change. Academic Press, New York.

READ, D.W., and S.A. LeBLANC

221   1978   Descriptive Statements, Covering Laws, and Theoretical
             Archaeology. Current Anthropology 19(2):307-335.

RENFREW, C.

222   1969   Trade and Culture Process in European Prehistory. Current
             Anthropology 10(2-3):151-169.

223   1970- The Revolution in Prehistory. The Listener 1970:897-900;
      1971   1971:12-15.

SABLOFF, J., and G.R. WILLEY

224   1967   The Collapse of Maya Civilization in the Southern Lowlands:
             A Consideration of History and Process. Southwestern
             Journal of Anthropology 23:311-336.

SCHIFFER, M.B.

225   1972   Archaeological Context and Systemic Context. American
             Antiquity 37(2):156-165.

TUGGLE, H.D., A.H. TOWNSEND, and T.J. RILEY

226   1972   Laws, Systems, and Research Designs: A Discussion of
             Explanation in Archaeology. American Antiquity 37(1):
             3-12.

WATSON, R.

227   1972   The "New Archaeology" of the 1960's. Antiquity 46(183):
             210-215.

WILSON, H.C.

228   1963   An Inquiry into the Nature of Plains Indian Cultural
             Development. American Anthropologist 65:335-369.

3. The Direct Historical Approach in Archaeology

BAERREIS, D.A.

229   1961   The Ethnohistoric Approach and Archaeology. Ethnohistory
             8:49-77.

BROSE, D.S.

230   1971   The Direct Historic Approach to Michigan Archaeology.
             Ethnohistory 18(1):51-61.

HEIZER, R.F.

231   1941   The Direct-Historical Approach in California Archaeology.
             American Antiquity 7:98-122.

STEWARD, J.H.

232   1942   The Direct Historical Approach in Archaeology. American
             Antiquity 7:337-343.

STRONG, W.D.

233   1940   From History to Prehistory in the Northern Great Plains.
             Smithsonian Institution, Miscellaneous Collections 100:
             353-394.

WRIGHT, J.V.

233a 1968   The Application of the Direct-Historical Approach to the
             Iroquois and Ojibwa. Ethnohistory 15:96-111.

4. Ecological Approaches in Archaeology

ALTHIN, C.A.

234   1954   Man and Environment: A View of the Mesolithic Material in
             Southern Scandinavia. K.G.L. Hum. Vetenskap, Lund
             Arsberrattesle 6:269-293.

BARTH, F.

235   1950   Ecologic Adaptation and Cultural Change in Archaeology.
             American Antiquity 15:338-339.

BATES, M.

236   1953   Human Ecology. In A.L. Kroeber, ed., Anthropology Today:
             700-713. University of Chicago Press, Chicago.

BROSE, D.S.

237   1970   The Summer Island Site; A Study of Prehistoric Cultural
             Ecology and Social Organization in the Northern Lake
             Michigan Area. Studies in Anthropology 1, Case Western
             Reserve University, Cleveland, Ohio.

BUTZER, K.

238 1971 Environment and Archeology: An Ecological Approach to
Prehistory. Aldine Publishing Co., Chicago.

CLARK, J.D.

239 1964 The Influence of Environment in Inducing Culture Change
at the Kalambo Falls Prehistoric Site. South African
Archaeological Bulletin 19(76), Pt. 4:93-101.

CLARK, J.G.D.

240 1952 Prehistoric Europe: The Economic Basis. Methuen, London.

241 1953 The Economic Approach to Prehistory. Proceedings, British
Academy 39:215-238. London.

EISELEY, L.

242 1963 Man: The Lethal Factor. American Scientist 51(1):71-83.

FLANNERY, K.V.

243 1965 The Ecology of Early Food Production in Mesopotamia.
Science 147:1247-1256.

FLANNERY, K.V., and J. SCHOENWETTER

244 1970 Climate and Man in Formative Oaxaca. Archaeology 23(2):
144-152.

FORBIS, R.G., et al.

245 1969 Post-Pleistocene Man and His Environment on the Northern
Plains. University of Calgary Archaeology Association.

GORMAN, F.

246 1969 The Clovis Hunters: An Alternate View of Their Environment
and Ecology. Kiva 35(2):12-14.

HAWLEY, A.H.

247 1944 Ecology and Human Ecology. Social Forces 22:399-405.

HEIZER, R.F.

248 1955 Primitive Man as an Ecologic Factor. Kroeber Anthropological
Society Papers 13:1-31.

249 1970 Environment and Culture: The Lake Mojave Case. Southwest
Museum Masterkey 44(2):68-72.

HELM, J.

250 1962 The Ecological Approach in Anthropology. American Journal
of Sociology 47:630-639.

HIGHAM, C.F.W.

251 1970 The Role of Economic Prehistory in the Interpretation of
the Settlement of Oceania. In R. Green and M. Kelly, eds.,

Studies in Oceanic Culture History 1. Pacific Anthropological Records 11:165-174.

HOBLER, P.M., and J.J. HESTER

252 1968 Prehistory and Environment in the Libyan Desert. South African Archaeological Bulletin 23(92), Pt. 4:120-130.

HOLE, F., K.V. FLANNERY, and J.A. NEELY

253 1969 Prehistory and Human Ecology of the Deh Luran Plain: An Early Village Sequence from Khuzistan, Iran. Museum of Anthropology, University of Michigan, Memoirs 1. Ann Arbor.

KOWTA, M.

254 1969 The Sayles Complex; a Late Milling Stone Assemblage from Cajon Pass and the Ecological Implications of Its Scraper Planes. University of California Publications in Anthropology 6.

LARSON, V.

255 1970 Ecological Interpretation in Archaeological Reconstruction. Bulletin, Archeological Society of Connecticut 36:25-34.

McILWRAITH, T.F.

256 1955 The Relation of Man to Nature Through the Ages. Canadian Field Naturalist 69:71-73.

MALDE, H.E.

257 1964 The Ecologic Significance of Some Unfamiliar Geologic Processes. Reconstruction of Past Environments. Fort Burgwin Research Center, Report 3:7-15.

MEGGERS, B.J.

258 1954 Environmental Limitation on the Development of Culture. American Anthropologist 56:801-824.

MEIGHAN, C.W., et al.

259 1958 Ecological Interpretation in Archaeology. American Antiquity 24:1-23, 131-150.

NETTING, R.M.

260 1971 The Ecological Approach in Cultural Study. Addison-Wesley Publishing Company, Reading, Mass.

PULESTON, D.E., and O.S. PULESTON

261 1971 An Ecological Approach to the Origins of Maya Civilization. Archaeology 24(4):330-336.

RANDS, R.L.

262 1969 Mayan Ecology and Trade: 1967-1968. Southern Illinois University Press, Carbondale.

ROHN, A.H.

263 1963 An Ecological Approach to the Great Pueblo Occupation of the Mesa Verde, Colorado. Plateau 36:1-17.

SAPIR, O.L. de, and A.J. RANERE

264 1971 Human Adaptation to the Tropical Forests of Western Panama. Archaeology 24(4):346-354.

SARMA, A.

265 1977 Approaches to Paleoecology. W.C. Brown, Co., Dubuque, Iowa.

SAXON, A., and C. HIGHAM

266 1969 A New Research Method for Economic Prehistorians. American Antiquity 34:303-311.

SCHROEDER, A.H.

267 1968 Tentative Ecological and Cultural Factors and Their Effects on Southwestern Farmers. Contributions to Southwestern Prehistory 4, Proceedings VII, Congress, International Association for Quaternary Research. Eastern New Mexico University. Portales.

SIMMONS, I.G.

268 1969 Environment and Early Man at Dartmoor, Devon, England. Proceedings, Prehistoric Society 35:203-219.

SMITH, P.E.L.

269 1970 Ecological Archeology in Iran. A Review of F. Hole, K.V. Flannery, and J.A. Neely, Prehistory and Human Ecology of the Deh Luran Plain. Science 168:707-709.

SMITH, R.A. and J.W.

270 1970 Early Man and Environments in Northwest North America. University of Calgary Archaeology Association.

STRYD, A.H., and R.A. SMITH

271 1971 Aboriginal Man and Environment on the Plateau of Northwest America. University of Calgary Archaeology Association.

TAYLOR, W.W.

272 1958 The Pueblo Ecology Study: Hail and Farewell. Museum of Northern Arizona, Bulletin 30:1-77.

THOMAS, W.L., ed.

273 1956 Man's Role in Changing the Face of the Earth. University of Chicago Press, Chicago.

THOMPSON, D.F.

274 1939 The Seasonal Factor in Human Culture. Proceedings, Prehistoric Society 5:209-221.

TRIGGER, B.G.

275   1970   Archaeology and Ecology.   World Archaeology 2:321-336.

VICKERY, D.

276   1970   Evidence Supporting the Theory of Climatic Change and the
             Decline of Hopewell.   Wisconsin Archaeologist 51(2):57-76.

WARREN, C.N.

277   1968   Cultural Tradition and Ecological Adaptation on the Southern
             California Coast.   Eastern New Mexico University Contribu-
             tions in Anthropology 1(3):1-14.

WATSON, R.A., and P.J. WATSON

278   1969   Man and Nature: An Anthropological Essay in Human Ecology.
             Harcourt, Brace, and World, Inc., New York.

WOODBURY, R.B.

279   1963   Indian Adaptations to Arid Environments.   In C. Hodge, ed.,
             Aridity and Man.   American Association for the Advancement
             of Science, Publication 74.   Washington, D.C.

B. KINDS OF ARCHAEOLOGY

1. Prehistoric (General Surveys)

BANDI, H.

280   1969   Eskimo Prehistory.   University of Alaska Press, College.

BENSON, E.P.

281   1972   The Mochica: A Culture of Peru.   Praeger, New York.

BEUCHAT, H.

282   1912   Manuel d'Archéologie Américaine.   Librairie Alphonse Picard,
             Paris.

BRAIDWOOD, R.J.

283   1958   Near Eastern Prehistory.   Science 127:1419-1430.

BROSE, D.S., and N. GREBER, eds.

284   1980   Hopewell Archaeology: The Chillicothe Conference.   Kent
             State University Press, Kent, Ohio.

CHANG, D.C.

285   1968   Archeology of Ancient China.   Science 162(3853):519-526.

CLARK, J.D.

286   1970   The Prehistory of Africa.   Praeger, New York.

COE, M.D.
287 1962 Mexico. Praeger, New York.

COLE, S.
288 1963 The Prehistory of East Africa. Macmillan & Co., New York.

CORNWALL, I.W.
289 1964 The World of Ancient Man. John Day Co., New York.

DANIEL, G.
290 1955 Prehistory and Protohistory in France. Antiquity 116: 209-214.

EHRICH, R.W., ed.
291 1965 Chronologies in Old World Archaeology. University of Chicago Press, Chicago.

FAGE, J.D., and R.A. OLIVER, eds.
292 1970 Papers in African Prehistory. Cambridge University Press, Cambridge.

FAIRSERVIS, W.A.
293 1971 The Roots of Ancient India; the Archaeology of Early Indian Civilization. Macmillan & Co., New York.

FRANKFORT, H.A.
294 1950 The Birth of Civilization in the Near East. Doubleday and Co., Garden City, N.Y.

GRIFFIN, J.B., ed.
295 1952 The Archeology of Eastern United States. University of Chicago Press, Chicago.

JENNINGS, J.D., ed.
296 1978 Ancient Native Americans. W.H. Freeman, San Francisco.

LAMBERG-KARLOVSKY, C.C., ed.
297 1972 Old World Archaeology: Foundations of Civilization; Readings from Scientific American. W.H. Freeman, San Francisco.

LANNING, E.P.
298 1967 Peru Before the Incas. Prentice-Hall, Englewood Cliffs, N.J.

McCARTHY, F.D.
299 1949 The Prehistoric Cultures of Australia. Oceania 19(4): 305-319.

MEGGERS, B.J.
300 1972 Prehistoric America. Aldine-Atherton, Chicago.

MELLAART, J.

301 1965 Earliest Civilizations of the Near East. McGraw-Hill
           (Library of the Early Civilizations), New York.

MULVANEY, D.J.

302 1969 The Prehistory of Australia. Thames and Hudson, London.

MYLONAS, G.E.

303 1966 Mycenae and the Mycenaean Age. Princeton University
           Press, Princeton, N.J.

PENDLEBURY, J.D.

304 1939 The Archaeology of Crete. Methuen, London.

PETRIE, W.M.F.

305 1974 Prehistoric Egypt. J.L. Malter, Encino, Cal. (reprinted).

PIGGOTT, S.

306 1954 Neolithic Cultures of the British Isles. Cambridge
           University Press, Cambridge.

307 1965 Ancient Europe, from the Beginnings of Agriculture to
           Classical Antiquity; a Survey. Aldine Publishing Co.,
           Chicago.

RENFREW, C.

308 1972 The Emergence of Civilisation: The Cyclades and the Aegean
           in the Third Millennium B.C. Methuen, London.

ROUSE, I.

309 1972 Introduction to Prehistory. McGraw-Hill, New York.

SANDERS, W.T., and J. MARINO

310 1970 New World Prehistory. Archaeology of the American Indian.
           Prentice-Hall, Englewood Cliffs, N.J.

SULIMIRSKI, T.

311 1970 Prehistoric Russia: An Outline. John Baker, London.

THOMPSON, J.E.S.

312 1966 The Rise and Fall of Maya Civilization. Civilization of
           American Indians Series 39, University of Oklahoma Press,
           Norman.

VERMEULE, E.

313 1964 Greece in the Bronze Age. University of Chicago Press,
           Chicago.

WILLEY, G.R.

314 1966 An Introduction to American Archaeology, Vol. 1: North and

Middle America. Prentice-Hall, Englewood Cliffs, N.J.

315 1971 An Introduction to American Archaeology, Vol. 2: South
America. Prentice-Hall, Englewood Cliffs, N.J.

2. Salvage Archaeology
(Cultural resource management archaeology of
the last decade is covered on pp. 60-63.)

AVELEYRA ARROYO de ANDA, L.

316 1961 Protecting Mexico's Heritage. Archaeology 14(4):261-267.

BRETERNITZ, D.A.

317 1969 Rescue Archaeology at the Kainji Dam, Northern Nigeria.
Current Anthropology 10:136.

BREW, J.O.

318 1961 Salvage in River Basins: A World View. Archaeology 14(4):
232-235.

BROWN, J.L.

319 1967 An Experiment in Problem-Oriented Highway Salvage Archaeology. Kiva 33(2):60-66.

CORBETT, J.M.

320 1961 River Basin Salvage in the United States. Archaeology
14(4):236-240.

FORBIS, R.G.

321 1961 Rescuing the Past in Canada. Archaeology 14(4):257-261.

GREMINGER, H.C.

322 1961 Papers from a Training Program in Salvage Archaeology.
Papers in Anthropology. Museum of New Mexico Press, Santa
Fe.

HEIZER, R.F.

323 1966 Salvage and Other Archaeology. Southwest Museum Masterkey
40(2):54-60.

HESTER, J.J.

324 1963 A Training Program for Salvage Archaeology. American
Antiquity 28:392-394.

KING, T.F.

325 1971 A Conflict of Values in American Archaeology. American
Antiquity 36(3):255-262.

KING, T.F., R.E. SCHENK, and L.E. WILDESEN

326 1970 Audio-Visual Techniques in Emergency Salvage Archaeology.
American Antiquity 35(2):220-223.

LANGE, F.W., and K.K. SCHEIDENHELM

327 1972 The Salvage Archaeology of a Zoned Bichrome Cemetery,
           Costa Rica. American Antiquity 37(2):240-244.

LINDSAY, A.J., Jr.

328 1961 Saving Prehistoric Sites in the Southwest. Archaeology
           14(4):245-249.

LININGTON, R.E.

329 1961 Physics and Archaeological Salvage. Archaeology 14(4):
           287-292.

NÖEL HUME, I.

330 1961 Preservation of English and Colonial American Sites.
           Archaeology 14(4):250-256.

RAINEY, F.

331 1960 Archaeological Salvage in Egypt: An Example of International
           Cooperation. Expedition 2(4):2-3.

RIDLEY, F.

332 1961 Archaeological Conservation in China. Archaeology 14(4):
           277-283.

RITCHIE, W.A.

333 1961 Highway Construction and Salvage Problems. Archaeology
           14(4):241-244.

ROBERTS, F.H.H., Jr.

334 1952 Inter-Agency Archaeological Salvage Program: Results of
           Research in Various River Basins of the United States--
           Foreword. American Antiquity 17:297-298.

ROSS, H.M.

335 1966 Salvage Archaeology at a Mississippian Burial Ground.
           Missouri Archaeological Society, Research Series 4.

SCHUMACHER, P.J.F.

336 1962 The Archaeological Salvage Program in the United States.
           Akten des 34 Internationalen Amerikanistenkongresses:
           294-297.

SEARS, W.H.

337 1958 Highway Salvage Archaeology: Its Background and the Florida
           Program. In C.H. Fairbanks, ed., Florida Anthropology.
           Joint Publication, Florida Anthropological Society and
           Florida State University:57-60.

STEEN, C.R.

338 1956 The Archaeological Salvage Program Today. Archaeology
           9(3):175-181.

STEPHENSON, R.L.

339 1954 Salvage Anthropology. Bible Archaeological Digest 9(2):2-11.

WASLEY, W.W.

340 1960 Salvage Archaeology on Highway 66 in Eastern Arizona.
           American Antiquity 26:30-42.

341 1961 Techniques and Tools of Salvage. Archaeology 14(40):283-
           286.

WENDORF, F.

342 1962 A Guide for Salvage Archeology. Museum of New Mexico
           Press, Santa Fe.

                        3. Historic Archaeology

ALLEN, J.

343 1973 The Archaeology of Nineteenth-Century British Imperialism:
           An Australian Case Study. World Archaeology 5(1):44-60.

ASCHER, R.

344 1974 Tin-Can Archaeology. Historical Archaeology 8:7-16.

ASCHER, R., and C.H. FAIRBANKS

345 1971 Excavation of a Slave Cabin: Georgia, U.S.A. Historical
           Archaeology 5:3-17.

BAKER, V.G.

346 1978 Historical Archaeology at Black Lucy's Garden, Andover,
           Massachusetts: Ceramics from the Site of a Free, 19th
           Century Afro-American. Papers of the Robert S. Peabody
           Foundation for Archaeology 8.

BENNYHOFF, J.A., and A.B. ELSASSER

347 1954 Sonoma Mission: An Historical and Archaeological Study of
           Primary Constructions, 1823-1913. University of California,
           Archaeological Survey Report 27.

BOWER, B.A.

348 1977 Historical Archeology Investigations: A Methodology for
           Developing Insights into Colonial-Early American Life.
           Technology and Conservation 2(3):32-37.

BROSE, D.S.

349 1967 The Custer Road Dump Site: An Exercise in Victorian Archae-
           ology. Michigan Archaeologist 13(2):37-128.

BULLEN, A.K., and R.P. BULLEN

350 1945 Black Lucy's Garden. Bulletin, Massachusetts Archaeological
           Society 6(2):17-28.

CLELAND, C.E., and J.E. FITTING

351 1967 The Crisis of Identity: Theory in Historic Sites
           Archaeology. Conference on Historic Site Archaeology,
           Papers 1, Pt. 2:124-138.

COMBES, J.D.

352 1972 Ethnography, Archaeology and Burial Practices Among Coastal
           South Carolina Blacks. Conference on Historic Site
           Archaeology, Papers 7:52-61.

COTTER, J.L.

353 1957 Rediscovering Jamestown. Archaeology 10(1):25-30.

354 1958 Archaeological Excavations at Jamestown, Virginia.
           National Park Service, Archeological Research Series 4.
           Washington, D.C.

355 1962 Perils and Pleasures of Historic Sites Archaeology. South-
           eastern Archaeological Conference, Newsletter 9(1):46-49.

356 1976 Historical Archaeology: An Introduction. Archaeology
           29(3):150-151.

COTTER, J.L., compiler

357 1968 Handbook for Historical Archaeology, Pt. 1. J.L. Cotter,
           Wyncote, Pa.

COTTER, J.L., and E.B. JELKS

358 1957 Historic Site Archaeology at Jamestown. American Antiquity
           22:387-389.

DAVIS, E.M., and J.E. CORBIN

359 1967 Archeological Investigations at Washington-on-the-Brazos
           State Park in 1966. State Building Commission Archaeologi-
           cal Program Report 5. Austin.

DEAGAN, K.

360 1975 Archaeology at the National Greek Orthodox Shrine, St.
           Augustine, Florida. The University Presses of Florida,
           Gainesville.

361 1978 The Material Assemblage of 16th Century Spanish Florida.
           Historical Archaeology 12:25-50.

DEETZ, J.J.F.

362 1976 Black Settlement at Plymouth. Archaeology 29:207.

363 1977 In Small Things Forgotten: The Archaeology of Early
           American Life. Doubleday and Co., Garden City, N.Y.

DOLLAR, C.

364 1968 Some Thoughts on Theory and Method in Historical Archaeo-
           logy. The Conference on Historic Site Archaeology, Papers
           2(2):3-30.

365 1977 An Archaeological Assessment of Historic Davidsonville,
           Arkansas. Arkansas Archeological Survey Research Report 17.

FAIRBANKS, C.H.

366 1972 The Kingsley Slave Cabins in Duval County, Florida, 1968.
           The Conference on Historic Site Archaeology, Papers 7:62-93.

367 1976 Spaniards, Planters, Ships and Slaves: Historical Archae-
           ology in Florida and Georgia. Archaeology 29(3):164-172.

FERGUSON, L., ed.

368 1977 Historical Archaeology and the Importance of Material
           Things. The Society for Historical Archaeology, Special
           Publication Series 2.

FLEMING, R.L.

369 1971 After the Report, What? The Uses of Historical Archaeology,
           a Planner's View. Historical Archaeology 5.

FONTANA, B.L.

370 1965 On the Meaning of Historic Sites Archaeology. American
           Antiquity 31:61-65.

FONTANA, B.L., and J.C. GREENLEAF

371 1962 Johnny Ward's Ranch: A Study in Historic Archaeology.
           Kiva 28(1-2):1-115.

GILMORE, K.

372 1973 The Keeran Site: The Probable Site of La Salle's Fort
           St. Louis in Texas. Texas Historical Commission, Office
           of the State Archeologist, Report 24.

GLASSIE, H.

373 1975 Folk Housing in Middle Virginia: Structural Analysis of
           Historic Artifacts. The University of Tennessee Press,
           Knoxville.

GRIFFITHS, D.M.

374 1978 Use-Marks on Historic Ceramics: A Preliminary Study.
           Historical Archaeology 12:78-81.

HANDLER, J.S., and F.W. LANGE

375 1979 Plantation Slavery on Barbados, West Indies. Archaeology
           32(4):45-52.

HARRINGTON, J.C.

376 1952 Historic Site Archeology in the United States. In J.B.
           Griffin, ed., Archeology of the Eastern United States:
           335-344. University of Chicago Press, Chicago.

HEIZER, R.F.

377 1950 Observations on Historic Sites and Archaeology in California.
           Papers in California Archaeology 6. University of
           California Archaeological Survey Reports 9.

378 1972 California's Oldest Historical Relic? Robert H. Lowie
           Museum of Anthropology, University of California, Berkeley.

HULAN, R., and S.S. LAWRENCE

379 1970 Guide to the Reading and Study of Historic Site Archaeology.
           University of Missouri, Museum of Anthropology, Museum
           Briefs 5. Columbia.

JELKS, E.B.

380 1968 Observations on the Scope of Historical Archaeology.
           Historical Archaeology 2:1-4.

KELSO, W.M.

381 1979 Rescue Archaeology on the James: Early Virginia Life.
           Archaeology 32(5):15-25.

KELSO, W.M., and E.A. CHAPPELL

382 1974 Excavation of a Seventeenth Century Pottery Kiln at Glebe
           Garbor, Westmoreland County, Virginia. Historical
           Archaeology 8:53-63.

KENNEDY, J.I.

383 1969 Settlement in the South East Bay of Islands, 1772; a
           Study in Text-Aided Field Archaeology. Anthropology
           Department, University of Otago, Studies in Prehistoric
           Anthropology 3.

KIDD, K.E.

384 1954 Trade Goods Research Techniques. American Antiquity 20:1-8.

LARRABEE, E. McM.

385 1969 Historic Site Archaeology in Relation to Other Archaeology.
           Historical Archaeology 3:67-74.

LEWIS, K.E.

386 1976 Camden, a Frontier Town. University of South Carolina,
           Anthropological Studies 1.

LISTER, F.C., and R.H. LISTER

387 1978 The First Mexican Majolicas: Imported and Locally Produced.
           Historical Archaeology 12:1-24.

LYMAN, R.L.

388 1979 Analysis of Historic Faunal Remains. Historical Archaeol-
           ogy 11:67-73.

MILLER, G.L.

389   1971   Time Expended for Archaeological Excavation vs. Technical
             Analysis of Artifacts from the Franklin Glass Works Site,
             Kent, Ohio. Michigan Archaeologist 17(2):91-95.

MILLS, J.E.

390   1960   Historic Sites Archeology in the Fort Randall Reservoir,
             South Dakota. Bureau of American Ethnology, Bulletin 176:
             25-48.

MONTGOMERY, R.G., W. SMITH, and J.O. BREW

391   1949   Franciscan Awatovi. Harvard University, Peabody Museum
             Papers 36.

MORAN, G.P.

392   1976   Trash Pits and Natural Rights in the Revolutionary Era:
             Excavations at the Narbonne House in Salem, Massachusetts.
             Archaeology 29(3):194-202.

NÖEL HUME, I.

393   1968   Historical Archaeology. Alfred A. Knopf, New York.

OTTO, J.S.

394   1977   Artifacts and Status Differences: A Comparison of Ceramics
             from Planter, Overseer, and Slave Sites on an Antebellum
             Plantation. In Stanley South, ed., Research Strategies
             in Historical Archaeology:91-118. Academic Press, New York.

POWELL, B.B.

395   1968   Some Practical Aspects of Historical Archaeology. Maryland
             Archaeology 4(1):14-19.

REESE, K.M.

396   1979   Newscripts. Nondestructive Test Devised for Historic
             Adobe Walls. Chemical and Engineering News 57(42):60.

RITCHIE, W.A.

397   1954   Dutch Hollow, an Early Historic Period Seneca Site in
             Livingston County, New York. Researches and Transactions
             of the New York State Museum, Circular 40. Albany, N.Y.

SALWEN, B., and G.M. GYRISCO

398   1978   An Annotated Bibliography, Archeology of Black American
             Culture. 11593 Sepplement 3(1):1-4. Heritage Conserva-
             tion and Recreation Service, Washington, D.C.

SCHMIDT, P.R.

399   1978   Historical Archaeology: A Structural Approach in an African
             Culture. Greenwood Press, Westport, Conn.

SCHUYLER, R.L.

400 1970 Historical and Historic Sites Archaeology as Anthropology:
           Basic Definitions and Relationships. Historical Anthro-
           pology 4:83-89.

401 1979 Archaeological Perspectives on Ethnicity in America.
           Baywood Publishing Company, Inc., Farmingdale, N.Y.

SCHUYLER, R.L., ed.

402 1978 Historical Archaeology, a Guide to Substantive and
           Theoretical Contributions. Baywood Publishing Co.,
           Farmingdale, N.Y.

SMITH, G.H.

403 1960 Archeological Investigations at the Site of Fort Stevenson
           (32M21), Garrison Reservoir, North Dakota. Bureau of
           American Ethnology, Bulletin 176:159-238.

404 1960 Fort Pierre II (39ST217), a Historic Trading Post in the
           Oake Dam Area, South Dakota. Bureau of American Ethnology,
           Bulletin 176:83-158.

SOUTH, S.A.

405 1968 Photography in Historical Archaeology. Historical Archae-
           ology 2:73-113.

406 1974 Palmetto Parapets. Anthropological Studies 1, University
           of South Carolina.

407 1976 Method and Theory in Historical Archeology. Academic
           Press, New York.

SOUTH, S., ed.

408 1977 Research Strategies in Historical Archeology. Academic
           Press, New York.

STOLTMAN, J.B.

409 1974 Groton Plantation: An Archaeological Study of a South
           Carolina Locality. Peabody Museum Monograph 1. Cambridge,
           Mass.

STONE, L.M.

410 1970 Formal Classification and the Analysis of Historic Arti-
           facts. Historical Archaeology 4:90-102.

411 1974 Fort Michilimackinac, 1715-1781: An Archaeological Per-
           spective on the Revolutionary Frontier. Publications of
           the Museum of Michigan State University 2.

TOULOUSE, J.H., Jr.

412 1949 The Mission of San Gregorio de Abo. School of American
           Research Monograph 13, Santa Fe.

TREGANZA, A.E.

413 1956 Sonoma Mission: An Archaeological Reconstruction of the Mission San Francisco de Solano Quadrangle. Kroeber Anthropological Society Papers 14:1-18. Berkeley.

TUNNELL, C.D., and W.W. NEWCOMB, Jr.

414 1969 A Lipan Apache Mission, San Lorenzo de la Santa Cruz 1762-1771. Texas Memorial Museum Bulletin 14.

WERTENBAKER, T.J.

415 1953 The Archaeology of Colonial Williamsburg. Proceedings, American Philosophical Society 97:44-50.

WHITE, J.R.

416 1978 Bottle Nomenclature: A Glossary of Landmark Terminology for the Archaeologist. Historical Archaeology 12:58-77.

WILLIAMS, S.

417 1962 Historic Archaeology in the Lower Mississippi Valley. Southeastern Archaeological Conference Newsletter 9(1): 53-63.

WOOD, W.R.

418 1971 Biesterfeldt: A Post-Contact Coalescent Site on the Northeastern Plains. Smithsonian Contributions to Anthropology 15.

4. Underwater Archaeology

ARNOLD, J.B., III

419 1974 A Magnetometer Survey of the Steamboat Black Cloud. Bulletin, Texas Archeological Society 45:225-230.

420 1976 An Underwater Archeological Magnetometer Survey and Site Test Excavation Project Off Padre Island, Texas. Texas Antiquities Committee, Underwater Archeology Series 3. Austin.

421 1978 1977 Underwater Site Test Excavations Off Padre Island, Texas. Texas Antiquities Committee, Underwater Archeology Series 5. Austin.

ARNOLD, J.B., III, ed.

422 1978 Beneath the Waters of Time: Proceedings of the Ninth Conference on Underwater Archeology. Texas Antiquities Committee, Underwater Archeology Series 6. Austin.

ARNOLD, J.B., III, and R.S. WEDDLE

423 1978 The Nautical Archeology of Padre Island: The Spanish Shipwrecks of 1554. Texas Antiquities Committee, Underwater Archeology Series 7. Austin.

BASCOM, W.

424   1971   Deep-Water Archeology. Science 174:261-269.

BASS, G.F.

425   1961   The Cape Gelidonya Wreck: Preliminary Report. American
              Journal of Archaeology 65(3):267-276.

426   1966   Archaeology Under Water. Praeger, New York.

427   1968   A Diversified Program for the Study of Shallow Water
              Searching and Mapping Techniques. University of Pennsyl-
              vania Museum, Philadelphia.

428   1975   Archaeology Beneath the Sea. Walker and Co., New York.

BASS, G.F., and P. THROCKMORTON

429   1961   Excavating a Bronze Age Shipwreck. Archaeology 14(2):78-87.

BLAVATSKY, V.D.

430   1963   An Underwater Expedition to the Azov and Black Seas.
              Archaeology 16(2):93-98.

BORHEGYI, S.F. de

431   1957   Aqualung Archaeology. Natural History 67(3):120-125.

432   1957   Underwater Research in Guatemala. Archaeology 10(4):282-
              283.

433   1959   Underwater Archaeology in Guatemala. Congreso Internacional
              de Americanistas, Actas 2:229-240.

434   1959   Underwater Archaeology in Guatemala. Scientific American
              200(3):100-115.

435   1959   Underwater Archaeology in the Maya Highlands. Scientific
              American 200(3):100-113.

BUKOWSKI, Z.

436   1965   Remarks on Archaeological Underwater Research Based on the
              Example of a Settlement Within the Lake Pilakno, Mragowo
              District (North-Eastern Poland). Archaeologia Polona
              VIII:105-124.

CASSON, L.

437   1957   More Sea-Digging. Archaeology 10(4):248-257.

CLAUSEN, C.J., and J.B. ARNOLD III

438   1975   Magnetic Delineation of Individual Shipwreck Sites: A New
              Control Technique. Bulletin, Texas Archeological Society
              46:69-86.

CLAUSEN, C.J., et al.

439   1979   Little Salt Spring, Florida: A Unique Underwater Site.
              Science 203 (4381):609-614.

DAVIS, J.L.

440 1977 Treasure, People, Ships and Dreams: A Spanish Shipwreck on
           the Texas Coast. Texas Antiquities Committee, Underwater
           Archeology Series 4. Austin.

DUMAS, F.

441 1962 Deep Water Archaeology. Routledge and Kegan Paul, London.

ELLIS, H.

442 1847 On the Ruins of a City Submerged in the Sea on the Coast
           of Pomerania. Archaeologia 32:419-422.

EMERY, K.O.

443 1966 Early Man May Have Roamed the Atlantic Shelf. Oceanus 12:
           3-4.

EMERY, K.O., and R.L. EDWARDS

444 1966 Archaeological Potential of the Atlantic Continental Shelf.
           American Antiquity 31:733-737.

ERICSSON, C.H.

445 1972 A Sunken Russian Frigate. Archaeology 25(3):172-179.

FOSTER, E.J.

446 1970 A Diver-Operated Underwater Metal Detector. Archaeometry
           12:161-166.

FROST, H.

447 1963 Under the Mediterranean. Prentice-Hall, Englewood Cliffs,
           N.J.

GOGGIN, J.M.

448 1960 Underwater Archaeology: Its Nature and Limitations.
           American Antiquity 25:348-354.

GREEN, J.N., and C. MARTIN

449 1970 Metal Detector Survey of the Wreck of the Armada Ship
           Santa Maria de la Rosa. Prospezioni Archeologiche 5:
           95-100.

HALL, E.T.

450 1966 The Use of the Proton Magnetometer in Underwater
           Archaeology. Archaeometry 9:32-44.

451 1970 Survey Techniques in Underwater Archaeology. In The
           Impact of the Natural Sciences on Archaeology:121-124.
           Oxford University Press, London.

HAMILTON, D.L.

452 1976 Conservation of Metal Objects from Underwater Sites: A
           Study in Methods. Texas Antiquities Committee, Underwater
           Archeology Series 1. Austin.

HARDING, A.F.

453 1970 Pavlopetri: A Mycenaean Town Underwater. Archaeology 23(3):
           242-250.

HOLMQUIST, J.D., and A.H. WHEELER, eds.

454 1963 Diving into the Past: Theories, Techniques and Applications
           of Underwater Archaeology. Minnesota Historical Society
           and Council of Underwater Archaeology, St. Paul.

HUDSON, D.T.

455 1976 Marine Archaeology Along the Southern California Coast.
           San Diego Museum Papers 9.

JEWELL, D.P.

456 1961 Fresh-Water Archaeology. American Antiquity 26(3):414-416.

KAPITAN, G.

457 1966 A Bibliography of Underwater Archaeology. Argonaut,
           Chicago.

KATZEV, M.L.

458 1970 Kyrenia 1969: A Greek Ship Is Raised. Expedition 12(4):
           6-14.

KEITH, D.H.

459 1980 A Fourteenth-Century Shipwreck at Sinan-gun. Archaeology
           33(2):33-43.

KEITH, D.H., and D.A. FREY

460 1979 Saturation Diving in Nautical Archaeology. Archaeology
           32(4):24-33.

LEWIS, J.D.

461 1971 Marine Archaeology Symposium at Bristol, England. Archae-
           ology 24(4):361.

McCANN, A.M.

462 1972 A Fourth Century B.C. Shipwreck near Taranto. Archaeology
           25(3):180-187.

McDONALD, D., and J.B. ARNOLD III

463 1978 Documentary Sources for the Wreck of the New Spain Fleet
           of 1554. Texas Antiquities Committee, Underwater
           Archeology Series 8. Austin.

McGEHEE, M.S., B.P. LUYDENDYK, and D.E. BOEGMAN

464 1967 Location of Ancient Roman Shipwreck by Modern Acoustic
           Techniques. Report MPL-U-98/67. Marine Physical Labora-
           tory, University of California, San Diego.

MARSDEN, P.

465 1972 Archaeology at Sea. Antiquity 46(183):198-202.

MARSHALL, N.F., and J.R. MORIARTY

466 1964 Principles of Underwater Archaeology. Pacific Discovery
17(5):18-25.

MERLIN, A.

467 1930 Submarine Discoveries in the Mediterranean. Antiquity
4:405-414.

OLDS, D.L.

468 1976 Texas Legacy from the Gulf: A Report on 16th Century
Shipwreck Materials from the Texas Tidelands. A Joint
Publication of the Texas Memorial Museum, Miscellaneous
Papers 5 and the Texas Antiquities Committee, Underwater
Archeology Series 2. Austin.

OLSEN, S.J.

469 1961 Scuba as an Aid to Archeologists and Paleontologists.
Curator 4:371-378.

OWEN, D.I.

470 1970 Picking Up the Pieces: The Salvage Excavation of a Looted
Fifth Century B.C. Shipwreck in the Straits of Messina.
Expedition 13(1):24-29.

PETERSON, M.

471 1965 History Under the Sea, a Handbook for Underwater Exploration. Smithsonian Institution Press, Washington, D.C.

RACKL, H.

472 1968 Diving into the Past: Archaeology Under Water. Charles
Scribner's Sons, New York.

RYAN, E.J., and G.F. BASS

473 1962 Underwater Surveying and Draughting--a Technique.
Antiquity 36(144):252-261.

ST. DAVID'S, LORD BISHOP OF

474 1859 On Some Traditions Relating to the Submersion of Ancient
Cities. Transactions of the Royal Society of Literature
and Science 6:387-415.

SHERIDAN, R.E.

475 1979 Site Charting and Environmental Studies of the Monitor
Wreck. Journal of Field Archaeology 6(3):253-264.

SILVERBERG, R.

476 1963 Sunken History: The Story of Underwater Archeology.
Chilton, Philadelphia.

TAYLOR, J., ed.

477 1965 Marine Archaeology. Hutchinson, London..

THROCKMORTON, P.

478 1970 More Lost Ships. Expedition 13(1):35-40.

479 1971 Shipwrecks and Archaeology. Little, Brown and Company,
           Boston.

TUTHILL, C., and A.A. ALLANSON

480 1954 Ocean Bottom Artifacts. Southwest Museum Masterkey 28:
           222-232.

WHEELER, R.C., W.A. KENYON, A.R. WOOLWORTH, and D.A. BIRK

481 1975 Voices from the Rapids: An Underwater Search for Fur Trade
           Artifacts, 1960-73. Minnesota Historical Society,
           Minnesota Prehistoric Archaeology Series 3. St. Paul.

5. Industrial Archaeology

BIDDLE, M.

482 1965 Winchester, the Archaeology of a City. Science Journal,
           March:55-61.

BUCHANAN, R.A.

483 1970 Industrial Archaeology: Retrospect and Prospect. Antiquity
           64:281-287.

FOLEY, V.P.

484 1968 On the Meaning of Industrial Archaeology. Historical
           Archaeology 2:66-68.

HUDSON, K.

485 1963 Industrial Archaeology: An Introduction. John Baker, London.

486 1966 Industrial Archaeology: An Introduction. Humanities Press,
           New York.

487 1967 A Handbook for Industrial Archaeologists. John Baker,
           London.

488 1971 A Guide to the Industrial Archaeology of Europe. Dickinson
           University Press, Cranbury, N.J.

489 1978 Food, Clothes and Shelter: Twentieth Century Industrial
           Archaeology. John Baker, London.

490 1979 World Industrial Archaeology. Cambridge University Press,
           New York.

LEAVITT, T.W.

491 1969 Five Years of Industrial Archaeology. Technology and
           Culture 10(4):587-592.

McCUTCHEON, W.A.

492 1969 Industrial Archaeology and Technological Conservation in Northern Ireland. Technology and Culture 10(3):412-421.

SANDE, T.A.

493 1979 Industrial Archaeology and the Cause for Historic Preservation in the United States. Historical Archaeology 11:39-44.

494 1979 Industrial Archaeology: A New Look at the American Heritage. Penguin Books, New York.

VOGEL, R.M.

495 1969 On the Real Meaning of Industrial Archaeology. Historical Archaeology 3:87-92.

6. Classical Archaeology

ANGEL, J.L.

496 1946 Some Interrelations of Classical Archaeology with Anthropology. American Journal of Archaeology 50:401.

BANTI, L.

497 1960 Il Mondo degli Etruschi. Editrice Primato, Roma.

498 1973 Etruscan Cities and Their Culture. Translated by E. Bizzarri. University of California Press, Berkeley.

BARTOLONI, G.

499 1972 Le Tombe da Poggio Buco nel Museo Archeologico di Firenze (Monumenti Etruschi ser., Vol. 3). Leo S. Olschki for Istituto di Studi Etruschi ed Italici.

BEAZLEY, J.D., and B. ASHMOLE

500 1966 Greek Sculpture and Painting to the End of the Hellenistic Period. Cambridge University Press, Cambridge.

BERNABÒ BREA, L.

501 1964 Poliochni, Città Preistorica nell'Isola de Lemnos. "L'Erma," Roma.

BETANCOURT, P.P.

502 1977 Marine-Life Pottery from the Aegean. Archaeology 30(1): 38-43.

BLEGEN, C.W.

503 1937 Prosymna. The University Press, Cambridge.

504 1954 An Early Tholos Tomb in Western Messenia. Hesperia 23(2): 158-163.

BLEGEN, C.W., et al.

505   1966, The Palace of Nestor at Pylos in Western Messenia.   3 vols.
      1969, Princeton University Press, Princeton, N.J.
      1973

BOARDMAN, J.

506   1974 Athenian Black Figure Vases. Oxford University Press, New
            York.

506a 1975 Attic Red Figure Vases, the Archaic Period.   Thames and
            Hudson, London.

BRADFORD, J.

507   1957 The Changing Face of Europe: Classical and Medieval Town
            Plans.   In Ancient Landscapes, Studies in Field Archaeology.
            G. Bell and Sons, London.

508   1957 Roman Centuriation: A Planned Landscape.   In Ancient Land-
            scapes, Studies in Field Archaeology. G. Bell and Sons,
            London.

BROGAN, O.

509   1953 Roman Gaul. G. Bell and Sons, London.

BROWNE, E.A.

510   1925 Greek Architecture. Black, London.

BUCHHOLZ, H., and V. KARAGEORGHIS

511   1973 Prehistoric Greece and Cyprus: An Archaeological Handbook.
            Phaidon, London.

BUFORD, A.

512   1972 Craftsmen in Greek and Roman Society. Thames and Hudson,
            London.

CARPENTER, R.

513   1932 New Material for the West Pediment of the Parthenon.
            Hesperia 1.

514   1960 Greek Sculpture: A Critical Review. University of Chicago
            Press, Chicago.

CERAM, C.W.

515   1951 Gods, Graves, and Scholars. Alfred A. Knopf, New York.
            (See Section I.)

CHADWICK, J., et al.

516   1963 The Mycenae Tablets III. Transactions of the American
            Philosophical Society 52(7), Philadelphia.

CHEVALLIER, R.

517   1976 Roman Roads. Batsford, London.

COLDSTREAM, J.N., and G.L. HUXLEY, eds.

518 1972 Kythera: Excavations and Studies Conducted by the University of Pennsylvania Museum and the British School at Athens. Faber, London.

COOK, R.M.

519 1972 Greek Art: Its Development, Character and Influence. Weidenfeld and Nicolson, London.

CORBETT, P.E.

520 1959 The Sculpture of the Parthenon. Penguin Books, Baltimore.

COTTRELL, L.

521 1963 The Lion Gate (American edition: Realms of Gold). Evans Brothers, London.

DEMARGNE, P.

522 1964 The Birth of Greek Art. Translated by S. Gilbert and J. Emmons. Golden Press, New York.

DENNIS, G.

523 1883 The Cities and Cemeteries of Etruria. 2 vols. John Murray, London.

DESBOROUGH, V.

524 1964 The Last Mycenaeans and Their Successors; an Archaeological Survey. Clarendon Press, Oxford.

du BOULAY, J.

525 1974 Portrait of a Greek Mountain Village. Clarendon Press, Oxford.

ERICH, R.W., ed.

526 1966 Chronologies in Old World Archaeology. University of Chicago Press, Chicago.

EVANS, A.J.

527 1964 The Palace of Minos; a Comparative Account of the Successive Stages of the Early Cretan Civilization as Illustrated by the Discoveries at Knossos. 4 vols. Biblo and Tannen, New York.

FURTWANGLER, A., and H.L. URLICHS

528 1914 Greek and Roman Sculpture. Dent and Sons, London.

GARDNER, E.A.

529 1897 A Handbook of Greek Sculpture. Macmillan and Co., London.

GREENHALGH, P.A.L.

530 1973 Early Greek Warfare. University Press, Cambridge.

HALL, H.R.

531   1928   The Civilization of Greece in the Bronze Age.   Methuen and
             Co., London.

HAMMOND, N.G.L.

532   1967   A History of Greece to 322 B.C.   2nd ed.   Clarendon Press,
             Oxford.

533   1972   A History of Macedonia.   Clarendon Press, Oxford.

534   1973   Studies in Greek History.   Clarendon Press, Oxford.

535   1976   Migrations and Invasions in Greece and Adjacent Areas.
             Noyes Press, Park Ridge, N.J.

HARRIS, H.A.

536   1972   Sport in Greece and Rome.   Thames and Hudson, London.

HARRISON, E.B.

537   1967   Athena and Athens in the East Pediment of the Parthenon.
             American Journal of Archaeology 71.

HAWKES, C., and S. HAWKES, eds.

538   1973   Greeks, Celts and Romans: Studies in Venture and Resistance.
             Dent, London.

HEURGON, J.

539   1964   Daily Life of the Etruscans.   Weidenfeld and Nicolson,
             London.

HOOD, S.

540   1961   Tholos Tombs of the Aegean.   Antiquity 135:166-176.

541   1971   The Minoans: Crete in the Bronze Age.   Thames and Hudson,
             London.

HOOKER, J.T.

542   1977   Mycenaean Greece.   Routledge and Kegan Paul, London.

HOOPER, R.J.

543   1976   The Early Greeks.   Weidenfeld and Nicolson, London.

HUGHES, J.D.

544   1975   Ecology in Ancient Civilisations.   University of New
             Mexico Press, Albuquerque.

HUTCHINSON, R.W.

545   1962   Prehistoric Crete.   Penguin Books, Baltimore.

JEFFERY, L.H.

546   1976   Archaic Greece: The City States c. 700–500 B.C.   Ernest
             Benn, London.

KRAAY, C.M.

547   1976   Archaic and Classical Greek Coins.   University of California
             Press, Berkeley.

KURTZ, D.C., and J. BOARDMAN

548   1971   Greek Burial Customs.   Cornell University Press, Ithaca.

LAING, L.B.

549   1969   Coins and Archaeology.   Weidenfeld and Nicolson, London.

LANG, A.

550   1908   Homer and Anthropology.   In R.R. Marett, ed., Anthropology
             and the Classics.   Clarendon Press, Oxford.

LEVI, D.

551   1964   The Recent Excavations at Phaistos.   Studies in Mediter-
             ranean Archaeology 11.   Lund.

LLEWELLYN, P.

552   1971   Rome in the Dark Ages.   Faber, London.

McKAY, A.G.

553   1975   Houses, Villas and Palaces in the Roman World.   Thames and
             Hudson, London.

MacKENDRICK, P.

554   1960   The Mute Stones Speak: The Story of Archaeology in Italy.
             St. Martin's Press, New York.

555   1962   The Greek Stones Speak: The Story of Archaeology in Greek
             Lands.   St. Martin's Press, New York.

556   1972   Roman France.   St. Martin's Press, New York.

557   1975   The Dacian Stones Speak.   University of North Carolina
             Press, Chapel Hill.

MARINATOS, S.

558   1960   Crete and Mycenae.   Translated by J. Boardman; M. Hirmer,
             photographer.   H.N. Abrams, New York.

MATZ, F.

559   1958   Creta, Micene, Troia.   Editrice Primato, Roma.

560   1962   The Art of Crete and Early Greece; the Prelude to Greek
             Art.   Translated by A.E. Keep.   Crown Publishers, New York.

MELAN, E., ed.

561 1973 Temples and Sanctuaries of Ancient Greece: A Companion
           Guide. Thames and Hudson, London.

MYLONAS, G.

562 1957 Ancient Mycenae. Princeton University Press, Princeton,
           N.J.

563 1966 Mycenae and the Mycenaean Age. Princeton University
           Press, Princeton, N.J.

PALLOTTINO, M.

564 1940 Gli Etruschi. Colombo, Roma.

565 1971 Civiltà Artistica Etrusca-Italica. Sansoni, Florence.

566 1975 The Etruscans. J. Cremona, transl.; D. Ridgway, ed.
           Indiana University Press, Bloomington.

PALMER, L.R.

567 1963 The Interpretation of Mycenaean Greek Texts. Clarendon
           Press, Oxford.

568 1965 Mycenaeans and Minoans: Aegean Prehistory in the Light of
           the Linear B Tablets. 2nd ed. Alfred A. Knopf, New
           York.

RENFREW, C.

569 1978 The Mycenaean Sanctuary at Phylakopi. Antiquity 52(204):
           7-15.

RICHARDSON, E.

570 1964 The Etruscans: Their Art and Civilization. University of
           Chicago Press, Chicago.

RICHARDSON, L., Jr.

571 1977 The Libraries of Pompeii. Archaeology 30(6):394-402.

RICHTER, G.M.A.

572 1950 The Sculpture and Sculptors of the Greeks. Yale University
           Press, New Haven.

RIDGWAY, D.

573 1967- Archaeological Reports 14. Hellenic Society and British
     1968   School at Athens, London.

SCHACHERMEYR, F.

574 1964 Die Minoische Kultur des Alten Kreta. W. Kohlhammer,
           Stuttgart.

SCHLIEMANN, H.

575 1878 Mycenae: A Narrative of Researches and Discoveries at
           Mycenae and Tiryns. John Murray, London.

576 1886 Tiryns; the Prehistoric Palace of the Kings of Tiryns,
           the Results of the Latest Excavations. John Murray,
           London.

SCULLARD, H.H.

577 1967 The Etruscan Cities and Rome. Thames and Hudson, London.

SIMPSON, R.H.

578 1965 A Gazetteer and Atlas of Mycenaean Sites. Bulletin of the Institute of Classical Studies, University of London, Supplement 16.

STRONG, D.

579 1968 The Early Etruscans. Evans Brothers, London.

STUBBINGS, F.

580 1964 The Expansion of Mycenaean Civilization. Cambridge Ancient History II, Chapter xxii. Cambridge University Press, Cambridge.

SULIMIRSKI, T.

581 1970 The Sarmatians. Praeger, New York.

TAYLOUR, W.

582 1958 Mycenaean Pottery in Italy, and Adjacent Areas. Cambridge University Press, Cambridge.

583 1964 The Mycenaeans. Praeger, New York.

TOYNBEE, J.M.C.

584 1973 Animals in Roman Life and Art. Thames and Hudson, London.

TRENDALL, A.D.

585 1972- Archaeological Reports 19. Hellenic Society and British
    1973 School at Athens, London.

VERMEULE, E.

586 1966 Greece in the Bronze Age. University of Chicago Press, Chicago. (See the extensive bibliography on classical archaeology in Greece:328-383.)

Von MACH, E.

587 1914 Handbook of Greek and Roman Sculpture. Stanhope Press, Boston.

WACE, A.J.B.

588 1949 Mycenae, an Archaeological History and Guide. Princeton University Press, Princeton, N.J.

WACE, A.J.B., and M.S. THOMPSON

589 1912 Prehistoric Thessaly. Cambridge University Press, London.

WARREN, P.

590 1972 Myrtos: An Early Bronze Age Settlement in Crete. Thames

and Hudson, London, for the British School of Archaeology
at Athens.

WEINBERG, S.S.

591 1965 The Stone in the Aegean. Cambridge Ancient History I,
           Chapter X. Cambridge University Press, Cambridge.

WELLS, C.M., and E.M. WIGHTMAN

592 1980 Canadian Excavations at Carthage, 1976 and 1978: The
           Theodosian Wall, Northern Sector. Journal of Field
           Archaeology 7(1):43-64.

7. Biblical Archaeology

AKERMAN, J.Y.

593 1966 Numismatic Illustrations of the Narrative Portions of the
           New Testament. Argonaut, Chicago.

ALBRIGHT, W.F.

594 1942 Archaeology and the Religion of Israel. Johns Hopkins
           Press, Baltimore.

595 1957 From the Stone Age to Christianity: Monotheism and the
           Historical Process. 2nd ed. Johns Hopkins Press, Baltimore.

596 1961 The Archaeology of Palestine. Penguin Books, Harmondsworth,
           England.

597 1968 Archaeology and the Religion of Israel. 5th ed. Doubleday,
           Garden City, N.Y.

BARROIS, A.G.

598 1939, Manuel d'Archéologie Biblique, Vols. 1, 2. A. Picard,
1953   Paris.

BARTON, G.A.

599 1937 Archaeology and the Bible. American Sunday-School Union,
           Philadelphia.

BURROWS, M.

600 1941 What Mean These Stones? American Schools of Oriental
           Research, New Haven.

FRANK, H.T.

601 1971 Bible, Archaeology and Faith. Abingdon Press, New York.

FRANKEN, H.J., and C.A. FRANKEN-BATTERSHILL

602 1963 Primer of Old Testament Archaeology. Brill, Leiden.

FREEDMAN, D.N., and J.C. GREENFIELD

603 1971 New Directions in Biblical Archaeology. Doubleday, Garden
           City, N.Y.

GOEDICKE, H.

604 1971 Near Eastern Studies in Honor of William Foxwell Albright. Johns Hopkins Press, Baltimore.

GRAY, J.

605 1962 Archaeology and the Old Testament World. Thomas Nelson and Sons, London.

HARKER, R.

606 1973 Digging Up the Bible Lands. Henry Z. Walck, New York.

KENYON, K.M.

607 1965 Archaeology in the Holy Land. Ernest Benn, London.

608 1972 Royal Cities of the Old Testament. Schocken Books, New York.

609 1976 Jerusalem: Excavating 3000 Years of History. McGraw-Hill, New York.

610 1978 The Bible and Recent Archaeology. John Knox Press, Atlanta.

NEGEV, A., ed.

611 1972 Archaeological Encyclopedia of the Holy Land. Putnam, New York.

PARROT, A.

612 1955 Discovering Buried Worlds. Philosophical Library, New York.

PFEIFFER, C.F.

613 1969 The Dead Sea Scrolls and the Bible. Baker Studies in Biblical Archaeology. Baker Book House, Grand Rapids, Mich.

PRITCHARD, J.B.

614 1958 Archaeology and the Old Testament. Princeton University Press, Princeton, N.J.

SANDERS, J.A., ed.

615 1970 Near Eastern Archaeology in the Twentieth Century; Essays in Honor of Nelson Glueck. Doubleday, Garden City, N.Y.

TEICHER, J.L.

616 1963 Archaeology and the Dead Sea Scrolls. Antiquity 37(145): 25-30.

THOMAS, D.W.

617 1961 Documents from Old Testament Times. Harper Torchbooks TB 85, New York.

THOMPSON, J.A.

618 1962 The Bible and Archaeology. Paternoster Press, Erdmans Publishing Company, Grand Rapids.

WILLIAMS, W.G.

619 1965 Archaeology in Biblical Research. Abingdon Press, New
           York.

WRIGHT, G.E.

620 1947 Biblical Archaeology Today. Biblical Archaeologist 10:7-24.

621 1947 Tell en-Nasbeh. Biblical Archaeologist 10:69-77.

622 1957 Bringing Old Testament Times to Life. National Geographic
           112:833-864.

WRIGHT, G.E., and D.N. FREEDMAN, eds.

623 1961 The Biblical Archaeologist Reader. Quadrangle Books,
           Chicago.

8. Ethnoarchaeology

ACKERMAN, R.E.

624 1970 Archaeoethnology, Ethnoarchaeology, and the Problems of
           Past Cultural Patterning. In M. Lantis, ed., Ethnohistory
           in Southwestern Alaska and the Southern Yukon. Studies in
           Anthropology. University Press of Kentucky, Lexington.

ACKERMAN, R.E., and L.A. ACKERMAN

625 1973 Ethnoarchaeological Interpretations of Territoriality and
           Land Use in Southwestern Alaska. Ethnohistory 20(4):
           315-334.

ADAMS, W.H.

626 1973 An Ethnoarchaeological Study of a Rural American Community:
           Silcott, Washington. 1900-1930. Ethnohistory 20(4):
           335-346.

ARNOLD, D.

627 1971 Ethnomineralogy in Ticul; Yucatan Potters: Etics and Emics.
           American Antiquity 36:20-40.

ASCHER, R.

628 1962 Ethnography for Archeology; a Case from the Seri Indians.
           Ethnology 1:306-369.

629 1968 Time's Arrow and the Archaeology of a Contemporary Com-
           munity. In K.C. Chang, ed., Settlement Archeology:43-52.
           Palo Alto, Cal.

BALFET, H.

630 1965 Ethnographical Observations in North Africa and Archaeolog-
           ical Interpretation: The Pottery of the Maghreb. In F.R.
           Matson, ed., Ceramics and Man:161-177. Viking Fund Publica-
           tions in Anthropology 41.

BINFORD, L.R.

631 1978 Dimensional Analysis of Behavior and Site Structure: Learning from an Eskimo Hunting Stand. American Antiquity 43(3):330-361.

632 1978 Nunamiut Ethnoarchaeology. Academic Press, New York.

BLACKBURN, R.H.

633 1973 Okiek Ceramics: Evidence for Central Kenya Prehistory. Azania 7:55-70.

BOSHIER, A.K.

634 1965 Effects of Pounding by Africans of North-West Transvaal on Hard and Soft Stones. South African Archaeological Bulletin 20(3):131-136.

BRAIN, C.K.

635 1967 Bone Weathering and the Problem of Bone Pseudo-Tools. South African Journal of Science 63:97-99.

636 1967 Hottentot Food Remains and Their Bearing on the Interpretation of Fossil Bone Assemblages. Scientific Papers of the Namib Desert Research Station 37.

637 1969 The Contribution of the Namib Desert Hottentots to an Understanding of Australopithecine Bone Accumulations. Scientific Papers of the Namib Desert Research Station 39.

BUTZER, K.W., et al.

638 1979 Dating and Context of Rock Engravings in Southern Africa. Science 203:1201-1214.

CARMACK, R.M.

639 1973 Quichean Civilization: The Ethnohistoric, Ethnographic, and Archaeological Sources. University of California Press, Berkeley.

CARNEIRO, R.L.

640 1979 Tree Felling with the Stone Ax: An Experiment Carried Out Among the Yanomamo Indians of Southern Venezuela. In C. Kramer, ed., Ethnoarchaeology:21-58. Columbia University Press, New York.

CARPENTER, R.

641 1974 The Flint Knapper. The American Rifleman 122(12).

CLARKE, R.

642 1935 The Flint-Knapping Industry at Brandon. Antiquity 9(33): 38-56.

CLEWLOW, C.W., and A.G. PASTRON

643 1974 Ethno-Archaeology and Acculturation: Problems in Historic Period Archaeology at Grass Valley and Ethnographic

Observations Among the Tarahumara of North Mexico. Nevada
Archeological Survey, Research Paper 5.

CRADER, D.C.

644 1974 The Effects of Scavengers on Bone Material from Large
           Mammals: An Experiment Conducted Among the Bisa of Luangwa
           Valley, Zambia. In C.B. Donnan and C.W. Clewlow, eds.,
           Ethnoarchaeology:161-173. UCLA Institute of Archaeology,
           Monograph 4.

CRANSTONE, B.A.L.

645 1971 The Tifalmin: A Neolithic People in New Guinea. World
           Archaeology 3(2):132-142.

DAVID, N.

646 1971 The Fulani Compound and the Archaeologist. World Archae-
           ology 3(2):111-131.

DAVID, N., and N. HENNIG

647 1972 The Ethnography of Pottery; a Fulani Case Seen in Archaeo-
           logical Perspective. Addison-Wesley Module in Anthropology
           21:1-29.

DeBOER, W., and D.W. LATHRAP

648 1979 The Making and Breaking of Shipibo-Conibo Ceramics. In
           C. Kramer, ed., Ethnoarchaeology:102-138. Columbia Univer-
           sity Press, New York.

DONNAN, C.B.

649 1971 Ancient Peruvian Potter's Marks and Their Interpretation
           Through Ethnographic Analogy. American Antiquity 36:460-
           465.

DONNAN, C.B., and C.W. CLEWLOW, Jr.

650 1974 Ethnoarchaeology. Monograph 4, Institute of Archaeology,
           University of California at Los Angeles.

EBERT, J.I.

651 1979 An Ethnoarchaeological Approach to Reassessing the Meaning
           of Variability in Stone Tool Assemblages. In C. Kramer,
           ed., Ethnoarchaeology:59-74. Columbia University Press,
           New York.

GALLAGHER, J.P.

652 1977 Contemporary Stone Tools in Ethiopia: Implications for
           Archaeology. Journal of Field Archaeology 4(4):407-414.

GIFFORD, D.P.

653 1978 Ethnoarchaeological Observations of Natural Processes
           Affecting Cultural Materials. In R.A. Gould, ed., Explora-
           tions in Ethnoarchaeology:77-102. University of New Mexico
           Press, Albuquerque.

GOULD, R.A.

654 1967 Notes on Hunting, Butchering and Sharing of Game Among the Ngatatjara and Their Neighbors in the West Australian Desert. Kroeber Anthropological Society, Papers 36:41-66.

655 1968 Chipping Stones in the Outback. Natural History 77:42-49.

656 1968 Living Archaeology: The Ngatatjara of Western Australia. Southwestern Journal of Anthropology 24:101-122.

657 1971 The Archaeologist as Ethnographer: A Case from the Western Desert of Australia. World Archaeology 3(2):143-178.

658 1973 Australian Archaeology in Ecological and Ethnographic Perspective. Warner Modular Publications in Anthropology 7:1-33.

659 1978 Beyond Analogy in Ethnoarchaeology. In R.A. Gould, ed., Explorations in Ethnoarchaeology:249-294. University of New Mexico Press, Albuquerque.

660 1978 From Tasmania to Tucson: New Directions in Ethnoarchaeology. In R.A. Gould, ed., Explorations in Ethnoarchaeology:1-10. University of New Mexico Press, Albuquerque.

661 1979 Review of Nunamiut Ethnoarchaeology. Science 204:737-739.

GOULD, R.A., ed.

662 1978 Explorations in Ethnoarchaeology. University of New Mexico Press, Albuquerque.

GOULD, R.A., D.A. KOSTER, and A.H.L. SONTZ

663 1971 The Lithic Assemblage of the Western Desert Aborigines. American Antiquity 36:149-169.

HEIDER, K.G.

664 1967 Archaeological Assumptions and Ethnographic Facts: A Cautionary Tale from New Guinea. Southwestern Journal of Anthropology 23:52-64.

HEIZER, R.F.

665 1962 Village Shifts and Tribal Spreads in California. Southwest Museum Masterkey 36:60-67.

HILTON-SIMPSON, M.W.

666 1920 Gun-Flint Making in Algeria. Man 20:33-34.

HOLE, F.

667 1978 Pastoral Nomadism in Western Iran. In R.A. Gould, ed., Explorations in Ethnoarchaeology: 127-168. University of New Mexico Press, Albuquerque.

668 1979 Rediscovering the Past in the Present: Ethnoarchaeology in Luristan, Iran. In C. Kramer, ed., Ethnoarchaeology:192-218. Columbia University Press, New York.

HOLLAND, W.R., and R.J. WEITLANER

669 1960 Modern Cuicatec Use of Prehistoric Sacrificial Knives.
           American Antiquity 25:392-396.

JAMES, C.D., III, and A.J. LINDSAY, Jr.

670 1973 Ethnoarchaeological Research at Canyon Del Muerto,
           Arizona: A Navajo Example. Ethnohistory 20(4):361-374.

KIRCH, P.V.

671 1978 Ethnoarchaeology and the Study of Agricultural Adaptation
           in the Humid Tropics. In R.A. Gould, ed., Explorations
           in Ethnoarchaeology:103-126. University of New Mexico
           Press, Albuquerque.

KLEINDIENST, M.R., and P.J. WATSON

672 1956 Action Archeology: The Archeological Inventory of a
           Living Community. Anthropology Tomorrow 5:75-78. Chicago.

KOHL, P.L.

673 1977 A Note on Chlorite Artefacts from Shahr-i Sokhta. East
           and West 27(1-4):111-127. Rome.

KRAMER, C.

674 1979 An Archaeological View of a Contemporary Kurdish Village:
           Domestic Architecture, Household Size, and Wealth. In
           C. Kramer, ed., Ethnoarchaeology:139-163. Columbia
           University Press, New York.

675 1979 Introduction. In C. Kramer, ed., Ethnoarchaeology:1-20
           (good bibliography, pp. 13-20). Columbia University Press,
           New York.

KRAMER, C., ed.

676 1979 Ethnoarchaeology: Implications of Ethnography for Archae-
           ology. Columbia University Press, New York.

LANGE, F.W., and C.R. RYDBERG

677 1972 Abandonment and Post-Abandonment Behavior at a Rural
           Central American House-Site. American Antiquity 37:419-434.

LEE, R., and I. DeVORE

678 1968 Man the Hunter. Aldine, Chicago.

LEES, S.H.

679 1979 Ethnoarchaeology and the Interpretation of Community
           Organization. In C. Kramer, ed., Ethnoarchaeology:265-
           276. Columbia University Press, New York.

LISTER, F.C., and R.H. LISTER

680 1972 Making Majolica Pottery in Modern Mexico. El Palacio 78:
           21-32.

LONGACRE, W.A.

681 1974 Kalinga Pottery-Making: The Evolution of a Research Design. In M.J. Leaf, Frontiers of Anthropology:51-67. Van Nostrand, New York.

LONGACRE, W.A., and J.E. AYRES

682 1968 Archeological Lessons from an Apache Wickiup. In S. Binford and L. Binford, eds., New Perspectives in Archeology:151-159. Aldine, Chicago.

LOVETT, E.

683 1877 Notice of the Gun Flint Manufactory at Brandon, with Reference to the Bearing of Its Processes upon the Modes of Flint-Working Practised in Prehistoric Times. Proceedings, Society of Antiquarians of Scotland 21:206-212.

McINTOSH, R.J.

684 1974 Archaeology and Mud Wall Decay in a West African Village. World Archaeology 6(2):154.

MALLOUF, R.J., and C. TUNNELL

685 1977 An Archeological Reconnaissance of the Lower Canyons of the Rio Grande. Office of the State Archeologist, Texas Historical Commission, Archeological Survey Report 22 (section on Ethnoarchaeology).

MANDEVILLE, M.

686 1974 A Study of Contemporary Ceramic Techniques at Tula and a Possible Archaeological Application. In R.A. Diehl, ed., Studies of Ancient Tollan: A Report of the University of Missouri Tula Archaeological Project. University of Missouri Monographs in Anthropology 1:122-129.

NISSEN, K., and M. DITTEMORE

687 1974 Ethnographic Data and Wear Pattern Analysis: A Study of Socketed Eskimo Scrapers. Tebiwa 17:67-88.

ORELLANA, S.L.

688 1977 Obsidian and Its Uses Among the Tzutujil Maya. Journal of New World Archaeology 2(1):17-29.

OSWALT, W.H., and J.W. VanSTONE

689 1967 The Ethnoarchaeology of Crow Village, Alaska. Bureau of American Ethnology Bulletin 199.

PASTRON, A.G., and C.W. CLEWLOW, Jr.

690 1974 The Ethno-Archaeology of an Unusual Tarahumara Burial Cave. Man 9(2):308-311.

PETERSON, N.

691 1971 Open Sites and the Ethnographic Approach to the Archae-
           ology of Hunters-Gatherers. In D.J. Mulvaney and J.
           Golson, eds., Aboriginal Man and Environment in Australia:
           239-248. Canberra.

692 1973 Camp Site Location Amongst Australian Hunters and Gatherers:
           Archaeological and Ethnographic Evidence for a Key Deter-
           minant. Archaeology and Physical Anthropology in Oceania
           8:173-193.

693 1977 Ethno-Archaeology in the Australian Iron Age. In G. de G.
           Sieveking, et al., eds., Problems in Economic and Social
           Archaeology:265-276. Westview Press, Boulder.

PRICE, C.

694 1972 Heirs of the Ancient Maya: The Lacandon Indians of Mexico.
           Scribner and Sons, New York.

ROBBINS, L.H.

695 1973 Turkana Material Culture Viewed from an Archaeological
           Perspective. World Archaeology 5:209-214.

SCHIFFER, M.B.

696 1978 Methodological Issues in Ethnoarchaeology. In R.A. Gould,
           ed., Explorations in Ethnoarchaeology:229-248. University
           of New Mexico Press, Albuquerque.

SCHRIRE, G.

697 1972 Ethno-Archaeological Models and Subsistence Behavior in
           Arnhem Land. In D.L. Clarke, ed., Models in Archaeology:
           653-670. Methuen and Co., London.

SOLECKI, R.S.

698 1979 Contemporary Kurdish Winter-Time Inhabitants of Shanidar
           Cave, Iraq. World Archaeology 10(3):318-330.

STANISLAWSKI, M.B.

699 1969 The Ethno-Archaeology of Hopi Pottery Making. Plateau 42:
           27-33.

700 1969 What Good Is a Broken Pot? An Experiment in Hopi-Tewa
           Ethnoarchaeology. Southwestern Lore 35:11-18.

701 1973 Ethnoarchaeology and Settlement Archaeology. Ethnohistory
           20(4):375-392.

702 1978 If Pots Were Mortal. In R.A. Gould, ed., Explorations in
           Ethnoarchaeology:201-229. University of New Mexico Press,
           Albuquerque.

THOMPSON, R.

703 1958 Modern Yucatecan Maya Pottery: A Study of the Nature of the
           Archeological Inference. Society for American Archaeology,
           Memoir 15.

TINDALE, N.B.

704   1950   Palaeolithic Kodj Axe of the Aborigines and Its Distribu-
             tion in Australia. Records, South Australian Museum 9(3):
             257-273.

TOWNSEND, J.B.

705   1973   Ethnoarchaeology in Nineteenth Century Southern and
             Western Alaska: An Interpretive Model. Ethnohistory 20(4):
             393-412.

TRINGHAM, R.

706   1978   Experimentation, Ethnoarchaeology and Leapfrogs in
             Archaeological Methodology. In R.A. Gould, ed., Explora-
             tions in Ethnoarchaeology:169-200. University of New
             Mexico Press, Albuquerque.

WATSON, P.J.

707   1979   The Idea of Ethnoarchaeology: Notes and Comments. In
             C. Kramer, ed., Ethnoarchaeology:277-288. Columbia
             University Press, New York.

WHITE, J.P.

708   1967   Ethno-Archaeology in New Guinea: Two Examples. Mankind
             6:409-414.

WOBST, H.M.

709   1978   The Archaeo-Ethnology of Hunter-Gatherers, or the Tyranny
             of the Ethnographic Record in Archaeology. American
             Antiquity 43(2):303-309.

YELLEN, J.E.

710   1976   Settlement of the !Kung: An Archaeological Perspective.
             In R.B. Lee and I. DeVore, eds., Kalahari Hunter-Gatherers:
             47-72. Harvard University Press, Cambridge, Mass.

711   1977   Archaeological Approaches to the Present. Academic Press,
             New York.

712   1977   Cultural Patterning in Faunal Remains: Evidence from the
             !Kung Bushmen. In D. Ingersoll, J.E. Yellen, and W.
             MacDonald, eds., Experimental Archaeology:271-331.
             Columbia University Press, New York.

713   1977   Long-Term Hunter-Gatherer Adaptation to Desert Environ-
             ments. World Archaeology 8(3):262-274.

YELLEN, J.E., and H. HARPENDING

714   1972   Hunter-Gatherer Populations and Archaeological Inference.
             World Archaeology 4:244-253.

9. Cultural Resource Management

AGOGINO, G.A., and S. SACHS

715 1960 Criticism of the Museum Orientation of Existing Antiquity
            Laws. Plains Anthropologist 5:31-35.

716 1960 The Failure of State and Federal Legislation to Protect
            Archaeological Resources. Tebiwa 3:43-46.

ANONYMOUS

717 1978 Oil Wells and Archaeology. COMARC Commentary, April:1-2.

BRACKEN, C.P.

718 1975 Antiquities Acquired. David and Charles, Newton Abbot,
            England.

BREW, J.O.

719 1964 Report on the Advisability of Drawing Up International
            Regulations Concerning the Preservation of Cultural Property
            Endangered by Public and Private Works. General Conference,
            Thirteenth Session, Programme Commission, UNESCO, PRG,
            13C/PRG/16, July 24, 1964, Paris.

CARRELL, T., S. RAYLE, and D. LENIHAN

720 1976 The Effects of Freshwater Inundation of Archeological
            Sites Through Reservoir Construction: A Literature Search.
            National Park Service, Cultural Resources Management
            Division, Washington, D.C.

CHAPMAN, C.H., ed.

721 1973 Archaeology in the 70s--Mitigating the Impact. The
            Missouri Archaeologist 35.

COLLINS, R.B., and D.F. GREEN

722 1978 A Proposal to Modernize the American Antiquities Act.
            Science 202:1055-1059.

DAVIS, H.A.

723 1971 Is There a Future for the Past? Archaeology 24(4):300-306.

724 1972 The Crisis in American Archaeology. Science 175:267-272.

DAWILL, T.C., M.P. PEARSON, R.W. SMITH, and R.M. THOMAS, eds.

725 1978 New Approaches to Our Past: An Archeological Forum.
            Southampton, England.

DIXON, K.A.

726 1977 Applications of Archaeological Resources: Broadening the
            Basis of Significance. In M. Schiffer and G. Gumerman,
            Conservation Archaeology:277-292. Academic Press, New
            York.

FAGAN, B.M.

727 1978 In the Beginning. 3rd ed. Little, Brown and Co.,
Boston. (See Chapter 11.)

FITTING, J.E.

728 1979 The Role of Market Analysis in Archaeological Planning.
Journal of Field Archaeology 6(2):229-235.

GARRISON, E.G.

729 1977 Modeling Inundation Effects for Planning and Prediction.
In M. Schiffer and G. Gumerman, eds., Conservation
Archaeology:151-156. Academic Press, New York.

GUNN, J, ed.

730 1978 Papers in Applied Archaeology. Center for Archaeological
Research, The University of Texas at San Antonio.

HOLDEN, C.

731 1977 Contract Archaeology: New Source of Support Brings New
Problems. Science 196:1070-1072.

KELLY, R.E., and R.A. FRANKEL

732 1974 An Annotated Bibliography for "Public Archaeology" in the
United States. Department of Anthropology, California
State University, Northridge.

KING, T.F.

733 1977 Resolving a Conflict of Values in American Archaeology.
In M. Schiffer and G. Gumerman, eds., Conservation
Archaeology:87-96. Academic Press, New York.

734 1978 The Archeological Survey: Methods and Uses. Heritage
Conservation and Recreation Service, U.S. Department of
the Interior, Washington, D.C.

KING, T.F., P.P. HICKMAN, and G. BERG

735 1977 Anthropology in Historic Preservation: Caring for Culture's
Clutter. Academic Press, New York.

LEE, R.F.

736 1970 The Antiquities Act of 1906. National Park Service,
Washington, D.C.

LIPE, W.D.

737 1974 A Conservation Model for American Archaeology. Kiva 39(3-
4):213-247.

LIPE, W.D., and A.J. LINDSAY, Jr., eds.

738 1975 Proceedings of the 1974 Cultural Resource Management
Conference, Denver, Colorado. Museum of Northern Arizona,
Flagstaff.

McGIMSEY, C.R., III

739 1972 Public Archeology. Seminar Press, New York.

McGIMSEY, C.R., III, and H.A. DAVIS, eds.

740 1977 The Management of Archeological Resources: The Airlie
           House Report. Special Publication, Society for American
           Archaeology. Washington, D.C.

McHARGUE, G., and M. ROBERTS

741 1977 A Field Guide to Conservation Archaeology in North America.
           J.B. Lippincott and Co., Philadelphia.

McNEIL, P.

742 1969 Legal Safeguards for Preserving the Past. Bulletin of the
           Texas Archeological Society 40:267-280.

MATHENY, R.T., and D.L. BERGE, eds.

743 1976 Symposium on Dynamics of Cultural Resource Management.
           U.S. Department of Agriculture, Forest Service, South-
           western Region, Archeological Report 10.

MORATTO, M.J., and R.E. KELLY

744 1978 Optimizing Strategies for Evaluating Archaeological
           Significance. In M. Schiffer, ed., Advances in Archae-
           ological Method and Theory, Vol. 1:1-31. Academic Press,
           New York.

PATTERSON, L.W.

745 1978 Basic Considerations in Contract Archaeology. Man in the
           Northeast 15-16:132-137.

746 1978 Contract Archaeology: Environmental and Practical Issues.
           Archaeology 31(1):60-61.

PLOG, F., ed.

747 1978 An Analytical Approach to Cultural Resource Management:
           The Little Colorado Planning Unit. Arizona State Univer-
           sity, Anthropological Research Papers 13. Tempe.

RAAB, L.M., and T.C. KLINGER

748 1977 A Critical Appraisal of "Significance" in Contract Archae-
           ology. American Antiquity 42(4):629-634.

SCHIFFER, M.B., and G.J. GUMERMAN, eds.

749 1977 Conservation Archaeology, a Guide for Cultural Resource
           Studies. Academic Press, New York. (Extensive bibliog-
           raphy, pp. 445-475.)

SCHIFFER, M.B., and J.H. HOUSE

750 1977 An Approach to Assessing Scientific Significance. In M.
           Schiffer and G. Gumerman, eds., Conservation Archaeology:
           249-258. Academic Press, New York.

SCHIFFER, M.B., and J.H. HOUSE, assemblers

751 1975 The Cache River Archeological Project: An Experiment in
           Contract Archeology. Arkansas Archeological Survey,
           Research Series 8.

SCOVILL, D.H., G.J. GORDON, and K.M. ANDERSON

752 1977 Guidelines for the Preparation of Statements of Environ-
           mental Impact on Archaeological Resources. In M. Schiffer
           and G. Gumerman, eds., Conservation Archaeology:43-62.
           Academic Press, New York.

SIEGEL, D.N.

753 1975 Legislation for the Protection and Preservation of
           Archaeological Remains in Arizona. Kiva 40(4):315-326.

SKINNER, S.A.

754 1979 Bid Solicitation and Award Protestation: A Case Study.
           Journal of Field Archaeology 6(1):108-111.

SPIESS, A.E., ed.

755 1978 Conservation Archaeology in the Northeast: Towards a Re-
           search Orientation. Peabody Museum Bulletin 3. Cambridge,
           Mass.

STUART, D.E.

756 1977 An Ethnologist's Perspective on Cultural Resource Manage-
           ment. In M. Schiffer and G. Gumerman, eds., Conservation
           Archaeology:73-78. Academic Press, New York.

TALMAGE, V., and O. CHESLER

757 1977 The Importance of Small, Surface and Disturbed Sites as
           Sources of Significant Archeological Data. Office of
           Cultural Resource Management, National Park Service,
           Washington, D.C.

VIELVOYE, R.

758 1979 How Pipeliners and Archaeologists Work Together. Oil and
           Gas Journal, October 22:45.

WEIL, M.E.

759 1978 A Canadian Perspective on Legislation and the Role of the
           Private Sector in Archaeology. Historical Archaeology 12:
           51-57.

10. Amateur Archaeology

ANONYMOUS

760 1978 Digging Up America--the Archaeology Craze. U.S. News and
           World Report, May 22:76-78.

BRENNAN, L.A.

761 1973 Beginner's Guide to Archaeology. Stackpole Books, Harris-
           burg, Pa.

BROOK, V.R.

762 1969 The Role of the Amateur Archaeologist. Southwestern Lore
           35(2):21-23.

CLARKE, D.V.

763 1978 Excavation and Volunteers: A Cautionary Tale. World Archae-
           ology 10(1):63-70.

CONNER, S.W.

764 1963 The Organization and Role of an Amateur Archeological
           Society. Plains Anthropologist 8(21):189-193.

COOKE, C.K.

765 1968 Presidential Address: What Does the Future Hold for the
           Amateur Archaeologist? South African Archaeological
           Bulletin 23(89), Pt. 1:3-8.

DUMONT, E.

766 1976 The Role of Amateur Societies. Southwestern Lore 42(4).

FELDMAN, M.

767 1977 Archaeology for Everyone. Quadrangle/The New York Times
           Book Co., New York.

FERGUSON, B.

768 1972 New Roles for the Amateur Archaeologist. American Antiquity
           37(1):1-2.

GRIFFIN, L.

769 1963 The Eisen Site: A New Concept in Amateur Archaeological
           Endeavor. Michigan Archaeologist 9(4):73-78.

HARGLE, D.D.

770 1956 Archeology and the Non Professional. Archeological Society
           of New Jersey, Bulletin 11:3-11.

HAYS, D.R.

771 1963 Published Materials for the Amateur Archaeologist.
           Michigan Archaeologist 9(4):58-72.

HESTER, T.R.

772 1980 Digging into South Texas Prehistory: A Guide for Amateur
           Archaeologists. Corona Publishing Company, San Antonio.

JONES, N.

773 1954 The Amateur in Archaeology. South African Archaeological
Bulletin 9(34):39-47.

KELLEY, J.H.

774 1963 Some Thoughts on Amateur Archaeology. American Antiquity
28:394-396.

LESLIE, V.

775 1961 Of Professionals, Semi-Professionals, Amateurs, Curio
Collectors and Pot Hunters. Pennsylvania Archaeologist
31(2):90-96.

NICKERSON, G.S.

776 1962 Status and Role in Archaeology: Professionals and Amateurs.
Plains Anthropologist 7(17):184-187.

NORDQUIST, D.

777 1965 Is There a Place for Both Professional and Amateur in
Archaeology? Washington Archaeologist 9(1):12-23.

ROBBINS, M., and M.B. IRVING

778 1973 The Amateur Archaeologist's Handbook. Thomas Y. Crowell
Co., New York.

STEEN, C.R.

779 1966 The Citizen and Archaeology. Southwestern Lore 32(3):66-69.

STRUEVER, S.

780 1963 The Amateur Archaeologist and the Relic Man--an Important
Distinction. Central State Archaeological Journal 10:
91-94, 100.

WEBB, C.H.

781 1936 The Role of the Nonprofessional in the Local Society.
American Antiquity 22:170-172.

C. COMMON KINDS OF SITES: SELECTED EXAMPLES

1. Open Occupation Sites

ALLEN, J.W., and C.H. McNUTT

782 1955 A Pit House Site Near Santa Ana Pueblo, New Mexico.
American Antiquity 20:241-255.

ANDERSON, D.D.

783 1968 A Stone Age Campsite at the Gateway to America. Scientific
American 218(6):24-33.

BELL, R.E.

784 1965 Investigaciones Arqueológicas en el Sitio El Inga, Ecuador.
           Editorial Casa de la Cultura Ecuatoriana, Quito.

CLARK, J.D.

785 1969 Kalambo Falls: Prehistoric Site 1: The Geology, Paleo-
           ecology and Detailed Stratigraphy of the Excavations.
           University Press, Cambridge.

786 1974 Kalambo Falls Prehistoric Site: The Later Prehistoric
           Cultures. University Press, Cambridge.

CLARK, J.G.D.

787 1972 Star Carr: A Case Study in Bioarchaeology. Addison-Wesley
           Module in Anthropology 10.

CLAUSEN, C.J., H.K. BROOKS, and A.B. WESOLOWSKY

788 1975 The Early Man Site at Warm Mineral Springs, Florida.
           Journal of Field Archaeology 2(3):191–213.

CURWEN, E.C.

789 1930 Neolithic Camps. Antiquity 4:22–54.

DAUGHERTY, R.D.

790 1956 Archaeology of the Lind Coulee Site, Washington. Proceedings,
           American Philosophical Society 100(3).

DeJARNETTE, D.L., and A.T. HANSEN

791 1960 The Archeology of the Childersburg Site, Alabama. Florida
           State University, Notes in Anthropology 6.

DORWIN, J.T.

792 1971 The Bowen Site: An Archaeological Study of Culture Process
           in the Late Prehistory of Central Indiana. Indiana His-
           torical Society, Prehistory Research Series 4.

EPSTEIN, J.F.

793 1969 The San Isidro Site: An Early Man Campsite in Nuevo Leon,
           Mexico. University of Texas, Anthropology Series 7.

FITTING, J.E., J. DeVISSCHER, and E.J. WAHLA

794 1966 The Paleo-Indian Occupation of the Holcombe Beach. Museum
           of Anthropology, University of Michigan, Anthropological
           Papers 27.

FUCHS, C., D. KAUFMAN, and A. RONEN

795 1977 Erosion and Artifact Distribution in Open-Air Epi-Palaeo-
           lithic Sites on the Coastal Plain of Israel. Journal of
           Field Archaeology 4(2):171–179.

GIMBUTAS, M.

796 1974 Achilleion: A Neolithic Mound in Thessaly; Preliminary
Report on 1973 and 1974 Excavations. Journal of Field
Archaeology 1(3/4):277-302.

HAURY, E.W.

797 1945 The Excavation of Los Muertos and Neighboring Ruins in the
Salt River Valley, Southern Arizona. Harvard University,
Papers of the Peabody Museum 24(1).

HEIZER, R.F., and A.B. ELSASSER

798 1956 Excavation of Two Northwestern California Coastal Sites.
University of California Archaeological Survey, Report
67:1-150.

HENRY, D.O., with a contribution by A. LEROI-GOURHAM

799 1976 The Excavation of Hayonim Terrace: An Interim Report.
Journal of Field Archaeology 3(4):391-406.

HESTER, J.J.

800 1972 Blackwater Locality No. 1, a Stratified, Early Man Site in
Eastern New Mexico. Fort Burgwin Research Center, Southern
Methodist University, Dallas.

HESTER, T.R.

801 1971 Burned Rock Midden Sites on the Southwestern Edge of the
Edwards Plateau, Texas. Plains Anthropologist 15(50):
237-250.

HIGGS, E.S.

802 1959 Excavations at a Mesolithic Site at Downton Near Salisbury,
Wiltshire. Proceedings, Prehistoric Society 25:209-232.

HOUART, G.L.

803 1971 Koster: A Stratified Archaic Site in the Illinois Valley.
Illinois State Museum, Report of Investigations 22, and
Illinois Valley Archaeological Program, Research Papers 4.

ISAAC, G.L.

804 1977 Olorgesailie: Archaeological Studies of a Middle Pleistocene
Lake Basin in Kenya. University of Chicago Press, Chicago.

JOHNSON, C.R.

805 1972 A Study of North Park Tipis. Southwestern Lore 37(4):93-
101.

KLÍMA, B.

806 1954 Palaeolithic Huts at Dolni Věstonice, Czechoslovakia.
Antiquity 28:4-14.

LEWIS, T.M.N., and M.K. LEWIS

807 1961 Eva: An Archaic Site. University of Tennessee Press, Knox-
           ville.

LUMLEY, H. de

808 1969 A Paleolithic Camp at Nice. Scientific American 222(5):
           42-59.

MacDONALD, G.F.

809 1968 Debert: A Paleo-Indian Site in Central Nova Scotia.
           Anthropology Papers, National Museum of Canada 16.

McPHERRON, A.

810 1967 The Juntunen Site and the Late Woodland Prehistory of the
           Upper Great Lakes Area. Museum of Anthropology, University
           of Michigan, Anthropological Papers 30.

MEACHAM, W., ed.

811 1978 Sham Wan, Lamma Island; an Archaeological Site Study.
           Journal Monograph III, Hong Kong Archaeological Society.

MONTET-WHITE, A., and A.E. JOHNSON

812 1976 Kadar: A Late Gravettian Site in Northern Bosnia, Yugo-
           slavia. Journal of Field Archaeology 3(4):407-424.

MULLOY, W.

813 1942 The Hagen Site. University of Montana Publications in
           Social Science 1.

OHEL, M.Y.

814 1977 Patterned Concentrations on Living Floors at Olduvai, Beds
           I and II: Experimental Study. Journal of Field Archaeology
           4(4):423-433.

PIDOPLITCHKO, I.G.

815 1969 Late Palaeolithic Dwellings of Mammoth Bones in the
           Ukraine. Moscow.

PITT-RIVERS, A.H. LANE-FOX

816 1876 Excavations in Cissbury Camp, Sussex: Being a Report of the
           Anthropological Institute for the Year 1875. Journal,
           Royal Anthropological Institute 5:357-390.

RAINEY, F.

817 1971 The Ipiutak Culture: Excavations at Point Hope, Alaska.
           Addison-Wesley Modules in Anthropology 8.

RITCHIE, W.A.

818 1940 Two Prehistoric Village Sites at Brewerton, New York.
           Researches and Transactions of the New York Archaeological
           Association 9(1).

SHUTLER, R., Jr.

819 1967 Archeology of Tule Springs, Nevada. State Museum Papers
           13(5).

SKINNER, S.A.

820 1971 Prehistoric Settlement of the De Cordova Bend Reservoir.
           Bulletin of the Texas Archeological Society 42:149–270.

STRUEVER, S., and J. CARLSON

821 1977 Koster Site: The New Archaeology in Action. Archaeology
           30(2):93–101.

Van NOTEN, F.

822 1978 Les Chasseurs de Meer. Dissertationes Archaeologicae
           Gandenses XVIII. De Tempel, Brugge (Belgium).

WEBB, W.S.

823 1946 Indian Knoll, Site Oh-2, Ohio County, Kentucky. University
           of Kentucky, Reports in Anthropology and Archaeology 4(3):1.

824 1974 Indian Knoll. University of Tennessee Press, Knoxville.

WEBB, W.S., and W.G. HAAG

825 1939 The Chiggerville Site. University of Kentucky Reports in
           Anthropology 4.

WILMSEN, E.N.

826 1974 Lindenmeier: A Pleistocene Hunting Society. Harper's
           Case Studies in Archaeology. Harper and Row, New York.

WINTERS, H.D.

827 1969 The Riverton Culture: A Second Millennium Occupation in the
           Central Wabash Valley. Illinois State Museum, Reports of
           Investigations 13.

WOOD, W.R., ed.

829 1969 Two House Sites in the Central Plains: An Experiment in
           Archaeology. Plains Anthropologist, Memoir 6.

829 1971 Biesterfeldt: A Post-Contact Coalescent Site on the North-
           eastern Plains. Smithsonian Contribution to Anthropology
           15. Smithsonian Institution, Washington, D.C.

2. Complex Sites: Selected References

ARMILLAS, P.

830 1951 Mesoamerican Fortifications. Antiquity 25(98):77–87.

BONOMI, J.

831 1853 Niveneh and Its Palaces. Ingram, Cooke, and Co., London.

BRENNAN, C.T.

832 1980 Cerro Arena: Early Cultural Complexity and Nucleation in
           North Coastal Peru. Journal of Field Archaeology 7(1):1-22.

BRUCE-MITFORD, R.L.S.

833 1951 The Sutton Hoo Ship-Burial. Scientific American 184(4):
           24-42.

BURL, A.

834 1976 The Stone Circles of the British Isles. Yale University
           Press, New Haven.

CATON-THOMPSON, G.

835 1929 Zimbabwe. Antiquity 3:424-433.

CRAVEN, R.C.

836 1974 Ceremonial Centers of the Maya. University Presses of
           Florida, Gainesville.

DIEHL, R.A., ed.,

837 1974 Studies of Ancient Tollan: A Report of the University of
           Missouri Tula Archaeological Project. University of
           Missouri Monographs in Anthropology 1.

Di PESO, C.

838 1974 Casas Grandes: A Fallen Trading Center of the Gran
           Chichimeca. 3 vols. Northland Press, Flagstaff.

DRUCKER, P., R.F. HEIZER, and R. SQUIER

839 1959 Excavations at La Venta, 1955. Bureau of American Ethnology,
           Bulletin 170.

EVANS, J.D.

840 1971 Neolithic Knossos: The Growth of a Settlement. Proceedings,
           Prehistoric Society 37(2):81-117.

FERDON, E.N., Jr.

841 1967 The Hohokam "Ball Court": An Alternate View of Its Function.
           Kiva 33(1):1-14.

FOLAN, W.J., L.A. FLETCHER, and E.R. KINTZ

842 1979 Fruit, Fiber, Bark and Resin: Social Organization of a
           Maya Urban Center. Science 204:697-701.

FOWLER, M.L.

843 1974 Cahokia: Ancient Capital of the Midwest. Addison-Wesley
           Module in Anthropology 48.

GHIRSHMAN, R.

844 1961 The Ziggurat of Tchoga-Zanbil. Scientific American 204(1):
           68-91.

GJERSTAD, E.

845 1952 Stratigraphic Excavations in the Forum Romanum. Antiquity 26(102):60-64.

HAMBLIN, D.J.

846 1973 The First Cities. Time-Life Books, New York.

HAMMOND, N.

847 1975 Lubaantun: A Classic Maya Realm. Peabody Museum Monograph 2. Cambridge, Mass.

HAURY, E.W.

848 1975 The Hohokam: Desert Farmers and Craftsmen: Excavations at Snaketown, 1964-65. University of Arizona Press, Tucson.

HEIZER, R.F., J.A. GRAHAM, and L.K. NAPTON

849 1968 The 1968 Investigations at La Venta. Contributions, University of California Research Facility 5:127-154.

HIBBEN, F.C.

850 1966 A Possible Pyramidal Structure and Other Mexican Influences at Pottery Mound, New Mexico. American Antiquity 31(4): 522-529.

KENYON, K.M.

851 1954 Excavations at Jericho. Royal Anthropological Institute of Great Britain and Ireland 84(1/2):103-110.

852 1956 Jericho and Its Setting in Near Eastern History. Antiquity 30:184-195.

853 1957 Digging Up Jericho. Ernest Benn, London.

854 1959 Earliest Jericho. Antiquity 33(129):5-9.

855 1970 Archaeology in the Holy Land. Praeger, New York.

856 1974 Digging Up Jerusalem. Praeger, New York.

LAYARD, A.H.

857 1849 Nineveh and Its Remains. Putnam, New York.

858 1853 Discoveries in the Ruins of Nineveh and Babylon. Putnam, New York.

LLOYD, S.

859 1963 Mounds of the Near East. Edinburgh University Press, Edinburgh.

LOFTUS, W.K.

860 1858 Warkah: Its Ruins and Remains. Transactions, Royal Society of Literature and Science 6:1-64.

MAIURI, A.

861 1958 Pompeii. Scientific American 189(4):68-82.

MAYER-OAKES, W.J.

862 1963 Complex Society Archaeology. American Antiquity 29:57-60.

MELLAART, J.

863 1970 Excavations at Hacilar. Edinburgh University Press, Edinburgh.

MILLON, R.

864 1960 The Beginnings of Teotihuacan. American Antiquity 26:1-10.

865 1967 Teotihuacan. Scientific American 216(6):38-63.

MILLON, R., and J.A. BENNYHOFF

866 1961 A Long Architectural Sequence at Teotihuacan. American Antiquity 26:516-523.

MILLON, R., and B. DREWITT

867 1961 Earlier Structures Within the Pyramid of the Sun at Teotihuacan. American Antiquity 26:371-380.

NEWELL, H.P., and A.D. KRIEGER

868 1949 The George C. Davis Site, Cherokee County, Texas. Society for American Archaeology, Memoir 5.

PLATON, N.E.

869 1971 Zakros: The Discovery of a Lost Palace of Ancient Crete. Scribner's, New York.

POPE, A.U.

870 1957 Persepolis as a Ritual City. Archaeology 10(2):123-130.

POZORSKI, T.

871 1980 The Early Horizon Site of Huaca de los Reyes: Societal Implications. American Antiquity 45(1):100-110.

REDFORD, D.B.

872 1978 The Razed Temple of Akhenaten. Scientific American 239(6): 136-147.

RODDEN, R.J.

873 1962 Excavations at the Early Neolithic Site at Nea Nikomedia, Greek Macedonia (1961). Proceedings, Prehistoric Society 28:267-288.

874 1965 An Early Neolithic Village in Greece. Scientific American 212:82-90.

SALVATORI, S.

875 1979 Sequential Analysis and Architectural Remains in the Central Quarters of Shahr-i Sokhta. Istituto Universitario Orientale Seminario di Studi Asiatici. South Asian

Archaeology 1977. Papers from the Fourth International Conference of South Asian Archaeologists in Western Europe, Naples.

SCHLIEMANN, H.

876 1875 Troy and Its Remains. John Murray, London.

877 1878 Mycenae. John Murray, London.

SCHROEDER, A.H.

878 1955 Ball Courts of Middle America and Arizona. Archaeology 8(3):156-161.

SHARER, R.J.

879 1978 Archaeology and History at Quirigua, Guatemala. Journal of Field Archaeology 5(1):51-70.

SMITH, A.L.

880 1950 Uaxactun, Guatemala: Excavations of 1931-1937. Carnegie Institution of Washington, Publication 588. Washington, D.C.

881 1962 Residential and Associated Structures at Mayapan. Carnegie Institution of Washington, Publication 619:165-320. Washington, D.C.

882 1972 Excavations at Altar de Sacrificios: Architecture, Settlement, Burials, and Caches. Harvard University, Peabody Museum Papers 62(2). Cambridge, Mass.

STONE, E.H.

883 1924 Stones of Stonehenge. Scott, London.

THOM, A.

884 1971 Megalithic Lunar Observatories. Oxford Press, New York.

TOBLER, A.J.

885 1950 Excavations at Tepe Gawra. Museum Monographs, University of Pennsylvania Museum, Philadelphia.

TODD, I.A.

886 1976 Catal Hüyük. Cummings Publishing Co., Menlo Park, Cal.

TRINGHAM, R., D. KRSTIĆ, T. KAISER, and B. VOYTEK

887 1980 The Early Agricultural Site of Selevac, Yugoslavia. Archaeology 33(2):24-32.

VENCL, S.

888 1971 Some Remarks on the Study of Prehistoric Structures. American Antiquity 36(4):451-454.

WAGNER, F.

889   1928   Prehistoric Fortifications in Bavaria. Antiquity 2:43-55.

WAUCHOPE, R.

890   1975   Zacualpa, El Quiche, Guatemala, an Ancient Provincial
             Center of the Highland Maya. Tulane University, Middle
             American Research Institute Publications 39. New Orleans.

WHEELER, M.

891   1954   The Stanwick Fortifications. Report of the Research
             Committee of the Society of Antiquities 17.

WICKE, C.R.

892   1963   Pyramids and Temple Mounds: Meso-American Ceremonial
             Architecture in Eastern North America. American Antiquity
             30:409-420.

WILLEY, G.R.

893   1973   The Altar de Sacrificios Excavations: General Summary and
             Conclusions. Harvard University, Peabody Museum Papers
             64(3).

WILLEY, G.R., ed.

894   1978   Excavations at Seibal, Department of Peten, Guatemala.
             Peabody Museum Memoirs 14(1, 2, 3).

WINLOCK, H.E.

895   1942   Excavations at Deir el Bahri, 1911-1931. Macmillan, New
             York.

WINTER, F.E.

896   1971   Greek Fortifications. University of Toronto Press,
             Toronto.

WISEMAN, J., and D. MANO-ZISSI, eds.

897   1974   Studies in the Antiquities of Stobi. University of Texas
             Press, Austin.

WOOLLEY, C.L.

898   1934   Ur Excavations. Publications of the Joint Expedition of
             the British Museum and the Museum of the University of
             Pennsylvania to Mesopotamia 2.

WYLIE, J.C.

899   1959   The Wastes of Civilization. Faber and Faber, London.

ZEUNER, F.E.

900   1954   The Neolithic Bronze Age Gap on the Tell of Jericho.
             Palestine Exploration Quarterly, May-October:64-68.

3. Shell Mounds and Middens

AMBROSE, W.R.

901 1967 Archaeology and Shell Middens. Archaeology and Physical Anthropology in Oceania 2:169-187.

BYERS, D.S., and F. JOHNSON

902 1939 Some Methods Used in Excavating Eastern Shell Heaps. American Antiquity 4:189-212.

COOK, S.F.

903 1946 A Reconsideration of Shellmounds with Respect to Population and Nutrition. American Antiquity 12:50-52.

GIFFORD, E.W.

904 1916 Composition of California Shellmounds. University of California Publications in American Archaeology and Ethnology 12(1). Berkeley.

905 1949 Diet and Age of the California Shellmounds. American Antiquity 14:223-224.

McGEEIN, D.J., and W.C. MUELLER

906 1955 A Shellmound in Marin County, California. American Antiquity 21:52-62.

MEIGS, P.

907 1938 Vegetation on Shell Mounds, Lower California. Science 87:346.

MELLARS, P.

908 1971 Excavation of Two Mesolithic Shell Middens on the Island of Oronsay (Inner Hebrides). Nature 231(5302): 397-398.

MOORE, E.S.

909 1925 Shell-Mounds and Changes in the Shells Composing Them. Scientific Monthly 21:429-440.

NELSON, N.C.

910 1909 Shell Mounds of the San Francisco Bay Region. University of California Publications in American Archaeology and Ethnology 7:309-348.

O'BRIEN, M.

911 1971 The Fullen Site, 41HR82. Bulletin, Texas Archeological Society 42:335-336.

SWANSON, E.H.

912 1959 The Whiskey Dick Shellmound, Washington. American Antiquity 25:122-123.

WALLACE, W.J., and D.W. LATHRAP

913 1975 West Berkeley (Ca-Ala-307): A Culturally Stratified Shell-
           mound on the East Shore of San Francisco Bay. Contributions,
           University of California Archaeological Research Facility
           29.

4. Mortuary Sites

ARTAMONOV, A.I.

914 1961 Frozen Tombs of the Scythians. Scientific American 212(5):
           100-104.

ATEN, L.E., C.K. CHANDLER, A.B. WESOLOWSKY, and R.M. MALINA

915 1976 Excavations at the Harris County Boys' School Cemetery;
           Analysis of Galveston Bay Area Mortuary Practices. Texas
           Archeological Society, Special Publication 3.

AVIGAD, N.

916 1955 The Necropolis of Beth She'arim. Archaeology 8(4):236-244.

CARTER, H.

917 1972 The Tomb of Tutankhamen. Barrie and Jenkins, London.

CASKEY, J.L.

918 1960 Royal Shaft Graves at Lerna. Archaeology 13(2):130-133.

CHILDE, V.G.

919 1932 Scottish Megalithic Tombs and Their Affinities. Transac-
           tions, Glasgow Archaeological Society 3:120-137.

CIANFARANI, V.

920 1972 The Necropolis of Campovalano--Mysteries of Middle Adriatic
           Culture. Expedition 14(4):27-32.

CLARK, G.

921 1949 Urn-Fields and Vital Statistics. Antiquity 23(89):46.

COE, M.D.

922 1956 The Funerary Temple Among the Classic Maya. Southwestern
           Journal of Anthropology 12:387-394.

COOK, B.F.

923 1966 An Alexandrian Tomb-Group Re-Examined. American Journal
           of Archaeology 70(4):325-330.

DANIEL, G.E., and T.G. POWELL

924 1949 The Distribution and Date of the Passage-Graves of the
           British Isles. Proceedings, Prehistoric Society 15:169-187.

DIMICK, J.

925 1958 The Embalming House of the Apis Bulls. Archaeology 11(3): 183–189.

DONNAN, C.B., and C.J. MACKEY

926 1978 Ancient Burial Patterns of the Moche Valley, Peru. University of Texas Press, Austin.

DUPREE, N.H.

927 1979 T'ang Tombs in Chien County, China. Archaeology 32(4): 34–44.

EMERY, W.B.

928 1938 Excavations at Saqqara; the Tomb of Hemaka. Government Press, Cairo.

929 1949, Great Tombs of the First Dynasty; Excavations at Saqqara;
     1954 I–II. Government Press, Cairo.

930 1955 Royal Tombs at Sakkara. Archaeology 8(1):2–9.

931 1957 The Tombs of the First Pharoahs. Scientific American 197: 106–117.

932 1958 Great Tombs of the First Dynasty; Excavations at Saqqara; III. Egypt Exploration Society, London.

GRINSELL, L.V.

933 1975 Barrow, Pyramid and Tomb: Ancient Burial Customs in Egypt, the Mediterranean, and the British Isles. Thames and Hudson, London.

GROHSKOPF, B.

934 1970 The Treasure of Sutton Hoo; Ship Burial for an Anglo-Saxon King. Atheneum Press, New York.

HENSHALL, A.S.

935 1972 The Chambered Tombs of Scotland 2. University Press, Edinburgh.

HESTER, T.R., M.B. COLLINS, F.A. WEIR, and F. RUECKING, Jr.

936 1969 Two Prehistoric Cemetery Sites in the Lower Rio Grande Valley of Texas. Bulletin, Texas Archeological Society 40:119–166.

KAPOSHINA, S.I.

937 1963 A Sarmatian Royal Burial at Novocherkassk. Antiquity 37(148):256–258.

KOROSEC, J.

938 1957 Roman Family Tombs in Yugoslavia. Archaeology 10(2): 117–122.

MACE, A.C.

939   1909   The Early Dynastic Cemeteries of Naga-ed-Dêr, Vol. II.
             J.C. Hinrichs, Leipzig.

MASSEY, W.C., and C.M. OSBORNE

940   1961   A Burial Cave in Baja California. In The Palmer Collection
             1887. University of California Anthropological Records
             16(8):338-353.

MATTHIAE, P.

941   1980   Two Princely Tombs at Tell Mardikh-Ebla. Archaeology
             33(2):8-17.

MENDELSSOHN, K.

942   1974   The Riddle of the Pyramids. Thames and Hudson, London.

MYRES, J.N.L.

943   1942   Cremation and Inhumation in the Anglo-Saxon Cemeteries.
             Antiquity 16(64):330-341.

POWELL, T.G.E., and G.E. DANIEL

944   1956   Barclodiad y Gawres (the excavation of a megalithic
             chamber tomb in Anglesey 1952-53). Liverpool University
             Press.

POWNALL, T.

945   1773   A Description of the Sepulchral Monument at New Grange,
             near Drogheda in the County of Meath, Ireland. Archaeologia
             2:236-275.

REISNER, G.A.

946   1908   The Early Dynastic Cemeteries of Naga-ed-Dêr, Vol. I.
             J.C. Hinrichs, Leipzig.

947   1932   A Provincial Cemetery of the Pyramid Age, Naga-ed-Dêr.
             University of California Publications in Egyptian Archaeol-
             ogy 3. University of California Press, Berkeley.

948   1936   The Development of the Egyptian Tomb down to the Accession
             of Cheops. Oxford University Press, London.

ROBINSON, W.J., and R. SPRAGUE

949   1965   Disposal of the Dead at Point of Pines, Arizona. American
             Antiquity 30:442-453.

SCHULTZ, F., and A.C. SPAULDING

950   1948   A Hopewellian Burial Site in the Lower Republican Valley,
             Kansas. American Antiquity 13:306-313.

SEARS, W.H.

951   1953   Kolomoki Burial Mounds and the Weeden Island Mortuary
             Complex. American Antiquity 18:223-229.

952   1958   Burial Mounds on the Gulf Coastal Plain.   American Antiq-
             uity 23:274-284.

      SKINNER, S.A., ed.

953   1969   Archaeological Investigations at the Sam Kaufman Site,
             Red River County, Texas.   Southern Methodist University,
             Contributions in Anthropology 5.   Dallas.

      SJOVOLD, T.

954   1958   A Royal Viking Burial.   Archaeology 11(3):190-199.

      TAYLOR, R.E.

955   1970   The Shaft Tombs of Western Mexico: Problems in the Inter-
             pretation of Religious Function in Nonhistoric Archaeological
             Contexts.   American Antiquity 35(2):160-169.

      TUCK, J.A.

956   1970   An Archaic Indian Cemetery in Newfoundland.   Scientific
             American 222(6):112-122.

      WHELAN, E.J.

957   1978   Dating of a Cemetery at Kish: A Reconsideration.   Journal
             of Field Archaeology 5(1):79-98.

      WHITEHOUSE, R.

958   1972   The Rock-Cut Tombs of the Central Mediterranean.
             Antiquity 46:275-281.

      WOOD, W.R.

959   1967   The Fristoe Burial Complex of Southwestern Missouri.
             Missouri Archaeologist 29:1-127.

      WOOLLEY, C.L.

960   1928   The Royal Tombs of Ur.   Antiquity 2:7-17.

5. Kill Sites

      AGENBROAD, L.D.

961   1978   The Hudson-Meng Site: An Alberta Bison Kill in the Nebraska
             High Plains.   University Press of America, Washington, D.C.

      AGOGINO, G.A., and W.D. FRANKFORTER

962   1960   A Paleo-Indian Bison-Kill in Northwestern Iowa.   American
             Antiquity 25:414-415.

      AVELEYRA ARROYO de ANDA, L.

963   1956   The Second Mammoth and Associated Artifacts at Santa Isabel
             Iztapan, Mexico.   American Antiquity 22:12-28.

BRYAN, A.L.

964   1978   An El Jobo Mastodon Kill at Taima-Taima, Venezuela.
             Science 200:1275-1277.

BUTLER, B.R.

965   1971   A Bison Jump in the Upper Salmon River Valley of Eastern
             Idaho. Tebiwa 14(1):4-32.

CLARK, J.D., and C.V. HAYNES, Jr.

966   1970   An Elephant Butchery Site at Mwanganda's Village, Karonga,
             Malawi, and Its Relevance for Paleolithic Archaeology.
             World Archaeology 1(3):390-411.

DAVIS, L.B., and M. WILSON, eds.

967   1978   Bison Procurement and Utilization: A Symposium. Plains
             Anthropologist, Memoir 14.

DIBBLE, D.S.

968   1970   On the Significance of Additional Radiocarbon Dates from
             Bonfire Shelter, Texas. Plains Anthropologist 15(50):
             251-254.

DIBBLE, D.S., and D. LORRAIN

969   1967   Bonfire Shelter: A Stratified Bison Kill-Site, Val Verde
             County, Texas. Miscellaneous Papers, Texas Memorial
             Museum 1. Austin.

EVERITT, C.

970   1975   Paleo-Indian Bison Kill Sites in North America. The Arti-
             fact 13(3):38-49. El Paso.

FORBIS, R.G.

971   1962   The Old Women's Buffalo Jump. National Museum of Canada,
             Contributions to Anthropology, Bulletin 180.

FRISON, G.C.

972   1970   The Glenrock Buffalo Jump, 48-CO-304. Plains Anthropologist
             15(50), Memoir 7.

973   1971   The Buffalo Pound in Northwestern Plains Prehistory: Site
             48-CA-302, Wyoming. American Antiquity 36(1):77-91.

974   1978   Prehistoric Hunters of the High Plains. Academic Press,
             New York.

FRISON, G.C., ed.

975   1974   The Casper Site: A Hell Gap Bison Kill on the High Plains.
             Academic Press, New York.

GRUHN, R.

976   1971   Preliminary Report on the Muhbach Site: A Besant Bison Trap
             in Central Alberta. Contributions to Anthropology 7:128-156.
             National Museum of Man of the National Museums of Canada.

HAURY, E.W.
977 1955 A Mammoth Hunt in Arizona. Archaeology 8(1):51-55.

HAURY, E.W., E. ANTEVS, and J.F. LANCE
978 1953 Artifacts with Mammoth Remains, Naco, Arizona. American Antiquity 19:1-14.

HAURY, E.W., E.B. SAYLES, and W.W. WASLEY
979 1959 The Lehner Mammoth Site, Southeastern Arizona. American Antiquity 25:2-30.

HAYNES, C.V.
980 1964 Fluted Projectile Points; Their Age and Dispersion. Science 145:1408-1413.

KEHOE, T.F.
981 1967 The Boarding School Bison Drive Site. Plains Anthropologist, Memoir 4.

982 1973 The Gull Lake Site: A Prehistoric Bison Drive Site in Southwestern Saskatchewan. Milwaukee Public Museum.

KEHOE, T.F., and A.B. KEHOE
983 1960 Observations on the Butchering Technique at a Prehistoric Bison-Kill in Montana. American Antiquity 25:421-423.

LEONHARDY, F.
984 1966 Domebo: A Paleo-Indian Kill in the Prairie-Plains. Contributions of the Museum of the Great Plains 1. Lawton, Okla.

MALOUF, C., and S. CONNER, eds.
985 1962 Symposium on Buffalo Jumps. Montana Archaeological Society, Memoir 1.

SCHULTZ, C.B., and L.C EISELEY
986 1935 Paleontological Evidence for the Antiquity of the Scottsbluff Bison Quarry and Its Associated Artifacts. American Anthropologist 3(2):306-318.

SELLARDS, E.H.
987 1952 Early Man in America. University of Texas Press, Austin.

SELLARDS, E.H., G.L. EVANS, and G.E. MEADE
988 1947 Fossil Bison and Associated Artifacts from Plainview, Texas, with Description of Artifacts by Alex D. Krieger. Bulletin of the Geological Society of America 58:927-954.

SHAY, C.T.
989 1971 Itasca Bison Kill Site: An Ecological Analysis. Minnesota Historical Society, St. Paul.

SPETH, J.D., and W.J. PARRY

990   1978   Late Prehistoric Bison Procurement in Southeastern New
             Mexico: The 1977 Season at the Garnsey Site. Research
             Reports in Archaeology, Contribution 4. Museum of Anthro-
             pology, University of Michigan.

TAMERS, M.A.

991   1972   Radiocarbon Dating of Kill Sites. Archaeometry 14(1):21-
             26.

TUNNELL, C.D., and J.T. HUGHES

992   1955   An Archaic Bison Kill Site in the Texas Panhandle.
             Panhandle-Plains Historical Society Bulletin 28:63-70.

WHEAT, J.B.

993   1967   A Paleo-Indian Bison Kill. Scientific American 216(1):
             44-52.

994   1972   The Olsen-Chubbuck Site, a Paleo-Indian Bison Kill.
             Memoirs, Society for American Archaeology 26.

995   1979   The Jurgens Site. Plains Anthropologist, Memoir 15.

6. Caves and Rockshelters

AIKENS, C.M.

996   1970   Hogup Cave. University of Utah Anthropological Papers 93.

ALEXANDER, R.K.

997   1970   Archaeological Investigations at Parida Cave, Val Verde
             County, Texas. Papers, Texas Archeological Salvage
             Project 19.

BLISS, W.L.

998   1950   Birdshead Cave, a Stratified Site in Wind River Basin,
             Wyoming. American Antiquity 15:187-196.

BORDES, F.

999   1972   A Tale of Two Caves. Harper and Row, New York.

BRYAN, K.

1000 1970   Geological Interpretation of the Deposits. In E.W. Haury,
             The Stratigraphy and Archaeology of Ventana Cave:75-125.
             University of Arizona Press, Tucson.

BUEHRER, T.F.

1001 1970   Chemical Study of the Material from Several Horizons of
             the Ventana Cave Profile. In E.W. Haury, The Stratigraphy
             and Archaeology of Ventana Cave:549-563. University of
             Arizona Press, Tucson.

CAMPBELL, J.B., and C.G. SAMPSON

1002 1971 A New Analysis of Kent's Cavern, Devonshire, England.
            University of Oregon Anthropological Papers 3.

CHAPMAN, C.H.

1003 1952 Recent Excavations in Graham Cave. Missouri Archaeological
            Society Memoir 2.

COLLCUTT, S.N.

1004 1979 The Analysis of Quaternary Cave Sediments. World Archae-
            ology 10(3):290-301.

COLLINS, M.B.

1005 1969 Test Excavations at Amistad International Reservoir,
            Fall 1967. Papers, Texas Archeological Salvage Project
            16.

COOKE, C.K.

1006 1963 Report on Excavations at Pomongwe and Tshangula Caves,
            Matopo Hills, Southern Rhodesia. South African Archae-
            ological Bulletin 18(71), Pt. 3:75-150.

COON, C.S.

1007 1951 Cave Explorations in Iran, 1949. University of Pennsyl-
            vania Museum, Museum Monographs, Philadelphia.

1008 1957 The Seven Caves. Alfred A. Knopf, New York.

1009 1968 Yengema Cave Report. University Museum, University of
            Pennsylvania. Philadelphia.

COSGROVE, C.B.

1010 1947 Caves of the Upper Gila and Hueco Areas in New Mexico and
            Texas. Papers of the Peabody Museum 24(2). Harvard
            University, Cambridge, Mass.

DORTCH, C.

1011 1979 Devil's Lair, an Example of Prolonged Cave Use in South-
            Western Australia. World Archaeology 10(3):258-279.

EPSTEIN, J.F.

1012 1963 Centipede and Damp Caves: Excavations in Val Verde County,
            Texas, 1958. Bulletin, Texas Archeological Society 33:
            1-130.

FENENGA, F., and F.A. RIDDELL

1013 1949 Excavation of Tommy Tucker Cave, Lassen County, California.
            American Antiquity 14:203-213.

FERDON, E.N.

1014 1946 Excavation of Hermit's Cave, New Mexico. University of
            New Mexico Press, Albuquerque.

FOWLER, M.L.

1015 1959 Summary Report of Modoc Rock Shelter, 1952, 1953, 1955,
            1956. Illinois State Museum, Report of Investigations 8.
            Springfield.

GLOVER, I.C.

1016 1979 The Effects of Sink Action on Archaeological Deposits in
            Caves: An Indonesian Example. World Archaeology 10(3):
            302-317.

GOODWIN, A.J.H.

1017 1929 The Montagu Cave: A Full Report of the Investigations of
            the Montagu Rock-Shelter. Annals, South African Museum
            24(1):1-16.

GRUHN, R.

1018 1961 The Archaeology of Wilson Butte Cave, South-Central
            Idaho. Occasional Papers of the Idaho State College
            Museum 6.

HARRINGTON, M.R.

1019 1933 Gypsum Cave, Nevada. Southwest Museum Papers 8, Los
            Angeles.

HAURY, E.W.

1020 1975 The Stratigraphy and Archeology of Ventana Cave.
            University of Arizona Press, Tucson.

HEIZER, R.F.

1021 1961 Preliminary Report of the Leonard Rockshelter Site,
            Pershing County, Nevada. American Antiquity 17:89-98.

HEIZER, R.F., and T.R. HESTER

1022 1973 The Archaeology of Bamert Cave, Amador County, California.
            University of California Archaeological Research Facility,
            Berkeley.

HIBBEN, F.C.

1023 1941 Evidences of Early Occupation in Sandia Cave, New Mexico,
            and Other Sites in the Sandia-Manzano Region. Smith-
            sonian Miscellaneous Collections 99:23.

JENNINGS, J.D.

1024 1957 Danger Cave. Memoirs of the Society for American Archae-
            ology 14. University of Utah Press, Salt Lake City.

KELLER, C.M.

1025 1973 Montagu Cave in Prehistory: A Descriptive Analysis.
            University of California Anthropological Records 28.
            Berkeley.

KIDDER, A.V., and S.J. GUERNSEY

1026 1921 Basket Maker Caves of Northeastern Arizona. Papers of the Peabody Museum, Harvard University 8(2).

LOGAN. W.D.

1027 1952 Graham Cave: An Archaic Site in Montgomery County, Missouri. Missouri Archaeological Society, Memoir 2, Columbia, Mo.

McBURNEY, C.B.M.

1028 1967 The Haua Fteah (Cyrenaica) and the Stone Age of the South-East Mediterranean. Cambridge University Press, London.

MOVIUS, H.L., Jr.

1029 1975 Excavation of the Abri Pataud, Les Eyzies (Dordogne). Peabody Museum of Archaeology and Ethnology, American School of Prehistoric Research Bulletin 30.

PARTRIDGE, T.C.

1030 1966 Ficus Cave: An Iron Age Living Site in the Central Transvaal. South African Archaeological Bulletin 21(83), Pt. 3:125-132.

PEARCE, J.E., and A.T. JACKSON

1031 1933 A Prehistoric Rock Shelter in Val Verde County, Texas. University of Texas Publication 3327.

SCHMID, E.

1032 1963 Cave Sediments and Prehistory. In D. Brothwell and E. Higgs, eds., Science in Archaeology:123-138. Thames and Hudson, London.

SERIZAWA, C.

1033 1979 Cave Sites in Japan. World Archaeology 10(3):340-349.

SHIPPEE, J.M.

1034 1966 The Archaeology of Arnold Research Cave, Callaway County, Missouri. Missouri Archaeologist 28:1-40.

SOLECKI, R.S.

1035 1957 Shanidar Cave. Scientific American 197(5):58-78.

1036 1971 Shanidar, the First Flower People. Alfred A. Knopf, New York.

van RIET LOWE, C.

1037 1954 The Cave of Hearths. South African Archaeological Bulletin 9(33):25-29.

WATSON, P.J.

1038 1969 The Prehistory of Salts Cave, Kentucky. Illinois State
            Museum, Report of Investigations 16. Springfield.

1039 1974 Archaeology of the Mammoth Cave Area. Academic Press,
            New York.

WATSON, P.J., and R.A. YARNELL

1040 1966 Archaeological and Paleoethnological Investigations in
            Salts Cave, Mammoth Cave National Park, Kentucky.
            American Antiquity 31:842-849.

WORD, J.H., and C.L. DOUGLAS

1041 1970 Excavations at Baker Cave, Val Verde County, Texas.
            Texas Memorial Museum, Bulletin 16.

ZORZI, F.

1042 1964 Palaeolithic Discoveries in the Grotta Paglicci.
            Antiquity 38(49):38-44.

7. Earthworks and Mounds

ANDERSEN, H.

1043 1951 Tomme Hoje (Empty Tumuli). Kuml 1951:91-135.

ASHBEE, P.

1044 1970 The Earthen Long Barrow in Britain. Dent, London.

BRAIDWOOD, R.J.

1045 1937 Mounds in the Plain of Antioch, an Archaeological
            Survey. Oriental Institute Publications 48. Chicago.

CHILDE, V.G., and I. SMITH

1046 1954 The Excavation of a Neolithic Barrow on Whiteleaf Hill,
            Bucks. Proceedings, Prehistoric Society n.s. 20(2):212-
            230.

CRAWFORD, O.G.S.

1047 1927 Barrows. Antiquity 1:419-434.

DENEVAN, W.M.

1048 1963 Additional Comments on Earthworks of Mojos in Northeastern
            Bolivia. American Antiquity 28:540-545.

FORD, J.A.

1049 1952 Mound Builders of the Mississippi. Scientific American
            186(3):22-27.

1050 1963 Hopewell Culture Burial Mounds Near Helena, Arkansas.
            Anthropological Papers, American Museum of Natural History
            50(1).

FOWLER, M., ed.

1051 1969 Explorations into Cahokia Archaeology. Illinois Archaeological Survey, Bulletin 7.

GARLAKE, P.S.

1052 1967 Seventeenth Century Portuguese Earthworks in Rhodesia. South African Archaeological Bulletin 21(4):157-170.

GROUBE, L.M.

1053 1970 The Origin and Development of Earthwork Fortifications in the Pacific. In R. Green and M. Kelly, eds., Studies in Oceanic Culture History 1. Pacific Anthropological Records 11:133-164.

HARDING, D.W., ed.

1054 1976 Hillforts, Later Prehistoric Earthworks in Britain and Ireland. Academic Press, London.

HARN, A.D.

1055 1971 The Prehistory of Dickson Mounds: A Preliminary Report. Illinois State Museum, Springfield.

HURLEY, W.M.

1056 1975 An Analysis of Effigy Mound Complexes in Wisconsin. Museum of Anthropology, University of Michigan, Anthropological Papers 59. Ann Arbor.

LEE, T.A.

1057 1974 Mound 4 Excavations at San Isidro, Chiapas, Mexico. New World Archeological Foundation Papers 34. Brigham Young University, Provo, Utah.

LLOYD, S.

1058 1954 Mound Surveys. Antiquity 112:214-228.

1059 1963 Mounds of the Near East. Edinburgh University Press, Edinburgh.

MOOREHEAD, W.K.

1060 1929 The Cahokia Mounds. University of Illinois Press, Urbana.

1061 1932 Exploration of the Etowah Site in Georgia. Department of Archaeology, Phillips Academy, Andover, Mass.

PEET, S.D.

1062 1891 The Great Cahokia Mound. American Antiquarian 13(1):3-31.

PIGGOTT, S.

1063 1973 The Dalladies Long Barrow: N.E. Scotland. Antiquity 47(185):32-36.

SHAW, T.

1064   1970   Methods of Earthwork Building. Proceedings, Prehistoric
              Society 36:380.

U.N. ECONOMIC COMMISSION FOR ASIA AND THE FAR EAST

1065   1961   Earthmoving by Manual Labour and Machines. United Nations,
              ST/ECAFE/SER.F/17. Bangkok.

VICINUS, J.

1066   1969   Annotated References to Excavated Burial Mound Sites in
              Wisconsin, Manitoba, North Dakota and South Dakota.
              Minnesota Archaeologist 30(3):55-72.

8. Monuments, Large Stone Structures, and Megaliths

ATKINSON, K.B.

1067   1968   The Recording of Some Prehistoric Carvings at Stonehenge.
              The Photogrammetric Record 6:24-31.

ATKINSON, R.J.C.

1068   1956   Stonehenge. Hamilton, London.

BAKKER, J.A.

1060   1979   Lucas de Heere's Stonehenge. Antiquity 53(208):107-111.

BALCER, J.M.

1070   1974   The Mycenaean Dam at Tiryns. American Journal of Archae-
              ology 78(2):141-150.

BELZONI, G.

1071   1820   Narrative of the Operations and Recent Discoveries
              Within the Pyramids, Temples, Tombs and Excavations in
              Egypt and Nubia. 2 vols. London.

BURL, A.

1072   1976   The Stone Circles of the British Isles. Yale University
              Press, New Haven.

CHILDE, V.G.

1073   1932   Scottish Megalithic Tombs and Their Affinities. Transac-
              tions, Glasgow Archaeological Society 3:120-137.

COE, W.R., and J.J. McGINN

1074   1963   Tikal: The North Acropolis and an Early Tomb. Expedition
              5(2):24-32.

CUTFORTH, RENÉ

1075   1970   Stonehenge at Midsummer. Antiquity 44:305-306.

DANIEL, G.E.

1076   1966   The Megalith Builders of the SOM. Palaeohistoria 12: 199-208.

EDWARDS, I.E.S.

1077   1961   The Pyramids of Egypt. Penguin Books, Baltimore.

ERASMUS, C.J.

1078   1965   Monument Building: Some Field Experiments. Southwestern Journal of Anthropology 21:277-301.

FERGUSSON, J.

1079   1872   Rude Stone Monuments in All Countries: Their Age and Uses. John Murray, London.

HAWKES, J.

1080   1953   Stonehenge. Scientific American 188(6):25-31.

HILL, P.A.

1081   1961   Sarsen Stones at Stonehenge. Science 133:1216-1222.

HOYLE, F.

1082   1966   Speculations on Stonehenge. Antiquity 46:262-276.

1083   1966   Stonehenge--an Eclipse Predictor. Nature 211(5048):454-456.

1084   1977   On Stonehenge. W.H. Freeman, San Francisco.

HUTCHINSON, G.E.

1085   1972   Long Meg Reconsidered. American Scientist 60(1):24-31.

HUTTON, J.H.

1086   1929   Assam Megaliths. Antiquity 3:324-388.

LOCKYER, N.

1087   1909   Stonehenge and Other British Stone Monuments Astronomically Considered. Macmillan and Co., London.

LUCAS, A.

1088   1938   Were the Giza Pyramids Painted? Antiquity 12(45):26-30.

MacKIE, E.W.

1089   1977   The Megalith Builders. Phaidon, Oxford.

MILLON, R., and B. DREWITT

1090   1961   Earlier Structures Within the Pyramid of the Sun at Teotihuacan. American Antiquity 26:371-380.

MILLON, R., B. DREWITT, and J. BENNYHOFF

1091 1965 The Pyramid of the Sun at Teotihuacan: 1959 Excavations.
            Transactions of the American Philosophical Society 55(6).

MOIR, G.

1092 1979 Hoyle on Stonehenge. Antiquity 53(208):124-129.

MULLOY, W.

1093 1970 A Speculative Reconstruction of Techniques of Carving,
            Transporting and Erecting Easter Island Statues.
            Archaeology and Physical Anthropology in Oceania 5(1):1-23.

NEWHALL, R.S.

1094 1929 Stonehenge. Antiquity 3:75-134.

NUALLAIN, S.O.

1095 1979 The Megalithic Tombs of Ireland. Expedition 21(3):6-15.

NYLANDER, C.

1096 1965 Old Persian and Greek Stone-Cutting and the Chronology of
            Achaemenian Monuments. American Journal of Archaeology
            69(1):49-56.

PEAKE, H.J., and H.J. FLEURE

1097 1930 Megaliths and Beakers. Journal of the Royal Anthropological
            Institute 9.

PEREZ, J.R.

1098 1935 Exploración del Tunel de la Piramide del Sol. El México
            Antiguo 3:91-95.

PIGGOTT, S.

1099 1954 The Druids and Stonehenge. South African Archaeological
            Bulletin 9(36):138-140.

POWELL, T.G.E., and others

1100 1969 Megalithic Enquiries in the West of Britain: A Liverpool
            Symposium. Liverpool University Monographs in Archae-
            ology and Oriental Studies.

RAUSING, G.

1101 1979 Moving Large Blocks of Stone in Pakistan. Antiquity
            53(208):143-144.

RENFREW, A.C.

1102 1967 Colonialism and Megalithismus. Antiquity 41:276-288.

RICKETSON, D.G., and E.B. RICKETSON

1103 1937 Uaxactun, Guatemala: Group E, 1926-1931. Carnegie Insti-
            tute of Washington 477.

SHOOK, E.M., and A.V. KIDDER

1104 1952 Mound E-III-3, Kaminaljuyu, Guatemala. Carnegie Institute
            of Washington 596.

SREJOVIC, D.

1105 1972 Europe's First Monumental Sculpture: New Discoveries at
            Lepenski Vir. Thames and Hudson, London.

STONE, E.H.

1106 1924 The Stones of Stonehenge. Scott, London.

THOM, A.

1107 1967 Megalithic Sites in Britain. Clarendon Press, Oxford.

THOM, A., and A.S. THOM

1108 1978 Megalithic Remains in Britain and Brittany. Clarendon
            Press, Oxford.

TROTTER, A.P.

1109 1927 Stonehenge as an Astronomical Instrument. Antiquity 1:
            42-53.

WERNICK, R.

1110 1973 The Monument Builders. Time-Life Books, New York.

WHEELER, N.F.

1111 1935 Pyramids and Their Purpose: II; the Pyramid of Khufu.
            Antiquity 9(34):161-189.

1112 1935 Pyramids and Their Purpose: III; Pyramid Mysticism and
            Mystification. Antiquity 9(35):292-304.

WISEMAN, J.R.

1113 1968 An Unfinished Colossus on Mt. Pendeli. American Journal
            of Archaeology 72(1):75.

9. Workshops and Quarries

ALTHIN, C.A.

1114 1951 The Scanian Flint Mines. Meddelanden fran Lunds Univer-
            sity Historiska Museum 1951:139-158.

ANDERSON, A.D.

1115 1975 The Cooperton Mammoth: An Early Man Bone Quarry. Great
            Plains Journal 14(2):130-173.

APPY, E.P.

1116 1889 Ancient Mining in America. American Antiquity and Oriental
            Journal 2:92-99.

BABBITT, F.E.

1117 1880   Ancient Quartz Workers and Their Quarries in Minnesota.
             American Antiquarian 3(1):18-23.

BALL, S.H.

1118 1941   The Mining of Gems and Ornamental Stones by American
             Indians. Bureau of American Ethnology, Bulletin 128:
             1-77.

BARCENAS GONZALEZ, J.G.

1119 1975   Las Minas de Obsidiana de la Sierra de las Navajas,
             Hidalgo, México. Actas, XLI Congreso Internacional de
             Americanistas I:369-377.

BECKER, C.J.

1120 1951   Late Neolithic Flint Mines at Aalborg. Acta Archaeologica
             22:135-152.

1121 1959   Flint-Mining in Neolithic Denmark. Antiquity 33:87-92.

BOLTON, R.P.

1122 1930   An Aboriginal Chert-Quarry in Northern Vermont. Indian
             Notes, Museum of American Indian, Heye Foundation 7:
             457-465.

BRESSLER, J.P.

1123 1960   The Penns Creek Archaic Workshops. Pennsylvania
             Archaeologist 30(1):25-29.

BRYAN, A.L., and TUOHY, D.R.

1124 1960   A Basalt Quarry in Northeastern Oregon. Proceedings,
             American Philosophical Society 104:488-510.

BRYAN, K.

1125 1938   Prehistoric Quarries and Implements of Pre-Amerindian
             Aspect in New Mexico. Science 87(2259).

1126 1950   Flint Quarries: The Sources of Tools, and at the Same
             Time, the Factories of the American Indian. Papers,
             Peabody Museum of American Archaeology and Ethnology 17(3).

CHARLTON, T.H.

1127 1969   On the Identification of Prehispanic Obsidian Mines in
             Southern Hidalgo. American Antiquity 34:176-177.

CLARK, J.G.D., and S. PIGGOTT

1128 1933   The Age of the British Flint Mines. Antiquity 7:166-183.

CLARKE, W.G.

1129 1915   A Prehistoric Flint-Pit at Ringland. Proceedings, Pre-
             historic Society, East Anglia 1:148-151.

CLASON, A.T.

1130 1971 The Flint-Mine Workers of Spiennes and Rijckholt-St.
             Geertruid and Their Animals. Helinium 2(1):3-33.

CRAWFORD, O.G.S., and J. RÖDER

1131 1955 The Quern-Quarries of Mayen in the Eifel. Antiquity 29:
             68-75.

FOWKE, G.

1132 1928 Archaeological Investigations, II. Aboriginal Flint
             Quarries. Bureau of American Ethnology, Annual Report
             (for 1926-1927):505-540.

HEIZER, R.F., and A.E. TREGANZA

1133 1944 Mines and Quarries of the Indians of California.
             California Journal of Mines and Geology 40:291-359.
             Reprinted 1972, Ballena Press, Ramona, Cal.

HOLMES, W.H.

1134 1879 Notes on an Extensive Deposit of Obsidian in Yellowstone
             National Park. American Naturalist 13(4):247-250.

1135 1890 Recent Work in the Quarry Workshops of the District of
             Columbia. American Anthropologist 3(o.s.):224-225.

1136 1890 A Quarry Workshop of the Flaked-Stone Implement Makers
             in the District of Columbia. American Anthropologist
             3(o.s.):1-26.

1137 1891 Aboriginal Novaculite Quarries in Garland Co., Arkansas.
             American Anthropologist 4(o.s.):313-315.

1138 1892 Modern Quarry Refuse and the Paleolithic Theory. Science
             20:295-297.

1139 1900 The Obsidian Mines of Hidalgo. American Anthropologist
             2(n.s.):405-416.

HORNKOHN, H.

1140 1947 Explotación Prehistórica de Pedernal en Chile. Publica-
             ciones de la Sociedad Arqueológica de la Serena, Boletin
             3:7-9.

HOULDER, C.H.

1141 1961 The Excavation of a Neolithic Stone Factory on Mynydd
             Rhiw in Caernarvonshire. Proceedings, Prehistoric
             Society 27:108-143.

IVES, D.J.

1142 1975 The Crescent Hills Prehistoric Quarrying Area. Museum
             Briefs, University of Missouri, Columbia.

JURY, W.W.

1143 1949 Report on Prehistoric Flint Work Shops at Port Franks.
             Ontario Museum of Indian Archaeology, University of
             Western Ontario, Bulletin 8.

KELLY, T.C., and T.R. HESTER

1144 1975 Archaeological Investigations at Four Sites in the Dry
            Comal Watershed, Comal County, South Central Texas.
            Center for Archaeological Research, The University of
            Texas at San Antonio, Archaeological Survey Report 15.

LEMELY, H.J.

1145 1942 Prehistoric Novaculite Quarries of Arkansas. Bulletin,
            Texas Archeological and Paleontological Society 14:32-37.

LOSEY, T.C.

1146 1971 The Stony Plain Quarry Site. Plains Anthropologist 16(52):
            138-154.

MacCALMAN, H.R., and A. VIERECK

1147 1967 Peperkorrel, a Factory Site of Lupemban Affinities from
            Central South West Africa. South African Archaeological
            Bulletin 22(86):41-50.

MARSDEN, J.G.

1148 1915 A Workshop Floor near Portcurno, Cornwall. Proceedings,
            Prehistoric Society, East Anglia 2:41-42.

MELLO, J.M.

1149 1884- On the Prehistoric Factory of Flints at Spiennes. Journal
      1885   of Transactions, Victoria Institute of London 18.

MERCER, H.C.

1150 1894 Indian Jasper Mines in the Lehigh Hills. American Anthro-
            pologist 7(o.s.):80-92.

MOIR, J.R.

1151 1911 The Discovery of a Flint Workshop in Ivry Street, Ipswich.
            Proceedings, Prehistoric Society, East Anglia 1:475-479.

MOYSEY, C.F.

1152 1918 A Flint Implement Factory Site Near Milverton, Somerset.
            Proceedings, Prehistoric Society, East Anglia 2:521-523.

PARKER, A.C.

1153 1924 The Great Algonkin Flint Mines at Coxsackie. Researches
            and Transactions of the New York State Archaeological
            Association, L.H. Morgan Chapter 4(4).

PEAKE, H.J.E., and O.G.S. CRAWFORD

1154 1922 A Flint Factory at Thatcham, Berks. Proceedings, Prehis-
            toric Society, East Anglia 3:499-514.

PHILLIPS, W.A.

1155 1900 Aboriginal Quarries and Shops at Mill Creek, Illinois.
            American Anthropologist 2(n.s.):37.

PROUDFIT, S.V.

1156 1889 Ancient Village Sites and Aboriginal Workshops in the
            District of Columbia. American Anthropologist 2(o.s.):
            241-246.

RANKINE, W.F.

1157 1952 A Mesolithic Chipping Floor at The Warren, Oakhanger,
            Selbourne, Hants. Proceedings, Prehistoric Society
            18(1):21-35.

1158 1960 Further Excavations at a Mesolithic Site at Oakhanger,
            Selbourne, Hants. Proceedings, Prehistoric Society 26:
            246-262.

SAINTY, J.E.

1159 1924- A Flaking Site on Kelling Heath, Norfolk. Proceedings,
1927   Prehistoric Society, East Anglia 4(1924):165-175;
       5(1925):56-61; 7(1927):283-287.

SETON-KARR, H.W.

1160 1898 Discovery of the Lost Flint Mines of Egypt. Journal,
            Royal Anthropological Institute 27:90-92.

SHAEFFER, J.B.

1161 1958 The Alibates Flint Quarry. American Antiquity 24:189-191.

SIEVEKING, G. de G., I.H. LONGWORTH, M.J. HUGHES, A.J. CLARK,
   and A. MILLET

1162 1973 A New Survey of Grimes's Graves, Norfolk. Proceedings,
            Prehistoric Society 39:182-218.

SINGER, C.A., and J.E. ERICSON

1163 1977 Quarry Analysis at Bodie Hills, Mono County, California:
            A Case Study. In J.E. Ericson, ed., Exchange Systems
            in Prehistory:171-187. Academic Press, New York.

SMITH, C.M.

1164 1885 A Descriptive Sketch of Flint Ridge, Licking County, Ohio.
            Smithsonian Institution--Annual Report for 1884:851-873.

SPENCE, M., and J. PARSONS

1165 1967 Prehistoric Obsidian Mines in Southern Hidalgo. American
            Antiquity 32:542-543.

STILES, D.N., R.L. HAY, and J.R. O'NEIL

1166 1974 The MNK Chert Factory Site, Olduvai Gorge, Tanzania. World
            Archaeology 5(3):285-308.

SULIMIRSKI, T.

1167 1960 Remarks Concerning the Distribution of Some Varieties
            of Flint in Poland. Swiatowit 23:281-307.

TUOHY, D.R.

1168 1970 The Coleman Locality: A Basalt Quarry and Workshop Near
            Falcon Hill, Nevada. Nevada State Museum, Anthropological
            Papers 15:143-205.

TURNER, C.H.

1169 1954 Indian Quarries. Missouri Archaeologist 16(2):6.

WAGNER, E., and C. SCHUBERT

1170 1972 Pre-Hispanic Workshop of Serpentine Artifacts, Venezuelan
            Andes and Possible Raw Material Source. Science 175(4204):
            888-890.

WEIGAND, P.C.

1171 1968 The Mines and Mining Techniques of the Chalchichuites
            Culture. American Antiquity 33:45-61.

WILSON, T.

1172 1896 Piney Branch (D.C.) Quarry Workshop and Its Implements.
            American Naturalist 30:855-873; 976-992.

WITTY, T.A.

1173 1967 A Greenwood County Quarry Site. Kansas Anthropological
            Association Newsletter 12(5):1-2.

ZUROWSKI, T.

1174 1960 Flint-Mining on the Kamienna River. Swiatowit 23:249-279.

10. Rock Art
(See E11.)

D. FIELD WORK

1. Preparation and Research Design

ADAMS, R. McC.

1175 1968 Archeological Research Strategies: Past and Present.
            Science 160:1187-1192.

BINFORD, L.R.

1176 1964 A Consideration of Archaeological Research Design.
            American Antiquity 29(4):425-441.

DANIELS, S.G.H.

1177 1972 Research Design Models. In D.L. Clarke, ed., Models in
            Archaeology:201-230. Methuen and Co., London.

DITTERT, A.E., Jr., and F. WENDORF

1178 1969 Procedural Manual for Archaeological Research Projects.
            Papers in Anthropology, Museum of New Mexico Press,
            Santa Fe.

HERSKOVITS, M.J.

1179 1950 The Hypothetical Situation: A Technique of Field Research.
            Southwestern Journal of Anthropology 6:32-40.

HESTER, T.R., R.F. HEIZER, and J.A. GRAHAM

1180 1975 Field Methods in Archaeology. 6th ed. Mayfield Pub-
            lishing Co., Palo Alto, Cal.

HILL, J.N.

1181 1972 The Methodological Debate in Contemporary Archaeology:
            A Model. In D.L. Clarke, ed., Models in Archaeology:
            61-108. Methuen and Co., London.

LOOFBOUROW, J.C., and D. PAPPAGIANIS

1182 1971 Coccidiodomycosis, an Occupational Hazard for Archae-
            ologists. Department of Anthropology, San Francisco
            State College, Special Report 2.

PERINO, G.

1183 1967 Use, Care, and Construction of Archaeological Tools.
            Newsletter, Oklahoma Anthropological Society 15(7):2-4.

PLOG, F.T.

1184 1974 The Study of Prehistoric Change. Academic Press, New York.

REDMAN, C.L.

1185 1973 Multistage Field Work and Analytical Techniques. American
            Antiquity 38(1):61-79.

SCHIFFER, M.B., and G.J. GUMERMAN

1186 1977 Part III. Research Design. In M.B. Schiffer and G.J.
            Gumerman, eds., Conservation Archaeology:130-133.
            Academic Press, New York.

SHARER, R.J., and W. ASHMORE

1187 1979 Fundamentals of Archaeology. Benjamin/Cummings Publishing
            Co., Inc., Menlo Park, Cal. (See pp. 114-142.)

STRUEVER, S.

1188 1971 Comments on Archaeological Data Requirements and Research
            Strategy. American Antiquity 36(1):9-19.

SWARTZ, B.K., Jr.

1189 1967 A Logical Sequence of Archaeological Objectives. American
            Antiquity 32:487-497.

WATSON, P.J., S.A. LeBLANC, and C.L. REDMAN

1190 1971 Explanation in Archeology. Columbia University Press,
            New York.

2. Methods in the Field

ADERMAN, J.Y.

1191 1844 Account of the Opening by Matthew Bell, Esq. of an Ancient
            British Barrow, in Iffins Wood, near Canterbury, in the
            Month of January, 1842. Archaeologia 30(IV):57-61. London.

BERNAL, I.

1192 1952 Introducción a la Arqueología. Fondo de Cultura
            Económica, Mexico.

BETTAREL, R.

1193 1964 Archaeological Field Technique: A Brief Look at Pre-
            historic Michigan Burials. Michigan Archaeologist
            10(4):74-82.

BIRD, J.B.

1194 1943 Excavations in Northern Chile. Anthropological Papers
            of the American Museum of Natural History 38(4). New
            York.

BRAIDWOOD, R.J., and B. HOWE

1195 1960 Prehistoric Investigations in Iraqi Kurdistan. Oriental
            Institute of the University of Chicago, Studies in
            Oriental Civilization 31.

BRUCE-MITFORD, R.L.S., ed.

1196 1956 Recent Archaeological Excavations in Britain. Routledge
            and Kegan Paul, London.

COLTON, H.S.

1197 1953 Field Methods in Archaeology, Prepared for Archaeological
            Expeditions of the Museum of Northern Arizona. Museum of
            Northern Arizona, Flagstaff.

COLYER, M., and D. OSBORNE

1198 1965 Screening Soil and Fecal Samples for Recovery of Small
            Specimens. American Antiquity 31(2), Pt. 2:186-192.

DeJARNETTE, D.L., and O.W. BROCK, Jr.

1199 1968 The Use of Polyethylene in Stratigraphic Profiles.
            Journal of Alabama Archaeology 14(1):38-40.

DICTIONNAIRE ARCHÉOLOGIQUE DES TECHNIQUES

1200 1963- Two volumes. Editions de l'Accueil, Paris.
      1964

DITTERT, A.E., and F. WENDORF

1201 1963 Procedural Manual for Archaeological Field Research
            Projects of the Museum of New Mexico. Museum of New
            Mexico, Papers in Anthropology 12. Santa Fe.

FORD, J., W. PHILLIPS, and W. HAAG

1202 1955 The Jaketown Site in West-Central Mississippi. American
            Museum of Natural History, Anthropological Papers Series
            45(1).

FOWLER, W.S.

1203 1972 Recommended Methods for Excavating a Site. Bulletin of
            the Massachusetts Archaeological Society 33(1, 2):29-32.

GOODWIN, A.J.H.

1204 1953 Method in Prehistory. South African Archaeological
            Society Handbook 1. 2nd ed. Capetown, South Africa.

GREEN, C.

1205 1948 Balks and the Open Field System. Antiquity 22(88):206.

HEIZER, R.F., and J.A. GRAHAM

1206 1967 A Guide to Field Methods in Archaeology: Approaches to
            the Anthropology of the Dead. National Press, Palo Alto,
            Cal.

HESTER, T.R., R.F. HEIZER, and J.A. GRAHAM

1207 1975 Field Methods in Archaeology. 6th ed. Mayfield Publishing
            Co., Palo Alto, Cal.

KENYON, K.M.

1208 1952 Beginning in Archaeology. Praeger, New York.

KIDDER, A.V.

1209 1958 Pecos, New Mexico: Archaeological Notes. Papers of the
            R.S. Peabody Foundation for Archaeology 5. Phillips
            Academy, Andover, Mass.

LAMING-EMPERAIRE, A.

1210 1963 L'Archéologie Préhistorique. Editions de Sevil, Paris.

PARROT, A.

1211 1953 Archéologie Mesopotamienne: II, Technique et Problèmes.
            Albin Michel, Paris.

PONCE SANGINES, C.

1212 1961 Informe de Labores. Centro de Investigaciones
            Arqueológicas en Tiwanaku. Publication 1. La Paz.

PYDDOKE, E.

1213 1961 Stratification for the Archaeologist. Phoenix House,
            London.

RITCHIE, P.R., and J. PUGH

1214 1963 Ultra-Violet Radiation and Excavation. Antiquity
            37(148):259-263.

SIMMONS, H.C.

1215 1969 Archaeological Photography. University of London Press,
            London.

SMITH, R.H.

1216 1975 Ethics in Field Archaeology. Journal of Field Archaeology
            1(3/4):375-384.

SORENSON, J.L.

1217 1964 Use of Automated Tools in Archaeology. American Antiquity
            30:205-206.

STRAFFIN, D.

1218 1971 A Device for Vertical Archaeological Photography.
            Plains Anthropologist 16(53):232.

THOMPSON, R.H.

1219 1955 Review of R.E.M. Wheeler, Archaeology from the Earth.
            American Antiquity 21:188-189.

WEDEL, W.R.

1220 1951 The Use of Earth-Moving Machinery in Archaeological
            Excavation. University of Michigan, Museum of Anthropology
            Anthropological Papers 8:17-28.

WHEELER, N.F.

1221 1930 Excavation. Antiquity 4:173-178.

WHEELER, R.E.M.

1222 1932 This Fieldwork. Antiquity 6:55-59.

1223 1956 Archaeology from the Earth. Pelican Books A 356,
            Baltimore.

WHITTLESEY, J.

1224 1966 Photogrammetry for the Excavator. Archaeology 19:273-276.

YANINE, V.L.

1225 1960 Modern Methods in Archaeology: The Novgorod Excavations.
            Diogenes 29:82-101.

a. GENERAL FIELD GUIDES

ALEXANDER, J.

1226   1970   The Directing of Archaeological Excavations.   John Baker,
              London.

ASHBEE, P., and I.W. CORNWALL

1227   1961   An Experiment in Field Archaeology.   Antiquity 35(138):
              129-134.

ATKINSON, R.J.C.

1228   1953   Field Archaeology.   2nd ed.   Methuen and Co., London.

BARKER, P.

1229   1977   Techniques of Archaeological Excavation.   Universe Books,
              New York.

BRENNAN, L.A.

1230   1973   Beginner's Guide to Archaeology: The Modern Digger's
              Step-by-Step Introduction to the Expert Ways of Un-
              earthing the Past.   Stackpole Books, Harrisburg, Pa.

BROWNE, D.

1231   1975   Principles and Practice in Modern Archaeology.   Teach
              Yourself Books, London.

COLES, J.M.

1232   1972   Field Archaeology in Britain.   Barnes and Noble, London.

COLTON, H.S.

1233   1953   Field Methods in Archaeology.   Museum of Northern
              Arizona, Technical Series 1.

CORCORAN, J.

1234   1966   The Young Field Archaeologist's Guide.   G. Bell and Sons,
              London.

CRAWFORD, O.G.S.

1235   1953   Archaeology in the Field.   Praeger, New York.

DeLAET, S.J.

1236   1957   Archaeology and Its Problems.   Phoenix House, London.

DINSMOOR, W.B., Jr.

1237   1977   The Archaeological Field Staff: The Architect.   Journal
              of Field Archaeology 4(3):309-328.

FLADMARK, K.R.

1238   1978   A Guide to Basic Archaeological Field Procedures.   Simon
              Fraser University, Department of Archaeology.   Burnaby, B.C.

HAMMOND, P.C.

1239   1963   Archaeological Techniques for Amateurs.   Van Nostrand,
              Princeton, N.J.

HESTER, T.R., R.F. HEISER, and J.A. GRAHAM

1240   1975   Field Methods in Archaeology.   6th ed.   Mayfield Pub-
              lishing Co., Palo Alto, Cal.

HRANICKY, W.J.

1241   1973   Archaeology: A Means to the Past.   The Artifact 11(3):
              1-83.

1242   1979   An Introduction to American Prehistoric Field Archaeology.
              Popular Archaeology, Technical Publication 1.   Arlington,
              Va.

MULVANEY, D.J.

1243   1968   Australian Archaeology: A Guide to Field Techniques.
              Australian Institute of Aboriginal Studies, Manual 4.
              Canberra.

PAPWORTH, M.L., and L.R. BINFORD

1244   1962   A Guide to Archaeological Excavations.   Southwestern Lore
              28:1-24.

PLACE, R.

1245   1955   Down to Earth: A Practical Guide to Archaeology.
              Philosophical Library, New York.

POTRATZ, J.A.H.

1246   1962   Einführung in die Archäologie.   A. Kröner, Stuttgart.

PYDDOKE, E.

1247   1961   Stratification for the Archaeologist.   Lawrence Verry,
              Mystic, Conn.

ROBBINS, M., and M.B. IRVING

1248   1973   The Amateur Archaeologist's Handbook.   Thomas Y. Crowell,
              New York.

ROWLETT, R.M.

1249   1963   Methods and Techniques of Medieval Village Archaeology.
              Southeastern Archaeological Conference Newsletter 9(2):
              6-14.

SCHWARZ, G.T.

1250   1967   Archäologische Feldmethode.   O. Verlag, Thus and München.

SCHWARZ, G.T., and G. JUNGHANS

1251   1967   A New Method of Three-Dimensional Recording of Archae-
              ological Finds.   Archaeometry 10:64-69.

SODAY, F.J.

1252 1962 An Archaeological Field and Excavation Manual. Quarterly
            Bulletin, Archeological Society of Virginia 16(2-3).

WALKER, I.C.

1253 1967 Excavation with a Backhoe. Ontario Archaeology 10:12-17.

WEBSTER, G.

1254 1974 Practical Archaeology: An Introduction to Archaeological
            Field Work and Excavation. 2nd ed. A. & C. Black, London.

WHEELER, N.F.

1255 1930 Excavation. Antiquity 4:173-178.

WOOD, E.S.

1256 1963 Collins Field Guide to Archaeology. Collins, London.

b. SITE SURVEY

BASSHAM, E.F.

1257 1971 Cave Surveying Techniques. El Paso Archaeological
            Society, Handbook Series 1.

BORDEN, C.E.

1258 1952 A Uniform Site Designation Scheme for Canada. British
            Columbia Provincial Museum, Anthropology in British
            Columbia 3:44-48. Victoria, B.C.

CARR, R.F., and J.E. HAZARD

1259 1961 Tikal Report 11; Map of the Ruins of Tikal, El Peten,
            Guatemala. Museum Monographs. University of Pennsylvania
            Museum, Philadelphia.

COOMBS, C.

1260 1978 Survey Methods for Spatially-Dispersed Excavation Sampling.
            Journal of Field Archaeology 5(3):371-374.

DETWEILER, A.H.

1261 1948 Manual of Archaeological Surveying. American Schools
            of Oriental Research, Publications of the Jerusalem School,
            Archaeology 2. New Haven.

DIEHL, R.A.

1262 1970 A Site Designation System for Latin America. American
            Antiquity 35(4):491-492.

DILLS, C.E.

1263 1970 Coordinate Location of Archaeological Sites. American
            Antiquity 35(3):389-390.

DRUCKER, P., and E. CONTRERAS

1264 1953 Site Patterns in the Eastern Part of Olmec Territory.
            Journal of the Washington Academy of Science 43:389-396.

FORD, J.A., and G.R. WILLEY

1265 1949 Surface Survey of the Viru Valley, Peru. American Museum
            of Natural History, Anthropological Papers Series 43(1).

GORDON, B.C.

1266 1978 Chemical and Pedological Delimiting of Deeply Stratified
            Archaeological Sites in Frozen Ground. Journal of Field
            Archaeology 5(3):331-338.

HADLEIGH-WEST, F.

1267 1967 A System of Archaeological Sites Designation for Alaska.
            American Antiquity 32(1):107-108.

HAYES, A.C.

1268 1964 The Archeological Survey of Wetherill Mesa. National
            Park Service, Archeological Research Service 7-A.
            Washington.

HEIZER, R.F.

1269 1968 Suggested Change in System of Site Designations.
            American Antiquity 33:254.

JUDGE, W.J.

1270 1973 Paleoindian Occupation of the Rio Grande Valley.
            University of New Mexico Press, Albuquerque.

JUDGE, W.J., J.I. EBERT, and R.K. HITCHCOCK

1271 1975 Sampling in Regional Archaeological Survey. In J.W.
            Mueller, ed., Sampling in Archaeology:82-123. University
            of Arizona Press, Tucson.

LININGTON, R.E.

1272 1970 Techniques Used in Archaeological Field Surveys. In
            The Impact of the Natural Sciences on Archaeology:89-108.
            Oxford University Press, London.

PALMER, L.S.

1273 1960 Geological Surveying of Archaeological Sites. Proceedings,
            Prehistoric Society 26:64-75.

PLOG, S.

1274 1976 The Efficiency of Sampling Techniques for Archaeological
            Surveys. In K.V. Flannery, ed., The Early Mesoamerican
            Village:136-158. Academic Press, New York.

ROWE, J.H.

1275   1971   Site Designation in the Americas. American Antiquity
36(4):477-479.

RUPPE, R.J.

1276   1966   The Archaeological Survey: A Defense. American Antiquity
31:313-333.

SCHIFFER, M.B., A.P. SULLIVAN, and T.C. KLINGER

1277   1978   The Design of Archaeological Surveys. World Archaeology
10(1):1-28.

SHAEFFER, J.B.

1278   1960   The County Grid System of Site Designation. Plains
Anthropologist 5(9):29-31.

SOLECKI, R.

1279   1949   The Trinomial Classification System (for Sites) for West
Virginia. West Virginia Archaeologist 1:5-6.

STAUB, G.

1280   1951   Die Geographische Fixierung Historischer Objekte und
Örtlichkeiten. Jahrbuch 41 die Schweizerischen Gesellschaft
für Urgeschichte:191-195.

TOLSTOY, P.

1281   1958   Surface Survey of the Northern Valley of Mexico: The
Classic and Post-Classic Periods. Transactions, American
Philosophical Society 48(5). Philadelphia.

TRUE, D.L., and R.G. MATSON

1282   1974   Random Sampling Procedures in Archaeological Surveying:
An Evaluation. In R. Kautz, ed., Readings in Archae-
ological Method and Technique. University of California,
Center for Archaeological Research at Davis, Publication 4.

WITTHOFT, J.

1283   1965   The Basic Problems of Archaeological Surveys. Journal,
Archaeological Society of Maryland 1(1):1-4.

3. Subsurface Detection

ABRAHAMSEN, N.

1284   1967   Some Archaeomagnetic Investigations in Denmark.
Prospezioni Archeologiche 2:95-98.

AITKEN, M.J.

1285   1963   Magnetic Location. In D. Brothwell and E. Higgs, eds.,
Science in Archaeology:555-568. Thames and Hudson, London.

1286 1970 Magnetic Prospecting. In R. Berger, ed., Scientific
            Methods in Medieval Archaeology:423-434. University of
            California Press, Berkeley.

1287 1971 Enkomi-Alasia: The Proton Magnetometer Survey. Alasia 4.

      ALLDRED, J.C., and M.J. AITKEN

1288 1966 A Fluxgate Gradiometer for Archaeological Surveying.
            Prospezioni Archeologiche 1:53-60.

      ALLDRED, J.C., and A. SHEPHERD

1289 1963 Trial of Neutron Scattering for the Detection of Buried
            Walls and Cavities. Archaeometry 6:89-92.

      ANDERSEN, H.

1290 1951 Det Femte Store Mosefund. Kuml:9-22. Aarhus, Denmark.

      ARNOLD, J.B., III, and G.B. KEGLEY III

1291 1977 Results of a Magnetometer Survey at Hueco Tanks, a
            Prehistoric Mogollon Village in Western Texas. Texas
            Journal of Science 28(1-4):201-208.

      ASPINALL, A., and J. LYNAM

1292 1968 Induced Polarization as a Technique for Archaeological
            Surveying. Prospezioni Archeologiche 3:91-94.

      ATKINSON, R.J.

1293 1963 Resistivity Surveying in Archaeology. In E. Pyddoke, ed.,
            The Scientist and Archaeology:1-30. Phoenix House Pub-
            lishers, London.

      BLACK, G.A., and R.B. JOHNSTON

1294 1962 A Test of Magnetometry as an Aid to Archaeology.
            American Antiquity 28:199-205.

      BREINER, S.

1295 1965 The Rubidium Magnetometer in Archeological Exploration.
            Science 150:185-193.

1295a 1973 Applications Manual for Portable Magnetometers. Geo-
            metrics, Palo Alto, Cal.

      BREINER, S., and M.D. COE

1296 1972 Magnetic Exploration of the Olmec Civilization. American
            Scientist 60:566-575.

      BULLITT, O.H.

1297 1969 Search for Sybaris. Lippincott, Philadelphia.

      CARABELLI, E.

1298 1966 A New Tool for Archaeological Prospecting: The Sonic
            Spectroscope for Detection of Cavities. Prospezioni
            Archeologiche 1:25-36.

CHALABI, M.

1299 1965 Applications of Geo-Electrical Methods in Archaeology.
            Sumer 21(1,2). Iraq.

1300 1969 Theoretical Resistivity Anomalies Across a Single Vertical
            Discontinuity. Geophysical Prospecting 17(1):63-81.

CHIKISHEV, A.G.

1301 1965 Plant Indicators of Soils, Rocks, and Subsurface Waters.
            Consultants Bureau, New York.

CLARK, A.

1302 1963   Resistivity Surveying. In D. Brothwell and E. Higgs, eds.,
            Science in Archaeology:569-581. Thames and Hudson, London.

COLANI, C.

1303 1966 A New Method and Wide-Range Apparatus for Locating Metal
            Objects in the Ground, Fresh Water and Salt Water.
            Prospezioni Archeologiche 1:15-24.

DABROWSKI, K., and W. STOPIŃSKI

1304 1962 The Application of the Electric-Resistivity Method to
            Archaeological Investigations Illustrated on the Example
            of an Early Mediaeval Hill-Fort Zawodzie in Kalisz.
            Archaeologia Polona V:21-30.

DUNK, A.J.

1305 1962 An Electrical Resistance Survey over a Romano-British
            Site. Bonner Jahrbucher 16:272-276.

FORD, R.I.

1306 1964 A Preliminary Report of the 1964 Resistivity Survey at
            the Schulz Site (20 SA 2). Michigan Archaeologist 10(3):
            54-58.

FORD, R.I., and R.O. KELSIN

1307 1969 A Resistivity Survey at the Norton Mound Group, 20 KT 1,
            Kent County. Michigan Archaeologist 15(3):86-92.

FRY, R.E.

1308 1972 Manually Operated Post Hole Diggers as Sampling Instru-
            ments. American Antiquity 37(2):259-260.

GRAMLY, R.M.

1309 1970 Use of a Magnetic Balance to Detect Pits and Postmolds.
            American Antiquity 35(2):217-220.

GRIFFITHS, D.W.

1310 1973 Local Archaeomagnetic Research. Bulletin of the New York
            State Archaeological Association 58:24-25.

GUMERMAN, G.J., and T.R. LYONS

1311 1971 Archeological Methodology and Remote Sensing. Science
            172:126-132.

HESSE, A.

1312 1966 The Importance of Climatologic Observations in Archae-
            ological Prospecting. Prospezioni Archeologiche 1:11-14.

1313 1973 Applications des Méthodes Géophysiques de Prospection à
            l'Étude des Sites Préhistoriques et Protohistoriques.
            Paleorient 1:11-20.

HOWELL, M.I.

1314 1968 The Soil Conductivity Anomaly Detector (SCM) in Archae-
            ological Prospection. Prospezioni Archeologiche 3:101-104.

HRDLIČKA, L.

1315 1969 Apparatus for the Investigation of Inaccessible Under-
            ground Cavities. Prospezioni Archeologiche 4:103-110.

JOHNSTON, R.B.

1316 1961 Archaeological Application of the Proton Magnetometer in
            Indiana (USA). Archaeometry 4:71-72.

LANGAN, L.

1317 1966 Use of New Atomic Magnetometers in Archaeology.
            Prospezioni Archeologiche 1:61-66.

LENKIEWICZ, T., and W. STOPIŃSKI

1318 1969 The Application of an Electric Resistivity Method to
            Archaeological Research in Towns. Archaeologia Polona
            XI:173-198.

LERICI, C.M.

1319 1961 Archaeological Surveys with the Proton Magnetometer in
            Italy. Archaeometry 4:76-82.

1320 1962 New Archaeological Techniques and International Coopera-
            tion in Italy. Expedition 4(3):5-10.

LININGTON, R.E.

1321 1966 Test Use of a Gravimeter on Etruscan Chamber Tombs at
            Cerveteri. Prospezioni Archeologiche 1:37-42.

1322 1967 An Electrical Resistivity Survey at Les Matignons.
            Prospezioni Archeologiche 2:91-93.

1323 1968 The Search for the Supposed Obelisk under Via Giustinani,
            Rome. Prospezioni Archeologiche 3:77-84.

1324 1970 A First Use of Linear Filtering Techniques on Archae-
            ological Prospecting Results. Prospezioni Archeologiche
            5:43-54.

McPHERSON, A., and E.K. RALPH

1325 1970 Magnetometer Location of Neolithic Houses in Yugoslavia.
Expedition 12(2):10-17.

MORRISON, F.

1326 1971 High-Sensitivity Magnetometers in Archaeological Exploration. University of California, Archaeological Research
Facility, Contribution 12:6-19.

MORRISON, F., C.W. CLEWLOW, Jr., and R.F. HEIZER

1327 1970 Magnetometer Survey of the La Venta Pyramid. University
of California, Archaeological Research Facility, Contribution 8:1-20.

OLSEN, S.J.

1328 1963 Metal Detectors as Archaeological Aids. Curator 6:321-324.

PALERM, L.S.

1329 1960 Geoelectrical Surveying of Archaeological Sites. Proceedings, Prehistoric Society 26:64-75.

PESCHEL, G.

1330 1967 A New Favourable Combination of Resistivity Sounding and
Profiling in Archaeological Survey. Prospezioni
Archeologiche 2:23-28.

PRICE, J.C., R.G. HUNTER, and E.V. McMICHAEL

1331 1964 Core Drilling in an Archaeological Site. American
Antiquity 30(2):219-222.

RALPH, E.K.

1332 1965 The Electronic Detective and the Case of the Missing City.
Expedition 7(2):4-8.

REED, N.A., J.W. BENNETT, and J.W. PORTER

1333 1968 Solid Core Drilling of Monks Mound: Technique and Findings.
American Antiquity 33(2):137-148.

ROBERTSON, R.

1334 1970 Beginning Archaeology in London--5 Resistivity Surveying.
The London Archaeologist 1(9):195-197.

SCHWARZ, G.T.

1335 1961 The "Zirkelsonde": A New Technique for Resistivity
Surveying. Archaeometry 4:67-70.

SCOLLAR, I.

1336 1962 Electromagnetic Prospecting Methods in Archaeology.
Archaeometry 5:146-153.

1337   1969   A Program for the Simulation of Magnetic Anomalies of
              Archaeological Origin in a Computer. Prospezioni
              Archeologiche 4:59-84.

1338   1970   Magnetic Methods of Archaeological Prospecting--Advances
              in Instrumentation and Evaluation Techniques. In The
              Impact of the Natural Sciences on Archaeology:109-120.
              Oxford University Press, London.

       TITE, M.S., and C. MULLINS

1339   1970   Electromagnetic Prospecting on Archaeological Sites Using
              Soil Conductivity Meter. Archaeometry 12:97-104.

       WEYMOUTH, J.W., and R. NICKEL

1340   1977   A Magnetometer Survey of the Knife River Indian Villages.
              Plains Anthropologist, Memoir 13:104-118.

       WHITWELL, J.B., and K.P. WOOD

1341   1969   Three Pottery Kiln Sites in Lincolnshire, Located by
              Proton Gradiometer (Maxbleep) Survey and Confirmed by
              Excavation. Prospezioni Archeologiche 4:125-130.

       WILCOCK, J.D.

1342   1969   Computer Analysis of Proton Magnetometer Readings from
              South Cadbury 1968. A Long Distance Exercise. Prospezioni
              Archeologiche 4:85-94.

       WILSON, A.E.

1343   1970   A Winter Survey with Proton Magnetometers of an Underwater
              Site. Prospezioni Archeologiche 5:89-94.

4. Site Mapping Methods

       BLAKESLEE, D.J.

1344   1979   Mapping with an Electronic Calculator. Journal of Field
              Archaeology 6(3):321-328.

       BOUCHARD, H., and F.H. MOFFITT

1345   1960   Surveying. International Textbook Company, Scranton, Pa.

       DEBENHAM, F.

1346   1955   Map Making. Blackie and Son, London.

       DILLS, C.E.

1347   1970   Coordinate Location of Archaeological Sites. American
              Antiquity 35(3):389-390.

       EDWARDS, R.L.

1348   1969   Archaeological Use of the Universal Transverse Mercator
              Grid. American Antiquity 34(2):180-182.

FORBES, R.A.

1349 1955 Forestry Handbook. Ronald Press, New York.

GANNETT, H.

1350 1906 Manual of Topographic Methods. USGS Ser. F., Geog. 56, Bulletin 307.

GREENHOOD, D.

1351 1964 Mapping. University of Chicago Press, Chicago.

KJELLSTROM, B.

1352 1967 Be Expert with Map and Compass. American Orienteering Service, La Porte, Ind.

LOW, J.W.

1353 1952 Plane Table Mapping. Harper and Row, New York.

MILLON, R.

1354 1964 The Teotihuacan Mapping Project. American Antiquity 29(3):345-352.

MUEHRCKE, P.

1355 1974 Beyond Abstract Map Symbols. Journal of Geography 73(8): 35-52.

NAPTON, L.K.

1356 1975 Site Mapping and Layout. In T.R. Hester, R.F. Heizer, and J.A. Graham, Field Methods in Archaeology, 6th ed.: 37-64. Mayfield Publishing Co., Palo Alto, Cal.

REYMAN, J.E.

1357 1978 Two Techniques for Better Theodolite and Transit Setups. American Antiquity 43(3):486-487.

STEVENS, D.J.

1358 1974 A Field Plan for Large-Scale Terrain Mapping. Journal of Geography 73(2):17-22.

WILSON, R.L.

1359 1972 Elementary Forest Surveying and Mapping. Oregon State University Bookstore, Corvallis.

5. Surface Collecting Methods

ALCOCK, L.

1360 1951 A Technique for Surface Collecting. Antiquity 25(98): 75-76.

DAVIS, E.L.

1361 1978 The Non-Destructive Archaeologist: Or How to Collect
            Without Collecting. Pacific Coast Archaeological Quar-
            terly 14(1):43-55.

FITTING, J.E.

1362 1964 Analysis and Reporting of Surface Collections. Michigan
            Archaeologist 10(3):58-65.

HAYDEN, J.D.

1363 1965 Fragile-Pattern Areas. American Antiquity 31(2):272-276.

REDMAN, C.L., and P.J. WATSON

1364 1970 Systematic, Intensive Surface Collection. American
            Antiquity 35(3):279-291.

VARNER, D.M.

1365 1968 The Nature of Non-Buried Archaeological Data: Problems in
            Northeast Mexico. Bulletin of the Texas Archeological
            Society 38:51-65.

6. Stratigraphy

ADAMS, R.E.W.

1366 1975 Stratigraphy. In T.R. Hester, R.F. Heizer, and J.A.
            Graham, Field Methods in Archaeology, 6th ed.:147-162.
            Mayfield Publishing Co., Palo Alto, Cal.

DRUCKER, P.

1367 1972 Stratigraphy in Archaeology: An Introduction. Addison-
            Wesley Module in Anthropology 30.

HARRIS, E.C.

1368 1975 The Stratigraphic Sequence: A Question of Time. World
            Archaeology 7:109-121.

PYDDOKE, E.

1369 1961 Stratification for the Archaeologist. Phoenix House,
            London.

SHARER, R.J., and W. ASHMORE

1370 1979 Archaeological Stratification and Stratigraphy. In R.J.
            Sharer and W. Ashmore, Fundamentals of Archaeology:214-
            220. Benjamin/Cummings Publishing Co., Menlo Park, Cal.

THOMAS, D.H.

1371 1979 Stratigraphy. In D.H. Thomas, Archaeology:166-168.
            Holt, Rinehart and Winston, New York.

WHEELER, M.

1372 1956 Archaeology from the Earth. Pelican, Baltimore.

WILLIAMS, R.B.G.

1373 1973 Frost and the Works of Man. Antiquity 47(185):19-31.

7. Sampling Methods and Recovery Techniques

BARKER, G.

1374 1975 To Sieve or Not to Sieve. Antiquity 49:61-63.

BINFORD, L.R., S. BINFORD, R. WHALLON, and M.A. HARDIN

1375 1970 Archaeology at Hatchery West. Memoirs, Society for American Archaeology 24.

BODNER, C.C., and R.M. ROWLETT

1376 1980 Separation of Bone, Charcoal, and Seeds by Chemical Flotation. American Antiquity 45(1):110-116.

BROOKS, R.H.

1377 1965 The Feasibility of Micro-Analysis in Southwestern Archaeological Sites. In D. Osborne, ed., Contributions of the Wetherill Mesa Archeological Project. Memoir, Society for American Archaeology 19:182-185.

BROWN, J.A.

1378 1975 Deep-Site Excavation Strategy as a Sampling Problem. In J.W. Mueller, ed., Sampling in Archaeology:155-169. University of Arizona Press, Tucson.

BROYLES, B.

1379 1969 The Sluicing System Used at the St. Albans Site. Southeastern Archaeological Conference Bulletin 9:45-52.

CASTEEL, R.W.

1380 1970 Core and Column Sampling. American Antiquity 35(4): 465-467.

CHARTKOFF, J.L.

1381 1978 Transect Interval Sampling in Forests. American Antiquity 43(1):46-52.

CHERRY, J.F.

1382 1975 Efficient Soil Searching: Some Comments. Antiquity 49: 217-219.

1383 1978 Questions of Efficiency and Integration in Assemblage Sampling. In J. Cherry, C. Gamble, and S. Shennan, eds., Sampling in Contemporary British Archaeology. BAR British Series 50:293-320.

CHERRY, J.F., C. GAMBLE, and S. SHENNAN, eds.

1384   1978   Sampling in Contemporary British Archaeology.   BAR
              British Series 50.

COCHRAN, W.G.

1385   1953   Sampling Techniques.   John Wiley and Sons, New York.

COWGILL, G.

1386   1970   Some Sampling and Reliability Problems in Archaeology.
              In Archéologie et Calculateurs:161-175.   Editions du
              Centre National de la Recherche Scientifique, Paris.

DAVIS, E.M., and A.B. WESOLOWSKY

1386a 1975   The Izum: A Simple Water Separation Device.   Journal of
              Field Archaeology 2:271-273.

DIAMANT, S.

1387   1979   A Short History of Archaeological Sieving at Franchthi
              Cave, Greece.   Journal of Field Archaeology 6(2):203-218.

FLANNERY, K.V.

1388   1976   Excavating Deep Communities by Transect Samples.   In K.V.
              Flannery, ed., The Early Mesoamerican Village:68-72.
              Academic Press, New York.

FRENCH, D.

1389   1971   An Experiment in Water-Sieving.   Anatolian Studies 21:
              59-64.

FRY, R.E.

1390   1972   Manually Operated Post-Hole Diggers as Sampling Instru-
              ments.   American Antiquity 37(2):259-260.

HILL, J.

1391   1967   The Problem of Sampling.   Field Museum of Natural History.
              Fieldiana, Anthropology 57:145-157.

JELKS, E.B.

1392   1975   The Use and Misuse of Random Sampling in Archaeology.
              Jett Publishing Company, Normal, Ill.

JOHNSON, D.L., and C.S. ALEXANDER

1393   1975   A Portable Coring Device for Rapid Site-Sampling.   Plains
              Anthropologist 20(68):135-137.

KRUMBEIN, W.C.

1394   1965   Sampling in Paleontology.   In B. Krummel and D. Raup, eds.,
              Handbook of Paleontological Techniques:137-149.   W.H.
              Freeman, San Francisco.

LANGE, F.W., and F.M. CARTY

1395 1975 Salt Water Application of the Flotation Technique.
Journal of Field Archaeology 2:119-124.

LIMP, W.F.

1396 1975 Water Separation and Flotation Processes. Journal of
Field Archaeology 1(3/4):337-342.

MORRIS, C.

1397 1975 Sampling in the Excavation of Urban Sites: The Case at
Huanuco Pampa. In J.W. Mueller, ed., Sampling in
Archaeology:192-208. University of Arizona Press, Tucson.

MUELLER, J.W., ed.

1398 1975 Sampling in Archaeology. University of Arizona Press,
Tucson.

PAYNE, S.

1399 1972 Partial Recovery and Sample Bias: The Results of Some
Sieving Experiments. In E. Higgs, ed., Problems in
Economic Prehistory:49-63. Cambridge University Press,
Cambridge.

PENDLETON, M.W.

1400 1979 A Flotation Apparatus for Archaeological Sites. Kiva
44(2-3):89-94.

RAGIR, S.

1401 1975 A Review of Techniques for Archaeological Sampling.
In T.R. Hester, R.F. Heizer and J.A. Graham, Field
Methods in Archaeology, 6th ed.:283-302. Mayfield
Publishing Co., Palo Alto, Cal.

REDMAN, C.L.

1402 1974 Archaeological Sampling Strategies. Addison-Wesley
Module in Anthropology 55.

REID, J.J., M.B. SCHIFFER, and J.M. NEFF

1403 1975 Archaeological Considerations of Intrasite Sampling.
In J.W. Mueller, ed., Sampling in Archaeology:209-226.
University of Arizona Press, Tucson.

ROOTENBERG, S.

1404 1964 Archaeological Field Sampling. American Antiquity 30:
181-188.

SCHOCK, J.M.

1405 1971 Indoor Water Flotation--a Technique for the Recovery of
Archaeological Materials. Plains Anthropologist 16(53):
228.

SCHWARZ, G.T.

1406   1967   A Simplified Chemical Test for Archaeological Field Work.
              Archaeometry 10:57-63.

STOCKTON, J.

1407   1974   Earth Moving Equipment in Archaeological Excavation.
              Archaeology and Physical Anthropology in Oceania 9(3):
              238-242.

STRUEVER, S.

1408   1968   Flotation Techniques for the Recovery of Small Scale
              Archaeological Remains. American Antiquity 33(3):353-
              362.

VESCELIUS, G.

1409   1955   Archaeological Sampling: A Problem in Statistical In-
              ference. In G.E. Dole and R.L. Carneiro, eds., Essays
              in the Science of Culture:457-470. Thomas Y. Crowell,
              New York.

WATSON, P.J.

1410   1974   Flotation Procedures Used on Salts Cave Sediments.   In
              P.J. Watson, ed., Archeology of the Mammoth Cave Area:
              107-108. Academic Press, New York.

1411   1976   In Pursuit of Prehistoric Subsistence: A Comparative
              Account of Some Contemporary Flotation Techniques.
              Midcontinental Journal of Archaeology 1(1):77-100.

WILLIAMS, D.

1411a 1974   Flotation at Siraf. Antiquity 47:288-292.

WINTER, M.C.

1412   1976   Excavating a Shallow Community by Random Sampling
              Quadrats. In K.V. Flannery, ed., The Early Mesoamerican
              Village:62-67. Academic Press, New York.

8. Site Disturbance and Destruction

ANDERSON, J.G.

1413   1934   Children of the Yellow Earth. Routledge and Kegan Paul,
              London.

ANONYMOUS

1414   1977   Legislation Against Bulldozing in New Mexico. Archaeology
              30(4):277.

BRAIDWOOD, R.J.

1415   1946   The Order of Incompleteness of the Archaeological Record.
              In Human Origins, Selected Readings, Series II:108-112.
              2nd ed. University of Chicago Press, Chicago.

BREW, J.O.

1416 1961 Emergency Archaeology: Salvage in Advance of Technological
            Progress. Proceedings, American Philosophical Society
            105:1-10.

BRUHNS, K.O.

1417 1972 The Methods of Guaqueria: Illicit Tomb Looting in
            Colombia. Archaeology 25(2):140-143.

CLEWLOW, C.W., Jr., P.S. HALLINAN, and R.D. AMBRO

1418 1971 A Crisis in Archaeology. American Antiquity 36(4):
            472-473.

COGGINS, C.

1419 1969 Illicit Traffic in Pre-Columbian Antiquities. The Art
            Journal 39:1.

DAVIS, H.A.

1420 1971 Is There a Future for the Past? Archaeology 24(4):300-
            306.

DIETZ, E.F.

1421 1955 Natural Burial of Artifacts. American Antiquity 20:273-
            274.

FAGAN, B.

1422 1973 Belzoni the Plunderer. Archaeology 26(1):48-51.

FAHKRY, A.

1423 1947 A Report on the Inspectorate of Upper Egypt. Annales du
            Service des Antiquities de l'Egypte 46:25-54.

FORD, J.L., M.A. ROLINGSON, and L.D. MEDFORD

1424 1972 Site Destruction Due to Agricultural Practices in South-
            east Arkansas (Ford and Rolingson) and Northeast Arkansas
            (Medford). Arkansas Archeological Survey Research Series
            3.

GORDON, D.H.

1425 1953 Fire and the Sword: The Technique of Destruction.
            Antiquity 27:149-153.

GRAYBILL, D.A.

1426 1977 Illegal Site Destruction in Southwestern New Mexico.
            Journal of Field Archaeology 4(4):481-484.

HAWLEY, F.M.

1427 1937 Reversed Stratigraphy. American Antiquity 2:297-299.

HEIZER, R.F.

1428   1944   Artifact Transport by Migratory Animals and Other Means.
              American Antiquity 9:395-400.

1429   1966   Salvage and Other Archaeology. Southwest Museum Masterkey
              40:54-60.

1430   1968   Migratory Animals as Dispersal Agents of Cultural
              Materials. Science 161:914-915.

HESTER, T.R.

1431   1968   Destruction of Archeological Sites in Uvalde County,
              Texas. Texas Archeology 12(1):13-15.

1432   1975   The Natural Introduction of Mollusca in Archaeological
              Sites: An Example from Southern Texas. Journal of Field
              Archaeology 2:273-275.

HUDOBA, M.

1433   1979   The Artifact Hunter's Handbook. Contemporary Books,
              Chicago.

JENNINGS, J.D.

1434   1963   Administration of Contract Emergency Archaeological
              Programs. American Antiquity 28:282-285.

JOHNSON, F.

1435   1966   Archeology in an Emergency. Science 152:1592-1597.

MARINATOS, S.

1436   1939   Volcanic Destruction of Minoan Crete. Antiquity 13(52):
              425-439.

MEYERS, K.

1437   1973   The Plundered Past. Atheneum Press, New York.

MOOREHEAD, A.

1438   1961   A Reporter at Large: The Temples of the Nile. New Yorker,
              (September 23):106-137. New York.

NANCE, C.R.

1439   1976   Artifact Attribute Covariation as the Product of Inter-
              Level Site Mixing. Midcontinental Journal of Archaeology
              1(2):229-235.

NEWMAN, T.M.

1440   1971   The Crisis in Oregon Archaeology. Tebiwa 14(1):1-3.

NICKERSON, G.S.

1441   1962   Considerations of the Problems of Vandalism and Pot-
              Hunting in American Archaeology. Anthropology and Soci-
              ology Papers 22. Montana State University, Missoula.

1442 1962 Professional, Amateur and Pot-Hunter: The Archaeological
          Hierarchy in the United States. The Washington Archae-
          ologist 6:8-12. University of Washington, Seattle.

PARROT, A.

1443 1939 Malédictions et Violations des Tombes. P. Geuthner, Paris.

PEET, T.E.

1444 1943 The Great Tomb Robberies of the Twentieth Egyptian
          Dynasty. Clarendon Press, Oxford.

PORTER, M.N.

1445 1953 Tlatilco and the Pre-Classic Cultures of the New World.
          Viking Fund Publications in Anthropology 19.

POWELL, J.W.

1446 1961 The Colorado River and Its Canyons. Dover Books, New
          York.

RASSAM, H.

1447 1897 Asshur and the Lands of Nimrod. Curts and Jennings,
          Cincinnati.

ROBERTSON, M.G.

1448 1972 Monument Thievery in Mesoamerica. American Antiquity
          37(2):147-155.

SHEETS, P.D.

1449 1973 The Pillage of Prehistory. American Antiquity 38(3):
          317-320.

SHUTLER, R., Jr.

1450 1973 Conservation of Archaeological Sites in the Pacific.
          Asian Perspectives 15:202-207.

van RIET LOWE, C.

1451 1954 Pitfalls in Prehistory. Antiquity 28:85-90.

WARD, J.

1452 1900 Pyramids and Progress. Eyre and Spottiswoode, London.

9. Handling Specimens in the Field

GARLAKE, M.

1453 1969 Recovery and Treatment of Fragile Artifacts from an Ex-
          cavation. South African Archaeological Bulletin 24(94),
          Pt. 2:61-62.

MOHD, K.B., and S. ULLAH

1454 1946 Notes on the Preservation of Antiquities in the Field.
            Ancient India 1:77-82.

RIGGS, E.S.

1455 1952 The Discovery of the Use of Plaster of Paris on Bandaging
            Fossils. Society of Vertebrate Paleontology News Bul-
            letin 34:24-25.

TOOMBS, H.A., and A.F. RIXON

1456 1950 Removal of Bones from Other Matrix. Antiquity 24:141.

10. Field Photography and Photogrammetry

BASCOM, W.R.

1457 1941 Possible Application of Kite Photography to Archaeology
            and Ethnology. Illinois Academy of Science Transactions
            34(2):62-63.

BLAKER, A.A.

1458 1965 Photography for Scientific Publication: A Handbook.
            W.H. Freeman, San Francisco.

BROSE, D.

1459 1964 Infra-Red Photography: An Aid to Stratigraphic Interpre-
            tation. Michigan Archaeologist 10(4):69-73.

BUETTNER-JANUSCH, J.

1460 1954 Use of Infrared Photography in Archaeological Field Work.
            American Antiquity 20:84-87.

CLARK, W.

1461 1946 Photography by Infrared, Its Principle and Application.
            John Wiley and Sons, New York.

COLE, J.R.

1462 1972 Time-Lapse Photography in Archaeological Data-Recording.
            Plains Anthropologist 17(58), Pt. 1:347-349.

COOKSON, M.B.

1463 1954 Photography for Archaeologists. Parrish, London.

CUMMER, W.W.

1464 1975 Photogrammetry at Ayia Irini on Keos. Journal of Field
            Archaeology 1(3/4):385-387.

DAFOE, T.

1465 1969 Artifact Photography. Archaeological Society of Alberta,
            Newsletter 19:1-17.

DODGE, D.

1466 1968 Laboratory Artifact Photography. Archaeology in Montana
9(1):17-23.

DORWIN, J.T.

1467 1967 Iodine Staining and Ultraviolet Photography Field Techniques. American Antiquity 32(1):105-107.

ERSKINE, C.A.

1468 1965 Photographic Documentation in Archaeological Research:
Increasing the Information Content. Science 148:1089-
1090.

FEININGER, A.

1469 1965 The Complete Photographer. Prentice-Hall, Englewood
Cliffs, N.J.

FRANTZ, A.

1470 1951 Truth Before Beauty; or the Incomplete Photographer.
Archaeology 3:202-215.

1471 1955 Photography for Archaeologists, a Review. Antiquity 113:
15-16.

GEBHARD, D.

1472 1960 Prehistoric Paintings of the Diablo Region of Western
Texas. Roswell Museum and Art Center Publications in
Art and Science 3.

GILLIO, D.A.

1473 1970 Uses of Infrared Photography in Archaeology. Colorado
Anthropologist 2(2):13-19.

GUY, P.L.O.

1474 1932 Balloon Photography and Archaeological Excavation.
American Antiquity 6:148-155.

HALLERT, B.

1475 1971 Photogrammetry and Culture History. Norwegian Archaeological Review 4(1):28-36.

HAMMOND, N.

1476 1973 A Giant Scale for Long-Distance Photography. Antiquity
48(186):144.

KNIGHT, H.

1477 1966 The Photography of Petroglyphs and Pictographs. Newsletter, New Zealand Archaeological Association 10(1):
62-64.

JELKS, E.B.

1478   1965   Some Pointers on Field Photography.   Newsletter, Oklahoma
               Anthropological Society 13(9):1-3.

LERICI, C.M.

1479   1959   Periscope Camera Pierces Ancient Tombs to Reveal 2,500
               Year Old Frescoes.   National Geographic Magazine CXVI:
               336-351.   Washington, D.C.

McFADGEN, B.G.

1480   1971   An Application of Stereo-Photogrammetry to Archaeological
               Recording.   Archaeometry 13(1):71-81.

MARE, E. de

1481   1962   Photography.   Penguin Handbook, Harmondsworth, Middlesex.

MATTHEWS, S.K.

1482   1968   Photography in Archaeology and Art.   John Baker, London.

MERRILL, R.H.

1483   1941   Photographic Surveying.   American Antiquity 6:343-346.

1484   1941   Photo-Surveying Assists Archaeologists.   Civil Engineering
               11:233-235.

PIGGOTT, S., and M. MURRAY

1485   1966   A New Photographic Technique at Croft Moraig.   Antiquity
               40:304.

SCHWARZ, G.T.

1486   1964   Stereoscopic Views Taken with an Ordinary Single Camera--
               a New Technique for Archaeologists.   Archaeometry 7:36-42.

SIMMONS, H.C.

1487   1969   Archaeological Photography.   University of London Press,
               London.

SOUTH, S.A.

1488   1968   Photography in Historical Archaeology.   Historical Archae-
               ology 2:73-113.

STRAFFIN, D.

1489   1971   A Device for Vertical Archaeological Photography.   Plains
               Anthropologist 16(53):232-234.

STRANDBERG, C.H., and R. TOMLINSON

1490   1969   Photoarchaeological Analysis of Potomac River Fish Traps.
               American Antiquity 34:312-319.

SWARTZ, B.K., Jr.

1491 1963 Aluminum Powder: A Technique of Photographically Recording
            Petroglyphs. American Antiquity 28:400-401.

TURPIN, S.A., et al.

1492 1979 Stereophotogrammetric Documentation of Exposed Archaeolog-
            ical Features. Journal of Field Archaeology 6(3):329-
            337.

WEBSTER, W.J.

1493 1962 Techniques of Field Photography for Archaeological Purposes.
            Oceania 33(2):139-142.

WOOD, F.D.

1494 1945 Color Photography Applied to Stratigraphy. Transactions,
            Connecticut Academy of Art and Science 36:879-882.

11. Photography in the Laboratory

DAFOE, T.

1495 1969 Artifact Photography. Archaeological Society of Alberta,
            Newsletter 19:1-7.

DODGE, D.

1496 1968 Laboratory Artifact Photography. Archaeology in Montana
            9(1):17-23.

GRIGGS, E.L., Jr.

1497 1967 Photography of Flaked Artifacts. Tennessee Archaeologist
            23(1):31-37.

IVES, R.L.

1498 1941 Photographing Translucent, Transparent and Multi-Colored
            Artifacts. American Antiquity 6:263-265.

JOSSELYN, D.W.

1499 1967 Photography of Flaked Artifacts. Tennessee Archaeologist
            22(1):12-30.

KRAFT, H.

1500 1971 A Simple Ammonium Chloride Generator for Use in Observing
            and Photographing Chipping Details and Wear Evidence on
            Artifacts. Bulletin, New York State Archaeological
            Association 51:6-8.

LUTZ, B.J., and D.L. SLABY

1501 1972 A Simplified Technique for Photographing Obsidian.
            American Antiquity 37(2):262-263.

McCAUGHEY, D.

1502 1968 Artifact Photography.   Nevada Archaeological Survey,
            Reporter 2(6-8):3-4.

MacDONALD, G.F., and D. SANGER

1503 1968 Some Aspects of Microscope Analysis and Photomicrography
            of Lithic Artifacts.   American Antiquity 33:237-240.

MIRAMBELL, S.L.

1504 1964 Estudio Microfotográfico de Artefactos Liticos.
            Instituto Nacional de Antropología e Historia, Departa-
            mento de Prehistoria 14. Mexico.

STERUD, E.L., and P.P. PRATT

1505 1975 Archaeological Intra-Site Recording with Photography.
            Journal of Field Archaeology 2(1/2):151-168.

TOUMEY, C.P.

1506 1979 Techniques for Photographing Artifacts.   Journal of
            Field Archaeology 6(1):122-123.

WEIDE, D.L., and G.D. WEBSTER

1507 1967 Ammonium Chloride Powder Used in the Photography of
            Artifacts.   American Antiquity 32(1):104-105.

WILKINSON, K.

1508 1968 A Method of Preparing Translucent Artifact for Photog-
            raphy. Nevada Archaeological Survey, Reporter 2(2):10-11.

12. Aerial Photography and Remote Sensing

AGACHE, R.

1509 1964 Aerial Reconnaissance in Picardy.   Antiquity 38(150):
            113-119.

1510 1972 New Aerial Research in Picardy and Artois.   Antiquity
            46:117-123.

ATKINS, H.

1511 1972 Spying on the Past.   The Sciences 12(6):22-24.

BEAZELEY, G.A.

1512 1919 Air Photography in Archaeology.   The Geographical
            Journal (February 20):331-335.

BERLIN, G.L., J.R. AMBLER, R.H. HEVLY, and G.G. SCHABER

1513 1977 Identification of a Sinagua Agricultural Field by Aerial
            Thermography, Soil Chemistry, Pollen/Plant Analysis, and
            Archaeology.   American Antiquity 42(4):588-600.

BRADFORD, J.

1514 1947 Etruria from the Air. Antiquity 21(82):74-83.

1515 1957 Ancient Landscapes: Studies in Field Archaeology. G. Bell
and Sons, London.

CAMPANA, D.V.

1516 1977 Making Stereo-Photomacrographs for Archaeological Studies.
Journal of Field Archaeology 4(4):435-440.

CAPPER, J.E.

1517 1907 Photographs of Stonehenge as Seen from a War Balloon.
Archaeologia 60:571.

CHART, D.A.

1518 1930 Air-Photography in Northern Ireland. Antiquity 4:453-460.

CHEVALLIER, R.

1519 1957 Bibliographie des Applications Archéologiques de la
Photographie Aérienne. Bulletin d'Archéologie Marocaine.
Tome II (Supplement), Edita-Casablanca.

1520 1964 L'Avion à la Découverte du Passé. Fayard, Paris.

CRAWFORD, O.G.S.

1521 1933 Some Recent Air Discoveries. Antiquity 7:290-296.

1522 1939 Air Reconnaissance of Roman Scotland. Antiquity 13(51):
280-292.

1523 1954 A Century of Air-Photography. Antiquity 112:206-210.

DASSIE, J.

1524 1978 Le Premier Manuel d'Archéologie Aérienne. Editions
Technip, Paris.

DEUEL, L.

1525 1969 Flights into Yesterday: The Story of Aerial Archaeology.
St. Martin's Press, New York.

EARDLEY, A.J.

1526 1942 Aerial Photographs: Their Use and Interpretation. Harper
and Bros., New York.

GUMERMAN, G.J.

1527 1971 The Identification of Archaeological Sites by False Color
Infrared Aerial Photography. Interagency Report USGS-211.

GUMERMAN, G.J., and J.A. NEELY

1528 1972 An Archaeological Survey of the Tehuacan Valley, Mexico:
A Test of Color Infrared Photography. American Antiquity
37(4):520-527.

GUY, P.L.O.

1529 1932 Balloon Photography and Archaeological Excavation.
Antiquity 6:148-155.

HAMLIN, C.L.

1530 1977 Machine Processing of Landsat Data: An Introduction for
Anthropologists and Archaeologists. MASCA Newsletter
13(1/2).

HARP, E., Jr.

1531 1968 Optimum Scales and Emulsions in Air Photography. Proceedings, 8th International Congress of Anthropological
Sciences 3:163-165.

LARRABEE, E. McM.

1532 1963 The Identification of a Village Site by Aerial Photography.
West Virginia Archaeologist 15:7-8.

LYONS, T.R., and R.K. HITCHCOCK

1553 1977 Aerial Remote Sensing Techniques in Archeology. Reports
of the Chaco Center 2. Washington, D.C.

MATHENY, R.T.

1534 1962 Value of Aerial Photography in Surveying Archaeological
Sites in Coastal Jungle Regions. American Antiquity 28:
226-230.

MERRILL, R.H.

1535 1941 Photographic Surveying. American Antiquity 6:343-346.

1536 1941 Photo-Surveying Assists Archaeologists. Civil Engineering
11:233-235.

MILLER, W.C.

1537 1957 Uses of Aerial Photographs in Archaeological Field Work.
American Antiquity 23:46-62.

NORMAN, E.R., and J.K. ST. JOSEPH

1538 1969 The Early Development of Irish Society: The Evidence of
Aerial Photography. Cambridge University Press, Cambridge.

PRINTUP, D.

1539 1970 Experiments in Aerial Photography. Proceedings, Arkansas
Academy of Science for 1969:24-28.

QUANN, J., and B. BEVAN

1540 1977 The Pyramids from 900 Kilometers. MASCA Newsletter
13(1/2):12-14.

RAJEWSKI, Z.

1541 1965 Aérophotographie Prise d'un Ballon. Archaeologia Polona VIII:125-130.

REEVES, D.M.

1542 1936 Aerial Photography and Archaeology. American Antiquity 2:102-107.

RICKETSON, O., Jr., and A.V. KIDDER

1543 1930 An Archaeological Reconnaissance by Air in Central America. The Geographical Review 20(2):177-206.

RILEY, D.N.

1544 1945 Aerial Reconnaissance of the Fen Basin. Antiquity 19(75): 145-153.

ST. JOSEPH, J.K.S.

1545 1961 Aerial Reconnaissance in Wales. Antiquity 35(140):263-275.

1546 1962 Air Reconnaissance in Northern France. Antiquity 36(144): 279-286.

1547 1966 The Uses of Air Photography. John Baker, London.

SCHABER, G.G., and G.J. GUMERMAN

1548 1969 Infrared Scanning Images: An Archeological Application. Science 164:712-713.

SCHODER, R.V.

1549 1974 Ancient Greece from the Air. Thames and Hudson, London.

SOLECKI, R.S.

1550 1957 Practical Aerial Photography for Archaeologists. American Antiquity 22:337-351.

TINNEY, L.R., J.R. JENSEN, and J.E. ESTES

1551 1977 Mapping Archaeological Sites from Historical Photography. Photogrammetric Engineering and Remote Sensing 43(1): 35-44.

VOGT, E.Z., ed.

1552 1974 Aerial Photography in Anthropological Field Research. Harvard University Press, Cambridge, Mass.

WHITTLESEY, J.

1553 1967 Balloon over Sardis. Archaeology 20:67-68.

WILLIAMS-HUNT, P.D.R.

1554 1948 Archaeology and Topographical Interpretation of Air Photographs. Antiquity 22(86):103-104.

E. ANALYSIS

1. Typology and Classification (Artifacts)

BECK, H.C.

1555   1928   Classification and Nomenclature of Beads and Pendants.
               Society of Antiquaries 77:1-74. London.

BELL, R.E.

1556   1958   Guide to the Identification of Certain American Indian
               Projectile Points. Oklahoma Anthropological Society,
               Special Publication 1.

BENFER, R.A.

1557   1967   A Design for the Study of Archaeological Characteristics.
               American Anthropologist 69:719-730.

BIBERSON, P.

1558   1967   Galets Aménagés du Maghreb et du Sahara. Types I.
               1-I. 8, II. 1-II. 16, III. 1-III. 6., Fiches Typo-
               logiques Africaines, 2e. Cahier, Paris.

BLACK, G.A., and P. WEER

1559   1936   A Proposed Terminology for Shape Classifications of
               Artifacts. American Antiquity 1:280-294.

BLACKWOOD, B.

1560   1970   The Classification of Artifacts in the Pitt Rivers Museum,
               Oxford. Oxford University, Pitt Rivers Museum, Occasional
               Papers on Technology 11.

BORDES, F.

1561   1953   Notules de Typologie Paléolithique. I. Outils Moustériens
               à Fracture Volontaire. Bulletin de la Société Préhis-
               torique Française 50:224-226.

1562   1953   Notules de Typologie Paléolithique. II. Pointes
               Levalloisiennes et Pointes Pseudo-Levalloisiennes.
               Bulletin de la Société Préhistorique Française 50:311-313.

1563   1954   Notules de Typologie Paléolithique. III. Pointes
               Moustériennes Racloirs, Convergents et Déjetés, Limaces.
               Bulletin de la Société Préhistorique Française 51:336-339.

1564   1957   La Signification du Microburin dans le Paléolithique
               Supérieur. L'Anthropologie 61:578-582.

1565   1961   Typologie du Paléolithique Ancien et Moyen. Publications
               de l'Institut de Préhistoire, Université de Bordeaux,
               Memoire 1. 2 vols. Imprimeries Delmas, Bordeaux.

1566   1969   Reflections on Typology and Technique in the Paleolithic.
               Arctic Anthropology 6(1):1-29.

BORDES, F., and D. de SONNEVILLE-BORDES

1567 1970 The Significance of Variability in Palaeolithic Assemblages. World Archaeology 2(1):61-73.

BRÉZILLON, M.N.

1568 1968 La Dénomination des Objets de Pierre Taillée: Matériaux pour un Vocabulaire des Préhistoriens de Langue Française. Supplement IV, Gallia Préhistoire.

BULLEN, R.P.

1569 1968 A Guide to the Identification of Florida Projectile Points. Florida State Museum, Gainesville.

DORAN, J.E., and F.R. HODSON

1570 1966 A Digital Computer Analysis of Palaeolithic Flint Assemblages. Nature 210:688-689.

EPSTEIN, J.F.

1571 1964 Towards the Systematic Description of Chipped Stone. Actas y Memorias, XXXV Congreso Internacional de Americanistas 1:155-169.

FINKELSTEIN, J.J.

1572 1937 A Suggested Projectile Point Classification. American Antiquity 2:197-203.

FORD, J.A.

1573 1954 Comment on A.C. Spaulding, Statistical Techniques for the Discovery of Artifact Types. American Antiquity 19:390-391.

1574 1954 On the Concept of Types: The Type Concept Revisited. American Anthropologist 56:42-54.

FOWLER, M.L.

1575 1957 Archaic Projectile Point Styles 7,000-2,000 B.C. in the Central Mississippi Valley. Missouri Archaeologist 19 (1-2):7-21.

GAHEN, D., and F. Van NOTEN

1576 1971 Stone Age Typology: Another Approach. Current Anthropology 12(2):211-215.

GARCIA COOK, A.

1577 1967 Análisis Tipológico de Artefactos. Instituto Nacional de Antropología e Historia, Investigaciones 12. Mexico.

GARDIN, C.

1578 1957 Methods for the Descriptive Analysis of Archaeological Material. American Antiquity 22:13-20.

GIFFORD, J.C.

1579 1960 The Type-Variety Method of Ceramic Classification as an
            Indicator of Cultural Phenomena. American Antiquity 25:
            341-347.

GLOVER, I.C.

1580 1969 The Use of Factor Analysis for the Discovery of Artifact
            Types. Mankind 7(1):36-51.

HEINZELIN de BRAUCOURT, J. de

1581 1960 Principes de Diagnose Numérique en Typologie. Mémoires
            d'Academie Royale de Belgique 14(1703):77.

1582 1962 Manuel de Typologie des Industries Lithiques. Institut
            Royal des Sciences Naturelles de Belgique, Bruxelles.

HEIZER, R.F., and T.R. HESTER

1583 1978 Great Basin Projectile Points: Forms and Chronology.
            Ballena Press Publications in Archaeology, Ethnology and
            History 10. Socorro, N.M.

HILL, J.N., and R.K. EVANS

1584 1972 A Model for Classification and Typology. In D.L. Clarke,
            ed., Models in Archaeology:231-274. Methuen, London.

HODSON, F.R.

1585 1969 Searching for Structure Within Multi-Variate Archaeological
            Data. World Archaeology 1:90-105.

JAZDZEWSKI, K., ed.

1586 1962 Glossarium Archaeologicum. Fascula 7-12. Rudolf Habelt
            Verlag, Bonn.

KANTMAN, S.

1587 1969 Experimental Import of Observation and the Significance
            of Functionalism in Paleolithic Typology. Quaternaria
            11:263-274.

KIDD, K.E., and M.A. KIDD

1588 1974 A Classification System for Glass Beads for the Use of
            Field Archaeologists. In Canadian Historic Sites: Oc-
            casional Papers in Archaeology and History 1:47-92.
            National Historic Sites Service, National and Historic
            Parks Branch, Department of Indian Affairs and Northern
            Development, Ottawa.

KRIEGER, A.D.

1589 1944 The Typological Concept. American Antiquity 9:271-288.

1590 1960 Archeological Typology in Theory and Practice. In Selected
            Papers of the Fifth International Congress of Anthropology
            and Ethnological Sciences:141-151. Philadelphia.

1591   1964   New World Lithic Typology Project: Part II. American
              Antiquity 29:489-493.

       LAPLACE-JAURETCHE, G.

1592   1957   Typologie Analytique. Application d'une Nouvelle
              Méthode d'Étude des Formes et des Structures aux Indus-
              tries à Lames et à Lamelles. Quaternaria 4:133-164.

1593   1966   Recherches sur l'Origine et l'Évolution des Complexes
              Leptolithiques. École Française de Rome. Mélanges
              d'Archéologie et d'Histoire, Supplément 4. E. de Boccard,
              Paris.

1594   1968   Recherches de Typologie Analytique 1968. In Origini II
              Preistoria e Protoistoria delle Civiltà Antiche:7-60.
              Istituto di Palentologia, Rome.

       LWOFF, S.

1595   1970   Nouvelle Méthode d'Investigation par l'Ordinateur: Les
              Abaques à Points Cumules. Archéocivilisation 7-8:10-38.

       MacCORD, H.A., and W.J. HRANICKY

1596   1979   A Basic Guide to Virginia Prehistoric Projectile Points.
              Archaeological Society of Virginia, College of William
              and Mary, Williamsburg.

       McKusick, M.

1597   1963   Identifying Iowa Projectile Points. Journal of the Iowa
              Archaeology Society 12(3-4).

       MARSHALL, R.A.

1598   1963   A Descriptive System for Projectile Points. Missouri
              Archaeological Society, Research Series 1.

       MERINO, J.M.

1599   1969   Tipologia Litica. Munibe 21:3-325.

       PARKINGTON, J.E.

1600   1967   Some Comments on the Comparison and Classification of
              Archaeological Specimens. South African Archaeological
              Bulletin 22(87), Pt. 3:73-79.

       PERINO, G.H., ed.

1601   1968   Guide to the Identification of Certain American Indian
              Projectile Points. Oklahoma Anthropological Society,
              Special Bulletin 3.

       POPE, G.D., Jr.

1602   1960   Aims and Methods of Projectile Point Typology. Eastern
              States Archaeological Federation, Bulletin 19:13.

RITCHIE, W.A.

1603   1961   A Typology and Nomenclature for New York Projectile
                Points. New York State Museum Bulletin 384.

ROE, D.

1604   1977   Typology and the Trouble with Hand-Axes. In G. de G.
                Sieveking, et al., eds., Problems in Economic and Social
                Archaeology:61-72. Westview Press, Boulder.

ROUSE, I.

1605   1944   On the Typological Method. American Antiquity 10:202-204.

1606   1960   The Classification of Artifacts in Archaeology. American
                Antiquity 25:313-323.

1607   1960   Theoretical Concepts Underlying Projectile Point Classi-
                fication. Eastern States Archeological Federation,
                Bulletin 19:20.

1608   1970   Classification for What? Norwegian Archaeological
                Review 3:4-34.

SEARS, W.H.

1609   1960   Ceramic Systems and Eastern Archaeology. American Antiquity
                25:324-329.

SMITH, P.E.L.

1610   1966   Le Solutréen en France. Publications de l'Institut de
                Préhistoire, Mémoire 5. Université de Bordeaux,
                Imprimerie Delmas, Bordeaux.

SMITH, W.A.

1611   1971   A Grooved Axe Typology. Wisconsin Archaeologist 52(1):
                20-41.

SONNEVILLE-BORDES, D. de, and J. PERROT

1612   1953   Essai d'Adaptation des Méthodes Statistiques au Paléo-
                lithique Supérieur. Premiers Resultats. Bulletin de
                la Société Préhistorique Française 50(5-6):323-333.

1613   1954   Lexique Typologique du Paléolithique Supérieur. Outillage
                Lithique. I. Grattoirs, II. Outils Solutréens. Bulletin
                de la Société Préhistorique Française 51(7):327-335.

1614   1955   Lexique Typologique du Paléolithique Supérieur. Outillage
                Lithique. III. Outils Composités. Percoirs. Bulletin
                de la Société Préhistorique Française 52(1-2):76-79.

1615   1956   Lexique Typologique du Paléolithique Supérieur. Outillage
                Lithique. IV. Burins. Bulletin de la Société Préhis-
                torique Française 53(7-8):408-412.

1616   1956   Lexique Typologique du Paléolithique Supérieur. Outillage
                Lithique. V. Outillage à Bord Abattu. VI. Pièces
                Tronquées. VII. Lames Retouchées. VIII. Pièces Variées.

        IX. Outillage Lamellaire. Pointe Azilienne. Bulletin de
        la Société Préhistorique Française 53(9):547-559.

SPAULDING, A.C.

1617 1953 Statistical Techniques for the Discovery of Artifact
         Types. American Antiquity 18:305-313.

1618 1973 The Concept of Artifact Type in Archaeology. Plateau
         45(4):149-164.

STEWARD, J.H.

1619 1954 Types of Types. American Anthropologist 56:54-57.

SUHM, D.A., and E.B. JELKS

1620 1962 Handbook of Texas Archeology: Type Descriptions. Texas
         Archeological Society Special Publication 1 and Texas
         Memorial Museum Bulletin 4.

SUHM, D.A., A.D. KRIEGER, and E.B. JELKS

1621 1954 An Introductory Handbook of Texas Archeology. Bulletin
         of the Texas Archeological Society 25.

SWANSON, E.H., and B.R. BUTLER

1622 1962 The First Conference of Western Archaeologists on Problems
         of Point Typology. Occasional Papers of the Idaho State
         College Museum 10. Pocatello.

TIXIER, J.

1623 1958 Les Burins de Noailles de l'Abri André Ragout. Bois-du-
         Roc, Vilhonneur (Charente). Bulletin de la Société
         Préhistorique Française 55:628-644.

1624 1963 Typologie de l'Epipaléolithique du Maghreb. Mémoire II
         du C.R.A.P.E. Arts et Métiers Graphiques, Paris.

1625 1967 Pièces Pedonculées Ateriennes du Maghreb et du Sahara.
         Types 1-30. Fiches Typologiques Africaines 3e Cahier,
         Paris.

TUGBY, D.J.

1626 1958 A Typological Analysis of Axes and Choppers from Southeast
         Australia. American Antiquity 24:24-33.

Van BUREN, G.E.

1627 1944 Arrowheads and Projectile Points. Arrowhead Publishing,
         Garden Grove, Cal.

VERTES, L.

1628 1964 Statistiques et Graphiques dans l'Étude des Industries
         Préhistoriques. VII. Analyse Statistique des Industries
         Paléolithiques. Palaeohistoria 10:15-62.

WEYER, E.M., Jr.

1629 1964 New World Lithic Typology Project: Part I. American
            Antiquity 29:487-489.

WHITEFORD, A.H.

1630 1947 Description for Artifact Analysis. American Antiquity
            12:226-237.

2. Basketry

ADOVASIO, J.M.

1631 1977 Basketry Technology: A Guide to Identification and
            Analysis. Aldine, Chicago.

AMBRO, R.D.

1632 1970 A Basket Maker's Work Kit from Lovelock Cave. University
            of California, Contributions of the Archaeological Re-
            search Facility 7:73-79.

BALFET, H.

1633 1952 Basketry: A Proposed Classification. L'Anthropologie 56:
            259-280. (Reprinted in English translation in University
            of California Archaeological Survey, Report 37:1-21.)

CHAPMAN, J., and J.M. ADOVASIO

1634 1977 Textile and Basketry Impressions from Icehouse Bottom,
            Tennessee. American Antiquity 42(4):620-625.

FAIRSERVIS, W.A.

1635 1956 Excavations in the Quetta Valley, West Pakistan. American
            Museum of Natural History, Anthropological Papers 45(2):
            372-377.

LAMB, F.W.

1636 1972 Indian Baskets of North America. Riverside Museum Press,
            Riverside, Cal.

MASON, O.T.

1637 1904 Aboriginal American Basketry: Studies in a Textile Art
            Without Machinery. U.S. National Museum Report for 1902:
            171-548.

MORRIS, E.H., and R.F. BURGH

1638 1941 Anasazi Basketry: Basket Maker II Through Pueblo III.
            Carnegie Institute of Washington, Publication 533.
            Washington, D.C.

MOSER, E.

1639 1973 Seri Basketry. Kiva 38(3-4):105-140.

MUNGER, P., and R.M. ADAMS

1640 1941 Fabric Impressions of Pottery from the Elizabeth Herrell Site, Missouri. American Antiquity 7:166–171.

ROSSBACH, E.

1641 1973 Baskets as Textile Art. Van Nostrand Reinhold, New York.

WALLACE, W.J.

1642 1954 A Basket-Weaver's Kit from Death Valley. Southwest Museum Masterkey 28:216–221.

WELTFISH, G.

1643 1930 Prehistoric North American Basketry Techniques and Modern Distributions. American Anthropologist 32:454–495.

1644 1932 Problems in the Study of Ancient and Modern Basketmakers. American Anthropologist 34:108–117.

3. Textiles and Fabrics

ADOVASIO, J.M.

1645 1977 The Textile and Basketry Impressions from Jarmo. Paleorient 3(1975–1977):223–230. Paris.

BELLINGER, L.

1646 1950 Textile Analysis; Early Techniques in Egypt and the Near East, Parts I–III. Workshop Notes, Papers, Textile Museum 2–3, 6. Washington, D.C.

D'HARCOURT, R.

1647 1974 Textiles of Ancient Peru and Their Techniques. University of Washington Press, Seattle.

DIXON, K.

1648 1957 Systematic Cordage Structure Analysis. American Anthropologist 59:135–136.

EMERY, I.

1649 1966 The Primary Structures of Fabrics: An Illustrated Classification. The Textile Museum, Washington, D.C.

GAYTON, A.H.

1650 1961 Early Paracas Style Textiles from Yauca, Peru. Archaeology 14(2):117–121.

GREEN, J.S.

1651 1971 Archaeological Chichuhuan and Modern Tarahumara Weaving. Ethnos 36(1–4):115–130.

HELBAEK, H.

1652 1963 Textiles from Catal Huyuk. Archaeology 16(1):39-47.

HENNING, A.E.

1653 1966 Fabrics and Related Materials from Arnold Research Cave.
            Missouri Archaeologist 28.

HENSHALL, A.S.

1654 1951 Textiles and Weaving Appliances in Prehistoric Britain.
            Proceedings, Prehistoric Society 16:130-162.

HEYN, A.N.J.

1655 1954 Fiber Microscopy. Interscience Publishers, New York.

HOLMES, W.H.

1656 1881 Prehistoric Textile Fabrics of the United States, Derived
            from Impressions on Pottery. Bureau of American Ethnology,
            Annual Report 3:393-425.

HURLEY, W.M.

1657 1978 Prehistoric Cordage: Identification of Impressions on
            Pottery. Aldine, Chicago.

JOHNSON, I.W.

1658 1971 Basketry and Textiles. Handbook of Middle American
            Indians 10(1):297-321.

1659 1975 Textiles from the Cuevas de Atzcala, Rio Mezcala,
            Guerrero. Actas, XLI Congreso Internacional de Ameri-
            canistas I:279-291.

KAMINSKA, J., and A. NAHLIK

1660 1960 Études sur l'Industrie Textile du Haut Moyen Age en
            Pologne. Archaeologia Polona III:89-119.

KARDARA, C.

1661 1961 Dyeing and Weaving Works at Isthmia. American Journal
            of Archaeology 65(3):261-266.

KING, M.E.

1662 1969 Some New Paracas Textile Techniques from Ocucaje, Peru.
            Verhandlungen des XXXVIII. Internationalen Amerikanisten-
            kongresses, Stuttgart-München 12. bis 18. August 1968 1:
            369-378. Kommissionsverlag Klaus Renner, München, Germany.

1663 1969 Textile Fragments from the Riverside Site, Menominee,
            Michigan. Verhandlungen des XXXVIII. Internationalen
            Amerikanistenkongresses, Stuttgart-München 12. bis 18.
            August 1968 1:117-123. Kommissionsverlag Klaus Renner,
            München, Germany.

1664 1974 The Salts Cave Textiles: A Preliminary Account. In P.J. Watson, ed., Archeology of the Mammoth Cave Area:31-40. Academic Press, New York.

1665 1978 Analytical Methods and Prehistoric Textiles. American Antiquity 43(1):89-96.

LOCKE, L.L.

1666 1912 The Ancient Quipu, a Peruvian Knot Record. American Anthropologist 14:325-332.

LUNIAK, H.

1667 1953 Identification of Textile Fibres. Pitman, London.

MINER, H.

1668 1936 The Importance of Textiles in the Archaeology of Eastern United States. American Antiquity 1:181-192.

MOELLER, W.O.

1669 1969 The Male Weavers at Pompeii. Technology and Culture 10(4):561-566.

O'NEALE, L.M.

1670 1937 Archaeological Explorations in Peru. Part III, Textiles of the Early Nazca Period. Field Museum of Natural History, Anthropology Memoirs 2(3).

1671 1947 Note on an Apocynum Fabric. American Antiquity 13:179-180.

O'NEALE, L.M., and A.L. KROEBER

1672 1930 Textile Periods in Ancient Peru: I. University of California, Publications in American Archaeology and Ethnology 28:23-56.

O'NEALE, L.M., et al.

1673 1949 Chincha Plain-Weave Cloths. University of California Anthropological Records 9(2).

PANG, H.

1674 1975 Archaeological Textiles from Chametla: Sinaloa. Actas, XII Congreso Internacional de Americanistas I:301-331.

SCHLOTZ, S.C.

1675 1975 Prehistoric Piles: A Structural and Comparative Analysis of Cordage, Netting, Basketry and Fabric from Ozark Bluff Shelters. Arkansas Archeological Survey, Research Series 9.

TEXTILE INSTITUTE

1676 1949 The Identification of Textile Materials. The Institute, Handbook of Textile Technology 3, Manchester, England.

VREELAND, J.

1677   1977   Ancient Andean Textiles: Clothes for the Dead.   Archaeology
              30(3):166-178.

WHITFORD, A.C.

1678   1941   Textile Fibers Used in Eastern Aboriginal North America.
              American Museum of Natural History, Anthropological
              Papers 38, Pt. 1.

WILDMAN, A.B.

1679   1947   The Microscopy of Textile Fibers--Aids to Their Identifi-
              cation.   Journal of the Textile Institute 38:468-473.

                    4. Chipped and Ground Stone Artifacts

a. GENERAL

AISTON, G.

1680   1929   Chipped Stone Tools of the Aboriginal Tribes East and
              Northeast of Lake Eyre, South Australia.   Papers and
              Proceedings, Royal Society of Tasmania for 1928:123-131.

BARNES, A.S.

1681   1947   The Production of Long Blades in Neolithic Times.
              American Anthropologist 49:625-630.

1682   1947   The Technique of Blade Production in Mesolithic and
              Neolithic Times.   Proceedings, Prehistoric Society 13:
              101-113.

BARTLETT, K.

1683   1933   Pueblo Milling Stones of the Flagstaff Region.   Museum of
              Northern Arizona, Flagstaff.

BENFER, A.N.

1684   1974   A Preliminary Analysis of the Obsidian Artifacts from
              Tula, Hidalgo.   In R.A. Diehl, ed., Studies of Ancient
              Tollan: A Report of the University of Missouri Tula
              Archaeological Project.   University of Missouri Monographs
              in Anthropology 1:56-87.   Columbia.

BIALOR, P.

1685   1962   The Chipped Stone Industry of Catal Huyuk.   Anatolian
              Studies 12:67.

BINFORD, L.R.

1686   1963   A Proposed Attribute List for the Description and Classi-
              fication of Projectile Points.   Anthropological Papers of
              the Museum of Anthropology, University of Michigan 19:
              193-221.   Ann Arbor.

BINFORD, L.R., and G.I. QUIMBY

1687 1963 Indian Sites and Chipped Stone Materials in the Northern
Lake Michigan Area. Chicago Natural History Museum,
Fieldiana: Anthropology 36(12):277-307.

BLACK, G.A., and P. WEER

1688 1936 A Proposed Terminology for Shape Classifications of
Artifacts. American Antiquity 1:280-294.

BORDAZ, J.

1689 1970 Tools of the Old and New Stone Age. Natural History
Press, Garden City, N.Y.

BORDES, F.

1690 1950 Principe d'une Méthode d'Étude des Techniques de Débitage
et de la Typologie du Paléolithique Ancien et Moyen.
L'Anthropologie 54:19-34.

1691 1968 The Old Stone Age. World University Library, New York.

1692 1969 Traitement Thermique du Silex au Solutréen. Bulletin de
la Société Préhistorique Française 66:197.

BORDES, F., and D. de SONNEVILLE-BORDES

1693 1970 The Significance of Variability in Palaeolithic Assemblages. World Archaeology 2(1):61-73.

BRADLEY, B.

1694 1974 Comments on the Lithic Technology of the Casper Site
Materials. In G.C. Frison, The Casper Site: A Hell Gap
Bison Kill on the High Plains:191-198. Academic Press,
New York.

BULGARELLI, G.M.

1695 1979 The Lithic Industry of Tepe Hissar at the Light of Recent
Excavations. South Asian Archaeology 1977:39-54. Naples.

BURGESS, R.J., and K.L. KVAMME

1696 1978 A New Technique for the Measurement of Artifact Angles.
American Antiquity 43(3):482-485.

BURKITT, M.C.

1697 1937 The Old Stone Age. Cambridge University Press, Cambridge,
England.

CALABRESE, F.A., R.E. PANGBORN, and R.J. YOUNG

1698 1970 Two Village Sites in Southwestern Missouri: A Lithic
Analysis. Missouri Archaeological Society, Research
Series 7.

COLLINS, M.B.

1699 1973 Observations on Thermal Treatment of Chert in the Solu-
            trean of Laugerie Haute, France. Proceedings, Prehistoric
            Society 39:461-466.

CORLISS, D.W.

1700 1972 Neck Width of Projectile Points: An Index of Culture
            Continuity and Change. Occasional Papers of the Idaho
            State University Museum 29.

CRABTREE, D.E.

1701 1972 An Introduction to Flint-Working. Occasional Papers of
            the Idaho State University Museum 28.

CURWEN, E.C.

1702 1930 Prehistoric Flint Sickles. Antiquity 4:179-186.

1703 1935 Agriculture and the Flint Sickle in Palestine. Antiquity
            9:62-66.

1704 1940 The White Patination of Black Flint. Antiquity 14:435-
            437.

De PRADENNE, A.V.

1705 1935 Fossil Tradition in Stone Implements. Antiquity 9(33):
            74-83.

ENGEL, C.G., and R.P. SHARP

1706 1958 Chemical Data on Desert Varnish. Bulletin, Geological
            Society of America 69:487-518.

EVANS, J.

1707 1872 The Ancient Stone Implements, Weapons, and Ornaments of
            Great Britain. D. Appleton, New York.

FITTING, J.E.

1708 1970 Chippage Analysis: In J. DeVisscher and E.J. Wahla,
            Additional Paleo-Indian Campsites Adjacent to the Holcombe
            Site. Michigan Archaeologist 16(1):1-25.

FLENNIKEN, J.J., and E.G. GARRISON

1709 1975 Thermally Altered Novaculite and Stone Tool Manufacturing
            Techniques. Journal of Field Archaeology 2(1):125-132.

GRIFFITH, F.L.

1710 1896 The Manufacture and Use of Flint Knives. Chapter II.
            In Beni Hasan, Part III. Archaeological Survey of Egypt,
            Memoir 5.

HEIZER, R.F.

1711 1951 The Sickle in Aboriginal Western North America. American
            Antiquity 16:247-252.

HESTER, T.R.

1712 1970 A Study of Wear Patterns on Hafted Bifaces from Two
            Nevada Caves. University of California, Contributions
            of the Archaeological Research Facility 7:44-54.

1713 1971 Hafted Unifaces from Southwestern Coahuila. Kiva 36(4):
            36-41.

1714 1972 Notes on Large Blade Cores and Core-Blade Technology in
            Mesoamerica. University of California, Contributions of
            the Archaeological Research Facility 14:95-105.

HESTER, T.R., ed.

1715 1978 Archaeological Studies of Mesoamerican Obsidian. Ballena
            Press, Socorro, N.M.

HESTER, T.R., and R.F. HEIZER

1716 1972 Problems in Functional Interpretation of Artifacts: Scraper
            Planes from Mitla and Yagul, Oaxaca. University of
            California, Contributions of the Archaeological Research
            Facility 14:107-123.

1717 1973 Review and Discussion of Great Basin Projectile Point
            Forms and Chronology. Non-serial publication, University
            of California, Archaeological Research Facility. Berkeley.

HESTER, T.R., R.F. HEIZER, and R.N. JACK

1718 1971 Technology and Geologic Sources of Obsidian from Cerro de
            las Mesas, Veracruz, Mexico, with Observations on Olmec
            Trade. University of California, Contributions of the
            Archaeological Research Facility 13:133-142.

HESTER, T.R., R.N. JACK, and R.F. HEIZER

1719 1971 The Obsidian of Tres Zapotes, Veracruz, Mexico. University
            of California, Contributions of the Archaeological Research
            Facility 13:65-131.

HODGES, H.

1720 1964 Artifacts. John Baker, London.

HOLMES, W.H.

1721 1919 Handbook of Aboriginal American Antiquities: 1. The
            Lithic Industries. Bureau of American Ethnology, Bulletin
            60.

HONEA, K.H.

1722 1964 The Patination of Stone Artifacts. Plains Anthropologist
            9(1):23.

1723 1965 The Bipolar Flaking Technique in Texas and New Mexico.
            Bulletin of the Texas Archeological Society 36:259-267.

1724 1965 Evolution in Lithic Traditions of the Southwest. El
            Palacio 72(4):32-36.

1725   1965   A Morphology of Scrapers and Their Methods of Production.
              Southwestern Lore 31(2):25-38.

1726   1966   Prehistoric Flaking Technologies in Texas. Sixth Inter-
              national Congress of Prehistoric and Protohistoric
              Sciences 3(1962):260-267.

       HOUGH, W.

1727   1897   Stone-Working at Tewa. American Anthropologist 10:191.

       HOWCHIN, W.

1728   1921   On the Methods Adopted by the Aborigines of Australia in
              the Making of Stone Implements Based on Actual Observa-
              tion. Transactions, Royal Society of South Australia
              45:28-281.

       HUMPHREYS, A.J.B.

1729   1970   The Role of Raw Material and the Concept of the Fauresmith.
              South African Archaeological Bulletin 25(99-100), Pts.
              3-4:139-144.

       HUMPHREYS, H.

1730   1952   Flint Tools and Their Makers. Antiquity 26(103):123-134.

       ISAAC, G.L., and C.M. KELLER

1731   1968   Note on the Proportional Frequency of Side- and End-Struck
              Flakes. South African Archaeological Bulletin 23(89),
              Pt. 1:17-19.

       KOWTA, M.

1732   1969   The Sayles Complex; a Late Milling Stone Assemblage from
              Cajon Pass and the Ecological Implications of Its Scraper
              Planes. University of California Press, Publications in
              Anthropology 6. Berkeley.

       LEAKEY, L.S.B.

1733   1950   Stone Implements: How They Were Made and Used. South
              African Archaeological Bulletin 5(18):71-74.

1734   1954   Working Stone, Bone, and Wood. In C. Singer, E.J. Holm-
              yard, and A.R. Hall, A History of Technology 1:128-143.
              Clarendon Press, Oxford.

       Le BAR, F.M.

1735   1964   The Material Culture of Truk. Yale University Publica-
              tions in Anthropology 68.

       LEGGE, R.W.

1736   1929   On Some Diminutive Types of Tasmanian Stone Implements.
              Papers and Proceedings, Royal Society of Tasmania for
              1928:87-92.

1737 1930 Tasmanian Stone Culture. Some Notes on Distinctive Types, Spokeshaves, Borers and Chipping Tools, and Their Probable Usages. Papers and Proceedings, Royal Society of Tasmania for 1929:39-43.

LEROI-GOURHAN, A., and M. BRÉZILLON

1738 1966 Habitation Magdalénienne 1 de Pincevent près Montereau (Seine-et-Marne). Gallia Préhistoire, C.N.R.S., Tome IX, Fascicule 2:263-385.

LINNÉ, S.

1739 1957 Technical Secrets of American Indians. Journal, Royal Anthropological Institute of Great Britain and Ireland 87(1-2):149-164.

LOSEY, T.C.

1740 1971 The Stony Plain Quarry Site. Plains Anthropologist 16(52): 138-154.

LOTHROP, S.K.

1741 1955 Jade and String Sawing in Northeastern Costa Rica. American Antiquity 21:43-51.

LUCAS, A.

1742 1962 Ancient Egyptian Materials and Industries. E. Arnold, London.

McGIMSEY, C.R., III

1743 1963 Stone Working: Fracturing or Chipping. Bulletin, Massachusetts Archaeological Society 24(3-4):60-64.

MacNEISH, R.S., A. NELKEN-TERNER, and I.W. JOHNSON

1744 1967 The Prehistory of the Tehuacan Valley 2, Non-Ceramic Artifacts. University of Texas Press, Austin.

MALIK, S.C.

1745 1961 Stone Age Techniques in Nineteenth Century India. Man 61: 163.

MAN, E.H.

1746 1883 Stone Implements. In On the Aboriginal Inhabitants of the Andaman Islands. Journal, Royal Anthropological Institute 12:379-381.

MEYERS, J.T.

1747 1970 Chert Resources of the Lower Illinois Valley. Reports of Investigations 18, Illinois State Museum, and Research Papers 2, Illinois Valley Archaeological Program.

MICHELS, J.W.

1748 1971 The Colonial Obsidian Industry of the Valley of Mexico.
            In R.H. Brill, ed., Science and Archaeology. MIT Press,
            Cambridge, Mass.

MITCHELL, S.R.

1749 1949 Stone-Age Craftsmen. Tait Book Co., Melbourne, Australia.

MOHOLY-NAGY, H.

1750 1975 Obsidian at Tikal, Guatemala. Actas, XLI Congreso
            Internacional de Americanistas I:519-521.

MOVIUS, H.L., Jr., and A.S. BROOKS

1751 1971 The Analysis of Certain Major Classes of Upper Palaeo-
            lithic Tools: Aurignacian Scrapers. Proceedings, Pre-
            historic Society 37(2):253-274.

MOVIUS, H.L., Jr., N.C. DAVID, H.M. BRICKER, and R.B. CLAY

1752 1968 The Analysis of Certain Major Classes of Upper Paleo-
            lithic Tools. American School of Prehistory Research,
            Peabody Museum, Harvard University Bulletin 26. Cam-
            bridge, Mass.

NANCE, J.D.

1753 1971 Functional Interpretations from Microscopic Analysis.
            American Antiquity 36(3):361-365.

NELSON, N.C.

1754 1916 Flint Working by Ishi. In F.W. Hodge, ed., William Henry
            Holmes Anniversary Volume:397-402. Smithsonian Institu-
            tion, Washington, D.C.

NEUMANN, T.W., and E. JOHNSON

1755 1979 Patrow Site Lithic Analysis. Midcontinental Journal of
            Archaeology 4(1):79-112.

NEWCOMER, M.H., and F. HIVERNEL-GUERRE

1756 1974 Nucléus sur Éclat: Technologie et Utilisation par
            Différentes Cultures Préhistoriques. Bulletin de la
            Société Préhistorique Française 71:119-128.

OAKLEY, K.P.

1757 1950 Man the Tool-Maker. British Museum, London.

1758 1956 The Earliest Tool-Makers. Antiquity 117:4-8.

1759 1957 Tools Makyth Man. Antiquity 124:199-209.

ODELL, G.H.

1760 1975 Micro-Wear in Perspective: A Sympathetic Response to
            Lawrence H. Kelley. World Archaeology 7(2):226-235.

PARKER, A.C.

1761 1924 The Great Algonkin Flint Mines at Coxsackie. Researches
            and Transactions of the New York State Archaeological
            Association, L.H. Morgan Chapter 4(4).

PARKINGTON, J.E.

1762 1967 Some Comments on the Comparison and Classification of
            Archaeological Specimens. South African Archaeological
            Bulletin 22(87), Pt. 3:73-79.

PEYRONY, D., H.H. KIDDER, and H.V.V. NOONE

1763 1949 Outils Ensilex Émoussés du Paléolithique Supérieur.
            Bulletin de la Société Préhistorique Française 46:298-301.

PIPERNO, M.

1764 1973 The Lithic Industry of Tepe Yahya: A Preliminary Typo-
            logical Analysis. East and West 23(1,2):59-74. Rome.

POND, G.G.

1765 1969 A Technique for Flaking Projectile Points. Kiva 34(4):
            237-241.

RANKINE, W.F.

1766 1952 A Mesolithic Chipping-Floor at Oakhenge, Selbourne Haits.
            Proceedings, Prehistoric Society (n.s.) 18(1):21-35.

RENAUD, E.B.

1767 1941 Classification and Description of Indian Stone Artifacts.
            Colorado Archaeological Society, Gunnison.

SANGER, D., ed.

1768 1971 Northern North American Core and Blade Industries
            (Conference Proceedings). Arctic Anthropology VII (2).

SANKALIA, H.D.

1769 1964 Stone Age Tools: Their Techniques, Names and Probable
            Functions. Deccan College, Poona.

1770 1970 Some Aspects of Prehistoric Technology in India. Indian
            National Science Academy, New Delhi.

SEMENOV, S.A.

1771 1964 Prehistoric Technology. Translated by M.W. Thompson.
            Cory, Adams and Mackay, London.

SHAFER, H.J., and T.R. HESTER

1772 1971 A Study of the Function and Technology of Certain Bifacial
            Tools from Southern Texas. Texas Historical Survey
            Commission, Archeological Report 20.

SHEETS, P.D.

1773 1978 From Craftsman to Cog: Quantitative Views of Mesoamerican
            Lithic Technology. In R. Sidrys, ed., Papers on the
            Economy and Architecture of the Ancient Maya. Institute
            of Archaeology, Monograph VIII, University of California,
            Los Angeles.

SKINNER, H.D.

1774 1948 Chisel, Wedge, Axe and Adze. Antiquity 22(88):208-209.

SOLLBERGER, J.B.

1775 1971 A Technological Study of Beveled Knives. Plains Anthro-
            pologist 16(53):209-218.

1776 1976 Bifacing on Prismatic Flakes. Bulletin of the Texas
            Archeological Society 47:261-268.

SONNENFELD, J.

1777 1962 Interpreting the Function of Primitive Implements: The
            Celt and the Hoe. American Antiquity 28:56-65.

1778 1962 Prehistoric Technology: Functional Interpretations and
            Geographical Implications. The Professional Geographer
            14:4-8.

SONNEVILLE-BORDES, D. de

1779 1960 Le Paléolithique Supérieur en Périgord. Imprimeries
            Delmas, Bordeaux.

SPENCE, M.W.

1780 1967 The Obsidian Industry of Teotihuacan. American Antiquity
            32:507-514.

SPETH, JOHN D.

1781 1972 Mechanical Basis of Percussion Flaking. American Antiquity
            37(1):34-60.

SPIER, R.F.G.

1782 1970 From the Hand of Man: Primitive and Preindustrial Tech-
            nologies. Houghton Mifflin, Boston, Mass.

SULIMIRSKI, T.

1783 1960 Remarks Concerning the Distribution of Some Varieties of
            Flint in Poland. Swiatowit 23:281-307. Warzawa.

SWANSON, E., ed.

1784 1975 Lithic Technology: Making and Using Stone Tools. Aldine
            Publishing Co., Chicago.

THOMSEN, E.G., and H.H. THOMSEN

1785 1970 Precolumbian Obsidian Ear Spools: An Investigation of
            Possible Manufacturing Methods. University of California,

Contributions of the Archaeological Research Facility 8: 41-53.

1786 1971 Litho-Mechanics in Archaeology. University of California, Contributions of the Archaeological Research Facility 12: 51-62.

THOMSON, D.F.

1787 1961 Some Wood and Stone Implements of the Bindibu Tribe of Central Western Australia. Proceedings, Prehistoric Society (n.s.) 30:400-422.

TOBIAS, P.V.

1788 1965 Australopithecus, Homo Habilis, Tool-Using and Tool-Making. South African Archaeological Bulletin 20(80), Pt. 4:167-192.

TOLSTOY, P.

1789 1971 Utilitarian Artifacts of Central Mexico. Handbook of Middle American Indians 10(1):270-296. University of Texas Press, Austin.

VAYSON de PRADENNE, A.

1790 1936 Sur l'Utilisation de Certains Microlithes Géometriques. Bulletin de la Société Préhistorique Française 33:217-232.

VERTES, L.

1791 1960 Observations on the Technique of Production of Szeletian Flint Implements. Proceedings, Prehistoric Society 26: 37-43.

WATSON, W.

1792 1950 Flint Implements: An Account of Stone Age Techniques and Cultures. British Museum, London.

WAYLAND, E.J.

1793 1950 Two Boulder-on-Boulder Flaking Techniques. South African Archaeological Bulletin 5(19):99-100.

WEYMOUTH, J.H., and W.O. WILLIAMSON

1794 1951 Some Physical Properties of Raw and Calcined Flint. Mineralogical Magazine 29(213):573-593. London.

WILLEY, G.R.

1795 1972 The Artifacts of Altar de Sacrificios. Peabody Museum Papers 64(1).

WILMSEN, E.N.

1796 1968 Lithic Analysis in Paleo-Anthropology. Science 161:982-987.

1797 1970 Lithic Analysis and Cultural Inference: A Paleo-Indian
            Case. Anthropological Papers of the University of
            Arizona 16. Tucson.

WITTHOFT, J.

1798 1967 The Art of Flint Chipping. Journal of the Archaeological
            Society of Maryland 3(1):123-144.

1799 1968 Stone Hammers: A Preliminary Report. Maryland Archaeology
            4(1):5-13.

WOODBURY, R.B.

1800 1954 Prehistoric Stone Implements of Northeastern Arizona.
            Reports of the Awatovi Expedition 6. Papers, Peabody
            Museum of American Archaeology and Ethnology, Harvard
            University 34.

WORMINGTON, H.M.

1801 1962 The Problems of the Presence and Dating in America of
            Flaking Techniques Similar to the Paleolithic in the Old
            World. Atti del VI Congresso Internazionale delle
            Scienze Preistoriche e Protohistoriche 1:273-283.

*b. NATURAL OBJECTS vs. MANMADE: STONE AND BONE (INCLUDING NATURAL
ALTERATION OF ARTIFACTS)*

ABBOTT, W.J.L.

1802 1915 Flint Fracture. Nature 94:198.

1803 1928 The Necessary Qualifications for the Study of Comparative
            Flint-Flaking. Man 28:101-103.

ASCHER, R., and M. ASCHER

1804 1965 Recognizing the Emergence of Man. Science 147:243-250.

BARNES, A.S.

1805 1939 De la Manière dont la Nature Imite le Travail Humain dans
            l'Éclatment du Silex. Bulletin, Société Préhistorique
            Française 36:74-89.

1806 1939 The Differences Between Natural and Human Flaking on
            Prehistoric Flint Implements. American Anthropologist
            41:99-112.

BELL, A.M.

1807 1894 Remarks on the Flint Implements from the Chalk Plateau
            of Kent. Journal, Royal Anthropological Institute 23:
            266-283.

BLACKMORE, H.P.

1808 1923 The Piltdown Flints. Man 23:98-99.

BLEED, P.

1809 1977 Early Flakes from Sozudai, Japan: Are They Man-Made?
            Science 197:1357-1359.

BOURDIER, F.

1810 1953 Pseudo-Industries Humaines sur Galets de Quartzite
            Glaciares. Bulletin, Société Préhistorique Française
            50:436.

BRAIN, C.K.

1811 1967 Bone Weathering and the Problem of Bone Pseudo Tools.
            South African Journal of Science 63(3):97-100.

BREUIL, H.

1812 1943 On the Presence of Quartzites Mechanically Broken in the
            Dwyka Tillites and Their Derivation in the Older Gravels
            of the Vaal. South African Journal of Science 40:285-286.

CARTER, G.F.

1813 1950 Evidence for Pleistocene Man in Southern California.
            Geographical Review 40:84-102.

1814 1957 Pleistocene Man at San Diego. Johns Hopkins Press,
            Baltimore.

1815 1967 Artifacts and Naturifacts: Introduction. Anthropological
            Journal of Canada 5(I):2-5.

CLARK, J.D.

1816 1958 The Natural Fracture of Pebbles from the Batoka Gorge,
            Northern Rhodesia, and Its Bearing on the Kafuan Indus-
            tries of Africa. Proceedings, Prehistoric Society (n.s.)
            24:64-77.

1817 1961 Fractured Chert Specimens from the Lower Pleistocene
            Bethlehem Beds, Israel. Bulletin of the British Museum
            (Natural History), Geology 5:4.

CLARKE, W.G.

1818 1914 Some Aspects of Striation. Proceedings, Prehistoric
            Society of East Anglia 1:434-438.

DART, R.A.

1819 1957 The Osteodontokeratic Culture of Australopithecus Pro-
            metheus. Transvaal Museum Memoir 10. Pretoria.

1820 1958 Bone Tools and Porcupine Gnawing. American Anthropologist
            60:715-724.

1821 1967 Mousterian Osteodontokeratic Objects from Geula Cave
            (Haifa, Israel). Quaternaria 9:105-140.

ENGERRAND, G.C.

1822 1912 L'État Actuel de la Question des Éolithes. Revue Générale
            des Sciences 23:541-548.

1823 1913 Estado Actual de la Cuestion de los Eolitos. Boletin del
            Museo Nacional Arqueología, Historia y Etnología,
            Tomo 2(8):150-160.

GREENMAN, E.F.

1824 1957 An American Eolithic? American Antiquity 22:298.

GRIST, C.J.

1825 1919 Some Eoliths from Dwilisk and the Question of Origin.
            Journal, Royal Anthropological Institute 40:192-208.

HARNER, M.J.

1826 1956 Thermo Facts vs. Artifacts: An Experimental Study of the
            Malpais Industry. University of California Archaeological
            Survey Reports 33:39-43.

HAWARD, F.N.

1827 1912 The Chipping of the Flint by Natural Agencies. Pro-
            ceedings, Prehistoric Society of East Africa 1:185.

1828 1919 The Origin of the Rostro-Carinate Implements and Other
            Chipped Flints from the Basement Beds of East Anglia.
            Proceedings, Prehistoric Society of East Anglia 3(1),
            for 1918-1919.

1829 1921 The Fracture of Flint. Proceedings, Prehistoric Society
            of East Anglia 3:448-452, for 1920-1921.

HESTER, T.R.

1830 1971 An "Eolith" from Lower Pleistocene Deposits in Southern
            Texas. Bulletin of the Texas Archeological Society 42:
            367-371.

JOHNSON, F., and J. MILLER

1831 1958 Review of G.F. Carter, Pleistocene Man at San Diego.
            American Antiquity 24:206-210.

JONES, F.W., and T.D. CAMPBELL

1832 1925 A Contribution to the Study of Eoliths. Journal, Royal
            Anthropological Institute 55:115-122.

KITCHING, J.W.

1833 1963 Bone, Tooth and Horn Tools of Paleolithic Man: An Account
            of the Osteodontokeratic Discoveries in Pin Hole Cave,
            Derbyshire. Manchester University Press, Manchester.

KRIEGER, A.D.

1834 1958 Review of George F. Carter, Pleistocene Man at San Diego.
            American Anthropologist 60:974-978.

LACAILLE, A.D.

1835 1931 Aspects of Intentional Fracture. Transactions of the
            Glasgow Archaeological Society 9:313-341.

LARTET, E.

1836 1960 Sur l'Ancienneté Géologique de l'Espèce Humaine. Comptes
            Rendus de l'Academie des Sciences 50:790-791. Paris.

LAUDERMILK, J.D., and T.G. KENNARD

1837 1938 Concerning Lightning Spalling. American Journal of
            Science 5(25):104-122.

LEAKEY, L.S.B.

1838 1960 Adam's Ancestors. 4th ed. Harper and Row, New York.

LEAKEY, L.S.B., R. SIMPSON, and T. CLEMENTS

1839 1968 Archaeological Investigations in the Calico Mountains,
            California: Preliminary Report. Science 160:1022-1023.

MacCURDY, G.G.

1840 1905 The Eolithic Problem--Evidences of a Rude Industry
            Antedating the Paleolithic. American Anthropologist
            7:425-479.

1841 1924 What is an Eolith? Natural History 24:656-658.

MASON, R.J.

1842 1965 Makapapsgat Limeworks Fractured Stone Objects and Natural
            Fracture in Africa. South African Archaeological Bulletin
            20:3-17.

MERCER, H.C.

1843 1872 Pebbles Chipped by Modern Indians as an Aid to the Study
            of the Trenton Gravel Implements (Abstract). Proceedings,
            American Association for the Advancement of Science 41:
            287-289.

1844 1893 Trenton and Somme Gravel Specimens Compared with Ancient
            Quarry Refuse in America and Europe. American Naturalist
            27:962-978.

MOIR, J.R.

1845 1912 The Natural Fracture of Flint and Its Bearing Upon Rudi-
            mentary Flint Implements. Proceedings, Prehistoric
            Society of East Anglia 1:171-184.

1846 1914 The Striation of Flint Surfaces. Man 14(90):177-181.

1847 1915 The Large Non-Conchoidal Fracture Surfaces of Early
            Flint Implements. Nature 94:89, 227, 288.

1848 1916 Flint Fracture and Flint Implements. Science Progress
            41:37-50.

1849 1927 The Antiquity of Man in East Anglia. The University
            Press, Cambridge.

1850 1935 The Darmsden Flint Implements. Proceedings, Prehistoric
            Society 10:93-100.

NELSON, N.C.

1851 1928 Pseudo-Artifacts from the Pliocene of Nebraska. Science
            67:316-317.

WHITNEY, M.I., and R.V. DIETRICH

1852 1973 Ventifact Sculpture by Windblown Dust. Geological Society
            of America Bulletin 84:2561-2582.

c. *STONE TOOL USE: BEHAVIORAL ASPECTS*

BARNES, A.S.

1853 1932 Modes of Prehension of Some Forms of Upper Paleolithic
            Implements. Proceedings, Prehistoric Society 7(1):43-56.

BINFORD, S.R., and L.R. BINFORD

1854 1969 Stone Tools and Human Behavior. Scientific American
            220(4):70-87.

BORDES, F.

1855 1969 Reflections on Typology and Techniques in the Palaeo-
            lithic. Arctic Anthropology 6(1):1-29.

CREUTZ, E., and J. MORIARTY

1856 1963 Inferences on the Use Position of San Dieguito Percussion-
            Flaked Artifacts. American Antiquity 29:82-89.

ISAAC, G.

1857 1977 Early Stone Tools--an Adaptive Threshold. In G. de G.
            Sieveking, et al., eds., Problems in Economic and Social
            Archaeology:39-48. Westview Press, Boulder.

JELINEK, A.J.

1858 1976 Form, Function, and Style in Lithic Analysis. In C.E.
            Cleland, ed., Cultural Change and Continuity: Essays in
            Honor of James Bennett Griffin. Academic Press, New York.

KRANTZ, G.S.

1859 1960 Evolution of the Human Hand and the Great Hand-Axe
            Tradition. Kroeber Anthropological Society Papers 23:
            114-128.

OYEN, O.J.

1860 1978 Stone-Eating and Tool-Use Among Olive Baboons. Texas
            Journal of Science 30(3):295.

SPURRELL, F.C.J.

1861 1884 On Some Palaeolithic Knapping Tools and Modes of Using
            Them. Journal, Royal Anthropological Institute 13:107-
            118.

TOBIAS, P.V.

1862 1965 Australopithecus, Homo Habilis, Tool-Using and Tool-
            Making. South African Archaeological Bulletin 20(80):167-
            192.

WATANABE, H., and Y. KUCHIKURA

1863 1973 Control Precision in the Flaking of Levallois Points
            from the Amud Cave; a Technological Approach to the
            Study of Early Man's Manual Dexterity. Paleorient 1.

WHITE, L.A.

1864 1948 Use and Manufacture of Tools by the Lower Primates.
            Antiquity 22(88):210-211.

d. STONE TOOL USE: FUNCTIONAL STUDIES

ALLAIN, J., and J. DESCOUTS

1865 1957 A Propos d'une Baguette à Rainure Armée de Silex
            Découverte dans le Magdaléinien de Saint-Marcel.
            L'Anthropologie 61(5-6):503-512.

AQUILAS-WAUTERS, R.F.

1866 1956 Une Pointe de la Gravette Fichée dans un Fragment de
            Mâchoire de Cervus Giganteus. Bulletin de la Société
            Royale Belge d'Anthropologie et de Préhistorie 67:31-36.

BIRKET-SMITH, K.

1867 1958 Boulder-Chip Scrapers in the Eastern Arctic. Man 58(157):
            113-114.

BORDES, F.

1868 1965 Utilisation Possible des Côtés de Burins. Fundberichte
            aus Schwaben 17:3-4.

1869 1969 Les Chasseurs. In La France au Temps des Mammouths:93-
            131. Hachette, Paris.

BORN, P.L.

1870 1971 Adze Wear Patterns. Newsletter, Missouri Archaeological
            Society 250:2-5.

BROSE, D.S.

1871 1970 The Archaeology of Summer Island: Changing Settlement
            Systems in Northern Lake Michigan. Museum of Anthropology,
            University of Michigan, Anthropological Papers 41.

CAMPANA, D.V.

1872 1979 A Natufian Shaft-Straightener from Mugharet El Wad,
            Israel: An Example of Wear Pattern Analysis. Journal
            of Field Archaeology 6(2):237-242.

COOKE, C.K.

1873   1969   A Re-Examination of the "Middle Stone Age" Industries of
              Rhodesia. Arnoldia 4(7):1-19.

COOKE, C.K., and P.S. GARLAKE

1874   1968   The Tshangula (Magosian) Site at Sitanda Dam, Tshipise
              Tribal Trust Lands, Beit Bridge, Rhodesia. Rhodesian
              Schools Exploration Society 18th Expedition, Siyanje.

CRABTREE, D.E.

1875   1977   The Obtuse Angle as a Functional Edge. In D. Ingersoll,
              J.E. Yellen, and W. MacDonald, eds., Experimental
              Archaeology:38-51. Columbia University Press, New York.

DAVIDSON, D.S.

1876   1935   Archaeological Problems of Northern Australia. Journal
              of the Royal Anthropological Institute 65:145-184.

DAVIS, D.D., ed.

1877   1978   Lithics and Subsistence: The Analysis of Stone Tool Use
              in Prehistoric Economies. Vanderbilt University Publica-
              tions in Anthropology 20. Nashville.

FRISON, G.C.

1878   1968   A Functional Analysis of Certain Chipped Stone Tools.
              American Antiquity 33:149-155.

GEIER, C.

1879   1970   The Lithic Assemblage in Archaeological Interpretation.
              Newsletter, Missouri Archaeological Society 238:2-7.

GILLESPIE, Dr.

1880   1877   On Flint Cores as Implements. Journal, Royal Anthropo-
              logical Institute 6:260-263.

GOULD, R.A., and J. QUILTER

1881   1972   Flat Adzes: A Class of Flaked Stone Tools from South-
              western Australia. American Museum of Natural History
              Novitates.

HAY, C.A.

1882   1977   Use-Scratch Morphology: A Functionally Significant Aspect
              of Edge Damage on Obsidian Tools. Journal of Field
              Archaeology 4(4):491-494.

HAYDEN B., ed.

1883   1979   Lithic Use-Wear Analysis. Academic Press, New York.

HESTER, T.R.

1884 1970 A Study of Wear Patterns on Hafted and Unhafted Bifaces from Two Nevada Caves. University of California, Contributions of the Archaeological Research Facility 7:45-54.

1885 1971 Hafted Unifaces from Southwestern Coahuila, Mexico. Kiva 36(4):36-41.

1886 1975 The Obsidian Industry of Beleh (Chinautla Viejo), Guatemala. Actas XLI Congreso Internacional de Americanistas I:473-488.

HESTER, T.R., and R.F. HEIZER

1887 1973 Arrow Points or Knives: Comments on the Function of Stockton Points. American Antiquity 38(2):220-221.

HESTER, T.R., D. GILBOW, and A.D. ALBEE

1888 1973 A Functional Analysis of "Clear Fork" Artifacts from the Rio Grande Plain, Texas. American Antiquity 38(1):90-96.

JELINEK, A.J.

1889 1967 A Prehistoric Sequence in the Middle Pecos Valley, New Mexico. Museum of Anthropology, University of Michigan, Anthropological Papers 31.

KEELEY, L.H.

1890 1974 Technique and Methodology in Microwear Studies: A Critical Review. World Archaeology 5(3):323-336.

1891 1976 Microwear on Flint: Some Experimental Results. Second International Symposium on Flint. Staringia 2:49-51. Nederlandse Geologische Vereniging, Maastricht.

KEELEY, L.H., and M.H. NEWCOMER

1892 1977 Microwear Analysis of Experimental Flint Tools: A Test Case. Journal of Archaeological Science 4:29-62.

KELLER, C.M.

1893 1966 The Development of Edge Damage Patterns on Stone Tools. Man 1(4):501-511.

LEGGE, R.W.

1894 1930 Tasmanian Stone Culture. Some Notes on Distinctive Types, Spokeshaves, Borers and Chipping Tools, and Their Probable Usages. Papers and Proceedings, Royal Society of Tasmania for 1929:39-43.

LEROI-GOURHAN, A., and M. BRÉZILLON

1895 1966 Habitation Magdalénienne 1 de Pincevent près Montereau (Seine-et-Marne). Gallia Préhistoire. C.N.R.S. IX(2): 263-385.

LORENZO, J.L.

1896   1958   Préhistoire et Quaternaire au Mexique.   État Actuel des
              Connaissances.   L'Anthropologie 62:62-83.

LOVE, J.R.B.

1897   1952   A Primitive Method of Making a Wooden Dish by Native
              Women of the Musgrave Range, South Australia.   Transac-
              tions of the Royal Society of South Australia 66:215-217.

McCRONE, A.W., D. WOUTH, R. ASCHER, and M. ASCHER

1898   1965   Stone Artifacts: Identification Problems.   Science 148:
              167-168.

MacDONALD, G.F.

1899   1968   Debert: A Paleo-Indian Site in Central Nova Scotia.
              Anthropology Papers, National Museum of Canada 16.

MOUNTFORD, CHARLES P.

1900   1941   An Unrecorded Method of Manufacturing Wooden Implements
              by Simple Stone Tools.   Transactions of the Royal Society
              of South Australia 65:312-316.

MUNRO, R.

1901   1892   On Prehistoric Saws vs. Sickles.   Archaeological Journal
              69:164-175.

NANCE, J.D.

1902   1971   Functional Interpretations from Microscopic Analysis.
              American Antiquity 36:361-366.

NERO, R.

1903   1948   Primary Flake Implements.   Wisconsin Archaeologist 29(2):
              23-27.

ODELL, G.H.

1904   1976   L'Analyse Fonctionnelle Microscopique des Pierres
              Taillées, un Nouveau Système.   Congrès Préhistorique
              de France, XXe Session, Provence:385-390.

1905   1978   Préliminaires d'une Analyse Fonctionnelle des Pointes
              Microlithiques de Bergumermeer (Pays-Bas).   Bulletin de
              la Société Préhistorique Française 75(2):37-49.

ORELLANA, S.L.

1906   1977   Obsidian and Its Uses Among the Tzutujil Maya.   Journal
              of New World Archaeology 2(1):17-29.

OVER, W.H.

1907   1937   The Use of the Thumb-Scraper.   American Antiquity 2:208-
              209.

PEYRONY, D., H.H. KIDDER, and H.V.V. NOONE

1908 1949 Outils Ensilex Émoussés du Paléolithique Supérieur. Bulletin de la Société Préhistorique Française 46:298-301.

PORSILD, P.

1909 1915 Studies on the Material Culture of the Eskimo in West Greenland. Meddelelser om Grønland 7:110-250.

ROSENFELD, A.

1910 1971 The Examination of Use-Marks on Some Magdalenian End Scrapers. In G. de G. Sieveking, ed., Prehistoric and Roman Studies:176-182. British Museum, London.

ROZOY, J.-G.

1911 1977 Les Derniers Chasseurs. L'Epipaléolithic en France et en Belgique. Charleville-Mezieres, France.

SEMENOV, S.A.

1912 1964 Prehistoric Technology. Cory, Adams and MacKay, London.

SINGER, C.A., and R.O. GIBSON

1913 1970 The Medea Creek Village Site (41 Lan-243v): A Functional Lithic Analysis. Annual Report, Archaeological Survey, Department of Anthropology, University of California, Los Angeles 12:186-203.

SONNENFELD, J.

1914 1962 Interpreting the Function of Primitive Implements. American Antiquity 28:56-65.

SPURRELL, F.C.J.

1915 1892 Notes on Early Sickles. Archaeological Journal 69:53-68.

STOCKTON, E.D.

1916 1970 Some Observations on Bondi Points. Mankind 7:227-229.

SWAUGER, J.L., and B.L. WALLACE

1917 1964 An Experiment in Skinning with Egyptian Paleolithic and Neolithic Stone Implements. Pennsylvania Archaeologist 34:1-7.

TINDALE, N.B.

1918 1945 A Microlithic Mounted Stone Engraver from Western Queensland. The Queensland Naturalist 12:83-84.

1919 1951 Palaeolithic Kodj Axe of the Aborigines. Further Notes. Records, South Australian Museum 9(4):371-374.

1920 1968 Nomenclature of Archaeological Cultures and Associated Implements in Australia. Records, South Australian Museum 15(4):615-640.

TRINGHAM, R., et al.

1921 1974 Experimentation in the Formation of Edge Damage: A New
            Approach to Lithic Analysis. Journal of Field Archaeology
            1(1/2):171-196.

Van NOTEN, F.

1922 1978 Les Chasseurs de Meer. Dissertationes Archaeologicae
            Gandenses, XVIII. De Tempel, Brugge (Belgium). (Section
            by L.H. Kelley on microwear.)

VAYSON de PRADENNE, A.

1923 1936 Sur l'Utilisation de Certains Microlithes Géometriques.
            Bulletin de la Société Préhistorique Française 33:217-232.

WALCOTT, C.F.

1924 1965 The Significance of Wear on Chipped Implements. Bulletin,
            Massachusetts Archaeological Society 27(1):12-14.

WALKER, P.L., and J.C. LONG

1925 1977 An Experimental Study of the Morphological Characteristics
            of Tool Marks. American Antiquity 42(4):605-616.

WEBB, C.H., J.L. SHINER, and E.W. ROBERTS

1926 1971 The John Pearce Site (16 CD 56): A San Patrice Site in
            Caddo Parish, Louisiana. Bulletin of the Texas Archeo-
            logical Society 42:1-50.

WHITE, J.P.

1927 1968 Fabricators, Outils Ecailles, or Scalar Cores? Mankind
            6(12):658-666.

1928 1969 Typologies for Some Prehistoric Flaked Stone Artifacts
            of the Australian New Guinea Highlands. Archaeology and
            Physical Anthropology of Oceania 4(1):18-46.

WHITE, J.P., and D.H. THOMAS

1929 1972 What Mean These Stones? Ethno-Taxonomic Models and
            Archaeological Interpretations in the New Guinea Highlands.
            In D. Clarke, ed., Models in Archaeology:275-308. Methuen
            and Co., London.

WILMSEN, E.N.

1930 1968 Functional Analysis of Flaked Stone Artifacts. American
            Antiquity 33:156-161.

1931 1970 Lithic Analysis and Cultural Inference: A Paleo-Indian
            Case. Anthropological Papers, University of Arizona 16.

WITTHOFT, J.

1932 1955 Worn Stone Tools from Southeastern Pennsylvania. Penn-
            sylvania Archaeologist 25(1):16-31.

1933 1967 Glazed Polish on Flint Tools. American Antiquity 32: 383-388.

1934 1969 Lithic Materials and Technology. Proceedings, 25th Southeastern Archaeological Conference 9:3-15.

e. EXPERIMENTAL STUDIES (FLINT-KNAPPING)

ACKERLY, N.W.

1935 1978 Controlling Pressure in Experimental Lithics Research. American Antiquity 43(3):436-443.

ALIMEN, H.

1936 1963 Enclumes (Percuteurs Dormants) Associés à l'Acheuleen Supérieur de l'Augartien. Bulletin de la Société Préhistorique Française 40(1-2):43-47.

ASCHER, R.

1937 1961 Experimental Archeology. American Anthropologist 63(4): 793-816.

BADEN-POWELL, D.F.W.

1938 1949 Experimental Clactonian Technique. Proceedings, Prehistoric Society 15:38-41.

BIXBY, L.B.

1939 1945 Flint Chipping. American Antiquity 10:356-361.

BORDES, F.

1940 1947 Étude Comparative des Différentes Techniques de Taille du Silex et des Roches Dures. L'Anthropologie 51:1-29.

1941 1955 Observations sur la Note de M.H. Kelley sur la Technique de Taille "Levalloisienne." Bulletin de la Société Préhistorique Française 52:113-114.

1942 1969 Reflections on Typology and Techniques in the Paleolithic. Arctic Anthropology 6(1):1-29.

1943 1970 Observations Typologiques et Techniques sur le Périgordien Supérieur de Corbiac (Dordogne). Bulletin, Société Préhistorique Française 67:105-113.

BORDES, F., and D. CRABTREE

1944 1969 The Corbiac Blade Technique and Other Experiments. Tebiwa 12(2):1-21.

CABROL, A., and L. COUTIER

1945 1931 L'Utilisation du Bois en Guise de Percuteur pour Tailler la Pierre. Bulletin, Société Préhistorique Française 28: 170.

COUTIER, L.

1946   1929   Experiences de Taille pour Rechercher les Anciennes Techniques Paléolithiques. Bulletin, Société Préhistorique Française 26:172-174.

CRABTREE, D.E.

1947   1966   A Stoneworker's Approach to Analyzing and Replicating the Lindenmeier Folsom. Tebiwa 9(1):3-39.

1948   1968   Mesoamerican Polyhedral Cores and Prismatic Blades. American Antiquity 33:446-478.

1949   1970   Flaking Stone with Wooden Implements. Science 169:146-153.

1950   1972   The Cone Fracture Principle and the Manufacture of Lithic Materials. Tebiwa 15(2):29-42.

1951   1973   Experiments in Replicating Hohokam Points. Tebiwa 16(1): 10-45.

CRABTREE, D.E., and B.R. BUTLER

1952   1964   Notes on Experiments in Flintknapping 1: Heat Treatment of Silica Minerals. Tebiwa 7(3):1-6.

CRABTREE, D.E., and R.A. GOULD

1953   1970   Man's Oldest Craft Recreated. Curator 13(3):179-188.

CRABTREE, D., and E.H. SWANSON, Jr.

1954   1968   Edge-Ground Cobbles and Blade-Making in the Northwest. Tebiwa 11(2):50-58.

DeVISSCHER, J.

1955   1955   Experiments in Flint Chipping. Cranbrook Institute of Science, Newsletter 25:23-24. Bloomfield Hills, Mich.

ELLIS, H.H.

1956   1940   Flint-Working Techniques of the American Indians: An Experimental Study. The Lithic Laboratory, Department of Archaeology, Ohio State Museum.

FLENNIKEN, J.J.

1957   1978   Reevaluation of the Lindenmeier Folsom: A Replication Experiment in Lithic Technology. American Antiquity 43(3):473-479.

GORODZOW, B.A.

1958   1914   Les Procédés de Fabrication des Instruments en Pierre. Bulletin, Société Préhistorique Française 11(4):229-239.

HEALY, J.A.

1959   1966   Applying the Ancient Craft of Knapping thru Controlled Fracturing. Archaeology in Montana 6(4):5-21.

HEWITT, H.D.

1960 1915 Some Experiments on Patination. Proceedings, Prehistoric
            Society of East Anglia 2(1):45-50.

JELINEK, A.J.

1961 1965 Lithic Technology Conference, Les Eyzies, France.
            American Antiquity 31:277-278.

JELINEK, A.J., B. BRADLEY, and B. HUCKELL

1962 1971 The Production of Multiple Secondary Flakes. American
            Antiquity 36:198-200.

JONES, P.R.

1963 1979 Effects of Raw Materials on Biface Manufacture. Science
            204:835-836.

KANTMAN, S.

1964 1970 Raclettes Mousteriennes: Une Étude Experimentale sur la
            Distinction de Retouche Intentionelle et les Modifications
            du Tranchant par Utilisation. Quaternaria 13:295-304.

KNOWLES, F.H.S.

1965 1944 The Manufacture of a Flint Arrowhead by Quartzite Hammer-
            Stone. Occasional Papers on Technology 1. Pitt Rivers
            Museum, Oxford.

KRAGH, A.

1966 1952 Stenalderens Flintteknik. Saertryk af Kuml, Arbog for
            Jysk Arkaeologisk Selskab:49-64.

1967 1964 Mand Og Flint. Copenhagen.

LANGFORD, R.R.

1968 1961 A Technique for Eden Collateral Flaking. Southwestern
            Lore 27(3):44-45.

LEAKEY, L.S.B.

1969 1950 Stone Implements: How They Were Made and Used. South
            African Archaeological Bulletin 5(18):71-74.

MARSHALL, R.

1970 1969 Some Comments on Hinge Fracture in Fluted Point Manufac-
            ture. Proceedings, 25th Southeastern Archaeological
            Conference Bulletin 9:22-31.

MASON, O.T.

1971 1894 North American Bows, Arrows and Quivers. Annual Report,
            Smithsonian Institution for 1893:631-680.

MEWHINNEY, H.

1972 1952 Plaint of the Flint Flaker. Tennessee Archeologist 8(3):
            77-80.

1973 1957 A Manual for Neanderthals. University of Texas Press,
            Austin.

1974 1963 Oddities of Flint. American Antiquity 28:299-400.

1975 1964 A Skeptic Views the Billet Flake. American Antiquity
            30:203-204.

NEILL, W.T.

1976 1952 The Manufacture of Fluted Points. Florida Anthropologist
            5:9-16.

NEWCOMER, M.H.

1977 1970 Conjoined Flakes from the Lower Loam, Barnfield Pit,
            Swanscombe (1970). Proceedings, Royal Anthropological
            Institute 970:51-59.

NICHOLS, G.W.

1978 1970 The Hinge Fracture Problem in Fluted Point Manufacture.
            Memoir, Missouri Archaeological Society 8:1-9.

ODELL, G.H., and F. ODELL-VEREECKEN

1979 1980 Verifying the Reliability of Lithic Use-Wear Assessments
            by "Blind Tests": The Low-Power Approach. Journal of
            Field Archaeology 7(1):87-120.

PAINTER, F.E.

1980 1965 The Cattail Creek Fluting Tradition. Chesopiean 3(1):
            11-18.

POND, A.W.

1981 1930 Primitive Methods of Working Stone, Based on Experiments
            of Halvor L. Skavlem. Logan Museum, Beloit College 2(1).

POND, G.G.

1982 1969 A Technique for Flaking Projectile Points. Kiva 34(4):
            237-241.

POPE, S.T.

1983 1913 Making Indian Arrow Heads. Forest and Stream 81:796.

SCHWARTZ, A.

1984 1914 Some Suggestions for Organised Research on Flint Imple-
            ments. Proceedings of the Prehistoric Society of East
            Anglia 1:449-454.

SELLERS, G.E.

1985 1886 Observations on Stone-Chipping. Annual Report, Smith-
            sonian Institution for 1885:871-891.

SHEETS, P.D., and G.R. MUTO

1986 1972 Pressure Blades and Total Cutting Edge: An Experiment in
            Lithic Technology. Science 175(4022):632-634.

SMITH, P.E.L.

1987 1966 Lithic Technology: Report on Conference, November 25-28, 1964, Les Eyzies. Current Anthropology 7:592-593.

SNYDER, J.F.

1988 1897 The Method of Making Stone Arrow Points. Antiquarian 1(9):231-234.

SOLLBERGER, J.B.

1989 1968 A Partial Report on Research Work Concerning Lithic Typology and Technology. Bulletin of the Texas Archeological Society 39:95-110.

1990 1969 The Basic Tool Kit Required to Make and Notch Arrow Shafts for Stone Points. Bulletin of the Texas Archeological Society 40:231-240.

1991 1970 Preforms Are Not Projectile Point Types. Bulletin, Oklahoma Anthropological Society 19:151-154.

1992 1971 A Technological Study of Beveled Knives. Plains Anthropologist 16(53):209-218.

1993 1977 On Fluting Folsom: Notes on Recent Experiments. Bulletin of the Texas Archeological Society 48:47-52.

SOLLBERGER, J.B., and L.W. PATTERSON

1994 1976 Prismatic Blade Replication. American Antiquity 41(4): 517-531.

SPETH, J.D.

1995 1972 Mechanical Basis of Percussion Flaking. American Antiquity 37:34-60.

STAFFORD, C.R., and B.D. STAFFORD

1996 1979 Some Issues Concerning the Design of Lithic Experiments. Lithic Technology 8(2):21-24.

SWANSON, E.H., Jr.

1997 1966 An Introduction to Crabtree's Experiments in Flint-Knapping. Tebiwa 9(1):1-2.

TINDALE, N.B., and H.V.V. NOONE

1998 1941 Analysis of an Australian Aboriginal's Hoard of Knapped Flint. Transactions, Royal Society of South Australia 65:116-122.

WITTHOFT, J.

1999 1957 The Human Factor in Flint Technology. Ohio Archaeologist 7(1).

2000 1967 The Art of Flint Chipping. Journal, Archaeological Society of Maryland 3(1):123-144.

2001 1969 Lithic Materials and Technology. Proceedings, 25th Southeastern Archaeological Conference, Bulletin 9:3-15.

5. Ceramics

ADAMS, R.E.W.

2002 1971 The Ceramics of Altar de Sacrificios. Peabody Museum
            Papers, Harvard University, 63(1).

ALBRIGHT, W.F.

2003 1939 Ceramics and Chronology in the Near East. In D.D. Brand
            and F.E. Harvey, eds., So Live the Works of Men:49-63.
            The University of New Mexico Press, Albuquerque.

ALVAREZ, L., F. FRANCO, and S. ESCOBAR

2004 1967 Análisis Químico de Cerámicas Arqueológicas. Instituto
            Nacional de Antropología e Historia, Tecnología 1.
            Mexico.

AMIRAN, R.

2005 1970 Ancient Pottery of the Holy Land: From Its Beginnings in
            the Neolithic Period to the End of the Iron Age. Rutgers
            University Press, New Brunswick, N.J.

ARNOLD, J.B., III

2006 1975 Porosity and Refiring Tests on Ceramics from the George
            C. Davis Site, Texas. Bulletin of the Texas Archeological
            Society 46:231-242.

ATEN, L.E., and C.N. BOLLICH

2007 1969 A Preliminary Report on the Development of a Ceramic
            Chronology for the Sabine Lake Area of Texas and Louisiana.
            Bulletin of the Texas Archeological Society 40:241-258.

BAUMHOFF, M.A., and R.F. HEIZER

2008 1959 Some Unexploited Possibilities in Ceramic Analysis.
            Southwestern Journal of Anthropology 15:308-316.

BENNET, A.

2009 1974 Basic Ceramic Analysis. Contributions in Anthropology,
            Eastern New Mexico University 6(1).

BENSON, J.L.

2010 1961 Observations on Mycenaean Vase-Painters. American Journal
            of Archaeology 65(4):337-348.

BRETERNITZ, D.A., A.H. ROHN, and E.A. MORRIS

2011 1974 Prehistoric Ceramics of the Mesa Verde Region. Museum
            of Northern Arizona Ceramic Series 5. Flagstaff.

BRODY, J.J.

2012 1977 Mimbres Painted Pottery. University of New Mexico Press,
            Albuquerque.

BULLEN, R.P., and J.B. STOLTMAN, eds.

2013 1972 Fiber Tempered Pottery in Southeastern United States and Northern Colombia: Its Origins, Context and Significance. Florida Anthropological Society Publication 6.

CATLING, H.W.

2014 1970 Analysis of Pottery from the Mycenaean Period. In The Impact of the Natural Sciences on Archaeology:85-178. Oxford University Press, Oxford.

CLARKE, G.

2015 1970 Beaker Pottery of Great Britain and Ireland. Western African Language Monograph Series 2. Cambridge University Press, Cambridge.

COLTON, H.S.

2016 1939 The Reducing Atmosphere and Oxidizing Atmosphere in Prehistoric Southwestern Ceramics. American Antiquity 4:224-231.

2017 1953 Potsherds. Museum of Northern Arizona Bulletin 25.

2018 1955 Check List of Southwestern Pottery Types. Museum of Northern Arizona, Flagstaff.

CONKLIN, H.C.

2019 1953 Buhid Pottery. University of Manila Journal of East Asiatic Studies 3:1-12.

COWGILL, G.L.

2020 1964 The Selection of Samples from Large Sherd Collections. American Antiquity 29:467-473.

CRONIN, C.

2021 1962 An Analysis of Pottery Design Elements, Indicating Possible Relationships Between Three Decorated Types. Chapters in the Prehistory of Eastern Arizona, I. Chicago Natural History Museum. Fieldiana, Anthropology 53:105-114.

DAVID, N.

2022 1972 The Ethnography of Pottery: A Fulani Case Seen in Archaeological Perspective. Addison-Wesley Module in Anthropology 21.

DAVID, N., and H. HENNIG

2023 1972 On the Life Span of Pottery, Type Frequencies, and Archaeological Inference. American Antiquity 37(1):141-142.

deBOOY, T.

2024 1915 Pottery from Certain Caves in Eastern Santo Domingo, West Indies. American Anthropologist 17:69-97.

DIXON, K.A.

2025 1963 The Interamerican Diffusion of a Cooking Technique: The
             Culinary Shoe-Pot. American Anthropologist 65:593-619.

ERICSON, J.E., and E.G. STICKEL

2026 1973 A Proposed Classification System for Ceramics. World
             Archaeology 4(3):357-367.

ERICSON, J.E., D.W. READ, and C. BURKE

2027 1971 Research Design: The Relationship Between the Primary
             Functions and the Physical Properties of Ceramic Vessels
             and the Implications for Ceramic Distribution on an
             Archaeological Site. Anthropology, UCLA 3(2):84-95.

FARNSWORTH, M.

2028 1959 Types of Greek Glaze Failure. Archaeology 12(4):242-250.

2029 1964 Greek Pottery: A Mineralogical Study. American Journal
             of Archaeology 68(3):221-228.

FEWKES, V.J.

2030 1951 The Function of Paddle and Anvil in Pottery Making.
             American Antiquity 7:162-164.

FISCHER, E.

2031 1963 Die Topferei bei den Westlichen Dah (of Liberia).
             Zeitschrift für Ethnologie 88:100-115.

FORD, J.A.

2032 1936 Analysis of Indian Village Site Collection from Louisiana
             and Mississippi. State of Louisiana, Department of
             Conservation Archaeological Study 2.

2033 1949 A Surface Survey of Viru Valley, Peru. American Museum
             of Natural History, Anthropological Papers 43(1).

FOSTER, G.M.

2034 1948 Some Implications of Modern Mold-Made Pottery. South-
             western Journal of Anthropology 4:356-370.

2035 1955 Contemporary Pottery Techniques in Southern and Central
             Mexico. Middle American Research Institute, Publication
             22:1-48. Tulane University, New Orleans.

2036 1956 Pottery-Making in Bengal. Southwestern Journal of
             Anthropology 12:395-405.

2037 1960 Archaeological Implications of the Modern Pottery of
             Acatáln, Puebla, Mexico. American Antiquity 26:205-214.

2038 1960 Life-Expectancy of Utilitarian Pottery in Tzintzuntzan,
             Michoacan, Mexico. American Antiquity 25:606-609.

FRANKEN, H.J.

2039 1974 In Search of the Jericho Potters: Ceramics from the Iron Age and from the Neolithicum. North Holland Publishing Co., Amsterdam.

FRANKFORT, H.

2040 1924 Studies in Early Pottery of the Near East. Royal Anthropological Institute of Great Britain and Ireland, London.

GARDNER, E.

2041 1979 Graphite Painted Ceramics. Archaeology 32(4):18-23.

GARLAKE, M.

2042 1967 A New Method of Restoring Pottery. South African Archaeological Bulletin 22(88), Pt. 4:156.

GIFFORD, J.C.

2043 1960 The Type-Variety Method of Ceramic Classification as an Indicator of Cultural Phenomena. American Antiquity 25:341-347.

GILLIN, J.

2044 1938 A Method of Notation for the Description and Comparison of Southwestern Pottery Sherds by Formula. American Antiquity 4:22-39.

GLADWIN, W., and H.S. GLADWIN

2045 1928 The Use of Potsherds in an Archaeological Survey of the Southwest. Medallion Papers 2, Gila Pueblo. Globe, Ariz.

GOLDMAN, H.

2046 1934 The Bronze Age Pottery of Greece. Bulletin, American Ceramic Society 13(11):301-308.

GOODYEAR, F.H.

2047 1971 Initial Firing Temperature, Composition and Provenance of Pottery. Science and Archaeology 6.

GUTHE, C.E.

2048 1925 Pueblo Pottery Making: A Study at the Village of San Ildefonso. Yale University Press, New Haven.

HAMMOND, P.C.

2049 1964 The Physical Nature of Nabataen Pottery. American Journal of Archaeology 68(3):259-268.

2050 1971 Ceramic Technology of South-West Asia, Syro-Palestine: Iron IIB Hebron. Science and Archaeology 5.

HARGRAVE, L.L.

2051 1974 Type Determinants in Southwestern Ceramics and Some of
            Their Implications. Plateau 46(3):76-95.

HARGRAVE, L.L., and W. SMITH

2052 1936 A Method of Determining the Texture of Pottery. American
            Antiquity 2:32-36.

HAYDEN, J.D.

2053 1959 Notes on Pima Pottery Making. Kiva 24:10-16.

HESTER, T.R., and T.C. HILL, Jr.

2054 1971 An Initial Study of a Prehistoric Ceramic Tradition in
            Southern Texas. Plains Anthropologist 16(53):195.

HILL, W.W.

2055 1937 Navajo Pottery Manufacture. University of New Mexico
            Bulletin, Anthropological Series 2(3).

HOUSTON, M., and J.C. WAINER

2056 1971 Pottery-Making Tools from the Valley and Coast of Oaxaca.
            Bulletin, Oaxaca Studies 36.

JANSMA, M.J.

2057 1977 Diatom Analysis of Pottery. In B.L. van Beek, et al.,
            eds., Ex Horreo:77-85. Albert Egges van Giffen Instituut,
            Amsterdam.

KELSON, J.L.

2058 1948 The Ceramic Vocabulary of the Old Testament. Bulletin,
            American School of Oriental Research, Supplementary
            Studies 5-6. New Haven.

KETCHUM, W.C.

2059 1971 The Pottery and Porcelain Collector's Handbook. Funk and
            Wagnalls, New York.

KIDDER, A.V.

2060 1915 Pottery of the Pajarito Plateau and of Some Adjacent
            Regions in New Mexico. American Anthropological
            Association, Memoirs 2(6).

KIRKMAN, J.

2061 1958 Potter's Marks from Medieval Arab Sites in Kenya. South
            African Archaeological Bulletin 13(52):156-159.

KROEBER, A.L.

2062 1916 Zuni Potsherds. American Museum of Natural History,
            Anthropological Papers 18(1).

KROEBER, A.L., and W.D. STRONG

2063 1942 The Uhle Pottery Collections from Ica. University of
California Publications in American Archaeology and
Ethnology 21(3). Berkeley.

LANDON, M.V.

2064 1959 Dimensional Determinations from Potsherds. Bulletin,
Massachusetts Archaeological Society 20(3):46-47.

LISTER, F.C., and R.H. LISTER

2065 1974 Maiolica in Colonial Spanish America. Historical
Archaeology 8:17-52.

LOTHROP, S.K.

2066 1942 Cocle, an Archaeological Study of Central Panama 2.
Memoirs of the Peabody Museum, Harvard University, 8.

MARCH, B.

2067 1934 Standards of Pottery Description. Occasional Contributions from the Museum of Anthropology of the University
of Michigan 3.

MATSON, F.R.

2068 1945 Technological Development of Pottery in Northern Syria
During the Chalcolithic Age. Journal, American Ceramic
Society 28(1):20-25.

2069 1951 Ceramic Technology as an Aid to Cultural Interpretation:
Techniques and Problems. Anthropological Papers of the
University of Michigan 8:102-116.

2070 1960 The Quantitative Study of Ceramic Materials. Viking Fund
Publications in Anthropology 28:34-51.

MATSON, F.R., ed.

2071 1965 Ceramics and Man. Viking Fund Publications in Anthropology 41.

PEACOCK, D.P.S.

2072 1969- Scientific Analysis of Ceramics; a Review. World Archae-
1970 ology 1:375-389.

PETRIE, W.M.F.

2073 1901 Diospolis Parva. Egyptian Exploration Fund Memoirs 20.
London.

PLANT, R.J.

2074 1970 A Study of Moisture Absorbed by Biscuit Pottery as a Means
of Determining the Approximate Firing Temperature.
Science and Archaeology 4.

POWELL, B.B.

2075 1962 Classification of Ceramics from Historic American Sites.
            Southeastern Archaeological Conference, Newsletter 9(1):
            34-45.

QUIMBY, G.I.

2076 1949 A Hopewell Tool for Decorating Pottery. American Antiquity
            14:344.

REICHEL-DOLMATOFF, G.

2077 1971 Early Pottery from Colombia. Archaeology 24(4):338-345.

REINA, R.E., and R.M. HILL II

2078 1978 The Traditional Pottery of Guatemala. University of
            Texas Press, Austin.

RICHTER, G.M.A., and M.J. MILNE

2079 1935 Shapes and Names of Athenian Vases. Planter Press, New
            York.

ROGERS, M.J.

2080 1936 Yuman Pottery Making. San Diego Museum Papers 2.

RUTTER, J.B.

2081 1975 Ceramic Evidence for Northern Intruders in Southern
            Greece at the Beginning of the Late Helladic IIIC Period.
            American Journal of Archaeology 79(1):17-32.

SANDERS, W.T.

2082 1960 Prehistoric Ceramics and Settlement Patterns in Quintana
            Roo, Mexico. Carnegie Institution of Washington,
            Contributions to American Anthropology and History 12(60).

SCHMIDT, E.F.

2083 1928 Time-Relations of Prehistoric Pottery Types in Southern
            Arizona. Anthropological Papers of the American Museum
            of Natural History 30(4). New York.

SHEPARD, A.O.

2084 1948 Plumbate: A Mesoamerican Trade Ware. Carnegie Institution
            of Washington, Publication 573.

2085 1956 Ceramics for the Archaeologist. Carnegie Institution of
            Washington, Publication 609.

2086 1963 Beginnings of Ceramic Industrialization: An Example from
            the Oaxaca Valley. Notes from a Ceramic Laboratory 2,
            Carnegie Institution of Washington.

2087 1965 Problems in Pottery Analysis. American Antiquity 31:
            870-871.

2088 1965 Rio-Grande Glaze-Paint Pottery: A Test of Petrographic
             Analysis. In F.R. Matson, ed., Ceramics and Man:62-87.
             Aldine, Chicago.

2089 1971 Ceramic Analysis; the Interrelations of Methods; the
             Relations of Analysts and Archaeologists. In R.H. Brill,
             ed., Science and Archaeology:55-64. MIT Press, Cambridge,
             Mass.

SMITH, R.E.

2090 1955 Ceramic Sequences at Uaxactun. Middle American Research
             Institute, Publication 20. Tulane University, New Orleans.

2091 1971 The Pottery of Mayapan, Including Studies of Ceramic
             from Uxmal, Kabah, and Chichen Itza. Papers, Peabody
             Museum of Archaeology and Ethnology 66. Harvard Univer-
             sity, Cambridge, Mass.

SMITH, R.E., G.R. WILLEY, and J.C. GIFFORD

2092 1960 The Type-Variety Concept as a Basis for the Analysis of
             Maya Pottery. American Antiquity 25:330-340.

SMITH, W.

2093 1962 Schools, Pots, and Potters. American Anthropologist 64:
             1165-1178.

SOLHEIM, W.G., II

2094 1960 The Use of Sherd Weights and Counts in the Handling of
             Archaeological Data. Current Anthropology 1:325-329.

STEENSBERG, A.

2095 1940 Hand-Made Pottery in Jutland. Antiquity 14(54):148-153.

STORY, D.A.

2096 1966 Indian Artifacts; Pottery Vessels. In E. Jelks, ed.,
             The Gilbert Site. Bulletin, Texas Archeological Society
             37:112-188.

STRONG, W.D., and J.M. CORBETT

2097 1943 A Ceramic Sequence at Pachacamac. Columbia University
             Studies in Archaeology and Ethnology 1(1).

SUGGS, R.C.

2098 1967 A Reanalysis of Galapagos Ceramics Data. Zeitschrift
             für Ethnologie 92(2):238-247.

THOMPSON, J.E.S.

2099 1941 A Coordination of the History of Chichen Itza with Ceramic
             Sequence in Central Mexico. Revista Mexicana de Estudios
             Antropológicas 5:97-111.

TITE, M.S.

2100 1969 Determination of the Firing Temperature of Ancient
            Ceramics by Measurement of Thermal Expansion: A Reassess-
            ment. Archaeometry 11:131-144.

TUNNELL, C.

2101 1966 A Description of Enameled Earthenware from an Archeological
            Excavation at Mission San Antonio de Valero (the Alamo).
            State Building Commission, Archeological Program Reports
            2. Austin, Tex.

Van der LEEUW, S.E.

2102 1977 Towards a Study of the Economics of Pottery Making.
            In B.L. van Beek, et al., eds., Ex Horreo:68-76. Albert
            Egges van Giffen Instituut, Amsterdam.

WARD, L.

2103 1948 Suggested Outline for Description of Pottery. Far Eastern
            Ceramic Bulletin 3:17-19.

WEAVER, E.C.

2104 1963 Technological Analysis of Prehistoric Lower Mississippi
            Ceramic Materials: A Preliminary Report. American
            Antiquity 29:49-56.

WHALLON, R.J.

2105 1969 Rim Diameter, Vessel Volume, and Economic Prehistory.
            Michigan Academician 2(2):89-98.

2106 1972 A New Approach to Pottery Typology. American Antiquity
            37(1):13-33.

WHITTLESEY, S.M.

2107 1974 Identification of Imported Ceramics Through Functional
            Analysis of Attributes. Kiva 40(1-2):101-112.

WILLEY, G.R.

2108 1939 Ceramic Stratigraphy in a Georgia Village Site. American
            Antiquity 5:140-147.

2109 1961 Volume in Pottery and the Selection of Samples. American
            Antiquity 27:230-231.

XANTHOUDIDES, S.

2110 1927 Some Minoan Potter's-Wheel Discs. In C.S. Casson, ed.,
            Essays in Aegean Archaeology; Presented to Sir Arthur
            Evans in Honour of His 75th Birthday:111-128. Clarendon,
            Oxford.

ZIMMERMAN, D.W.

2111 1971 Uranium Distributions in Archeologic Ceramics: Dating of
            Radioactive Inclusions. Science 174:818-819.

6. Petrographic Analysis

a. GENERAL

BELL, R.E.

2112   1955   Lithic Analysis and Archaeological Method.   American
              Anthropologist 55:299-301.

BOWMAN, H.R., F. ASARO, and I. PERLMAN

2113   1973   Composition Variations in Obsidian Sources and the
              Archaeological Implications.   Archaeometry 15(1):123-138.

DESMAISONS, H.

2114   1935   La Minéralogie en Préhistoire.   Bulletin de la Société
              Préhistorique Française 32:87-96.

ELLIS, H.H.

2115   1938   Lithic Problems.   American Antiquity 4:63-64.

FISCHER, H.

2116   1878   Die Mineralogie als Hilfswissenschaft für Archäologie,
              Ethnographie, u.j.w. mit Specieller Berücksichtigung
              Mexicanischer Sculpturen.   Archiv für Anthropologie
              10:177-214.

2117   1879   Mineralogisch-Archäologische Studien.   Mitteilungen der
              Anthropologischen Gesellschaft in Wien 8:148-183.

FITTING, J.E., and L.M. STONE

2118   1969   Distance and Utility in the Distribution of Raw Materials
              in the Cedar Mountains of New Mexico.   Kiva 34:207-212.

GILBERT, R.I., Jr.

2119   1977   Applications of Trace Element Research to Problems of
              Archeology.   In R.L. Blakeley, ed., Biocultural Adaptation
              in Prehistoric America:85-100.   University of Georgia
              Press, Athens, Ga.

GORDUS, A.A.

2120   1970   Neutron Activation Analysis of Archaeological Artefacts.
              The Impact of the Natural Sciences on Archaeology:165-
              174.   Oxford University Press, London.

GROUT, F.F.

2121   1932   Petrography and Petrology.   McGraw, New York.

HERZ, N.

2122   1955   Petrofabrics and Classical Archaeology.   American Journal
              of Science 253:299-305.

HERZ, N., and W.K. PRITCHETT

2123   1953   Marble in Attic Epigraphy.   American Journal of Archaeology
              57:71–83.

JOHNSON, R.A., and F.H. STROSS

2124   1965   Laboratory-Scale Instrumental Neutron Activation for
              Archaeological Analysis.   American Antiquity 30:345–347.

JOPE, E.M.

2125   1948– Abingdan Abbey Craftsmen and Building Supplies.   Berkshire
       1949   Archaeological Journal 51:53–64.

2126   1953   History, Archaeology and Petrography.   Advancement of
              Science 9:432–435.

KEMP, J.F.

2127   1940   A Handbook of Rocks, for Use Without the Petrographic
              Microscope.   6th ed.   D. Van Nostrand Co., New York.

LUEDTKE, B.E.

2128   1978   Chert Sources and Trace-Element Analysis.   American
              Antiquity 43(3):413–423.

MALINA, J.

2129   1970   Die Jungpaläolithische Steinindustrie aus Mahren, Ihre
              Rohstoffe und Ihre Patina.   Acta Praehistorica et
              Archaeologica 1:157–173.

MUNCK, E. de

2130   1886   Une Méthode à Suivre pour l'Étude des Migrations des
              Peuplades des Âges de la Pierre.   Annales de la Fédération
              Archéologique et Historique de Belgique 2:3–13.

NEGBI, O.

2131   1964   A Contribution of Mineralogy and Paleontology to an
              Archaeological Study of Terracottas.   Israel Exploration
              Quarterly 14:187–189.

NORTH, F.J.

2132   1938   Geology for Archaeologists.   Archaeological Journal 94:
              73–115.

OBENAUER, K.

2133   1933   Die Verwendung Petrographischer Methoden in der
              Vorgeschichte.   Nachrichtenblatt für Deutsche Vorzeit
              9:188–190.   Leipzig.

OTTO, H.

2134   1961   Mineralogische und Petrographische Untersuchungen an
              vor-und Frühgeschichtlichen Gegenständen.   Ausgrabungen
              und Funde 6:314–316.   Berlin.

ROSENFELD, A.

2135   1965   The Inorganic Raw Materials of Antiquity. Praeger, New
              York.

SCHMITT, F.R.

2136   1938   Petrographische Untersuchungen in der Vorgeschichts-
              forschung. Rheinische Vorzeit in Wort und Bild 1:130-133.
              Dusseldorf.

2137   1939   Moglichkeiten und Grenzen des Einsatzes der Petrographie
              bei der Untersuchung von Vorzeitfunden. Nachrichtenblatt
              für Deutsche Vorzeit 15:47-51. Leipzig.

SEDGLEY, J.P.

2138   1970   Petrographic Examination of Stone Artifacts. Science and
              Archaeology 2-3:10-12.

SHOTTEN, F.W.

2139   1969   Petrological Examination. In D. Brothwell and E. Higgs,
              eds., Science in Archaeology:571-577. 2nd ed. Thames
              and Hudson, London.

SIEVEKING, G. de G.

2140   1972   Prehistoric Flint Mines and Their Identification as
              Sources of Raw Material. Archaeometry 14(2):151-176.

SIEVEKING, G. de G., et al.

2141   1970   Characterization of Prehistoric Flint Mine Products.
              Nature 228(5628):251-254.

STEIN, M.

2142   1915   Ein Mineralogisches Erkennungszeichen Prähistorischer
              Feuersteinartefakte. Korrespondenz-Blatt der Deutschen
              Gesellschaft für Anthropologie. Ethnologie und
              Urgeschichte 46:30-31.

ŠTELCL, J., and J. MALINA

2143   1969   Petrographie in der Archäologie. Wissenschaftliche
              Zeitschrift der Philosophischen Fakultät der Universität
              Brno, E14:223-227. Brno.

2144   1970   Anwendung der Petrographie in der Archäologie. Folia
              Facultatis Scientiarum Naturalium Universitatis Purkynianae
              Brunensis XI-10. Brno.

ŠTELCL, J., J. MALINA, and T. VELIMSKY

2145   1971   Zur Terminologie und Methodik der Petroarchäologischen
              Untersuchung von Steindenkmalern. Folia Facultatis
              Naturalium Universitatis Purkynianae Brunensis, Brno.

ŠTELCL, J., M. MASKA, and J. MALINA

2146   1970   Zur Entwicklung der Petroarchäologischen Forschung. In
              Sborník J. Poulíkovi k Sědesátinám:149-152. Brno.

STONE, J.F.S.

2147   1952   L'Identification Pétrographique des Instruments de Pierre.
              In A. Laming, ed., La Découverte du Passé:247-262.
              A. and J. Picard, Paris.

TAYLOR, R.E., ed.

2148   1976   Advances in Obsidian Glass Studies: Archaeological and
              Geochemical Perspectives. Noyes Press, Park Ridge, N.J.

ULRICH, F.

2149   1935   Mineralogische Untersuchung des Obsidians. In S. Janšák,
              Prähistorische Siedlungen mit Obsidiankultur in der
              Ostslowakei:11-16, 147-150. Bratislava.

WALLIS, F.S.

2150   1955   Petrology as an Aid to Prehistoric and Medieval Archaeology.
              Endeavor 14(55):146-151.

2151   1963   Petrological Examination. In E. Pyddoke, ed., The Scien-
              tist and Archaeology:80-100. Phoenix House, London.

WEISS, L.E.

2152   1954   Fabric Analysis of Some Greek Marbles and Its Application
              to Archaeology. American Journal of Science 252:641-662.

WILLIAMS, H., and R.F. HEIZER

2153   1965   Sources of Rocks Used in Olmec Monuments. University of
              California, Contributions of the Archaeological Research
              Facility 1:1-40.

WITTHOFT, J., and E.S. WILKINS

2154   1967   Petrographic Studies; Lateritic Flints. MASCA Newsletter
              3:3-4.

*b. RESULTS OF PETROGRAPHIC AND TRACE ELEMENT ANALYSIS OF ROCKS AND
   MINERALS*
_____

AHLFELD, F.

2155   1946   Estudios sobre la Procedencia de las Piedras Semipreciosas
              y las Rocas Encontradas en las Ruinas Preincaicos de
              Tiahanacu. Boletin de la Sociedad Geológica del Peru
              19:34-44.

AHLFELD, F., and R.N. WEGNER

2156   1931   Über die Herkunft der im Bereich Altperuanischer Kulturen
              Gefundenen Schmuckstucke aus Sodalith. Zeitschrift für
              Ethnologie 63:288-296.

ASARO, F., et al.

2157   1978   High-Precision Chemical Characterization of Major Obsidian
              Sources in Guatemala. American Antiquity 43(3):436-443.

ASPINALL, A., and S.W. FEATHER

2158 1972 Neutron Activation Analysis of Prehistoric Flint Mine
            Products. Archaeometry 14(1):41–53.

BARCLAY, E.

2159 1911 The Ruined Temple, Stonehenge. St. Catherine Press,
            London.

BAUER, M.

2160 1904 Jadeit und Chloromelanit in Form Prähistorischer Artefacts
            aus Guatemala. Centralblatt für Mineralogie, Geologie
            und Palaeontologie:65–79. Stuttgart.

BAUTSCH, H.J., and H. KELCH

2161 1960 Mineralogischpetrographische Untersuchungen an Einigen
            in der Antike als Baumaterial Verwendeten Gesteinnen.
            Geologie 9:691–700. Berlin.

BECKER, M., and P. BETANCOURT

2162 1977 New Techniques for Analyzing Minoan Stonework. Archaeology
            30(4):276–277.

BELL, R.E.

2163 1947 Trade Materials at Spiro Mound as Indicated by Artifacts.
            American Antiquity 12:181–184.

BERGT, W.

2164 1894 Die Gesteine der Ruinenstätte von Tiahuanaco im Alten Peru
            (Bolivia). Abhandlungen der Naturwissenschaftlichen
            Gesellschaft Isis 5:35–52. Dresden.

BINNS, R.A., and I. McBRYDE

2165 1972 A Petrographic Analysis of Groundedge Artifacts from
            Northern New South Wales. Australian Aboriginal Studies
            47:1–130.

BODMER-BEDER, A.

2166 1903 Petrographische Untersuchungen von Steinwerkzischen
            Pfahlbaustätten. Neues Jahrbuch für Mineralogie, Geologie
            und Palaeontologie 16, Beilage B:166–198. Stuttgart.

CAMPBELL SMITH, A.

2167 1967 Source of the Stone Used in a Mace-Head from Dorchester,
            England. Proceedings, Prehistoric Society 33:455–456.

CANN, J.R., and C. RENFREW

2168 1964 The Characterization of Obsidian and Its Application to
            the Mediterranean Region. Proceedings, Prehistoric
            Society 30:111–131.

CHARLTON, T.H., D.C. GROVE, and P.H. HOPKE

2169 1978 The Paredon, Mexico, Obsidian Source and Early Formative
            Exchange. Science 201:807–809.

COBEAN, R.H., M.D. COE, E.A. PERRY, Jr., K.H. TUREKIAN, and
D.P. KHARKAR

2170 1971 Obsidian Trade at San Lorenzo Tenochtitlan, Mexico.
            Science 174:666–671.

COGNE, J., and P.R. GIOT

2171 1953 Étude Pétrographique des Haches Polies de Bretagne.
            Bulletin de la Société Préhistorique Française 50:37–39.

2172 1954 L'Étude Pétrographique des Haches Polies. Bulletin de
            la Société Préhistorique Française 51:28.

2173 1957 L'Étude Pétrographique des Haches Polies de Bretagne.
            Bulletin de la Société Préhistorique Française 54:240–
            241.

COURTOIS, L.

2174 1963 Examen Minéralogique de Quelques Roches de Monuments
            Grèco-Bourddhiques. Arts Asiatiques 9:107–113.

COUYAT, M.J.

2175 1908 Détermination et Nomenclature de Quelques Roches du Musée
            Égyptien du Caire. Bulletin de l'Institut Français
            d'Archéologie Orientale du Caire 6:49–59.

CRAIG, H., and V. CRAIG

2176 1972 Greek Marbles: Determination of Provenance by Isotopic
            Analysis. Science 176:601–603.

CUMMINS, W.A., and C.N. MOORE

2177 1973 Petrological Identification of Stone Implements from
            Lincolnshire, Nottinghamshire and Rutland. Proceedings,
            Prehistoric Society 39:219–255.

CURTIS, G.H.

2178 1959 The Petrology of Artifacts and Architectural Stone at La
            Venta. Bureau of American Ethnology, Bulletin 170:284–289.

DAMOUR, A.

2179 1863 Sur la Composition des Haches en Pierre Trouvées dans les
            Monuments Celtiques et Chez les Tribus Sauvages. Comptes
            Rendus des Seances de l'Académie des Inscriptions et
            Belles-Lettres, Paris.

2180 1864 Sur la Callais, Nouveau Phosphate d'Alumine Hydrate
            Recueilli dans un Tombeau Celtique de Morbihan. Comptes
            Rendus de l'Académie des Sciences 59:936–940.

2181 1865 Sur la Composition des Haches en Pierre Trouvées dans les
            Monuments Celtiques et Chez les Tribus Sauvages. Comptes
            Rendus de l'Académie des Sciences 63:1038–1050.

2182   1867   Sur la Composition des Haches en Pierre. Revue
               Archéologique 15:249-260.

DAVIS, E.L., et al.

2183   1969   The Western Lithic Co-Tradition. San Diego Museum of
               Man, Papers 6.

De BRUIN, M., P.J.M. KORTHOVEN, C.C. BAKELS, and F.C.A. GROEN

2184   1972   The Use of Non-Destructive Activation Analysis and
               Pattern Recognition in the Study of Flint Artefacts.
               Archaeometry 14(1):55-63.

DEECKE, W.

2185   1933   Die Mitteleuropäischen Silices nach Vorkommen. Eigen-
               schaften und Verwendung in der Prähistorie. Jena.

DIESELDORF, A.

2186   1902   Die Petrographische Beschreibung Einiger Steinartefacte
               von den Chatham-Inseln. Zeitschrift für Ethnologie 34:
               25-29. Berlin.

EVANS, E.D., L.V. GRINSELL, S. PIGGOTT, and F.S. WALLIS

2187   1962   Fourth Report of the Sub-Committee of the Southwestern
               Group of Museums and Art Galleries on the Petrological
               Identification of Stone Axes. Proceedings, Prehistoric
               Society 28:209-266.

FELLENBERG, L.R.

2188   1866   Analysen Einiger Nephrite aus des Schweizerischen
               Pfahlbauten. Mitteilungen der Naturforschenden
               Gesellschaft Bern aus dem Jahre 1865:112-125. Berlin.

FISCHER, H.

2189   1875   Nephrit und Jadeit nach Ihren Mineralogischen Eigen-
               schaften Sowie nach Ihrer Urgeschichtlichen und Ethno-
               graphischen Bedeutung. Schweizerbart, Stuttgart.

2190   1879   Mineralogisch-Archäologische Studien. Mitteilungen der
               Anthropologischen Gesellschaft in Wien 8:148-183. Wien.

FRECHEN, J.

2191   1965   Petrographische Untersuchung von Steingeräte bzw. Dessen
               Rohmaterial. In Schietzel K. Muddersheim, Eine Ansiedlung
               der Jüngeren Bandkeramik im Rheinland:39-43. Koln.

FRISON, G., G. WRIGHT, J. GRIFFIN, and A. GORDUS

2192   1968   Neutron Activation Analysis of Obsidian: An Example of
               Its Relevance to Northwestern Plains Archaeology.
               Plains Anthropologist 13(41):209-217.

GESCHWENDT, F.

2193   1941   Der Schlesische Nephrit und Seine Verwendung in Vor-
               geschichtlicher Zeit. Altschlesien 10:26-44. Breslau.

GIOT, P.R.

2194 1951 A Petrological Investigation of Breton Stone Axes. Pro-
             ceedings, Prehistoric Society 17:228.

2195 1964 Résultats de l'Identification Pétrographique des
             Matériaux des Haches Polies en France Septentrionale.
             Studien aus Alteuropa 1:123-133. Koln.

GOODMAN, M.E.

2196 1944 The Physical Properties of Stone Tool Materials. American
             Antiquity 9:415-433.

GORDUS, A.A., J.B. GRIFFIN, and G.A. WRIGHT

2197 1971 Activation Analysis Identification of the Geologic Origins
             of Prehistoric Obsidian Artifacts. In R.H. Brill, ed.,
             Science and Archaeology:222-234. MIT Press, Cambridge,
             Mass.

GORDUS, A.A., G.A. WRIGHT, and J.B. GRIFFIN

2198 1968 Characterization of Obsidian Sources by Neutron Activation
             Analysis. Science 161:382-384.

GORDUS, A.A., W. FINK, M. HILL, J. PURDY, and T. WILCOX

2199 1967 Identification of the Geologic Origins of Archaeological
             Artifacts: An Automated Method of Na and Mn Neutron
             Activation Analysis. Archaeometry 10:87-96.

GRAHAM, J.A., T.R. HESTER, and R.N. JACK

2200 1972 Sources for the Obsidian at the Ruins of Seibal, Peten,
             Guatemala. University of California, Contributions of
             the Archaeological Research Facility 16:11-116.

GREEN, R.C., R.R. BROOKS, and R.D. REEVES

2201 1967 Characterization of New Zealand Obsidians by Emission
             Spectroscopy. New Zealand Journal of Science 10(3):
             675-682.

GRIFFIN, J.B., A.A. GORDUS, and G.A. WRIGHT

2202 1969 Identification of the Sources of Hopewellian Obsidian in
             the Middle West. American Antiquity 34:1-14.

HEIZER, R.F., and H. WILLIAMS

2203 1963 Geologic Notes on the Idolo de Coatlinchan. American
             Antiquity 29:95-98.

2204 1965 Stones Used for Colossal Sculpture at or near Teotihuacan.
             University of California, Contributions of the Archaeo-
             logical Research Facility 1:55-70.

2205 1968 Archaeological Research in Peru and Bolivia. National
             Geographic Society Research Reports, 1963 Projects:127-134.

HEIZER, R.F., H. WILLIAMS, and J.A. GRAHAM

2206   1965   Notes on Mesoamerican Obsidians and Their Significance
              in Archaeological Studies. University of California,
              Contributions of the Archaeological Research Facility
              1:94-103.

HERZ, N.

2207   1955   Petrofabrics and Classical Archaeology. American Journal
              of Science 253:299-305.

HESTER, T.R., R.F. HEIZER, and R.N. JACK

2208   1971   Technology and Geologic Sources of Obsidian Artifacts from
              Cerro de Las Mesas, Veracruz, with Observations on Olmec
              Trade. University of California, Contributions of the
              Archaeological Research Facility 13:133-141.

HESTER, T.R., R.N. JACK, and R.F. HEIZER

2209   1971   The Obsidian of Tres Zapotes, Veracruz, Mexico. University
              of California, Contributions of the Archaeological Research
              Facility 13:65-131.

2210   1972   Trace Element Analysis of Obsidian from the Site of
              Cholula, Mexico. University of California, Contributions
              of the Archaeological Research Facility 16:105-110.

HUGI, Th.

2211   1947   Petrographische Untersuchungen an Steinwerkzeugen des
              Pfahlbautes Burgaschisee Ost. Jahrbuch für Solothurnische
              Geschichte 20:108-115. Solothurn.

2212   1948   Chemische Untersuchungen an Steinwerkzeugen. Schweizerische
              Mineralogische und Petrographische Mitteilungen 28:157-
              164. Zurich.

HURTADO de MENDOZA, L., and W.A. JESTER

2213   1978   Obsidian Sources in Guatemala: A Regional Approach.
              American Antiquity 43(3):424-435.

JACK, R.N., and I.S.E. CARMICHAEL

2214   1969   The Chemical Fingerprinting of Acid Volcanic Rocks.
              California Journal of Mines, Short Contributions S.R.
              100:17-32.

JACK, R.N., and R.F. HEIZER

2215   1968   Fingerprinting of Some Mesoamerican Obsidian Artifacts.
              University of California, Contributions of the Archaeological
              Research Facility 5:81-100.

JACK, R.N., T.R. HESTER, and R.F. HEIZER

2216   1972   Geologic Sources of Archaeological Obsidian from Sites
              in Northern and Central Veracruz, Mexico. University of
              California, Contributions of the Archaeological Research
              Facility 16:117-122.

JONES, T.R.

2217 1886 History of the Sarsens of Stonehenge. 1. Wilts Archaeo-
             logical and Historical Magazine 23:122-154.

JOPE, E.M., and J. PRESTON

2218 1954 An Axe of Stone from Great Langdale, Lake District,
             Found in County Antrim. Ulster Journal of Archaeology
             16:31-36.

JOPE, E.M., J.E. MOREY, and P.A. SABINE

2219 1953 Porcellanite Axes from Factories in North-East Ireland:
             Tievebulliagh and Rathlin. Ulster Journal of Archaeology
             16:31-36.

JUDD, W.A.

2220 1902 Notes on the Nature and Origin of the Rock Fragments
             Found in the Excavation Made at Stonehenge by Mr. Gowland
             in 1901. Archaeologia 58:106-118.

KEILLER, A., S. PIGGOTT, and F.S. WALLIS

2221 1941 First Report of the Sub-Committee of the Southwestern
             Group of Museums & Art Galleries on the Petrological
             Identification of Stone Axes. Proceedings, Prehistoric
             Society 7:50-72.

KEY, C.A.

2222 1969 The Identification of New Guinea Obsidians. Archaeology
             and Physical Anthropology in Oceania 4(1):47-55.

KOLDERUP, N.H.

2223 1925 Petrologische Untersuchungen über das Material für
             Werkzeuge im Westlichen Norwegen. Tschermaks
             Mineralogische und Petrographische Mitteilungen 38:165-174.
             Wien.

KOZLOWSKI, J.K.

2224 1958 Contribution to the Knowledge of the Palaeolithic and
             Neolithic Flint Material in Czechoslovakia. Wiadomosci
             Archeologiczne 25:355-359. Warsaw.

LEITMEIER, H.

2225 1932 Mineralogische Untersuchungen an den Werkzeugen von
             Willendorf. Mitteilungen der Anthropologischen
             Gesellschaft in Wien 62:361-366.

LeROUX, C.T.

2226 1971 A Stone Axe-Factory in Brittany. Antiquity 45(180):
             282-288.

LITTLE, O.H.

2227 1933 Preliminary Report on Some Geological Specimens from the
             Chephren Diorite Quarries, Western Desert. Service
             d'Antiquités de l'Egypte, Annales 33:75-80.

LUCAS, A., and J.R. HARRIS

2228 1962 Ancient Egyptian Materials and Industries. Edward Arnold Publishers, London.

MASKELYNE, N.S.

2229 1887 Petrology of Stonehenge. Wilts Archaeological and Natural History Magazine 17:147-160.

MICHELS, J.W.

2230 1971 The Colonial Obsidian Industry of the Valley of Mexico. In R.H. Brill, ed., Science and Archaeology:251-271. MIT Press, Cambridge, Mass.

MILLE, M., and C. PONCE SANGINES

2231 1968 Las Andesitas de Tiwanaku. Academia Nacional de Ciencias de Bolivia, Publicación 18. La Paz.

MISIK, M.

2232 1966 Die Petrographische Zugehörigkeit von Siliziten aus Paläolithischen und Neolithischen Artefakten der Slowakei. Acta Geologica et Geographica Universitatis Comenianae, Geologica 18:117-135. Bratislava.

MONTGOMERY, A.

2233 1963 The Source of the Fibrolite Axes. El Palacio 70:34-48.

MOORE, C.N., and W.A. CUMMINS

2234 1974 Petrological Identification of Stone Implements from Derbyshire and Leicestershire. Proceedings, Prehistoric Society 40:59-78.

MOREY, J.E.

2235 1950 Petrographical Identification of Stone Axes. Proceedings, Prehistoric Society 16:191-193.

NELSON, F.W., et al.

2236 1977 Preliminary Studies of the Trace Element Composition of Obsidian Artifacts from Northern Campeche, Mexico. American Antiquity 42(2):209-224.

OAKLEY, K.P.

2237 1939 The Nature and Origin of Flint. Scientific Progress 34:277-286.

ORDONEZ, E.

2238 1892 La Roca del Calendario Azteca. Memorias de la Sociedad Cientifica Antonio Alzate 6:327-332.

OTTO, H.

2239 1961 Mineralogische und Petrographische Untersuchungen an Vor- und Frühgeschichtlichen Gegenständen. Ausgrabungen und Funde 6:314-316. Berlin.

PARKS, G.A., and T.T. TIEH

2240 1967 Identifying the Geographical Sources of Artifact Obsidian.
            Nature 211(5046):289-290.

POSNANSKY, A.

2241 1904 Petrografía de Tiahanacu. Boletin de la Sociedad
            Geografía de La Paz 18-20:207-211.

PURDY, B.A., and F.N. BLANCHARD

2242 1973 Petrography as a Means of Tracing Stone Tools from Florida.
            Florida Anthropologist 25(1):121-125.

RENFREW, C., and J. DIXON

2243 1977 Obsidian in Western Asia: A Review. In G. de. G.
            Sieveking, et al., eds., Problems in Economic and Social
            Archaeology:137-152. Westview Press, Boulder.

RENFREW, C., J.R. CANN, and J.E. DIXON

2244 1965 Obsidian in the Aegean. Annual of the British School of
            Archaeology at Athens 60:225.

ROSICKÝ, V., and K. ZAPLETAL

2245 1935 Über die Petrographische Beschaffenheit der Otaslavicer
            Steinartefacte. In K. Absolon, Otaslavice, eine Neue,
            Grosse Palaeolithische Station in Mahren mit Quarzit
            Aurignacien. Studien aus dem Gebiete der Allgemeinen
            Karstforschung, der Wissenschaftlichen Hohlenkunde und den
            Nachbargebieten, Palaeoethnologische Serie 2:13-14. Brno.

SHOTTEN, F.W.

2246 1959 New Petrological Groups Based on Axes from the West
            Midlands. Proceedings, Prehistoric Society 25:135-143.

SIDRYS, R.

2247 1977 Trace Element Analysis of Obsidian Artifacts from
            Portezuelo, Mexico. Journal of New World Archaeology
            2(1):47-51.

SIDRYS, R., and J. KIMBERLIN

2248 1979 Use of Mayan Obsidian Sources Through Time: Trace-
            Element Data from El Balsamo, Guatemala. Journal of
            Field Archaeology 6(1):116-122.

SIGLEO, A.C.

2249 1975 Turquoise Mine and Artifact Correlation for Snaketown
            Site, Arizona. Science 189:459-460.

STAUTZ, P.

2250 1910 Petrographische Untersuchung von Steinartefakten aus dem
            Vogelsberge. Giessen.

ŠTELCL, J., F. KALOUSEK, and J. MALINA

2251 1970 A Petro-Archaeological Study of a Deposit of Neolithic
          Stone Tools at Stara Breclav, Czechoslovakia. Proceedings,
          Prehistoric Society 36:233-240.

STEVENSON, D.P., F.H. STROSS, and R.F. HEIZER

2252 1971 An Evaluation of X-ray Fluorescence Analysis as a Method
          for Correlating Obsidian Artifacts with Source Location.
          Archaeometry 13(1):17-25.

STONE, J.F.S.

2253 1952 Reconstitution des Voies de Commerce: L'Identification
          Pétrographique des Instruments de Pierre. In A. Laming,
          ed., La Découverte du Passé:247-262, 330-331. A. and J.
          Picard, Paris.

STONE, J.F.S., and F.S. WALLIS

2254 1947 Second Report of the Sub-Committee of the Southwestern
          Group of Museums and Art Galleries on the Petrological
          Identification of Stone Axes. Proceedings, Prehistoric
          Society 13:47-55.

STRATHERN, A.M.

2255 1965 Axe Types and Quarries. Journal, Polynesian Society 74:
          182-191.

STROSS, F.H., T.R. HESTER, R.F. HEIZER, and R.N. JACK

2256 1976 Chemical and Archaeological Studies of Mesoamerican
          Obsidians. In R.E. Taylor, ed., Advances in Obsidian
          Glass Studies: Archaeological and Geochemical Perspectives:
          240-258. Noyes Press, Park Ridge, N.J.

STROSS, F.H., D.P. STEVENSON, J.R. WEAVER, and G. WYLD

2257 1971 Analysis of American Obsidians by X-ray Fluorescence and
          Neutron Activation Analysis. In R.H. Brill, ed., Science
          and Archaeology:210-221. MIT Press, Cambridge, Mass.

STROSS, F.H., J.R. WEAVER, G. WYLD, R. HEIZER, and J. GRAHAM

2258 1968 Analysis of American Obsidians by X-ray Fluorescence and
          Neutron Activation Analysis. Contribution, University of
          California Archaeological Research Facility 5:59-79.

TEALL, J.J.H.

2259 1894 Notes on Sections of Stonehenge Rocks Belonging to Mr.
          Cunnington. Wilts Archaeological and Natural History
          Magazine 27:66-68.

THOMAS, H.H.

2260 1923 The Source of the Stones of Stonehenge. Antiquaries
          Journal 3:239-260.

VÉGH, A., and I. VICZIAN

2261 1964 Petrographische Untersuchungen an den Silexwerkzeugen.
            In L. Vértes, Tata, eine Mittelpaläolithische Travertin
            Siedlung in Ungarn:129-131. Budapest.

WALTHALL, J.A., S.H. STOW, and M.J. KARSON

2262 1980 Copena Galena: Source Identification and Analysis.
            American Antiquity 45(1):21-42.

WARNICA, J.M.

2263 1966 New Discoveries at the Clovis Site. American Antiquity
            31:345-357.

WEAVER, J.R., and F.H. STROSS

2264 1965 Analysis by X-ray Fluorescence of Some American Obsidians.
            University of California, Contributions of the Archaeo-
            logical Research Facility 1:89-103.

WEYMOUTH, J.H., and W.O. WILLIAMSON

2265 1951 Some Physical Properties of Raw and Calcinated Flint.
            Mineralogical Magazine 29(213):573-593.

WIEGERS, F.

2266 1950 Rohstoffversorgung im Paläolithikum. Praehistorische
            Zeitschrift 34-35:225-230. Berlin.

WILLIAMS, H., and R.F. HEIZER

2267 1965 Geological Notes in the Ruins of Mitla and Other Oaxacan
            Sites, Mexico. University of California, Contributions
            of the Archaeological Research Facility 1:41-54.

2268 1965 Sources of Rocks Used in Olmec Monuments. University of
            California, Contributions of the Archaeological Research
            Facility 1:1-40.

WRIGHT, F.E.

2269 1920 A Petrographic Description of the Material of the Copan
            Monuments. In S.G. Morley, The Inscriptions of Copan.
            Carnegie Institution of Washington, Publication 219:
            463-464.

WRIGHT, G.A.

2270 1969 Obsidian Analyses and Prehistoric Near Eastern Trade:
            7500-3500 B.C. Museum of Anthropology, University of
            Michigan, Anthropological Papers 37.

WRIGHT, G.A., and A.A. GORDUS

2271 1969 Source Areas for Obsidian Recovered at Munhata, Beisamoun,
            Hazorea and el-Khiam. Israel Exploration Journal 19(2):
            79-88.

ZIRKL, E.

2272   1955   Zur Herkunft der Rohstoffe Einiger Latenezeitlicher
              Handmühlen. Archaeologia Austriaca 18:90-92. Wien.

2273   1956- Das Gesteinsmaterial der Artefakte von Willendorf in dem
       1959   Wachau, N.O. Mitteilungen der Prähistorischen Kommission
              der Österreichischen Akademie der Wissenschaften 8-9:98-
              108. Wien.

c. PETROGRAPHIC ANALYSIS OF CERAMICS

ACCOLA, R.M.

2274   1977   Análisis de la Difracción de Rayos X: Su Aplicación
              Experimental en el Estudio de la Cerámica Policromada de
              Nicoya, Costa Rica. Vinculos 3(1-2):37-45. San José.

ARNOLD, D.E.

2275   1972   Mineralogical Analysis of Ceramic Materials from Quinua,
              Department of Ayacucho, Peru. Archaeometry 14(1):93-102.

ASPINALL, A., S.E. WARREN, J.G. CRUMMET, and R.G. NEWTON

2276   1972   Neutron Activation Analysis of Faience Beads. Archaeology
              14(1):27-41.

BENNYHOFF, J.A., and R.F. HEIZER

2277   1965   Neutron Activation Analysis of Some Cuicuilco and
              Teotihuacan Pottery: Archaeological Interpretation of
              Results. American Antiquity 30:348-349.

BUTTLER, W.

2278   1933   Dünnschliffuntersuchungen an Vorgeschichtlicher Keramik.
              Nachrichtenblatt für Deutsche Vorzeit 9:186-188. Leipzig.

CATLING, H.W., E.E. RICHARDS, and A.E. BLYN-STOYLE

2279   1963   Correlations Between Composition and Provenance of
              Mycenaean and Minoan Pottery. Annual of the British
              School of Archaeology at Athens 58:94-115.

CORNWALL, I., and H.W.M. HODGES

2280   1964   Thin Sections of British Neolithic Pottery: Windmill
              Hill--a Test Site. Bulletin, University of London Insti-
              tute of Archaeology 4:29-33.

COWGILL, U.M., and G.E. HUTCHINSON

2281   1969   A Chemical and Mineralogical Examination of the Ceramic
              Sequence from Tikal, El Peten, Guatemala. American
              Journal of Science 267:465-477.

DICKINSON, W.R.

2282   1971   Temper Sands in Lapita Style Potsherds in Malo. Journal
              of the Polynesian Society 80(2):244-246.

DICKINSON, W.R., and R. SHUTLER, Jr.

2283 1971 Temper Sands in Prehistoric Pottery of the Pacific
             Islands. Archaeology and Physical Anthropology in
             Oceania 6(3):191-203.

2284 1974 Probable Fijian Origins of Quartzose Temper Sands in
             Prehistoric Pottery from Tonga and the Marquesas.
             Science 185:454-457.

GOODYEAR, F.H.

2285 1970 Application of Scientific Techniques to the Problem of
             Provenance for Romano-British Coarse Ware. Science and
             Archaeology 2 and 3.

HARBOTTLE, G.

2286 1970 Neutron Activation Analysis of Potsherds from Knossos
             and Mycenae. Archaeometry 12:23-24.

HENSHALL, A.S.

2287 1963 The Chambered Tombs of Scotland. Vol. 1:107. Edinburgh
             University Press, Edinburgh.

HODGES, H.W.M.

2288 1962 Thin Sections of Prehistoric Pottery: An Empirical Study.
             Bulletin, University of London Institute of Archaeology
             3:58-68.

2289 1963 The Examination of Ceramic Materials in Thin Section. In
             E.W. Pyddoke, ed., The Scientist and Archaeology:101-110.
             Phoenix House, London.

KOHLER, A.

2290 1928 Mikroskopische Untersuchungen an Römischer und Vor-
             geschichtlicher Keramik von Hallstatt. Mikroskopie
             4:368.

LINNÉ, S.

2291 1929 Darien in the Past. Goteburgs Kungl. Vetenskaps-och
             Vitterhets-Samhalles Handlingar, Femte Foljden, Ser. A
             1(3).

PERLMAN, I., and F. ASARO

2292 1967 Deduction of Provenience of Pottery from Trace Element
             Analysis. E.O. Lawrence Radiation Laboratory, University
             of California, Publication UCRL-17937.

2293 1970 Deduction of Provenience of Pottery from Trace Element
             Analysis. In R. Berger, ed., Scientific Methods in
             Medieval Archaeology:389-408. University of California
             Press, Berkeley.

2294 1971 Pottery Analysis by Neutron Activation. In R.H. Brill,
             ed., Science and Archaeology:182-195. MIT Press, Cam-
             bridge, Mass.

PHILLIPS, Ċ.W.

2295 1934 The Examination of a Hut Group at Pant-y-Saes in the Parish of Llanfair-Mathafarm-Eithaf, Anglesey. Archaeologia Cambrensis 89, Pt. I:1-36.

SAYRE, E.V., and L.H. CHAN

2296 1971 High-Resolution Gamma Ray Spectroscopic Analyses of Fine Orange Pottery. In R.H. Brill, ed., Science and Archaeology:165-177. MIT Press, Cambridge, Mass.

SAYRE, E.V., and R.W. DODSON

2297 1957 Neutron Activation Study of Mediterranean Potsherds. American Journal of Archaeology 61(1):35-42.

SAYRE, E.V., A. MURRENHOFF, and C.F. WEICK

2298 1958 The Non-Destructive Analysis of Ancient Potsherds Through Neutron Activation. Brookhaven National Laboratory BNL 508(T-122).

SHEPARD, A.O.

2299 1957 Ceramics for the Archaeologist. Carnegie Institution of Washington, Publication 609:157ff.

STONE, J.F.S., and L.C. THOMAS

2300 1956 The Use and Distribution of Faience in the Ancient East and Prehistoric Europe. Proceedings, Prehistoric Society 22:37-84.

WILLIAMS, H.

2301 1956 Petrographic Notes on Tempers of Pottery from Chupicuaro, Cerro del Topalcate and Ticoman, Mexico. Transactions, American Philosophical Society 45:576-580.

7. Metals and Metallurgy

ALLAN, J.C.

2302 1970 Considerations of the Antiquity of Mining in the Iberian Peninsula. Royal Anthropological Institute Occasional Paper 27.

ALLEN, E.M., D. BRITTON, and H.H. COGHLAN

2303 1970 Metallurgical Reports on British and Irish Bronze Age Implements and Weapons in the Pitt Rivers Museum. Pitt Rivers Museum, Oxford University, Occasional Papers on Technology 10.

ARSANDAUX, H., and P. RIVET

2304 1921 Contribution à l'Étude de la Metallurgie Mexicaine. Journal, Société des Americanistes de Paris 13:261-280.

BARNARD, N., and S. TAMOTSU

2305 1975 Metallurgical Remains of Ancient China. Nichiosha, Tokyo.

BASTIAN, T.

2306 1961 Trace Element and Metallographic Studies of Prehistoric Copper Artifacts in North America: A Review. Museum of Anthropology, University of Michigan, Anthropological Papers 17:151–189.

BAUS, P.J.

2307 1965 The Art of Lost-Wax Casting: Men, Beeswax, and Molten Metal. Natural History 74(7):18–25.

BAYARD, D.T.

2308 1972 Early Thai Bronzes: Analysis and New Dates. Science 176:1411–1412.

BEARZI, B.

2309 1966 Bronze in Antiquity (Its Uses in Statuary and Its Analysis). Fonderia Ital 15(2):65–67.

BERGSOE, P.

2310 1937 The Metallurgy and Technology of Gold and Platinum Among the Pre-Columbian Indians. Ingeniorvidenskabelige Skrifter 44. Copenhagen.

BETANCOURT, P., et al.

2311 1978 Metallurgy at Gournia. MASCA Journal 1:7–9.

BRAIDWOOD, R.J., J.E. BURKE, and N.H. NACHTRIEB

2312 1951 Ancient Syrian Coppers and Bronzes. Journal, Chemical Education 28(2):87–96.

BRANIGAN, K.

2313 1968 Silver and Lead in Prepalatial Crete. American Journal of Archaeology 72(3):219–230.

BRAY, W.

2314 1971 Ancient American Metal-Smiths. Proceedings, Royal Anthropological Institute of Great Britain and Ireland for 1971:25–43.

BRIGHT, A.L.

2315 1972 A Goldsmith's Blowpipe from Colombia. Man 7(2):311–313.

BRITTON, D.

2316 1963 Traditions of Metal-Working in the Later Neolithic and Early Bronze Age of Britain: Part I. Proceedings, Prehistoric Society 29:258–325.

BROMEHEAD, C.N.

2317 1942 Ancient Mining Processes as Illustrated by a Japanese
            Scroll. Antiquity 16(63):193-207.

BRUHNS, K.O.

2318 1970 A Quimbaya Gold Furnace? American Antiquity 35(2):202-203.

2319 1972 Two Prehispanic Cire Perdue Casting Moulds from Colombia.
            Man 7(2):308-311.

BUTLER, J.J., and J.D. Van der WAALS

2320 1964 Metal Analysis, SAM I and European Prehistory. Helinium
            4.

2321 1966 Bell Beakers and Early Metal-Working in the Netherlands.
            Palaeohistoria 12:41-140.

CALEY, E.R., and D.T. EASBY, Jr.

2322 1959 The Smelting of Sulfide Ores of Copper in Preconquest
            Peru. American Antiquity 25:59-65.

2323 1967 Indium as an Impurity in Ancient Western Mexican Tin and
            Bronze Artifacts and in Local Tin Ore. Science 155:686-
            687.

CARROLL, D.L.

2324 1974 A Classification for Granulation in Ancient Metalwork.
            American Journal of Archaeology 78(1):33-40.

CASE, H.J.

2325 1966 Were Beaker-People the First Metallurgists in Ireland?
            Palaeohistoria 12:141-178.

CHAPLIN, J.H.

2326 1961 Notes on Traditional Smelting in Northern Rhodesia.
            South African Archaeological Society Bulletin 16(62):
            53-60.

CHARLES, J.A.

2327 1967 Early Arsenical Bronzes--a Metallurgical View. American
            Journal of Archaeology 71(1):21-26.

CHENG, C.F., and C.M. SCHWITTER

2328 1957 Nickel in Ancient Bronzes. American Journal of Archaeology
            61(4):351-366.

CHILDE, V.G.

2329 1948 The Technique of Prehistoric Metal Work: A Review.
            Antiquity 22(85):29-32.

CLARKE, R.R.

2330 1951 A Hoard of Metalwork of the Early Iron Age from Ringstead,
            Norfolk. Proceedings, Prehistoric Society 17(2):214-225.

COGHLAN, H.H.

2331 1942 Some Fresh Aspects of the Prehistoric Metallurgy of
            Copper. Antiquaries Journal 22:22-38.

2332 1951 Notes on the Prehistoric Metallurgy of Copper and Bronze
            in the Old World. Pitt Rivers Museum, Oxford University,
            Occasional Papers on Technology 4.

2333 1956 Notes on Prehistoric and Early Iron in the Old World.
            Pitt Rivers Museum, Oxford University, Occasional Papers
            on Technology 8.

2334 1960 Metallurgical Analysis of Archaeological Materials. In
            Viking Fund Publications in Anthropology 28:21-33.

2335 1962 A Note Upon Native Copper: Its Occurrence and Properties.
            Proceedings, Prehistoric Society 28:58-67.

COGHLAN, H.H., and H. CASE

2336 1957 Early Metallurgy of Copper in Ireland and Britain.
            Proceedings, Prehistoric Society 23:91-123.

COGHLAN, H.H., J.J. BUTLER, and G. PARKER

2337 1963 Ores and Metals; a Report of the Ancient Mining and
            Metallurgy Committee. Royal Anthropological Institute
            Occasional Papers 17:64. Royal Anthropological Institute
            of Great Britain and Ireland, London.

CONGDON, L.O.K.

2338 1967 Metallic Analyses of Three Greek Caryatid Mirrors.
            American Journal of Archaeology 71(2):149-154.

COOKE, C.K.

2339 1966 Account of Iron Smelting Techniques Once Practised by the
            Manyubi of the Matopo District of Rhodesia. South
            African Archaeological Bulletin 21(82), Pt. 2:86.

CRAWFORD, H.E.W.

2340 1974 The Problem of Tin in Mesopotamian Bronzes. World
            Archaeology 6(2):242.

CRÉQUI-MONTFORT, G., and P. RIVET

2341 1919 Contribution à l'Étude de l'Archéologie et de la
            Métallurgie Colombiennes. Journal, Société des
            Americanistes de Paris 11:525-591.

DART, R.A., and P. BEAUMONT

2342 1969 Evidence of Iron Ore Mining in Southern Africa in the
            Middle Stone Age. Current Anthropology 10:127.

DAVEY, P.J.

2343 1971 The Distribution of Later Bronze Age Metalwork from
            Lincolnshire. Proceedings, Prehistoric Society 37(1):
            96-111.

DOUGHERTY, R.C., and J.R. CALDWELL

2344 1966 Evidence of Early Pyrometallurgy in the Kerman Range in Iran. Science 153:984-985.

DRIER, R.W.

2345 1961 Archaeology and Some Metallurgical Investigative Techniques. Anthropological Papers, Museum of Anthropology, University of Michigan 17:134-147.

EASBY, D.T., Jr.

2346 1962 Two "South American" Metal Techniques Found Recently in Western Mexico. American Antiquity 28:19-24.

2347 1966 Early Metallurgy in the New World. Scientific American 214:73-81.

FALLAIZE, E.N.

2348 1937 Mineral Sources in Prehistoric Times. Science 86(2220): 6-7.

FRAIKOR, A.L., J.J. HESTER, and F.J. FRAIKOR

2349 1971 Metallurgical Analysis of a Hopewell Copper Earspool. American Antiquity 36(3):358-361.

FRANK, LEONARD

2350 1951 A Metallographic Study of Certain Precolumbian American Implements. American Antiquity 17:57-59.

FRIEDMAN, A.M., E. OLSEN, and J.B. BIRD

2351 1972 Moche Copper Analysis: Early New World Metal Technology. American Antiquity 37(2):254-258.

FRIEDMAN, A.M., et al.

2352 1966 Copper Artifacts: Correlations with Source Types of Copper Ores. Science 152:1504-1506.

GORDON, D.H.

2353 1950 The Early Use of Metals in India and Pakistan. Journal, Royal Anthropological Institute of Great Britain and Ireland 80(1-2):55-78.

GRIFFIN, J.B., ed.

2354 1961 Lake Superior Copper and the Indians: Miscellaneous Studies of Great Lakes Prehistory. Museum of Anthropology, University of Michigan, Anthropological Papers 17.

HAMILTON, H.W., J.T. HAMILTON, and E.F. CHAPMAN

2355 1974 Spiro Mound Copper. Memoir, Missouri Archaeological Society 11.

HARRISON, R., S. QUERO, and M.C. PRIEGO

2356   1975   Beaker Metallurgy in Spain. Antiquity 49(196):273-278.

HARRISSON, T.H., and S.J. O'CONNOR

2357   1969   Excavations of the Prehistoric Iron Industry in West
              Borneo. Cornell University, Southeast Asia Program,
              Data Paper 72.

HEINE-GELDERN, R.

2358   1954   Die Asiatische Herkunft der Sudamerikanischen Metall-
              technik. Paideuma 5:347-423.

HILL, D.K.

2359   1958   Chairs and Tables of the Ancient Egyptians. Archaeology
              11(4):276-280.

HILL, W.E., Jr., and R.W. NEUMAN

2360   1966   Copper Artefacts from Prehistoric Archaeological Sites
              in the Dakotas. Science 154:1171-1173.

IBARRA GRASSO, D.E.

2361   1969   La Imitación de Objetos Metálicos en Otros Materiales
              por Pueblos Precolombinos que no Trabajaban los Metales.
              Verhandlungen des XXXVIII. Internationalen Amerikanisten-
              kongresse. Stuttgart-München 12. bis 18. August 1968(1):
              79-84. Kommissionsverlag Klaus Renner, München, Germany.

IRABARREN CHARLIN, J.

2362   1969   Análisis Metalúrgico de Discos Metálicos de la Cultura de
              El Molle. Museo Arquelógico, Boletin 13:49-51. La
              Serena, Chile.

KLEIN, J.

2363   1971   A Greek Metalworking Quarter. Expedition 14(2):34-39.

KOLCHIN, B.A.

2364   1967   Metallurgy and Metal-Working in Ancient Russia. Clearing-
              house for Scientific and Technical Information TT6751343.
              Washington, D.C.

LANGE, F.W., and R.M. ACCOLA

2365   1979   Metallurgy in Costa Rica. Archaeology 32(5):26-33.

LONG, S.

2366   1964   Cire Perdue Copper Casting in Precolumbian Mexico: An
              Experimental Approach. American Antiquity 30:189-192.

LOTHROP, S.K.

2367   1950   Metalworking Tools from the Central Coast of Peru.
              American Antiquity 16:160-164.

LOWERY, P.R., R.D.A. SAVAGE, and R.L. WILKINS

2368   1971   Scriber, Graver, Scorper, Tracer: Notes in Experiments
              in Bronzeworking Technique. Proceedings, Prehistoric
              Society 37(1):167-182.

MACK, D.J.

2369   1959   A Short Tour of Archaeological Metallurgy. Metal
              Progress (Dec.):94-98.

MARYON, H.

2370   1965   Early Near Eastern Steel Swords. American Journal of
              Archaeology 65(2):173-185.

MATTUSCH, C.C.

2371   1977   Molds for an Archaic Bronze Statue from the Athenian
              Agora. Archaeology 30(5):326-332.

MEIGHAN, C.W.

2372   1960   Prehistoric Copper Objects from Western New Mexico.
              Science 131(3412):1534.

MELLICHAMP, J.W., and M. LEVEY

2373   1963   Silver from Ur of Ancient Mesopotamia. Science 142:44-45.

MOOREY, P.R.S., and F. SCHWEIZER

2374   1972   Copper and Copper Alloys in Ancient Iraq, Syria and
              Palestine: Some New Analyses. Archaeometry 14(2):177-198.

MOUNTJOY, J.B.

2375   1969   On the Origin of West Mexican Metallurgy. Mesoamerican
              Studies 4:26-42.

MUNUNA, A.N.

2376   1955   Etruscan Metallurgy. Scientific American 193(5):90-100.

NOBLE, J.V.

2377   1975   The Wax of the Lost Wax Process. American Journal of
              Archaeology 79(4):368-369.

OLSEN, E.J.

2378   1962   Copper Artifact Analysis with the X-ray Spectrometer.
              American Antiquity 28:234-238.

PALMER, H., and C. VERMEULE

2379   1959   Ancient Gold and Silver in the Museum of Fine Arts,
              Boston. Archaeology 12(1):2-7.

PATTERSON, C.E.

2380   1971   Native Copper, Silver and Gold Accessible to Early
              Metallurgists. American Antiquity 36(3):286-321.

PEACOCK, D.P.S.

2381 1976 The Petrography of Certain Glozelian Ceramics. Journal
            of Archaeological Science 3(3):271-274.

PHILLIPS, G.B.

2382 1925 The Primitive Copper Industry of America. American
            Anthropologist 27:284-289.

PITTIONI, R.

2383 1957 Urzeitlicher Bergban auf Kupfererz und Spurenanalyse.
            Österreichischen Akad. der Wissenschaften 7:97-99.

2384 1958 Zum Erzevhungsgebut der Bronzeitlichen Sichelnadeln.
            Archaeologia Austriaca 3:70-74.

2385 1960 Metallurgical Analysis of Archaeological Materials: II.
            Viking Fund Publications in Anthropology 28:21-23.

PLEINER, R.

2386 1963 Rediscovering the Techniques of Early European Black-
            smiths. Archaeology 16(4):234-242.

RAJPITAK, W., and N.J. SEELEY

2387 1979 The Bronze Bowls from Ban Don Ta Phet, Thailand: An
            Enigma of Prehistoric Metallurgy. World Archaeology
            11(1):26-31.

READ, T.E.

2388 1934 Metallurgical Fallacies in Archaeological Literature.
            American Journal of Archaeology 38:382-389.

RENFREW, C.

2389 1967 Cycladic Metallurgy and the Aegean Early Bronze Age.
            American Journal of Archaeology 71(1):1-20.

RICHTER, G.M.

2390 1958 Ancient Plaster Casts of Greek Metalware. American
            Journal of Archaeology 62(4):369-378.

RICKARD, T.A.

2391 1932 The Nomenclature of Copper and Its Alloys. Journal, Royal
            Anthropological Institute 62:281-290.

2392 1941 The Use of Meteoric Iron. Journal, Royal Anthropological
            Institute 71:55-66.

ROOT, W.C.

2393 1949 The Metallurgy of the Southern Coast of Peru. American
            Antiquity 15:10-37.

2394 1951 Metallurgical Analyses and Their Aid to Archaeology. In
            Essays on Archaeological Methods, Museum of Anthropology,
            University of Michigan, Anthropological Papers 8:85-93.

ROWLANDS, M.J.

2395 1971 The Archaeological Interpretation of Prehistoric Metal-
working. World Archaeology 3(2):210–224.

SASSOON, H.

2396 1963 Early Sources of Iron in Africa. South African Archaeological Bulletin 18(72), Pt. 4:176–180.

SAYCE, A.H.

2397 1928 The Antiquity of Iron-Working. Antiquity 2:224–227.

SCHROEDER, D.L., and K.C. RUHL

2398 1968 Metallurgical Characteristics of North American Prehistoric Copper Work. American Antiquity 33(2):162–169.

SCHWEIZER, F., and A.M. FRIEDMAN

2399 1972 Comparison of Methods of Analysis of Silver and Gold in
Silver Coins. Archaeometry 14(1):103–108.

SELIMKHANOV, I.R.

2400 1964 Was Native Copper Used in Transcaucasia in Eneolithic
Times? Proceedings, Prehistoric Society 30:66–74.

SENSE, R.

2401 1967 A Prehistoric Quarry near Ray, Arizona. Kiva 32(4):
170–174.

SHEPARD, A.O.

2402 1936 Metallographic Study of Copper Artifacts. American
Antiquity 2:139–140.

SHERRATT, A.

2403 1977 Resources, Technology and Trade in Early European
Metallurgy. In G. de G. Sieveking, et al., eds., Problems
in Economic and Social Archaeology:557–582. Westview
Press, Boulder.

SHINNIE, P.L., ed.

2404 1971 The African Iron Age. Oxford University Press, New York.

SLATER, E.A., and J.A. CHARLES

2405 1970 Archaeological Classification by Metal Analysis.
Antiquity 44:207–213.

SNODGRASS, A.M.

2406 1967 Arms and Armour of the Greeks. Cornell University
Press, New York.

SORENSON, J.L.

2407 1954 Preclassic Metal? American Antiquity 20:64.

TANABE, G.

2408   1962   A Study on the Chemical Compositions of Ancient Bronze
               Artifacts Excavated in Japan. Journal, Faculty of
               Science, University of Tokyo, Sec. V(2), Pt. 3:261-319.

TAYLOR, J.J.

2409   1979   Early Bronze Age Technology and Trade. Expedition 21(3):
               23-32.

THOMPSON, F.

2410   1958   The Early Metallurgy of Copper and Bronze. Man 58:1-7.

TYLECOTE, R.F.

2411   1970   The Composition of Metal Artifacts: A Guide to Provenance?
               Antiquity 44(173):19-25.

TYLECOTE, R.F., and P.J. BOYDELL

2412   1979   Experiments on Copper Smelting. In Chalcolithic Copper
               Smelting. Institute for Archaeo-Metallurgical Studies,
               London.

TYLECOTE, R.F., A. LUPU, and B. ROTHENBERG

2413   1967   A Study of Early Copper Smelting and Working Sites in
               Israel. Institute of Metals, Journal XCV(8):235-243.

UNDERWOOD, L.

2414   1958   Bronze Age Technology in Western Asia and Northern Europe:
               Part I. Man 58:17-22.

2415   1958   Bronze Age Technology in Western Asia and Northern Europe:
               Part II. Man 58:58-65.

WAINWRIGHT, G.A.

2416   1944   Early Tin in the Aegean. Antiquity 18(70):57-64.

WERNER, A.E.A.

2417   1970   Analysis of Ancient Metals. In The Impact of the Natural
               Sciences on Archaeology:179-185. Oxford University Press,
               London.

WERTIME, T.A.

2418   1964   Man's First Encounters with Metallurgy. Science 146:
               1257-1267.

2419   1973   The Beginnings of Metallurgy: A New Look. Science 182:
               875-894.

WEST, G.A.

2420   1929   Copper: Its Mining and Use by the Aborigines of the Lake
               Superior Region. Bulletin, Public Museum of the City of
               Milwaukee 10(1).

WILLOUGHBY, C.C.

2421 1903 An Early Experiment. In J. McQuire, ed., Primitive Metal
            Working, Discussion as to Copper from the Mounds:55-57.
            American Anthropologist, Special Publication.

WILSON, C.L., and M. SAYRE

2422 1935 A Brief Metallographic Study of Primitive Copper.
            American Antiquity 1:109-112.

8. Prehistoric Technologies: Selected References

ADAMSON, D., J.D. CLARK, and M.A.J. WILLIAMS

2423 1974 Barbed Bone Points from Central Sudan and the Age of the
            "Early Khartoum" Tradition. Nature 249(5453):120-123.

ALLAN, J.C.

2424 1970 Considerations of the Antiquity of Mining in the Iberian
            Peninsula. Royal Anthropological Institute Occasional
            Paper 27. London.

ATKINSON, R.J.C.

2425 1961 Neolithic Engineering. Antiquity 35(140):292-299.

BALL, S.H.

2426 1941 The Mining of Gems and Ornamental Stones by American
            Indians. Bureau of American Ethnology, Bulletin 128:
            1-77.

BANNOLD, A.H.

2427 1888 Account of the Manner in Which Two Colossal Statues of
            Rameses II at Memphis Were Raised. Proceedings, Society
            of Biblical Archaeology 18th Session, 1887-1888:452-463.

BARBER, F.M.

2428 1900 The Mechanical Triumphs of the Ancient Egyptians.
            Kegan Paul, Trench, Trubner, London.

BECKER, C.J.

2429 1959 Flint Mining in Neolithic Denmark. Antiquity 33(130):
            87-92.

BELL, R.E.

2430 1971 Bison Scapula Skin-Dressing Tools? Plains Anthropologist
            16(52):125-127.

BLACKWOOD, B.

2431 1950 The Technology of a Modern Stone Age People in New Guinea.
            Pitt Rivers Museum, Oxford University, Occasional Papers
            on Technology 3.

BORDAZ, J.

2432   1970   Tools of the Old and New Stone Age. American Museum of
              Natural History Press, Garden City, N.Y.

BORDES, F.

2433   1969   Reflections on Typology and Techniques in the Palaeo-
              lithic. Arctic Anthropology 6(1):1-29.

2434   1969   Traitement Thermique du Silex au Solutréen. Bulletin de
              la Société Préhistorique Française 66:197.

BOSHIER, A.K.

2435   1965   Effects of Pounding by Africans of North-West Transvaal
              on Hard and Soft Stones. South African Archaeological
              Bulletin 20(79), Pt. 3:131-136.

BRAIDWOOD, R.J.

2436   1967   Prehistoric Men. 7th ed. Scott, Foresman and Co.,
              Glenview, Ill.

BREUIL, A.H.

2437   1938   The Use of Bone Implements in the Old Palaeolithic Period.
              Antiquity 12(45):56-67.

2438   1939   Bone and Antler Industry of the Choukoutien Sinanthropus
              Site. Palaeontologica Sinica 6.

BRILL, R.H.

2439   1963   Ancient Glass. Scientific American 209(5):120-131.

BROMEHEAD, C.

2440   1954   Mining and Quarrying. In C. Singer, et al., eds., A
              History of Technology I:558-571. Clarendon Press, Oxford.

BROWN, J.L.

2441   1967   The Use of Atlatl Weights: A Suggestion. Southwestern
              Lore 32(4):84-85.

BRYAN, B.

2442   1961   The Manufacture of Stone Mortars. Southwest Museum
              Masterkey 35:134-139.

BRYAN, K.

2443   1950   Flint Quarries--the Sources of Tools and, at the Same
              Time, the Factories of the American Indian. Papers of
              the Peabody Museum, Harvard University 17(3). Cambridge,
              Mass.

BUNCH, B., and C.I. FELL

2444   1949   A Stone-Axe Factory at Pike of Stickle, Great Langdale,
              Westmorland. Proceedings, Prehistoric Society 15:1-20.

BUNKER, E.C., and J. TERNBACK

2445 1970 A Variation of the "Lost-Wax" Process. Expedition 12(3): 41-43.

CARPENTER, R.

2446 1968 The Unfinished Colossus of Mt. Pendeli. American Journal of Archaeology 72(3):279.

CAZENEUVE, J.

2447 1959 Technical Methods in the Prehistoric Age. Diogenes 27: 102-124.

CHARLESWORTH, D.

2448 1972 Tell El-Fara 'In, Egypt: An Industrial Site in the Nile Delta. Archaeology 25(1):44-47.

CHENG, T.K.

2449 1966 Ancient Kiln Sites in Szechwan. Archaeology 9(4):244-251.

CHILDE, V.G.

2450 1942 The Antiquity and Function of Antler Axes and Adzes. Antiquity 16(63):258-264.

2451 1944 Archaeological Ages as Technological Stages. Royal Anthropological Institute of Great Britain and Ireland, London. Huxley Lecture, London.

CLARK, G.

2452 1962 Prehistoric Ancestors of the Weapons Which Brought England Victory at Crecy: Neolithic Longbows of 4500 Years Ago, Found in the Somersetshire Peat. Illustrated London News, Feb. 10:219-221.

CLARK, G., and S. PIGGOTT

2453 1933 The Age of the British Flint Mines. Antiquity 7:166-183.

CLARK, J.D.

2454 1972 Paleolithic Butchery Practices. In P.J. Ucko, R. Tringham, and G.W. Dimbleby, eds., Man, Settlement and Urbanism. G. Duckworth, London.

CLARK, J.G.D.

2455 1963 Neolithic Bows from Somerset, England and the Prehistory of Archery in Northwest Europe. Proceedings, Prehistoric Society 29:50-98.

CLARK, J.G.D., and M.W. THOMPSON

2456 1954 The Groove and Splinter Technique of Working Antler in Upper Palaeolithic and Mesolithic Europe, with Special Reference to the Material from Star Carr. Proceedings, Prehistoric Society 19:148-160.

CLARKE, S., and R. ENGELBACH

2457 1930 Ancient Egyptian Masonry; the Building Craft. Oxford
            University Press, London.

COLES, J.

2458 1962 European Bronze Age Shields. Proceedings, Prehistoric
            Society 28:156-190.

2459 1963 Irish Bronze Age Horns and Their Relations with Northern
            Europe. Proceedings, Prehistoric Society 29:326-356.

COLLINS, M.B., and T.R. HESTER

2460 1968 A Wooden Mortar and Pestle from Val Verde County, Texas.
            Bulletin, Texas Archeological Society 39:1-8.

COSGROVE, H.S., and C.B. COSGROVE

2461 1932 The Swarts Ruin. Papers of the Peabody Museum, Harvard
            University 15(1).

COSNER, A.J.

2462 1951 Arrowshaft Straightening with a Grooved Stone. American
            Antiquity 17:147-148.

CRABTREE, D.E.

2463 1968 Mesoamerican Polyhedral Cores and Prismatic Blades.
            American Antiquity 33:446-478.

CRAWFORD, O.G.S.

2464 1955 How Things Are Made and Done. Antiquity 114:95-101.

CRESSEY, P.J.

2465 1975 Pre- and Post-Conquest Obsidian Tools in the Teotihuacan
            Valley. Actas, XLI Congreso Internacional de Americanistas
            I:208-218.

CURTIS, F.

2466 1964 Microdrills in the Manufacturing of Shell Beads in
            Southern California. Southwest Museum Masterkey 38(3):
            98-105.

CURWEN, E.C.

2467 1937 Querns. Antiquity 11(42):113-151.

2468 1941 Some Food-Gathering Implements: Study in Mesolithic
            Tradition. Antiquity 15(60):320-336.

2469 1943 Harvesting Implements in Denmark. Antiquity 17(68):
            196-206.

2470 1946 The Furrows in Prehistoric Fields in Denmark. Antiquity
            20:38-39.

DART, R.A.

2471 1949 The Predatory Implemental Technique of Australopithecus.
            American Journal of Physical Anthropology 7:1-38.

2472 1957 The Osteodontokeratic Culture of Australopithecus
            Prometheus. Transvaal Museum Memoir 10. Pretoria.

2473 1960 The Persistence of Some Tools and Utensils Found First
            in the Makapansgat Grey Breccia. South African Journal
            of Science 56:71-74.

2474 1965 Pounding as a Process and the Producer of Other Artefacts.
            South African Archaeological Bulletin 20(79), Pt. 3: 141-
            147.

DART, R.A., and J.W. KITCHING

2475 1958 Bone Tools at the Kalkbank Middle Stone Age Site and the
            Makapangsgat Australopithecine Locality, Central Transvaal;
            Part 2, The Osteodontokeratic Contribution. South
            African Archaeological Bulletin 13:94-116.

DAUMAS, M.

2476 1961 Histoire Générale des Techniques; I, Les Origines de la
            Civilisation Technique. Presses Universitaires de
            France, Paris.

DAVIES, O.

2477 1959 The Equipment of an Acheulian Man in Africa. Archaeology
            12(3):172-177.

DICKSON, F.P.

2478 1972 Ground Edge Axes. Mankind 8(3):206-211.

DONKIN, R.A.

2479 1970 Pre-Columbian Field Implements and Their Distribution
            in the Highlands of Middle and South America. Anthropos
            65(3/4):505-529.

DUNHAM, D.

2480 1956 Building an Egyptian Pyramid. Archaeology 9(3):159-165.

EATON, J.D.

2481 1976 Ancient Fishing Technology on the Gulf Coast of Yucatan,
            Mexico. Bulletin, Texas Archeological Society 47:231-244.

ELLIS, H.H.

2482 1965 Flint-Working Techniques of the American Indians: An
            Experimental Study. Ohio Historical Society, Columbus.

EVANS, J.

2483 1897 The Ancient Stone Implements, Weapons, and Ornaments, of
            Great Britain. 2nd ed. Longman, Green and Co., London.

EVANS, O.F.

2484 1957 Probable Use of Stone Projectile Points. American
            Antiquity 23:82-84.

FITTING, J.E.

2485 1972 Use and Techniques of Manufacture of Antler Implements
             from the Schultz Site. In J.E. Fitting, ed., The Schultz
             Site at Green Point. Memoirs of the Museum of Anthropology,
             University of Michigan 4.

FORBES, R.J.

2486 1955– Studies in Ancient Technology; I-VI. Brill, Leiden,
      1958   Netherlands.

FOWLER, W.S.

2487 1945 Tool-Making at the Westfield Quarry. American Antiquity
            11:95–101.

2488 1946 Stone Age Methods of Woodworking in the Connecticut
            Valley. Bulletin, Archeological Society of Connecticut
            2:1–32.

2489 1962 Woodworking: An Important Industry. Bulletin, Massachu-
            setts Archaeological Society 23(3–4):29–40.

2490 1967 Oaklawn Quarry: Stone Bowl and Pipe Making. Bulletin,
            Massachusetts Archaeological Society 29(1).

2491 1968 Stone Making at the Westfield Quarry. Bulletin, Massa-
            chusetts Archaeological Society 30(1):6–16.

2492 1971 Some Sources of New England Flints. Bulletin, Massachu-
            setts Archaeological Society 32(3–4):23–27.

2493 1972 Bone Implements: How They Were Used. Bulletin, Massachu-
            setts Archaeological Society 33(1–2):12–20.

2494 1972 Some Aboriginal Stone Works in New England. Bulletin,
            Massachusetts Archaeological Society 33(3–4):18–28.

FRANCO, C., and J.L. FRANCO

2495 1968 Objetos de Hueso de la Epoca Precolombina. Museo Nacional
            de Antropología e Historia, Cuadernos 4. Mexico City.

GARROD, D.A.E.

2496 1955 Paleolithic Spearthrowers. Proceedings, Prehistoric
            Society 21:21–35.

GIBSON, J.L.

2497 1968 Cad Mound: A Stone Bead Locus in East Central Louisiana.
            Bulletin, Texas Archeological Society 38:1–17.

GOETZ, H.

2498 1963 Building and Sculpture Techniques in India: Part II.
            Archaeology 16(1):47–53.

GOURDIN, W.H., and W.D. KINGERY

2499 1975 The Beginnings of Pyrotechnology: Neolithic and Egyptian
            Lime Plaster. Journal of Field Archaeology 2:133–150.

GREENHILL, B., ed.

2500 1976 Archaeology of the Boat. Wesleyan University Press,
            Middletown, Conn.

HAMMATT, H.H.

2501 1970 A Paleo-Indian Butchering Kit. American Antiquity 35: 141-152.

HAMY, E.T.

2502 1885 The Fishook Industry of the Ancient Inhabitants of the Archipelago of California. Revue d'Ethnographie 4:6-13. (English translation in University of California Archaeological Survey, Report 59:61-69.)

HARDEN, D.B.

2503 1933 Ancient Glass. Antiquity 7:419-428.

HARRISSON, T., and LORD MEDWAY

2504 1962 A First Classification of Prehistoric Bone and Tooth Artifacts (Based on Material from Niah Great Cave). Sarawak Museum Journal 10:335-362.

HARTENBERG, R.S., and J. SCHMIDT, Jr.

2505 1969 The Egyptian Drill and the Origin of the Crank. Technology and Culture 10(2):155-165.

HAURY, E.W.

2506 1931 Minute Beads from Prehistoric Pueblos. American Anthropologist 33:80-87.

2507 1937 Shell Artifacts from Snaketown Site. Gila Pueblo, Medallion Papers XXV:135-153. Globe, Ariz.

HEIZER, R.F.

2508 1963 Domestic Fuel in Primitive Society. Journal, Royal Anthropological Institute 93(2):186-192.

2509 1966 Ancient Heavy Transport, Methods and Achievements. Science 153:821-830.

HESTER, T.R.

2510 1969 Human Bone Artifacts from Southern Texas. American Antiquity 34(3):326-328.

2511 1972 Ethnographic Evidence for the Thermal Alteration of Siliceous Stone. Tebiwa 15(2):63-65.

HESTER, T.R., and R.F. HEIZER

2512 1973 Bibliography of Archaeology: 1. Experiments in Archaeology, Lithic Technology, and Petrography in Archaeology. Addison-Wesley Module in Anthropology 29.

HILL, J.N., and J. GUNN

2513 1977 The Individual in Prehistory; Studies of Variability in Style in Prehistoric Technologies. Academic Press, New York.

HO, P.

2514 1975 The Cradle of the East: An Inquiry into the Indigenous
             Origins of Techniques and Ideas of Neolithic and Early
             Historic China, 5000-1000 B.C. University of Chicago
             Press, Chicago.

HODGES, H.

2515 1964 Artifacts. John Baker, London.

2516 1974 Technology in the Ancient World. Alfred A. Knopf, New
             York.

HORNELL, J.

2517 1940 Old English Dead-Fall Traps. Antiquity 14(56):395-403.

2518 1943 The Sailing Ship in Ancient Egypt. Antiquity 17(65):
             27-42.

INIZAN, M.-L., H. ROCHE, and J. TIXIER

2519 1976 Avantages d'un Traitement pour la Taille des Roches
             Siliceuses. Quaternaria XIX:1-18.

JOHNSON, J.K.

2520 1959 Archaic Biface Manufacture: Production Failures, a
             Chronicle of the Misbegotten. Lithic Technology 8(2):
             25-35.

KEELEY, L.H.

2521 1977 The Functions of Paleolithic Flint Tools. Scientific
             American 237(5):108-126.

KELLAR, J.H.

2522 1955 The Atlatl in North America. Indiana Historical Society,
             Prehistory Research Series 3(3).

LAMPERT, R.J., and G.E. BURNBULL

2523 1970 The Manufacture of Shell Fish Hooks on the South Coast of
             N.S.W. Mankind 7(4):312-313.

LIGABUE, G., and S. SALVATORI

2524 1979 L'Alimentazione nella Preistoria. Centro Studi e
             Ricerche Ligabue, Venice.

LITTMANN, E.R.

2525 1958 Ancient Mesoamerican Mortars, Plasters and Stuccos: The
             Composition and Origin of Sascab. American Antiquity 24:
             172-176.

2526 1959 Ancient Mesoamerican Mortars, Plasters and Stuccos: Las
             Flores, Tampico. American Antiquity 25:117-119.

2527 1959 Ancient Mesoamerican Mortars, Plasters and Stuccos:
             Palenque Chiapas. American Antiquity 25:264-266.

LOVE, J.R.B.

2528 1942 A Primitive Method of Making a Wooden Dish by Native
Women of the Musgrave Ranges, South Australia. Transactions, Royal Society of South Australia 66:215-217.

LUCAS, A., and J.R. HARRIS

2529 1962 Ancient Egyptian Materials and Industries. St. Martin's
Press, New York.

MARX, E.

2530 1946 Ancient Egyptian Woodworking. Antiquity 20(79):127-133.

MASON, O.T.

2531 1966 The Origins of Invention. MIT Press, Cambridge, Mass.
(Reprint of 1895 London edition.)

MATHIASSEN, T.

2532 1935 Blubber Lamps in the Ertobolle Culture? Acta Archaeologica
9:224-228.

MATSON, F.R.

2533 1951 The Composition and Working Properties of Ancient Glasses.
Journal, Chemical Education 28(2):82-87.

MENCKEN, A.

2534 1963 Designing and Building the Great Pyramid. Privately
printed in Baltimore.

MEWHINNEY, H.

2535 1957 A Manual for Neanderthals. University of Texas Press,
Austin.

MICHELS, J.W.

2536 1971 The Colonial Obsidian Industry of the Valley of Mexico.
In R.H. Brill, ed., Science and Archaeology:251-271.
MIT Press, Cambridge, Mass.

MONTGOMERY, A.

2537 1962 The Source of the Fibrolite Axes. Museum of New Mexico,
El Palacio 70:34-48.

MOUNTFORD, C.P.

2538 1941 An Unrecorded Method of Manufacturing Wooden Implements
by Simple Stone Tools. Transactions, Royal Society of
South Australia 65:312-317.

MOVIUS, H.L.

2539 1950 A Wooden Spear of Third Interglacial Age from Lower
Saxony. Southwestern Journal of Anthropology 6:139-142.

MULLER-BECK, H.

2540   1965   Seeberg Burgaschisee-Sud; Part 5, Holzgerate und Holz-
              bearbeitung. Acta Bernensia 2(5).

NERO, R.W.

2541   1957   A "Graver" Site in Wisconsin. American Anthropologist 22:
              300-304.

NEWCOMER, M.H., and F. HIVERNEL-GUERRE

2542   1974   Nucléus sur Éclat: Technologie et Utilisation par
              Différentes Cultures Préhistoriques. Bulletin de la
              Société Préhistorique Française 71:119-128.

OAKLEY, K.

2543   1955   Fire as Palaeolithic Tool and Weapon. Proceedings,
              Prehistoric Society 21:36-48.

2544   1956   The Earliest Fire-Makers. Antiquity 118:102-117.

2545   1959   Man the Tool-Maker. University of Chicago Press, Chicago.

ORCHARD, W.C.

2546   1929   Beads and Beadwork of the American Indians. Museum of
              the American Indian, Heye Foundation, Contributions II.

OSWALT, W.H.

2547   1973   Habitat and Technology: The Evolution of Hunting. Holt,
              Rinehart and Winston, New York.

OUTWATER, J.O., Jr.

2548   1957   Pre-Columbian Wood-Cutting Techniques. American Antiquity
              22:410-411.

PATTERSON, L.W.

2549   1979   Quantitative Characteristics of Debitage from Heat-Treated
              Chert. Plains Anthropologist 24(58):255-260.

PITZER, J.M.

2550   1977   Basic Sources for the Study of Burins. Archaeological
              Research Facility, Department of Anthropology, University
              of California, Berkeley.

2551   1977   A Guide to the Identification of Burins in Prehistoric
              Chipped Stone Assemblages. Center for Archaeological
              Research, The University of Texas at San Antonio, Guide-
              books in Archaeology 1.

POND, A.W.

2552   1930   Primitive Methods of Working Stone, Based on Experiments
              of Halvor L. Skavlem. Logan Museum Bulletin 2(1). Beloit
              College, Wis.

POPE, S.T.

2553   1923   A Study of Bows and Arrows. University of California
              Publications in American Archaeology and Ethnology 13(9).
              (Reprinted by University of California Press, Berkeley,
              1962.)

PURDY, B.A., and H.K. BROOKS

2554   1971   Thermal Alteration of Silica Minerals: An Archaeological
              Approach. Science 173:322-325.

PURDY, B.A., and D.E. CLARK

2555   1979   Weathering of Thermally Altered Prehistoric Stone
              Implements. Lithic Technology 8(2):20-21.

RAUSING, G.

2556   1967   The Bow. Some Notes on Its Origin and Its Development.
              Acta Archaeologica Lundensia. Series 8º(6). Gleerup,
              Lund.

RIEHM, K.

2557   1961   Prehistoric Salt-Boiling. Antiquity 35(139):181-191.

ROBERTSON, M.G.

2558   1975   Stucco Techniques Employed by Ancient Sculptors of the
              Palenque Piers. Actas, XLI Congreso Internacional de
              Americanistas I:449-472.

ROBINSON, E.

2559   1942   Shell Fishhooks of the California Coast. Occasional
              Papers of the Bernice P. Bishop Museum 17(4).

ROCHE, J.

2560   1969   Les Industries Paléolithiques de la Grotte de Taforalt
              (Maroc Oriental) Méthodes d'Étude. Evolution Technique
              et Typologique. Quarternaria 11:89-100.

RODER, J.

2561   1944- Bilder sum Megalithen Transport. Paideuma 3:84-87.
       1949

ROSENFELD, A.

2562   1965   The Inorganic Raw Materials of Antiquity. Praeger, New
              York.

ROSENTHAL, E.J.

2563   1977   Sierra Pinacate Percussion--Flaked Shell Tool Manufacture.
              Journal of Field Archaeology 4(3):372-375.

SALEH, S.A., A.W. GEORGE, and F.H. HELMI

2564 1972 Study of Glass and Glass-Making Processes at Wadi el
            Natrun, Egypt, in the Roman Period 30 B.C. to 359 A.D.
            Studies in Conservation 17(4):143-172.

SAMOLIN, W.

2565 1965 Technical Studies of Chinese and Eurasian Archeological
            Objects. Technology and Culture 6:249-255.

SCHMIDER, B.

2566 1971 Les Industries Lithiques du Paléolithique Supérieur en
            Ile-de-France. Centre National de la Recherche Scien-
            tifique, Paris.

SCHULER, F.

2567 1959 Ancient Glassmaking Techniques: The Blowing Process.
            Archaeology 12(2):116-122.

2568 1959 Ancient Glassmaking Techniques: The Molding Process.
            Archaeology 12(1):47-52.

2569 1962 Ancient Glassmaking Techniques: The Egyptian Core Vessel
            Process. Archaeology 15(1):32-37.

SEMENOV, S.A.

2570 1964 Prehistoric Technology. Cory, Adams and Mackay,
            London.

SHAW, C.T.

2571 1945 Bead-Making with a Bow-Drill in the Gold Coast. Journal,
            Royal Anthropological Institute of Great Britain and
            Ireland 75(1-2):45-50.

SINGER, C., et al., eds.

2572 1958 A History of Technology. 5 vols. Clarendon Press,
            Oxford.

SMITH, G.V.

2573 1893 The Use of Flint Blades to Work Pine Wood. Smithsonian
            Institution Annual Report for 1891:601-605.

SMITH, R.W.

2574 1958 Technological Research on Ancient Glass. Archaeology
            11(2):111-116.

SPENCE, M.W.

2575 1967 The Obsidian Industry at Teotihuacan. American Antiquity
            32(4):507-514.

SPETH, J.D.

2576 1972 Mechanical Basis of Percussion Flaking. American
            Antiquity 37(1):34-69.

SPIER, R.F.G.

2577 1973 Material Culture and Technology. Burgess Publishing Co.,
            Minneapolis.

STEINBERG, J.

2578 1966 The Manufacture and Use of Bone Defleshing Tools.
            American Antiquity 31:575-581.

SWANSON, E., ed.

2579 1975 Lithic Technology: Making and Using Stone Tools. Mouton,
            The Hague.

THOMPSON, M.W.

2580 1954 Azilian Harpoons. Proceedings, Prehistoric Society 20(2):
            193-211.

TIEMANN, H.D.

2581 1947 Wood Technology. Pitman, London.

TIXIER, J.

2582 1972 Obtention de Lames par Debitage "Sous le Pied."
            Bulletin de la Société Préhistorique Française 69:134-139.

VASTAGH, G., and E.I. VASTAGH

2583 1948 The Chemistry of the Ancient Roman Mortars of Lime and
            Powdered Brick. Magyar Kemiai Folyoirat 54:42-45.

VOGT, E.

2584 1949 The Birch as a Source of Raw Material During the Stone
            Age. Proceedings, Prehistoric Society 15:50-51.

WASHBURN, S.L.

2585 1960 Tools and Human Evolution. Scientific American 203(3):
            62-75.

WEINBERG, G.D.

2586 1962 Evidence for Glass Manufacture in Ancient Thessaly.
            American Journal of Archaeology 66(2):129-134.

WHITE, K.D.

2587 1967 Agricultural Implements of the Roman World. Cambridge
            University Press, London.

WOODBURY, R.B.

2588 1954 Prehistoric Stone Implements from Northeastern Arizona.
            Papers of the Peabody Museum 34. Harvard University,
            Cambridge, Mass.

WYLIE, H.G.

2589 1975 Pot Scrapers and Drills from Southern Utah. Kiva 40(3):
            121-130.

ZIERHUT, N.

2590   1967   Bone Breaking Activities of the Calling Lake Cree.
              Atlanta Anthropologist 1(3):33-36.

9. Ecological and Environmental Analyses

a. ECOLOGY: GENERAL REFERENCES

ALLEN, D.C., and E.P. CHEATUM

2591   1961   Ecological Implications of Fresh-Water and Land Gastropods
              in Texas Archeological Studies. Bulletin, Texas Archeo-
              logical Society 31:293-316.

ANONYMOUS

2592   1970   Insects and Archaeology. Science and Archaeology 1.

ASCHMANN, H.

2593   1959   The Central Desert of Baja California: Demography and
              Ecology. Ibero-Americana 42. Berkeley.

BAUMHOFF, M.A.

2594   1963   Ecological Determinants of Aboriginal California Popula-
              tions. University of California, Papers in American
              Archaeology and Ethnology 49(2):155-236. Berkeley.

BLANK, T.P.

2595   1953   Ecology of Prehistoric Aleutian Village Sites. Ecology
              34:246-264.

BOHRER, V.L.

2596   1971   Paleoecology of Snaketown. Kiva 36(3):11-19.

BRAIDWOOD, R.J., and C.A. REED

2597   1957   The Achievement and Early Consequences of Food Production:
              A Consideration of the Archeological and Natural His-
              torical Evidence. Cold Spring Harbor Symposia on Quanti-
              tative Biology 22:19-32. Cold Spring Harbor, N.Y.

BROOKS, C.E.P.

2598   1927   The Climate of Prehistoric Britain. Antiquity 1:412-418.

BROSE, D.S.

2599   1970   The Summer Island Site; a Study of Prehistoric Cultural
              Ecology and Social Organization in the Northern Lake
              Michigan Area. Case Western Reserve University, Studies
              in Anthropology 1.

CLARK, J.D.

2600 1964 The Influence of Environment in Inducing Culture Change at the Kalambo Falls Prehistoric Site. South African Archaeological Bulletin 19:93-101.

2601 1965 Culture and Ecology in Prehistoric Africa. In D. Brokensha, ed., Ecology and Economic Development in Tropical Africa:13-28. University of California Press, Berkeley.

CLARK, J.G.D.

2602 1952 Prehistoric Europe: The Economic Basis. Methuen, London.

CONKLIN, H.C.

2603 1961 The Study of Shifting Cultivation. Current Anthropology 2:27-61. Chicago.

COWGILL, U.M., and G.E. HUTCHINSON

2604 1963 Ecological and Geochemical Archaeology in the Southern Maya Lowlands. Southwestern Journal of Anthropology 19: 267-283.

CRAIG, A.K., and N.P. PSUTY

2605 1971 Paleoecology of Shell Mounds at Otuma, Peru. Geographical Review 61(1):125-132.

EULER, R.C., et al.

2606 1979 The Colorado Plateaus: Cultural Dynamics and Paleoenvironment. Science 205:1089-1107.

EVANS, J.G.

2607 1978 An Introduction to Environmental Archaeology. Cornell University Press, Ithaca, N.Y.

FORD, R.I.

2608 1972 Salvaging Biological Remains from Archaeological Sites. Michigan Archaeologist 18(4):223-230.

FOSTER, J.W.

2609 1975 Shell Middens, Paleoecology, and Prehistory: The Case from Estero Morua, Sonora, Mexico. Kiva 41(2):185-194.

FREIMUTH, G., and W. LaBERGE

2610 1977 Dating and Environmental Reconstruction from Prehistoric Mud-Dauber Nests: Some Possibilities. Plains Anthropologist 21(72):111-114.

GODWIN, H.

2611 1946 The Relationship of Bog Stratigraphy to Climatic Change in Archaeology. Proceedings, Prehistoric Society 12: 1-11.

GRIEDER, T.

2612   1970   Ecology Before Columbus. Americas 22(5):21-28.

HACK, J.T.

2613   1942   The Changing Physical Environment of the Hopi Indians
              of Arizona. Peabody Museum Papers 35(1). Harvard
              University, Cambridge, Mass.

HEIZER, R.F.

2614   1960   Agriculture and the Theocratic State in Lowland South-
              eastern Mexico. American Antiquity 26:215-222.

HEUSSER, C.J.

2615   1960   Late Pleistocene Environments of North Pacific North
              America. American Geographical Society, Special Publica-
              tion 35.

IVERSON, J.

2616   1949   The Influence of Prehistoric Man on Vegetation. Dann,
              Geol. Unders, Raekke IV, 3(6). Copenhagen.

LaMARCHE, V.C., Jr.

2617   1974   Paleoclimatic Inferences from Long Tree-Ring Records.
              Science 183:1043-1048.

LANTIS, M.

2618   1955   Problems of Human Ecology in the North American Arctic.
              Arctic 7:307-320.

LEAKEY, L.S.B.

2619   1966   Africa and Pleistocene Overkill? Nature 212:1615-1616.

LEFTIN, H.

2620   1968   Ecology in the Archaeology and Ethnohistory of Panama.
              Panamanian Notes in Anthropology 13:51-56. Florida State
              University.

McDONALD, W.A., and G.R. RAPP, Jr., eds.

2621   1972   Minnesota Messenia Expedition: Reconstructing a Bronze
              Age Regional Environment. University of Minnesota Press,
              Minneapolis.

MACKEY, J.C., and S.J. HOLBROOK

2622   1978   Environmental Reconstruction and the Abandonment of the
              Largo-Gallina Area, New Mexico. Journal of Field
              Archaeology 5(1):29-49.

MacNEISH, R.S.

2623   1961   First Annual Report of the Tehuacan Archaeological-Botani-
              cal Project. R.S. Peabody Foundation for Archaeology,
              Andover, Mass.

MARTIN, P.S.

2624 1966 Africa and Pleistocene Overkill. Nature 212:339-342.

MATTESON, M.R.

2625 1960 Reconstruction of Prehistoric Environments Through the
            Analysis of Molluscan Collections from Shell Middens.
            American Antiquity 26:117-120.

MOUNTFORD, C.P.

2626 1960 Anthropology and Nutrition. In Records of the American-
            Australian Scientific Expedition 2:1-144. Melbourne
            University Press, Victoria.

PHILLIPS, C.W.

2627 1947 An Interesting Effect of Drought on Barren Land.
            Antiquity 21(84):212.

PILCHER, J.R., et al.

2628 1971 Land Clearance in the Irish Neolithic. Science 172:560-
            562.

RAIKES, R.

2629 1967 Water, Weather and Prehistory. John Baker, London.

ROTTLANDER, R.C.A.

2630 1976 Variation in the Chemical Composition of Bone as an
            Indicator of Climatic Change. Journal of Archaeological
            Science 3(1):83-88.

SAMPSON, C.G., ed.

2631 1978 Paleoecology and Archeology of an Acheulian Site at
            Caddinton, England. Department of Anthropology, Southern
            Methodist University, Dallas.

SANDERS, W.T.

2632 1965 The Cultural Ecology of the Teotihuacan Valley. Depart-
            ment of Anthropology, Pennsylvania State University.

SANDERS, W.T., J.R. PARSONS, and R.S. SANTLEY

2633 1979 The Basin of Mexico: Ecological Processes in the Evolution
            of a Civilization. Academic Press, New York.

SAYCE, R.U.

2634 1961 The Ecological Study of Culture. In G.A. Theodorson, ed.,
            Studies in Human Ecology. Row, Peterson, New York.

SEARS, P.B.

2635 1932 The Archaeology of Environment in Eastern North America.
            American Anthropologist 34:610-622.

2636 1953 An Ecological View of Land Use in Middle America. Ceiba
            3:157-165.

2637 1963 Vegetation, Climate, and Coastal Submergence in Connecti-
            cut. Science 140:59-60.

SNOW, D.R.

2638 1972 Rising Sea Level and Prehistoric Cultural Ecology in
            Northern New England. American Antiquity 37(2):211-221.

STEWARD, J.H.

2639 1937 Ecological Aspects of Southwestern Society. Anthropos
            32:87-104.

WATANABE, H.

2640 1964 The Ainu: A Study of Ecology and the System of Social
            Solidarity Between Man and Nature in Relation to Group
            Structure. Journal of the Faculty of Science, University
            of Tokyo, Section V, Anthropology 2(6).

2641 1966 Ecology of the Jomon People: Stability of Habitation and
            Its Biological and Ethnohistorical Implications. Journal
            of the Anthropological Society of Japan 74:21-32.

WEDEL, W.R.

2642 1953 Some Aspects of Human Ecology in the Central Plains.
            American Anthropologist 55:499-514.

WELLS, P., and C. JORGENSEN

2643 1964 Pleistocene Wood Rat Middens and Climatic Change in the
            Mohave Desert: A Record of Juniper Woodlands. Science
            143:1171-1173.

WENDORF, F., ed.

2644 1961 Paleoecology of the Llano Estacado. Fort Burgwin Research
            Center, Publication 1. University of New Mexico Press,
            Santa Fe.

WILKE, P.J.

2645 1978 Late Prehistoric Human Ecology at Lake Cahuilla Coachella
            Valley, California. Contributions of the University of
            California Archaeological Research Facility 38.

WRIGHT, H.E.

2646 1968 Natural Environment of Early Food Production North of
            Mesopotamia. Science 161:334-339.

b. PALYNOLOGY AND PHYTOLITHS

ANDERSON, R.Y.

2647 1955 Pollen Analysis, a Research Tool for the Study of Cave
            Deposits. American Antiquity 21:84-85.

BEISWENGER, J.

2648 1974 Pollen Report on the Casper Site. In G.C. Frison, The Casper Site: A Hell Gap Bison Kill on the High Plains: 247-249. Academic Press, New York.

BRYANT, V.M., Jr.

2649 1975 Pollen as an Indicator of Prehistoric Diets in Coahuila, Mexico. Bulletin, Texas Archeological Society 46:87-106.

BRYANT, V.M., Jr., and R.K. HOLTZ

2650 1968 The Role of Pollen in the Reconstruction of Past Environments. Pennsylvania Geographer 6(1):11-19.

CASIN, S.A.

2651 1939 Pollen Analysis as a Paleoecological Research Method. Botanical Review 5:583-591.

CLENDENING, J.A.

2652 1963 Palynology and Archaeology. West Virginia Archaeologist 16:24-28.

CULLY, A.C.

2653 1979 Some Aspects of Pollen Analysis in Relation to Archaeology. Kiva 44(2-3):95-100.

DAVIS, M.B.

2654 1963 On the Theory of Pollen Analysis. American Journal of Science 261:897-912.

2655 1965 A Method for Determination of Absolute Pollen Frequencies. In R. Kummell and D. Raup, eds., Handbook of Palaeontologic Techniques:674-686. W.H. Freeman, San Francisco.

DEEVEY, E.S., Jr.

2656 1944 Pollen Analysis and Mexican Archaeology: An Attempt to Apply the Method. American Antiquity 10:135-149.

DIMBLEBY, G.W.

2657 1954 Pollen Analysis as an Aid to the Dating of Prehistoric Monuments. Proceedings, Prehistoric Society 20(2):231-236.

2658 1963 Pollen Analysis. In D. Brothwell and E. Higgs, eds., Science in Archaeology:139-149. Thames and Hudson, London.

DIMBLEBY, G.W., and J.G. EVANS

2659 1974 Pollen and Land-Snail Analysis of Calcareous Soils. Journal of Archaeological Science 1(2):117-134.

EISELEY, L.C.

2660 1939 Pollen Analysis and Its Bearing upon American Prehistory: A Critique. American Antiquity 5:115-139.

ERDTMAN, G.

2661   1943   An Introduction to Pollen Analysis.   Ronald Press, New
              York.

FAEGRI, K., and J. IVERSEN

2662   1964   Textbook of Modern Pollen Analysis.   E. Munksgaard,
              Copenhagen.

GISH, J.W.

2663   1979   Palynological Research at Pueblo Grande Ruin.   Kiva 44
              (2-3):159-172.

GRAY, J., and W. SMITH

2664   1962   Fossil Pollen and Archaeology.   Archaeology 15(1):16-26.

GREIG, J.R.A., and J. TURNER

2665   1974   Some Pollen Diagrams from Greece and Their Archaeological
              Significance.   Journal of Archaeological Science 1(2):
              177-194.

HEUSSER, C.J.

2666   1963   Postglacial Palynology and Archaeology in the Naknek
              River Drainage Area, Alaska.   American Antiquity 29:74-81.

JELINEK, A.J.

2667   1966   Correlation of Archeological and Palynological Data.
              Science 152:1507-1509.

KAUTZ, R.R.

2668   1974   On Palynology and Its Application to Archaeological
              Problems.   In R. Kautz, ed., Readings in Archaeological
              Method and Technique:9-20.   Center for Archaeological
              Research at Davis Publication 4.   University of California,
              Davis.

KAUTZ, R.R., and D.H. THOMAS

2669   1972   Palynological Investigations of Two Prehistoric Cave
              Middens in Central Nevada.   Tebiwa 15(2):43-54.

KURTZ, E.B., Jr., and R.Y. ANDERSON

2670   1955   Pollen Analysis.   Physical Science Bulletin 2:113-135.
              University of Arizona, Tucson.

LEWIS, R.C.

2671   1978   Use of Opal Phytoliths in Paleo-Environmental Reconstruc-
              tion.   Wyoming Contributions to Anthropology 1:127-132.

MARTIN, P.S.

2672   1961   Pollen Analysis of (Animal) Coprolites.   In M.F. Lambert
              and R. Ambler, A Survey and Excavation of Caves in Hidalgo

County, New Mexico:101-104. School of American Research, Monograph 25. Santa Fe, N.M.

2673 1963 Early Man in Arizona: The Pollen Evidence. American Antiquity 29:67-73.

2674 1963 The Last 10,000 Years: A Fossil Pollen Record of the American Southwest. University of Arizona Press, Tucson.

MARTIN, P.S., and J. GRAY

2675 1962 Pollen Analysis and the Cenozoic. Science 137:103-111.

MARTIN, P.S., and F.W. SHARROCK

2676 1964 Pollen Analysis of Prehistoric Human Feces: A New Approach to Ethnobotany. American Antiquity 30:168-180.

MEHRINGER, P.J., Jr.

2677 1967 Pollen Analysis and the Alluvial Chronology. Kiva 32(3): 96-101.

2678 1967 Pollen Analysis of the Tule Springs Area, Nevada. Nevada State Museum, Anthropological Papers 13(3).

MEHRINGER, P.J., Jr., E. BLINMAN, and K.L. PETERSEN

2679 1977 Pollen Influx and Volcanic Ash. Science 198(4314):257-261.

NICHOLS, H.

2680 1967 The Suitability of Certain Categories of Lake Sediments for Pollen Analysis. Pollen et Spores 9:375-401.

PAQUEREAU, M.M.

2681 1969 Analyse Palynologique des Niveaux Moustériens de Caminade (Dordogne). Quarternaria 11:237-240.

2682 1969 Étude Palynologique du Wurm I du Pech de l'Aze (Dordogne). Quarternaria 11:227-236.

2683 1970 Étude Palynologique des Niveaux Aurignaciens de Caminade-Est (Dordogne). Quaternaria 13:133-136.

PEARSALL, D.M.

2684 1978 Phytolith Analysis of Archeological Soils: Evidence for Maize Cultivation in Formative Ecuador. Science 199: 177-178.

RISKIND, D.H.

2685 1970 Pollen Analysis of Human Coprolites from Parida Cave. In R.K. Alexander, Archeological Investigations at Parida Cave, Val Verde County, Texas:89-101. Papers, Texas Archeological Salvage Project 19.

RITTER, E.W., and B.W. HATOFF

2686 1977 Late Pleistocene Pollen and Sediments: An Analysis of a Central California Locality. Texas Journal of Science 29(3-4):195-208.

ROBINSON, R.L.

2687 1980 The Study of Biosilica: Reconstructing the Paleoenviron-
            ment of the Central Coastal Plain of Texas. Center for
            Archaeological Research, The University of Texas at San
            Antonio, Special Report 7 (in press).

SCHOENWETTER, J.

2688 1962 The Pollen Analysis of Eighteen Archaeological Sites in
            Arizona and New Mexico. Fieldiana, Anthropology 53.
            Chicago Natural History Museum, Chicago.

2689 1974 Pollen Analysis of Sediments from Salts Cave Vestibule.
            In P.J. Watson, ed., Archeology of the Mammoth Cave Area:
            97-106. Academic Press, New York.

SEARS, P.B.

2690 1952 Palynology in Southern North America. I: Archaeological
            Horizons in the Basin of Mexico. Bulletin of the Geo-
            logical Society of America 63:225-240.

SEARS, P.B., and A. ROOSMA

2691 1961 A Climatic Sequence from Two Nevada Caves. American
            Journal of Science 259:669-678.

SHUTLER, R., Jr.

2692 1961 Application of Palynology to Archaeological and Environ-
            mental Problems in the Pacific. Asian Perspectives 5:
            188-192.

Van Der SPOEL-WALVIUS, M.R.

2693 1964 Pollen Analytical Studies on Disc Wheels, with a Reference
            to the Radiocarbon Dates. Palaeohistoria 10.

Van DUINEN, L., and W. Van ZEIST

2694 1960 Some Pollen Diagrams from the Clay District in the
            Provinces of Groningen, Friesland, and North-Halland
            (Netherlands). Palaeohistoria 8:127-138.

Van ZINDEREN BAKKER, E.M.

2695 1951 Archaeology and Palynology. South African Archaeology
            Bulletin 23(6):80-87.

WATERBOLK, H.T.

2696 1956 Pollen Spectra from Neolithic Grave Monuments in the
            Northern Netherlands. Palaeohistoria 5:39-52.

WILKINSON, P.F.

2697 1971 Pollen, Archaeology and Man. Archaeology and Physical
            Anthropology in Oceania 6(1):1-20.

WODEHOUSE, R.P.

2698   1959   Pollen Grains: Their Structure, Identification and Sig-
                nificance in Science and Medicine. Hafner, New York.

WOOSLEY, A.I.

2699   1978   Pollen Extraction for Arid-Land Sediments. Journal of
                Field Archaeology 5(3):349-355.

c. FAUNAL REMAINS

  i. Methodology

AGENBROAD, L.D., and C.V. HAYNES

2700   1974   *Bison bison* Remains at Murray Springs, Arizona. Kiva 40
                (4):309-314.

AKAZAWA, T., and H. WATANABE

2701   1968   Restoration of Body Size of Jomon Shellmound Fish (Pre-
                liminary Report). Proceedings, 8th International Congress
                of Anthropological and Ethnological Sciences 3:193-197.

ANGRESS, S., and C.A. REED

2702   1962   An Annotated Bibliography on the Origin and Descent of
                Domestic Animals, 1900-1955. Chicago Natural History
                Museum, Fieldiana, Anthropology 54(1):1962.

ARTZ, J.A.

2703   1980   Inferring Season of Occupation from Fish Scales: An
                Archaeological Approach. Plains Anthropologist 25(87):
                47-62.

BOGNAR-KUTZIAN, I.

2704   1971   Zoology and Chronology in Prehistory. American Anthro-
                pologist 73(3):675-679.

BOKONYI, S.

2705   1971   The Development and History of Domestic Animals in
                Hungary: The Neolithic Through the Middle Ages. American
                Anthropologist 73(3):647-674.

2706   1972   Zoological Evidence for Seasonal or Permanent Occupation
                of Prehistoric Settlements. Warner Module Publication R4,
                Andover.

BONNICHSEN, R.

2707   1973   Some Operational Aspects of Human and Animal Bone Altera-
                tion. In B.M. Gilbert, Mammalian Osteo-Archaeology: North
                America:9-24. Special Publication, Missouri Archaeological
                Society.

BOURQUE, B.J., K. MORRIS, and A. SPIESS

2708 1978 (Comments on) Cementum Annuli in Mammal Teeth from
            Archeological Sites (M. Wilson). Science 202:542.

2709 1978 Determining the Season of Death of Mammal Teeth from
            Archaeological Sites: A New Sectioning Technique.
            Science 199(4328):530-531.

BRAIN, C.K.

2710 1969 The Probable Role of Leopards as Predators of the Swart-
            krans Australopithecines. South African Archaeological
            Bulletin 24(95-96), Pt. 3-4:170-171.

BRAINERD, G.W.

2711 1940 An Illustrated Field Key for the Identification of Mammal
            Bones. Ohio State Archaeological and Historical Quarterly
            48:324-328.

BRODRICK, A.H., ed.

2712 1972 Animals in Archaeology. Praeger, New York.

BROTHWELL, D.

2713 1976 Further Evidence of Bone Chewing by Ungulates: The Sheep
            of North Ronaldsay, Orkney. Journal of Archaeological
            Science 3(2):179-182.

BROTHWELL, D.R., K.D. THOMAS, and J. CLUTTON-BROCK, eds.

2714 1978 Research Problems in Zooarchaeology. Institute of
            Archaeology Occasional Papers 3, London.

BYERS, D.S.

2715 1951 On the Interpretation of Faunal Remains. American
            Antiquity 16:262-263.

CASTEEL, R.W.

2716 1971 Differential Bone Destruction: Some Comments. American
            Antiquity 36(4):466-468.

2717 1972 A Key, Based on Scales, to the Families of Native
            California Freshwater Fishes. Proceedings of the
            California Academy of Sciences (4th series) 39(7):75-86.

2718 1972 Some Biases in the Recovery of Archaeological Faunal
            Remains. Proceedings, Prehistoric Society 38:382-388.

2719 1973 Incremental Growth Zones in Mammals and Their Archaeo-
            logical Value. Kroeber Anthropological Society Papers 47:
            1-27. University of California, Berkeley.

2720 1976 Fish Remains in Archaeology and Paleo-Environmental
            Studies. Academic Press, New York.

2721 1976 Incremental Growth Zones in Mammals and Their Archaeo-
            logical Value. Kroeber Anthropological Society Papers
            47:1-27.

2722 1977 Characterization of Faunal Assemblages and the Minimum
            Number of Individuals Determined from Paired Elements:

Continuing Problems in Archaeology. Journal of Archaeological Science 4:125-134.

2723 1978 Faunal Assemblages and the Wiegemethode or Weight Method. Journal of Field Archaeology 5(1):71-78.

CASTEEL, R.W., and D.K. GRAYSON

2724 1977 Terminological Problems in Quantitative Faunal Analysis. World Archaeology 9(2):235-242.

CHAPLIN, R.E.

2725 1965 Animals in Archaeology. Antiquity 39(155):204-211.

2726 1971 The Study of Animal Bones from Archaeological Sites. Seminar Press, New York.

CLASON, A.T., and W. PRUMMEL

2727 1977 Collecting, Sieving and Archaeozoological Research. Journal of Archaeological Science 4:171-175.

CORNWALL, I.W.

2728 1956 Bones for the Archaeologist. Phoenix House, London.

DALLEMAGNE, M.J., C.A. BAUD, and P.W. MORGENTHALER

2729 1956 Réaction d'Échange du Calcium dans les Os Fossils. Bulletin de la Société de Chemi Biologique 38:1207-1211.

DALY, P.

2730 1969 Approaches to Faunal Analysis in Archaeology. American Antiquity 34:146-153.

DAWSON, E.W.

2731 1963 Bird Remains in Archaeology. In D. Brothwell and E. Higgs, eds., Science in Archaeology:279-293. Thames and Hudson, London.

DREW, I.M., D. PERKINS, and P. DALY

2732 1971 Prehistoric Domestication of Animals: Effects on Bone Structure. Science 171:280-282.

DYSON, R.H.

2733 1953 Archaeology and the Domestication of Animals in the Old World. American Anthropologist 55:661-673.

ELDER, W.H.

2734 1965 Primeval Deer Hunting Pressures Revealed by Remains from American Indian Middens. Journal of Wildlife Management 29(2):366-370.

FOLLETT, W.I.

2735 1976 Fish Remains from La Pitia, an Archaeological Site on the Guajira Peninsula in Venezuela. In Yale University Publications in Anthropology 76:235-249.

GIFFORD, D.P., and D.C. CRADER

2736 1977 A Computer Coding System for Archaeological Faunal Remains.
            American Antiquity 42(2):225-237.

GILBERT, B.M.

2737 1973 Mammalian Osteo-Archaeology: North America. Special
            Publication, Missouri Archaeological Society, Columbia.

GILLESPIE, R., et al.

2738 1978 Lancefield Swamp and the Extinction of the Australian
            Megafauna. Science 200:1044-1047.

GILMORE, R.M.

2739 1946 To Facilitate Cooperation in the Identification of
            Mammal Bones from Archaeological Sites. American
            Antiquity 12:49-50.

2740 1949 The Identification and Value of Mammal Bones from
            Archaeologic Excavations. Journal of Mammalogy 30(2):
            163-169.

GLASS, B.P.

2741 1951 A Key to the Skulls of North American Mammals. Burgess,
            Minneapolis.

GOURLAY, K.A.

2742 1971 The Ox and Identification. Man (n.s.) 7(2):244-254.

GRAYSON, D.K.

2743 1978 Minimum Numbers and Sample Size in Vertebrate Faunal
            Analysis. American Antiquity 43(1):53-64.

GRAYSON, D.K., and C. MASER

2744 1978 An Efficient, Inexpensive Dermestid Colony for Skeleton
            Preparation. Journal of Field Archaeology 5(2):246-247.

GUILDAY, J.E.

2745 1977 Animal Remains from Archeological Excavations at Fort
            Ligonier. In Experimental Archaeology. Columbia Univer-
            sity Press, New York.

HARGRAVE, L.L.

2746 1970 Mexican Macaws: Comparative Osteology. University of
            Arizona Press, Tucson.

2747 1972 Comparative Osteology of the Chicken and the American
            Grouse. Prescott College Press, Prescott, Ariz.

HEERE, W.

2748 1963 The Science and History of Domestic Animals. In D. Broth-
            well and E. Higgs, eds., Science in Archaeology:235-249.
            Thames and Hudson, London.

HENKE, R.A.

2749 1971 Antlered Deer Skull Remains in Archaeological Sites: A
Useful Indicator of Settlement Pattern. The Bulletin,
New York State Archaeological Association 51:8-11.

HERRE, W.

2750 1963 The Science and History of Domesticated Animals. In
D. Brothwell and E. Higgs, eds., Science in Archaeology:
235-249. Thames and Hudson, London.

HILDERBRAND, M.

2751 1955 Skeletal Differences Between Deer, Sheep, and Goats.
California Fish and Game 41(4):327-346.

HOKR, Z.

2752 1951 A Method of the Quantitative Determination of the Climate
in the Quaternary Period by Means of Mammal Association.
Sbornik Geological Survey, Czechoslovakia, Paleontology
18:209-218.

HUBBS, C., ed.

2753 1958 Zoogeography. American Association for the Advancement
of Science, Special Publications 51.

IJZEREEF, G.F.

2754 1978 Faunal Remains from the El Abra Rock Shelters (Colombia).
Palaeography, Palaeoclimatology, Palaeoecology 25:163-
177. Amsterdam.

JELINEK, A.J.

2755 1956 Pleistocene Faunas and Early Man. Papers of the Michigan
Academy of Science, Arts and Letters 42:225-237. Ann
Arbor.

JEWELL, P.A.

2756 1958 Buzzards and Barrows. South African Archaeological
Bulletin 13:153-155.

KEHOE, T.F., and A.B. KEHOE

2757 1960 Observations on the Butchering Technique at a Prehistoric
Bison Kill in Montana. American Antiquity 25:420-423.

KRANTZ, G.S.

2758 1968 A New Method of Counting Mammal Bones. American Journal
of Archaeology 73(3):286-288.

LEROI-GOURHAN, A.

2759 1952 L'Étude des Vestiges Zoologiques. In A. Laming, ed.,
La Découverte du Passé:127-150. A. and J. Picard, Paris.

LEWIS, S.D., and A. REDFIELD

2760 1970 Care of Osteological Collections. University of Missouri-
            Columbia, Museum of Anthropology Publication 4.

LORD, K.J.

2761 1977 Numerical Analysis of Faunal Remains of the Little
            Bethlehem (41 AU 38) and Leonard K (41 AU 37) Sites.
            Plains Anthropologist 22(78):291-298.

LOSEY, T.C.

2762 1971 Notes on Athapaskan Butchering Techniques 1. Newsletter,
            Archaeological Society of Alberta 26:1-9.

LYMAN, R.L.

2763 1979 Analysis of Historic Faunal Remains. Historical Archae-
            ology 11:67-73.

LYMAN, R.L., compiler

2764 1979 Archaeological Faunal Analysis: A Bibliography. Occasional
            Papers of the Idaho Museum of Natural History 31. Poca-
            tello.

LYON, P.J.

2765 1970 Differential Bone Destruction: An Ethnographic Example.
            American Antiquity 35(2):213-215.

MEADOW, R.H., and M.A. ZEDER, eds.

2766 1978 Approaches to Faunal Analysis in the Middle East.
            Peabody Museum Bulletin 2. Cambridge, Mass.

MODELL, W.

2767 1969 Horns and Antlers. Scientific American 220(4):114-122.

MORI, J.L.

2768 1970 Procedures for Establishing a Faunal Collection to Aid in
            Archaeological Analysis. American Antiquity 35(3):387-
            389.

MURIE, O.J.

2769 1951 The Elk of North America. Wildlife Management Institute,
            Washington, D.C.

NANCE, J.D.

2770 1969 Some Significant Differences in Certain Foot Elements
            of Elk and Bison. Newsletter, Archaeological Society of
            Alberta 22:3-9.

NOE-NYGAARD, N.

2771 1974 Mesolithic Hunting in Denmark Illustrated by Bone Injuries
            Caused by Human Weapons. Journal of Archaeological
            Science 1(3):217-248.

OLSEN, S.J.

2772 1960 Post-Cranial Skeletal Characteristics of Bison and Bos.
Papers of the Peabody Museum, Harvard University 35(3).
Cambridge, Mass.

2773 1961 The Relative Value of Fragmentary Mammalian Remains.
American Antiquity 26:538-540.

2774 1964 Mammal Remains from Archaeological Sites, Part I:
Southeastern and Southwestern United States. Papers of
the Peabody Museum, Harvard University 56(1). Cambridge,
Mass.

2775 1971 Zooarchaeology: Animal Bones in Archaeology and Their
Interpretation. Addison-Wesley Module in Anthropology 1.

2776 1972 Osteology for the Archaeologist. Papers of the Peabody
Museum, Harvard University 56(3-4). Cambridge, Mass.

2777 1975 The Early Domestic Dogs in North America and Their
Origins. Journal of Field Archaeology 1(3-4):343-346.

OLSEN, S.J., and R.P. WHEELER

2778 1978 Bones from Awatovi. Papers of the Peabody Museum,
Harvard University 70(1-2). Cambridge, Mass.

OSBORN, H.F.

2779 1906 The Causes of Extinction of Mammalia. American
Naturalist 40:769-795, 829-859.

ØSTERGÅRD, M.

2780 1980 X-ray Diffractometer Investigations of Bones from Domestic
and Wild Animals. American Antiquity 45(1):59-63.

PAYNE, S.

2781 1972 On the Interpretation of Bone Samples from Archaeological
Sites. In E. Higgs, ed., Papers in Economic Prehistory:
65-82. Cambridge University Press, London.

2782 1973 Kill-off Patterns in Sheep and Goats: The Mandibles from
Asvan Kale. Anatolian Studies 23:281-303.

PERKINS, D., and P. DALY

2783 1968 The Potential of Faunal Analysis: An Investigation of
the Faunal Remains from Suberde, Turkey. Scientific
American 219(5):96-106.

REED, C.A.

2784 1959 Animal Domestication in the Prehistoric Near East.
Science 130:1629-1639.

2785 1960 A Review of the Archaeological Evidence on Animal
Domestication in the Prehistoric Near East. Studies in
Ancient Oriental Civilization 31:119-145. Oriental
Institute of the University of Chicago.

2786 1961 Osteological Evidences for Prehistoric Domestication in
            Southwestern Asia. Zeitschrift für Tierzuchtung und
            Zuchtungs Biologie 76:31-38.

2787 1963 Osteo-Archaeology. In D. Brothwell and E. Higgs, eds.,
            Science in Archaeology:204-216. Thames and Hudson, London.

RIDDELL, W.H.

2788 1943 The Domestic Goose. Antiquity 17(67):148-155.

RYDER, M.L.

2789 1969 Animal Bones in Archaeology. Blackwell Scientific Pub-
            lications, Oxford & Edinburgh.

SCHMID, E.F.

2790 1972 Atlas of Animal Bones: For Prehistorians, Archaeologists
            and Quaternary Geologists. Elsevier Publishing Co., New
            York.

SEDDON, J.D.

2791 1966 The Origins of Domestication: Some Developments in the
            Last Five Years. South African Archaeological Bulletin
            21(83), Pt. 3:101-107.

SEVERINGHAUS, C.W.

2792 1949 Tooth Development and Wear as Criteria of Age in White-
            Tailed Deer. Journal of Wildlife Management 13(2).

SMITH, P.W.

2793 1965 Recent Adjustments in Animal Ranges. In H.E. Wright,
            Jr., and D.G. Frey, eds., The Quaternary of the United
            States:637-642. Princeton University Press, Princeton,
            N.J.

STEIN, W.T.

2794 1963 Mammal Remains from Archaeological Sites in the Point of
            Pines Region, Arizona. American Antiquity 29:213-220.

SUTCLIFFE, A.

2795 1970 Spotted Hyena: Crusher, Gnawer, Digester and Collector of
            Bones. Nature 227:1110-1113.

TAYLOR, W.W., ed.

2796 1957 The Identification of Non-Artifactual Archaeological
            Materials. National Academy of Sciences, National Re-
            search Council, Publication 565.

THENIUS, E.

2797 1961 Palaeozoologie und Prähistorie. Mitteilungen der Ur-
            geschichte und Anthropol. Gesellschaft 12(3-4):39-61.
            Wien.

2798 1961 Über die Bedeutung der Palokölogie für die Anthropologie und Urgeschichte. In J. Hackel, ed., Theorie und Praxis der Zusammenarbeit Zwischen den Anthropologischen Disziplinen:80-103. Niederösterreich, Horn.

THOMAS, D.H.

2799 1971 On Distinguishing Natural from Cultural Bone in Archaeological Sites. American Antiquity 36(3):366-371.

UCKO, P.J., and G.W. DIMBLEBY, eds.

2800 1969 The Domestication and Exploitation of Plants and Animals. Gerald Duckworth and Co. Ltd., London.

UERPMANN, H.P.

2801 1973 Animal Bone Finds and Economic Archaeology: A Critical Study of "Osteo-Archaeological" Method. World Archaeology 4(3):307-322.

WATSON, J.P.N.

2802 1972 Fragmentation Analysis of Animal Bone Samples from Archaeological Sites. Archaeometry 14(2):221-228.

WHITE, T.E.

2803 1952 Observations on the Butchering Techniques of Some Aboriginal Peoples 1. American Antiquity 17:337-338.

2804 1953 Aboriginal Utilization of Food Animals. American Antiquity 18:396-398.

2805 1954 Observations on the Butchering Techniques of Some Aboriginal Peoples 2. American Antiquity 19:160-164.

2806 1954 Observations on the Butchering Techniques of Some Aboriginal Peoples 3, 4, 5 and 6. American Antiquity 19:254-264.

2807 1955 Observations on the Butchering Techniques of Some Aboriginal Peoples 7, 8 and 9. American Antiquity 21:170-178.

2808 1955 The Technique of Collecting Osteological Materials. American Antiquity 21:85-87.

2809 1956 The Study of Osteological Materials in the Plains. American Antiquity 21:401-404.

WILSON, M.

2810 1978 Cementum Annuli in Mammal Teeth from Archeological Sites. Science 202:541-542.

YELLEN, J.E.

2811 1977 Cultural Patterning in Faunal Remains: Evidence from the !Kung Bushmen. In D. Ingersoll, J.E. Yellen, and W. MacDonald, eds., Experimental Archaeology:271-331. Columbia University Press, New York.

ZEUNER, F.E.

2812   1963   A History of Domesticated Animals.   Hutchinson, London.

ZIEGLER, A.C.

2813   1965   The Role of Faunal Remains in Archaeological Investiga-
              tions. Sacramento Anthropological Society, Paper 2:47-75.
              Sacramento State College, Sacramento, Cal.

2814   1973   Inference from Prehistoric Faunal Remains. Addison-Wesley
              Module in Anthropology 43.

2815   1975   Recovery and Significance of Unmodified Faunal Remains.
              In T.R. Hester, R.F. Heizer, and J.A. Graham, Field
              Methods in Archaeology:183-206. Mayfield Publishing
              Co., Palo Alto, Cal.

ii. Results of Faunal Research: Selected References

ADLER, K.

2816   1968   Turtles from Archaeological Sites in the Great Lakes
              Region. Michigan Archaeologist 14:147-163.

BARBER, M.B.

2817   1974   Analysis of Fauna from the Riker Site. Ohio Archaeologist
              24(4):42-44.

BERQUIST, H., and J. LEPIKSAAR

2818   1957   Animal Skeletal Remains from Medieval Lund. Archaeologica
              Lundensia 1. Museum of Cultural History, Lund.

BIESELE, M.

2819   1968   Faunal Remains (from the Spring Creek Site). Museum of
              Anthropology, University of Michigan, Anthropological
              Papers 32:54-64.

BOKONYI, S.

2820   1974   History of Domestic Mammals in Central and Eastern Europe.
              Adademiai Kiado, Budapest.

BRAIN, C.K.

2821   1969   Faunal Remains from the Bushman Rock Shelter, Eastern
              Transvaal. South African Archaeological Bulletin 24(94),
              Pt. 2:52-55.

CARTER, P.L., and C. FLIGHT

2822   1972   A Report on the Fauna from the Sites of Ntereso and Kin-
              tampo Rock Shelter 6 in Ghana; with Evidence for the Prac-
              tice of Animal Husbandry During the Second Millennium
              B.C. Man 7(2):277-282.

CLARK, J.D.

2823 1972 Paleolithic Butchery Practices. In P.J. Ucko, R. Tringham, and G.W. Dimbleby, eds., Man, Settlement and Urbanism:
149-156. G. Duckworth, London.

CLASON, A.T.

2824 1966 The Animal Remains and Implements of Bone and Antler
from Niederwil. Palaeohistoria 12:181-198.

CLASON, A.T., ed.

2825 1975 Archaeozoological Studies. Elsevier Publishing Co.,
New York.

CLELAND, C.E.

2826 1965 Faunal Remains from Bluff Shelters in Northwest Arkansas.
Arkansas Archaeologist 6(2-3):39-63.

2827 1968 Analysis of the Fauna of the Indian Point Site on Isle
Royale in Lake Superior. Michigan Archaeologist 14(3-4):
143-146.

CLELAND, C.E., and J. KEARNY

2828 1966 An Analysis of the Animal Remains from the Schmidt Site.
Michigan Archaeologist 12(2):81-83.

CLUTTON-BROCK, J., and H.P. UERPMANN

2829 1974 The Sheep of Early Jericho. Journal of Archaeological
Science 1(3):261-274.

DAVIS, S.

2830 1976 Mammal Bones from the Early Bronze Age City of Arad,
Northern Negev, Israel: Some Implications Concerning
Human Exploitation. Journal of Archaeological Science
3(2):153-164.

DEGERBØL, M.

2831 1961 On a Find of a Preboreal Domestic Dog (Canis familiaris
L.) from Star Carr, Yorkshire, with Remarks on other
Mesolithic Dogs. Proceedings, Prehistoric Society 27:
35-55.

DIBBLE, D.S., and D. LORRAIN

2832 1968 Bonfire Shelter: A Stratified Bison Kill Site, Val Verde
County, Texas. Texas Memorial Museum, Miscellaneous
Papers 1. Austin.

DORNSTREICH, M.D.

2833 1973 Food Habits of Early Man: Balance Between Hunting and
Gathering. Science 179:306-307.

DUFFIELD, L.F.

2834   1974   Nonhuman Vertebrate Remains from Salts Cave Vestibule.
                In P.J. Watson, ed., Archeology of the Mammoth Cave
                Area:123-134. Academic Press, New York.

FA⸍ ⸍ B.M., and D.W. PHILLIPSON

2835   1965   Sebanzi: The Iron Age Sequence at Lochinvar, and the
                Tonga. Journal, Royal Anthropological Institute 95:
                253-294.

FITCH, J.E.

2836   1969   Fish Remains, Primarily Otoliths, from a Ventura,
                California Chumash Village Site (Ven-3). Memoirs of the
                Southern California Academy of Sciences 8:56-71.

FITTING, J.E.

2837   1968   The Spring Creek Site. Museum of Anthropology, Univer-
                sity of Michigan Anthropological Papers 32(1):1-78.

FLANNERY, K.V.

2838   1967   The Vertebrate Fauna and Hunting Patterns in the Tehuacan
                Valley. In D.S. Byers, ed., The Prehistory of the Tehuacan
                Valley 1:132-177. University of Texas Press, Austin.

2839   1969   An Analysis of Animal Bones from Chiapa de Corzo,
                Chiapas. In The Artifacts of Chiapa de Corzo, Chiapas,
                Mexico. Papers, New World Archaeology Foundation 26:
                209-218.

FOLLETT, W.I.

2840   1957   Fish Remains from a Shellmound in Marin County, California.
                American Antiquity 23:68-71.

2841   1967   Fish Remains from Coprolites and Midden Deposits at
                Lovelock Cave, Churchill County, Nevada. University of
                California Archaeological Survey Report 70:93-116.
                Berkeley.

FORBIS, R.G.

2842   1956   Early Man and Fossil Bison. Science 123:327-328.

FRIEDMAN, E.

2843   1973   Preparation of Faunal Specimens. American Antiquity
                38(1):113-114.

GARROD, D., and D.M.A. BATE

2844   1937   The Stone Age of Mount Carmel. Oxford University
                Press, London.

GILMORE, R.M.

2845   1946   Mammals in Archaeological Collection from Southwestern
                Pennsylvania. Journal of Mammalogy 27(3):227-234.

GOULD, S.J.

2846 1971 The Paleontology and Evolution of Cerion II Age and the
            Fauna of Indian Shell Middens on Curaçao and Aruba.
            Breviora 372.

GRAYSON, D.K.

2847 1973 The Nightfire Island Avifauna and the Altithermal.
            Nevada Archeological Survey, Research Paper 6.

GRIFFIN, J.W., and P.E. WRAY

2848 1945 Bison in Illinois Archaeology. Transactions, Illinois
            Academy of Science 38:21-26.

GUILDAY, J.E.

2849 1961 Vertebrate Remains from the Varner Site. Pennsylvania
            Archaeologist 31(3-4):119-123.

2850 1963 Bone Refuse from the Oakfield Site. Pennsylvania
            Archaeologist 33(1-2):12-15.

2851 1963 Evidence for Buffalo in Prehistoric Pennsylvania.
            Pennsylvania Archaeologist 33(3):135-139.

GUILDAY, J.E., and D.P. TANNER

2852 1962 Animal Remains from the Quaker State Rockshelter.
            Pennsylvania Archaeologist 32(3-4):131-137.

GUILDAY, J.E., P.W. PARMALEE, and D.P. TANNER

2853 1962 Aboriginal Butchering Techniques at the Eschelman Site
            (36 LA 12), Lancaster County, Pennsylvania. Pennsylvania
            Archaeologist 32(2):59-83.

HARGRAVE, L.

2854 1939 Bird Remains from Abandoned Indian Dwellings in Arizona
            and Utah. The Condor 41:206-210.

HARRIS, A.H.

2855 1963 Vertebrate Remains and Past Environmental Reconstruction
            in the Navajo Reservoir District. Museum of New Mexico,
            Papers in Anthropology 11. Santa Fe.

HATT, R.T.

2856 1953 Faunal and Archaeological Researches in Yucatan Caves.
            Institute of Science, Bulletin 33. Cranbrook.

HEERE, W., ed.

2857 1962 Zur Domestikation und Fruhgeschichte der Haustiere:
            Internationales Symposium in Kiel 1961. Zeitschrift für
            Tierzuchtung und Zuchtungsbiologie 76(1-3), 77(1-2).

HENDEY, Q.B., and R. SINGER

2858 1965 The Faunal Assemblages from the Gamoos Valley Shelters.
            South African Archaeological Bulletin 20(80), Pt. 4:
            206-213.

HIGGS, E.S.

2859 1965 Faunal Fluctuations and Climate in Libya. In W.J. Bishop
            and J.D. Clark, eds., Background to Evolution in Africa:
            149-163. University of Chicago Press, Chicago.

HILZHEIMER, M.

2860 1941 Animal Remains from Tell Asmar. University of Chicago
            Press, Chicago.

ISAAC, G.L.

2861 1971 The Diet of Early Man: Aspects of Archaeological Evidence
            from Lower and Middle Pleistocene Sites in Africa. World
            Archaeology 2:278-299.

KOYOMA, S.

2862 1974 Correlation of Faunal Remains and Selected Artifacts at
            Hogup Cave, Utah. In R. Kautz, ed., Readings in
            Archaeological Method and Technique. Center for Archaeo-
            logical Research at Davis Publication 4:21-29. University
            of California, Davis.

LARTET, E., and C. GAILLARD

2863 1907 La Faune Momifiée de l'Ancienne Egypte. Archives de
            Musée Histoire Naturelle de Lyon 9:1-130.

LAWRENCE, B.

2864 1951 Mammals Found at the Awatovi Site. Papers of the Peabody
            Museum, Harvard University 35(3). Cambridge, Mass.

LEAKEY, L.S.B.

2865 1964 Olduvai Gorge 1951-61. I: Fauna and Background.
            University Press, Cambridge.

LUXENBERG, B.

2866 1972 Faunal Remains. In J.E. Fitting, ed., The Schultz Site
            at Green Point. Memoirs of the Museum of Anthropology,
            University of Michigan 4. Ann Arbor.

MILLER, L.

2867 1957 Bird Remains from an Oregon Indian Midden. The Condor
            59(1):59-63.

MORSE, D.F., and P.A. MORSE

2868 1963 Perforated Deer Phalanges. Tennessee Archaeologist 19(2):
            47-56.

NEILL, W.T., et al.

2869 1956 Animal Remains from Four Preceramic Sites in Florida. American Antiquity 21:383-395.

NIMMO, B.W.

2870 1971 Population Dynamics of a Wyoming Pronghorn Cohort from the Eden-Farson Site, 48SW304. Plains Anthropologist 16 (54), Pt. 1:285-288.

OLSEN, S.J.

2871 1964 Mammal Remains from Archaeological Sites: Part I, Southeastern and Southwestern United States. Harvard University, Papers of the Peabody Museum of Archaeology and Ethnology 56(1). Cambridge, Mass.

2872 1972 The Small Indian Dogs of Black Mesa, Arizona. Plateau 45(2):47-54.

OLSEN, S.J., and J.W. OLSEN

2873 1970 A Preliminary Report on the Fish and Herpeto-Fauna of Grasshopper Ruin. Kiva 36(2):41-43.

OSBORNE, D.

2874 1953 Archaeological Occurrences of Pronghorn Antelope, Bison and Horse in the Columbia Plateau. Scientific Monthly 67(5):260-269.

PARMALEE, P.W.

2875 1959 The Use of Mammalian Skulls and Mandibles by Prehistoric Indians of Illinois. Transactions, Illinois Academy of Science 52:85-95.

2876 1960 Vertebrate Remains from the Chucalissa Site, Tennessee. Tennessee Archaeologist 16(2):84-89.

PARMALEE, P.W., and G. PERINO

2877 1970 A Prehistoric Archaeological Record of the Roseate Spoonbill in Illinois. Transactions, Illinois Academy of Science 63(3):254-257.

PARMALEE, P.W., A.A. PALOUMPIS, and N. WILSON

2878 1972 Animals Utilized by Woodlands Peoples Occupying the Apple Creek Site, Illinois. Illinois State Museum, Reports of Investigations 23.

PEI, W.C.

2879 1938 Le Rôle des Animaux et des Causes Naturelles dans la Cassure des Os. Paleontologica Sinica, (n.s.) D. 7, Whole Series 118, Geological Survey of China, Nanking.

PERKINS, D.

2880 1969 Fauna of Catal Hüyük: Evidence for Early Cattle Domestication in Anatolia. Science 164:177-179.

PRAHL, E.J.

2881 1967 Prehistoric Dogs of Michigan. Michigan Archaeologist
            13(1):13-27.

REHER, C.A.

2882 1974 Population of the Casper Site Bison. In G.C. Frison,
            The Casper Site: A Hill Gap Bison Kill on the High
            Plains:113-124. Academic Press, New York.

RYDER, M.L.

2883 1968 Caprovine Foot-Prints in a Roman Tile. Proceedings,
            Society of Antiquaries of Scotland, Session 1966-1967;
            99:259ff.

SADEK, H.

2884 1965 Distribution of Bird Remains at Jaguar Cave. Tebiwa 8:
            20-29.

SANSON, A.

2885 1974 Le Cheval de Solutré. Matériaux pour l'Histoire de
            l'Homme 2(5):332-342.

SAXON, E.C.

2886 1974 The Mobile Herding Economy of Kebarah Cave, Mt. Carmel:
            An Economic Analysis of the Faunal Remains. Journal
            of Archaeological Science 1(1):27-46.

SCHULZ, P.D., and D.D. SIMONS

2887 1973 Fish Species Diversity in a Prehistoric Central
            California Indian Midden. California Fish and Game
            59(2):107-113.

Van BUREN, E.D.

2888 1939 The Fauna of Ancient Mesopotamia as Represented in Art.
            Analecta Orientalia 18:1-113.

WATERS, J.H.

2889 1962 Animals Used as Food by Late Archaic and Woodland
            Cultural Groups in New England. Science 137:283-284.

WELLS, L.H.

2890 1970 The Fauna of the Aloes Bone Deposit: A Preliminary Note.
            South African Archaeological Bulletin 25(97), Pt. 1:
            22-23.

WILMSEN, E.N., and J.T. MEYERS

2891 1972 The Mercury Content of Prehistoric Fish. Ecology of
            Food and Nutrition 1:179-186.

WOOD, W.R.

2892 1968 Mississippian Hunting and Butchering Patterns; Bone from the Vista Shelter. American Antiquity 33(2):170-179.

WRIGHT, G.A., and S.J. MILLER

2893 1976 Prehistoric Hunting of New World Wild Sheep: Implications for the Study of Sheep Domestication. In C.E. Cleland, ed., Cultural Change and Continuity: Essays in Honor of James Bennett Griffin. Academic Press, New York.

d. MOLLUSCAN ANALYSIS

BAERREIS, D.A.

2894 1969 A Preliminary Analysis of Gastropods from the Mill Creek Sites. Journal of the Iowa Archaeological Society 15: 333-343.

BAKER, F.C.

2895 1929 The Use of Molluscan Shells by the Cahokia Mound Builders. In W.K. Moorehead, The Cahokia Mounds:147-154. University of Illinois Press, Urbana.

2896 1932 Molluscan Shells from the Etowah Mounds. In W.K. Moorehead, Exploration of the Etowah Site in Georgia:145-150. Department of Archaeology, Phillips Academy, Andover, Mass.

BROSE, D.S.

2897 1972 The Mollusc Fauna. In J.E. Fitting, ed., The Schultz Site at Green Point. Memoirs of the Museum of Anthropology, University of Michigan 4. Ann Arbor.

CLARK, J.W., Jr.

2898 1969 Implications of Land and Fresh-Water Gastropods in Archeological Sites. Arkansas Academy of Science, Proceedings 23:38-52.

COAN, E.V.

2899 1965 Kitchen Midden Mollusks of San Luis Gonzaga Bay. Veliger 7(4):216-218.

COUTTS, P.J.F.

2900 1969 The State of Preservation of Shell Material in Midden Sites. Transactions, Royal Society of New Zealand, General 2:135-137.

2901 1971 Recent Techniques of Midden Analysis and Studies of Modern Shellfish Populations in New Zealand. Transactions, Royal Society of New Zealand, General 2:143-156.

EISELEY, L.C.

2902 1937 Index Mollusca and Their Bearing on Certain Problems of
            Prehistory: A Critique. In 25th Anniversary Studies,
            Philadelphia Anthropological Society:77-94.

FELDMAN, L.H.

2903 1969 Panamic Sites and Archaeological Mollusks of Lower
            California. Veliger 12(2):165-168.

JAEHNIG, M.E.W.

2904 1971 The Study of Gastropods: Methodology. Plains Anthro-
            pologist 16(54), Pt. 1:289-297.

JOPE, M.

2905 1960 The Mollusca and Animal Bones from the Excavations at
            Ringneill Quay. In N. Stephens and A.E.P. Collins, eds.,
            The Quaternary Deposits at Ringneill Quay and Ardmillan,
            Co. Down. Proceedings, Royal Irish Academy 61, Sec. 6(3):
            41-77.

MATTESON, M.R.

2906 1959 Land Snails in Archeological Sites. American Anthro-
            pologist 61:1094-1096.

2907 1960 Reconstruction of Prehistoric Environments Through the
            Analysis of Molluscan Collections from Shell Middens.
            American Antiquity 26:117-120.

MOHOLY-NAGY, H.

2908 1978 The Utilization of Pomacea Snails at Tikal, Guatemala.
            American Antiquity 43(1):65-72.

MORTON, B.

2909 1978 Molluscan Evidence of Environmental Changes at Sham Wan.
            In W. Meacham, ed., Sham Wan, Lamma Island; an Archaeo-
            logical Site Study:45-50. Journal Monograph III, Hong
            Kong Archaeological Society.

REED, C.A.

2910 1962 Snails on a Persian Hillside. Postilla, Yale Peabody
            Museum of Natural History 66.

SHAW, L.C.

2911 1978 The Use of Mollusk Shell for Ecological and Cultural
            Reconstruction. Wyoming Contributions to Anthropology
            1:61-66. Laramie.

e. PLANT REMAINS

ALLISON, A.P.

2912 1966 Analysis of Plant Remains from the Schmidt Site. Michigan
            Archaeologist 12(2):76-80.

2913   1972   Plant Remains.   In J.E. Fitting, ed., The Schultz Site
              at Green Point.   Memoirs of the Museum of Anthropology,
              University of Michigan 4.   Ann Arbor.

       ANONYMOUS

2914   1945   Identification of Fibers.   National Institute of Cleaning
              and Dyeing, Bulletin T-145, Silver Spring, Md.

       ASCH, N.B., R.I. FORD, and D.L. ASCH

2915   1972   Paleoethnobotany of the Koster Site.   Illinois State
              Museum Reports of Investigation 24.

       BALSER, C.

2916   1962   Notes on Resin in Aboriginal Central America.   Akten
              des 34 Internationalen Amerikanistenkongresses:374-380.

       BARGHOORN, E.S., Jr.

2917   1944   Collecting and Preserving Botanical Materials of
              Archaeological Interest.   American Antiquity 9:289-294.

       BELL, W.H., and C.J. KING

2918   1944   Methods for the Identification of the Leaf Fibers of
              Mescal (Agave), Yucca (Yucca), Beargrass (Nolina) and
              Sotol (Dasylirion).   American Antiquity 10:150-160.

       BRAZIER, J.D., and G.L. FRANKLIN

2919   1961   Identification of Hardwoods, a Microscope Key.   Forest
              Products Research Bulletin 46, London.

       BRUNETT, F.V.

2920   1972   Wood from Schultz and Other Prehistoric Sites in the
              Great Lakes Area.   In J.E. Fitting, ed., The Schultz
              Site at Green Point.   Memoirs of the Museum of Anthro-
              pology, University of Michigan 4.   Ann Arbor.

       CALLEN, O.E.

2921   1967   The First New World Cereal.   American Antiquity 32:4.

       CONKLIN, H.C.

2922   1959   Ecological Interpretations and Plant Domestication.
              American Antiquity 25:260-262.

       CONRAD, L.A., and R.C. KEOPPEN

2923   1972   An Analysis of Charcoal from the Brewster Site (13CK15),
              Iowa.   Plains Anthropologist 17(55):52-54.

       CUTLER, H.

2924   1952   A Preliminary Study of the Plant Remains of Tularosa
              Cave.   Fieldiana 40:461-480.   Natural History Museum,
              Chicago.

CUTLER, H.C., and L.W. BLAKE

2925 1971 Floral Remains from the Knoll Spring Site, Cook County,
            Illinois. In Mississippian Site Archaeology in Illinois:
            I. Illinois Archaeological Survey Bulletin 8:244-246.

DENNELL, R.W.

2926 1974 Botanical Evidence for Prehistoric Crop Processing Ac-
            tivities. Journal of Archaeological Science 1(3):275-284.

2927 1974 The Purity of Prehistoric Crops. Proceedings, Prehistoric
            Society 40:132-156.

DERING, J.P., and H.J. SHAFER

2928 1976 Analysis of Matrix Samples from a Crockett County Shelter:
            A Test for Seasonality. Bulletin, Texas Archeological
            Society 47:209-230.

DIMBLEBY, G.

2929 1967 Plants and Archaeology. John Baker, London.

FAULKNER, C.K., and J.B. GRAHAM

2930 1967 Plant Food Remains on Tennessee Sites: A Preliminary
            Report. Bulletin, Southeastern Archaeological Conference
            5:36-40.

FEWKES, J.W.

2931 1896 A Contribution to Ethnobotany. American Anthropologist
            9:14-21.

GORCZYNSKI, T., and B. MOLSKI

2932 1969 Anatomical Changes of Commonly Used Wood Species from an
            Archaeological Excavation. Archaeologia Polona XI:147-
            172.

GRIESS, E.A.M.

2933 1957 Anatomical Identification of Some Ancient Egyptian Plant
            Material. Mémoires de l'Institut d'Egypte. Cairo.

HARLAN, J., and D. ZOHARY

2934 1966 Distribution of Wild Wheats and Barley. Science 153:
            1074-1080.

HAURY, E.W., and C.M. CONRAD

2935 1938 The Comparison of Fiber Properties of Arizona Cliff-
            Dweller and Hopi Cotton. American Antiquity 3:224-227.

HELBAEK, H.

2936 1951 Seeds of Weeds as Food in the Pre-Roman Iron Age. Kuml,
            Arbog f yysk Arkaeol. Sels., 1951:65-74. Aarhus, Denmark.

2937 1955 Ancient Egyptian Wheats. Proceedings, Prehistoric Society
            21:93-96.

2938 1959 Domestication of Food Plants in the Old World. Science
130:365-372.

2939 1961 Studying the Diet of Ancient Man. Archaeology 14(2):
95-101.

HEVLY, R.H.

2940 1970 Botanical Studies of Sealed Storage Jar Cached near
Grand Falls, Arizona. Plateau 42(4):150-156.

HEYERDAHL, T.

2941 1964 Plant Evidence for Contacts with America Before Columbus.
Antiquity 38(150):120-133.

HRDLIČKA, A.

2942 1937 Man and Plants in Alaska. Science 86:559-560.

HUBBARD, B.

2943 1878 Ancient Garden Beds in Michigan. American Antiquarian
1:1-9.

HUBBARD, R.N.L.B.

2944 1976 On the Strength of the Evidence for Prehistoric Crop
Processing Activities. Journal of Archaeological
Science 3(3):257-266.

MABY, J.C.

2945 1932 The Identification of Wood and Charcoal Fragments. The
Analyst 57:2-8.

McMICHAEL, E.

2946 1965 Ethnobotanical Material from the Ohio Valley. Bulletin,
Southeastern Archaeological Conference 3:36-37.

MacNEISH, R.S.

2947 1955 Ancient Maize and Mexico. Archaeology 8(2):108-115.

MEHRINGER, P.J.

2948 1965 Late Pleistocene Vegetation in the Mohave Desert of
Southern Nevada. Journal, Arizona Academy of Science 3:
172-188.

MULLER-STOLL, W.R.

2949 1936 Untersuchungen Urgenschichtlicher Holzreste nebst
Anleitung zur Ihrer Bestimmung. Praehistorischer
Zeitschrift 27:1-57.

PHILLIPS, E.W.J.

2950 1948 Identification of Softwoods by Their Microscopic Structure.
Great Britain Forest Products Research Laboratory Bulletin
22. London.

ROMANS, R.C.

2951   1973   A History of Paleobotany in Arizona. Plateau 45(3):93–
              101.

ROOT, M.J.

2952   1979   The Paleoethnobotany of the Nebo Hill Site. Plains
              Anthropologist 24(58):239–248.

ROSENDAHL, P., and D.E. YEN

2953   1971   Fossil Sweet Potato Remains from Hawaii. Journal of
              the Polynesian Society 80(3):379–385.

SPECTOR, J.S.

2954   1970   Seed Analysis in Archaeology. Wisconsin Archaeologist
              51(4):153–190.

STEPHENS, S.G.

2955   1970   The Botanical Identification of Archaeological Cotton.
              American Antiquity 35(3):367–373.

TOWLE, M.A.

2956   1961   The Ethnobotany of Pre-Columbian Peru. Viking Fund
              Publications in Anthropology 30.

WELLS, M.J.

2957   1965   An Analysis of Plant Remains from Scott's Cave in the
              Camtoos Valley. South African Archaeological Bulletin
              20(78), Pt. 2:79–84.

WESTERN, A.C.

2958   1963   Wood and Charcoal in Antiquity. In D. Brothwell and
              E. Higgs, eds., Science in Archaeology:150–158. Thames
              and Hudson, London.

WETTSTEIN, E.

2959   1924   Die Tierreste aus dem Pfahlbau am Alpenquas in Zurich.
              Vierteljahrschaft der Naturforschenden Gesellschaft
              Zurich 69:79–127.

WHITAKER, T.W., H.C. CULTER, and R.S. MacNEISH

2960   1957   Cucurbit Materials from Three Caves near Tamaulipas.
              American Antiquity 22:352–358.

WILD, J.P.

2961   1966   Papyrus in Pre-Roman Britain. Antiquity 40:139–141.

WINTER, J.

2962   1971   A Summary of Owasco and Iroquois Maize Remains. Pennsyl-
              vania Archaeologist 41(3):1–11.

YARNELL, R.A.

2963 1964 Aboriginal Relationships Between Culture and Plant Life in the Upper Great Lakes Region. Museum of Anthropology, University of Michigan, Anthropological Papers 23.

2964 1965 Implications of Distinctive Flora on Pueblo Ruins. American Anthropologist 67:662-674.

ZEINER, H.M.

2965 1946 Botanical Survey of the Angel Mounds Site, Evansville, Indiana. American Journal of Botany 33:83-90.

f. FECAL ANALYSIS

AMBRO, R.D.

2966 1967 Dietary-Technological-Ecological Aspects of Lovelock Cave Coprolites. University of California Archaeological Survey, Report 70:37-48.

BRYANT, V.M., Jr.

2967 1974 Pollen Analysis of Prehistoric Human Feces from Mammoth Cave Area. In P.J. Watson, ed., Archaeology of the Mammoth Cave Area:203-210. Academic Press, New York.

2968 1974 The Role of Coprolite Analysis in Archaeology. Bulletin, Texas Archeological Society 45:1-28.

BRYANT, V.M., Jr., and G. WILLIAMS-DEAN

2969 1975 The Coprolites of Man. Scientific American 232(1):100-109.

CALLEN, E.O.

2970 1963 Diet as Revealed by Coprolites. In D. Brothwell and E. Higgs, eds., Science in Archaeology:186-194. Thames and Hudson, London.

2971 1965 Food Habits of Some Pre-Columbian Mexican Indians. Economic Botany 19:335-343.

2972 1967 Analysis of Tehuacan Coprolites. In D.S. Byers, ed., The Prehistory of Tehuacan Valley I:261-289. University of Texas Press, Austin.

CALLEN, E.O., and T.W.M. CAMERON

2973 1960 A Prehistoric Diet Revealed in Coprolites. The New Scientist, July 7:35-40.

COLYER, M., and D. OSBORNE

2974 1965 Screening Soil and Fecal Samples for Recovery of Small Specimens. American Antiquity 31(2), Pt. 2:186-192.

COWAN, R.A.

2975 1967 Lake Margin Exploitation in the Great Basin as Demonstrated
            by Analysis of Coprolites from Lovelock Cave, Nevada.
            University of California Archaeological Survey, Report
            70:21-36.

HEIZER, R.F.

2976 1967 Analysis of Human Coprolites from a Dry Nevada Cave.
            University of California Archaeological Survey, Report
            70:1-20.

2977 1970 The Anthropology of Prehistoric Great Basin Coprolites.
            In D. Brothwell and E. Higgs, eds., Science and Archae-
            ology:244-250. 2nd ed. Praeger, New York.

HEIZER, R.F., and L.K. NAPTON

2978 1970 Archaeology and the Prehistoric Great Basin Subsistence
            Regime as Seen from Lovelock Cave, Nevada. Contributions,
            University of California Archaeological Research Facility
            10.

KLIKS, M.

2979 1975 Paleoepidemiological Studies on Great Basin Coprolites:
            Estimation of Dietary Intake and Evaluation of the In-
            gestion of Anthelmintic Plant Substances. Archaeological
            Research Facility, University of California, Berkeley.

2980 1976 Paleodietetics: A Review of the Role of Dietary Fiber in
            Preagricultural Human Diets. In G.A. Spiller and R.J.
            Amen, eds., Fiber in Human Nutrition. C.C. Thomas,
            Springfield, Ill.

deLUMLEY, H.

2981 1969 Les Coprolithes de la Cabane Acheuleene du Lazaret, I:
            Étude Morphologique. In H. deLumley, Une Cabane
            Acheuleene dans la Grotte du Lazaret:121-122. Société
            Préhistorique Française, Mémoires 7. Paris.

2982 1969 A Paleolithic Camp at Nice. Scientific American 220(5):
            42-50.

McCLARY, A.

2983 1972 Notes on Some Late Middle Woodland Coprolites. In J.E.
            Fitting, ed., The Schultz Site at Green Point: A Strati-
            fied Occupation Area in the Saginaw Valley of Michigan:
            131-136. University of Michigan, Museum of Anthropology,
            Memoir 4. Ann Arbor.

MARQUARDT, W.H.

2984 1974 A Statistical Analysis of Constituents in Human Paleofecal
            Specimens from Mammoth Cave. In P.J. Watson, ed.,
            Archeology of the Mammoth Cave Area:193-202. Academic
            Press, New York.

NAPTON, L.K.

2985 1969 Archaeological and Paleobiological Investigations in Lovelock Cave, Nevada: Further Analysis of Human Coprolites. Kroeber Anthropological Society, Special Papers 2.

PIKE, A.W.

2986 1967 The Recovery of Parasite Eggs from Ancient Cesspit and Latrine Deposits: An Approach to the Study of Early Parasite Infections. An A.T. Sandison and D. Brothwell, eds., Diseases in Antiquity:184–188. C.C. Thomas, Springfield, Ill.

ROUST, N.L.

2987 1967 Preliminary Examination of Prehistoric Human Coprolites from Four Western Nevada Caves. University of California Archaeological Survey, Report 70:49–88.

SAMUELS, R.

2988 1965 Parasitological Study of Long-Dried Fecal Samples. American Antiquity 31(2), Pt. 2:175–179.

SCHOENWETTER, J.

2989 1974 Pollen Analysis of Human Paleofeces from Upper Salts Cave. In P.J. Watson, ed., Archeology of the Mammoth Cave Area:49–58. Academic Press, New York.

STEWART, R.B.

2990 1974 Identification and Quantification of Components in Salts Cave Paleofeces, 1970–1972. In P.J. Watson, ed., Archeology of the Mammoth Cave Area:41–48. Academic Press, New York.

WAKEFIELD, E.G., and S.C. DELLINGER

2991 1936 Diet of the Bluff Dwellers of the Ozark Mountains and Its Skeletal Effects. Annals of Internal Medicine 9:1412–1418.

WATSON, P.J.

2992 1974 Theoretical and Methodological Difficulties in Dealing with Paleofecal Material. In P.J. Watson, ed., Archeology of the Mammoth Cave Area:239–241. Academic Press, New York.

WILKE, P.J., and H.J. HALL

2993 1975 Analysis of Ancient Feces: A Discussion and Annotated Bibliography. Archaeological Research Facility, Department of Anthropology, University of California, Berkeley.

YARNELL, R.A.

2994 1969 Contents of Human Paleofeces. In P.J. Watson, The Prehistory of Salts Cave, Kentucky. Illinois State Museum, Report of Investigations 16:44–55.

g. THE STUDY OF SOILS/GEOARCHAEOLOGY

ANONYMOUS

2995 1968 Phosphatuntersuchungen zur Topographischen Lokalisation
            von Ortswustunge. Geographica Helvetica 5:185-190.

ARRHENIUS, O.

2996 1963 Investigation of Soil from Old Indian Sites. Ethnos
            2-3:122-136.

BERGER, K.C., and R.J. MUCKENHIRN

2997 1945 Soil Profiles of Natural Appearance Mounted with Vinglite
            Resin. Soil Science Society of America, Proceedings 10:
            368-370.

BIEK, L.

2998 1963 Soil Silhouettes. In D. Brothwell and E. Higgs, eds.,
            Science in Archaeology:108-112. Thames and Hudson,
            London.

BUTZER, K.W., and C.L. HANSEN

2999 1968 Desert and River in Nubia: Geomorphology and Prehistoric
            Environments in the Aswan Reservoir. University of
            Wisconsin Press, Madison.

CARTER, G.F.

3000 1956 On Soil Color and Time. Southwestern Journal of Anthro-
            pology 12:295-324.

CARTER, G.F., and R.L. PENDLETON

3001 1956 The Humid Soil: Process and Time. Geographical Review
            46:488-507.

COOK, S.F.

3002 1963 Erosion Morphology and Occupation History in Western
            Mexico. University of California Anthropological Records
            17(3):281-334. Berkeley.

COOK, S.F., and R.F. HEIZER

3003 1962 Chemical Analysis of the Hotchkiss Site (CCo-138).
            University of California Archaeological Survey, Report
            57(1):1-24. Berkeley.

3004 1965 Studies on the Chemical Analysis of Archaeological
            Sites. University of California Publications in Anthro-
            pology 2. Berkeley.

CORNWALL, I.W.

3005 1954 Soil Science and Archaeology with Illustrations from
            Some British Bronze Age Monuments. Proceedings, Prehis-
            toric Society 19(2):129-147.

3006   1958   Soils for the Archaeologist. Phoenix House, London.

3007   1960   Soil Investigations in the Service of Archaeology.
              Viking Fund Publications in Anthropology 28:265-299.

COWGILL, U.M.

3008   1961   Soil Fertility and the Ancient Maya. Transactions,
              Connecticut Academy of Arts and Sciences 42:1-56.

COWGILL, U.M., C. GOULDEN, G.E. HUTCHINSON, R. PATRICK,
A. RACEK, and M. TSUKADA

3009   1966   The History of Laguna de Petenxil. Memoirs, Connecticut
              Academy of Arts and Sciences 17.

COYLER, M., and D. OSBORNE

3010   1965   Screening Soil and Fecal Samples for Recovery of Small
              Specimens. American Antiquity 31(2), Pt. 2:186-192.

CROCKER, R.L.

3011   1952   Soil Genesis and the Pedogenic Factors. Quarterly Review
              of Biology 27:139-168.

CURWEN, E.C.

3012   1930   The Silting of Ditches in Chalk. Antiquity 4:97-100.

DAUNCEY, K.D.M.

3013   1952   Phosphate Content of Soils on Archaeological Sites. The
              Advancement of Science 9:33-36.

DAVIDSON, D.A.

3014   1973   Particle Size and Phosphate Analysis--Evidence for the
              Evaluation of a Tell. Archaeometry 15:143-152.

DAVIDSON, D.A., and M.L. SHACKLEY, eds.

3015   1977   Geoarchaeology: Earth Science and the Past. Westview
              Press, Boulder.

DEETZ, J., and E. DETHLEFSEN

3016   1963   Soil pH as a Tool in Archaeological Site Interpretation.
              American Antiquity 29:242-243.

DIETZ, E.F.

3017   1957   Phosphorus Accumulation in Soil of an Indian Habitation
              Site. American Antiquity 22:405-409.

DIMBLEBY, G.W.

3018   1957   Pollen Analysis of Terrestrial Soils. New Phytologist
              56:12-28.

DUFFIELD, L.F.

3019 1970 Vertisols and Their Implications for Archaeological
            Research. American Anthropologist 72(5):1055-1062.

DUMOND, D.E.

3020 1963 A Practical Field Method for the Preservation of Soil
            Profiles from Archaeological Cuts. American Antiquity
            29:116-118.

ECKBLAW, E.W.

3021 1936 Soil Geography and Relationship of Soils to Other Dynamic
            Processes. Soil Science Society of America, Proceedings
            1:1-5.

EDDY, F.W., and H.E. DREGNE

3022 1964 Soil Tests on Alluvial and Archaeological Deposits,
            Navajo Reservoir District. El Palacio 71:5-21.

EIDT, R.C.

3023 1977 Detection and Examination of Anthrosols by Phosphate
            Analysis. Science 197(4311):1327-1339.

EMERY, K., R.L. WIGLEY, A.S. BARTLETT, M. RUBIN, and E. BARGHOORN

3024 1967 Freshwater Peat on the Atlantic Continental Shelf.
            Science 158:1301-1307.

ERICSON, D.B., and G. WOLLIN

3025 1964 The Deep and the Past. Alfred A. Knopf, New York.

ERICSON, D.B., M. EWING, and G. WOLLIN

3026 1964 The Pleistocene Epoch in Deep-Sea Sediments. Science
            146:723-732.

FELGENHAUER, F., and F. SAUTER

3027 1959 Phosphatanalytische Untersuchungen an Paläolithischen
            Kulturschichten in Willendorf i.d. Wachau. Archaeologia
            Austriaca 25:25-34.

FENWICK, I.M.

3028 1968 Pedology as a Tool in Archaeological Investigations.
            Ontario Archaeology 11:27-38.

FISK, H.N.

3029 1944 Summary of the Geology of the Lower Alluvial Valley of
            the Mississippi River. War Department, Corps of Engineers,
            U.S. Army, Mississippi River Commission. Vicksburg, Miss.

GLADFELTER, B.G.

3030 1977 Geoarchaeology: The Geomorphologist and Archaeology.
            American Antiquity 42(4):519-538.

GODWIN, H.

3031 1946 Relationship of Bog Stratigraphy to Climatic Change and Archaeology. Proceedings, Prehistoric Society 12:1-11. London.

GOLDBERG, P.S.

3032 1975 Sediment Peels from Prehistoric Sites. Journal of Field Archaeology 1(3-4):323-328.

GRIFFITH, M.A., and F. MARK

3033 1978 The Use of Soil Analysis in Archeological Research. Man in the Northeast 15-16:118-123.

GRIMES, W.F.

3034 1945 Early Man and the Soils of Anglesey. Antiquity 19(76): 169-174.

GUNDLACH, H.

3035 1961 Tüpfelmethode auf Phosphat Angewandt in Prähistorischer Forschung (als Feldmethode). Mikrochimica et Ochnoanalytica Acta 5:735-737.

GUY, P.L.O.

3036 1954 Archaeological Evidence of Soil Erosion and Sedimentation in Wadi Musrara (Israel). Israel Exploration Journal 4: 77-87.

HARRADINE, F.F.

3037 1949 The Variability of Soil Properties in Relation to Stages of Profile Development. Soil Science Society of America, Proceedings 14:302-311.

HASSAN, F.A.

3038 1978 Sediments in Archaeology: Methods and Implications for Palaeoenvironmental and Cultural Analysis. Journal of Field Archaeology 5(2):197-214.

HAY, R.L.

3039 1976 Geology of the Olduvai Gorge: A Study of Sedimentation in a Semiarid Basin. University of California Press, Berkeley.

HORTON, R.E.

3040 1945 Erosional Development of Streams and Their Drainage Patterns. Bulletin, Geological Society of America 56:275-370.

HOWELL, F.C.

3041 1959 Upper Pleistocene Stratigraphy and Early Man in the Levant. Proceedings, American Philosophical Society 103:1-65.

HYAMS, E.

3042 1952 Soil and Civilization. Thames and Hudson, London.

JACKSON, M.L.

3043 1958 Soil Chemical Analysis. Prentice-Hall, Englewood Cliffs,
            N.J.

JAKOB, H.

3044 1955 Bedeutung der Phosphatmethode für die Urgeschichte und
            Bodenforschung. Deutsche Akademie der Landwirt. Wiss.
            Ab. 15:67-85.

JENNY, H.

3045 1941 Factors of Soil Formation: A System of Quantitative
            Pedology. McGraw-Hill, New York.

JOEFFE, J.S.

3046 1941 Climatic Sequence of the Post-Wisconsin Glacial Age as
            Revealed by the Soil Profile. Soil Science Society of
            America, Proceedings 6:368-372.

JUDSON, S.

3047 1953 Geology of the San Jon Site, Eastern New Mexico. Smith-
            sonian Institution, Miscellaneous Collections 121(1).

LEE, G.B.

3048 1969 Pedological Investigations at Mill Creek, Iowa, Archaeo-
            logical Sites. Journal of the Iowa Archaeological
            Society 15:318-332.

LIEBOWITZ, H., and R.L. FOLK

3049 1980 Archaeological Geology of Tel Yin'am, Galilee, Israel.
            Journal of Field Archaeology 7(1):23-42.

LISTITSINA, G.N.

3050 1976 Arid Soils--the Source of Archaeological Information.
            Journal of Archaeological Science 3(1):55-60.

LORCH, W.

3051 1939 Methodische Untersuchungen zur Wüstungsforschung.
            Arbeiten zur Landes und Volksforschung 4. Jena.

LORD, A.C., Jr.

3052 1961 An Introduction to Soils. Bulletin, Massachusetts
            Archaeological Society 23(1):14-18.

LOTSPEICH, F.B.

3053 1961 Soil Science in the Service of Archaeology. Fort Burgwin
            Research Center, Publication 1:137-139. Museum of New
            Mexico Press, Santa Fe.

LUTZ, H.J.

3054 1951 The Concentration of Certain Chemical Elements in the Soils of Alaska Archaeological Sites. American Journal of Science 249:925-928.

MATTINGLY, S.E.G., and R.J.B. WILLIAMS

3055 1962 A Note on the Chemical Analysis of a Soil Buried Since Roman Times. Journal of Soil Science 13:254-258.

NIKIFOROFF, C.C.

3056 1942 Fundamental Formula of Soil Formation. American Journal of Science 240:847-866.

NORTH, F.J.

3056a 1938 Geology for Archaeologists. Archaeological Journal 94: 73-115. London.

OVERSTREET, D.

3057 1974 A Rapid Chemical Field Test for Archaeological Site Surveying: An Application and Evaluation. Wisconsin Archeologist 55:262-270.

PARSONS, R.B.

3058 1962 Indian Mounds in Northeast Iowa as Soil Genesis Benchmarks. Journal of the Iowa Archaeological Society 12(1).

PEARSALL, W.H.

3059 1952 The pH of Natural Soils and Its Ecological Significance. Journal of Soil Science 3:41-51.

PROVAN, D.M.J.

3060 1971 Soil Phosphate Analysis as a Tool in Archaeology. Norwegian Archaeological Review 4:37-50.

RAPPAPORT, R.A., and A. RAPPAPORT

3061 1967 Analysis of Coastal Deposits for Midden Content. American Museum of Natural History, Anthropological Papers 51(2): 201-215.

RITTER, E.W., and B.W. HATOFF

3062 1974 Geomorphology and Archaeology. In R. Kautz, ed., Readings in Archaeological Method and Technique:1-8. Center for Archaeological Research at Davis Publication 4, University of California, Davis.

RUHE, R.V.

3063 1965 Quaternary Paleopedology. In H.G. Wright and D. Frey, eds., The Quaternary of the United States:755-764. Princeton University Press, Princeton, N.J.

SAUCIER, R.T.

3064   1966   Soil-Survey Reports and Archaeological Investigation.
              American Antiquity 31:419-422.

SCHOBINGER, J.

3065   1966   El Análisis de Sedimentos. Una Técnica Moderna al
              Servicio de la Datación del Paleolitico Alpino. Acta
              Praehistorica V/VII (1961-1963):223-239.

SCHWARZ, G.T.

3066   1967   A Simplified Chemical Test for Archaeological Field
              Work. Archaeometry 10:57-63.

SHACKLEY, M.L.

3067   1975   Archaeological Sediments: A Survey of Analytical Methods.
              John Wiley & Sons, New York.

SHAW, C.F.

3068   1928   Profile Development and the Relationship of Soils in
              California. Proceedings of the First International
              Congress of Soil Science 4:291-317.

SHORER, P.

3069   1964   A Method for the Transfer of Archaeological Soil Sections
              on to a Flexible Rubber Backing. Studies in Conservation
              9.

SIMONSEN, R.W.

3070   1954   Identification and Interpretation of Buried Soils.
              American Journal of Science 252:705-722.

SJOBERG, A.

3071   1976   Phosphate Analysis of Anthropic Soils. Journal of Field
              Archaeology 3:447-454.

SMITH, D.F.

3072   1963   Erosion and Deposition of Italian Stream Valleys During
              Historic Times. Science 140:898-900.

SOIL SURVEY STAFF

3073   1962   Soil Survey Manual: Identification and Nomenclature of
              Soil Horizons. Supplement to U.S. Department of Agricul-
              ture Handbook 18:173-188.

SOKOLOFF, V.P., and J.L. LORENZO

3074   1953   Modern and Ancient Soils at Some Archaeological Sites
              in the Valley of Mexico. American Antiquity 19:50-55.

SOLECKI, R.S.

3075 1951 Notes on Soil Analysis and Archaeology. American Antiquity 16:254-256.

SPORRONG, U.

3076 1966 Phosphatkartierung und Siedlungsanalyse. Geografiska Annaler 50B:62-64.

THROP, J.

3077 1941 The Influence of Environment on Soil Formation. Soil Science Society of America, Proceedings 6:39-46.

TITE, M.S.

3078 1972 The Influence of Geology on the Magnetic Susceptibility of Soils on Archaeological Sites. Archaeometry 14(2): 229-236.

Van der MERWE, N.J., and P.H. STEIN

3079 1972 Soil Chemistry of Postmolds and Rodent Burrows: Identification Without Excavation. American Antiquity 37(2): 245-253.

VOIGT, E., and G. GITTINS

3080 1977 The "Lackfilm" Method for Collecting Sedimentary Peels: Archaeological Applications. Journal of Field Archaeology 4(4):449-458.

WARD, T.

3081 1965 Correlation of Mississippian Sites and Soil Types. Bulletin, Southeastern Archaeological Conference 3:42-48.

WHITE, E.M.

3082 1978 Cautionary Note on Soil Phosphate Data Interpretation for Archaeology. American Antiquity 43(3):507-508.

WHITE, E.M., and J.K. LEWIS

3083 1967 Recent Gully Formation in Prairie Areas of the Northern Great Plains. Plains Anthropologist 12(37):318-322.

WOODS, W.I.

3084 1977 The Quantitative Analysis of Soil Phosphate. American Antiquity 42(2):248-251.

ZEUNER, F.E.

3085 1955 Loess and Palaeolithic Chronology. Proceedings, Prehistoric Society 21:51-64.

10. Human Skeletal Analysis

a. METHODOLOGY, GENERAL SURVEYS, AND IMPORTANT RESULTS

ALLISON, M.J., D. MENDOZA, and A. PEZZIA

3086 1974 A Radiographic Approach to Childhood Illness in Precolum-
            bian Inhabitants of Southern Peru. American Journal of
            Archaeology 40:409-416.

ANDERSON, J.E.

3087 1962 The Human Skeleton; a Manual for Archaeologists. National
            Museum of Canada, Ottawa.

3088 1968 Late Paleolithic Skeletal Remains from Nubia. In F.
            Wendorf, ed., The Prehistory of Nubia II:996-1040.
            Southern Methodist University Press, Dallas.

ANGEL, L.

3089 1944 Greek Teeth: Ancient and Modern. Human Biology 16:283-297.

ARMELAGOS, G.J., J.H. MIELKE, and J. WINTER

3090 1971 Bibliography of Human Paleopathology. Department of
            Anthropology, University of Massachusetts. Research
            Reports 8.

ATKINSON, R.J.C., C.M. PIGGOTT, and N.K. SANDERS

3091 1951 Excavations at Dorchester, Oxon. Ashmolean Museum,
            Oxford.

BABY, R.S.

3092 1954 Hopewell Cremation Practices. Ohio Historical Society,
            Papers in Archaeology 1. Columbus.

BAESSLER, A.

3093 1906 Peruanische Mumien. Untersuchunger mit X-Strahlen. 15
            plates with explanatory text. E. Scheuer, Inc., New York.

BARRINGTON, D.

3094 1783 Particulars Relative to a Human Skeleton, and the Garments
            That Were Found Thereon When Dug Out of a Bog at the Foot
            of Drumkeragh, a Mountain in the County of Moira's
            Estate, in the Autumn of 1780. Archaeologia 7:90-110.

BASS, W.M., III

3095 1964 The Variation in Physical Types of the Prehistoric Plains
            Indians. Plains Anthropologist, Memoir 1:9-24.

3096 1972 Human Osteology: A Laboratory and Field Manual of the
            Human Skeleton. Special Publication, Missouri Archaeo-
            logical Society.

BENTZEN, C.B.

3097   1942   An Inexpensive Method of Recovering Skeletal Material
              for Museum Display. American Antiquity 8:176-178.

BROTHWELL, D.R.

3098   1961   Cannibalism in Early Britain. Antiquity 35:304-307.

3099   1961   The People of Mount Carmel. Proceedings, Prehistoric
              Society 27:155-159.

3100   1962   Digging up Bones. British Museum of Natural History,
              London.

BROTHWELL, D.R., T. MOLLESON, and C. METREWELI

3101   1968   Radiological Aspects of Normal Variation in Earlier
              Skeletons: An Explanatory Study. In D.R. Brothwell, ed.,
              The Skeletal Biology of Earlier Human Populations:149-
              172. Pergamon Press, New York.

BUDGE, E.A.W.

3102   1977   The Mummy. Collier Books, New York.

COCKBURN, A., et al.

3103   1975   Autopsy of an Egyptian Mummy. Science 187:1155-1160.

COLLINS, M.B.

3104   1975   Excavation and Recording of Human Physical Remains. In
              T.R. Hester, R.F. Heizer, and J.A. Graham, Field Methods
              in Archaeology:163-182. Mayfield, Palo Alto, Cal.

COOK, S.F.

3105   1951   The Fossilization of Human Bone: Calcium, Phosphate and
              Carbonate. University of California Publications in
              American Archaeology and Ethnology 40(6).

COOK, S.F., and R.F. HEIZER

3106   1952   The Fossilization of Bone: Organic Components and Water.
              University of California Archaeological Survey, Report 17.
              Berkeley.

3107   1959   The Chemical Analysis of Fossil Bone: Individual Variation.
              American Journal of Physical Anthropology 17:109-115.

COOK, S.F., S.T. BROOKS, and H. EZRA-COHN

3108   1961   The Process of Fossilization. Southwestern Journal of
              Anthropology 17:355-364.

CRAIN, J.B.

3109   1971   Human Paleopathology: A Bibliographic List. Sacramento
              Anthropological Society Paper 12.

DAHLBERG, A.A.

3110   1951   Dentition of the American Indian. In W.S. Laughlin, ed.,

Papers on the Physical Anthropology of the American
Indian:137-176. Viking Fund, New York.

DERRY, D.E.

3111   1934   An X-ray Examination of the Mummy of King Amenophis I.
              Annales du Service des Antiquités de l'Égypte 34:47-48.

FEJFAR, O.

3112   1969   Human Remains from the Early Pleistocene in Czechoslo-
              vakia. Current Anthropology 10(2-3):170-174.

GEJUALL, N.G.

3113   1963   Cremations. In D. Brothwell and E. Higgs, eds., Science
              in Archaeology:379-390. Thames and Hudson, London.

GENOVÉS, S.

3114   1962   Introducción al Diagnóstico de la Edad y del Sexo en
              Restos Oseos Prehistóricos. Universidad Nacional
              Autonoma de México. Cuidad Universitaria, México.

GOULD, R.A.

3115   1963   Aboriginal California Burial and Cremation Practices.
              University of California Archaeological Survey, Report
              60:149-168. Berkeley.

HAMY, E.T.

3116   1870   Précis de Paléontologie Humaine. J.B. Baillière, Paris.

HANNA, R.E., and S.L. WASHBURN

3117   1953   The Determination of the Sex of Skeletons as Illustrated
              by a Study of the Eskimo Pelvis. Human Biology 25:21-27.

HARRIS, J.E., et al.

3118   1978   Mummy of the "Elder Lady" in the Tomb of Amenhotep II:
              Egyptian Museum Catalog Number 61070. Science 200:1149-
              1151.

HARRISON, R.G., and A.B. ABDALLA

3119   1972   The Remains of Tutankhamun. Antiquity 46(181):8-14.

HOOTEN, E.A.

3120   1930   The Indians of Pecos Pueblo: A Study of Their Skeletal
              Remains. Yale University Press, New Haven.

HOWELLS, W.W.

3121   1938   Prehistoric Craniology of Britain. Antiquity 12(47):
              332-388.

HOYME, L.E., and W.M. BASS

3122   1962   Human Skeletal Remains from the Tollifero (Ha 6) and
              Clarksville (Mc 14) Sites, John H. Kerr Reservoir Basin,
              Virginia. Bureau of American Ethnology, Bulletin 182:
              329-400. Washington, D.C.

HRDLIČKA, A.

3123 1930 The Skeletal Remains of Early Man. Smithsonian Institu-
            tion, Washington, D.C.

HUMPHREYS, H.

3124 1951 Dental Evidence in Archaeology. Antiquity 25(97):16-18.

KEEN, J.A.

3125 1950 A Study of the Difference Between Male and Female Skulls.
            American Journal of Physical Anthropology 8:65-79.

KENNEDY, K.A.R.

3126 1960 The Dentition of Indian Crania of the Early and Late
            Archaeological Horizons in Central California. University
            of California Archaeological Survey, Report 50:41-50.
            Berkeley.

3127 1965 Human Skeletal Material from Ceylon, with an Analysis
            of the Island's Prehistoric and Contemporary Populations.
            Bulletin, British Museum (Natural History) Geology 11(4):
            137-213.

KROEBER, A.L.

3128 1927 Disposal of the Dead. American Anthropologist 29:308-315.

LENGYEL, I.

3129 1968 Biochemical Aspects of Early Skeletons. In D.R. Brothwell,
            ed., The Skeletal Biology of Earlier Human Populations:
            271-287. Pergamon Press, New York.

LYNE, W.C.

3130 1916 The Significance of the Radiographs of the Piltdown Teeth.
            Proceedings, Royal Society of Medicine 9(3):33-62.

McKERN, T.W., and E.H. MUNRO

3131 1959 A Statistical Technique for Classifying Human Skeletal
            Remains. American Antiquity 24:375-382.

McLEAN, F.C.

3132 1968 Bone; Fundamentals of the Physiology of Skeletal Tissue.
            University of Chicago Press, Chicago.

MATSON, A.G.

3133 1936 A Procedure for the Serological Determination of Blood
            Relationship of Ancient and Modern People with Special
            Reference to the American Indians. Journal of Immunology
            30(6):359-370.

MOLNAR, S.

3134 1972 Tooth Wear and Culture: A Survey of Tooth Functions Among
            Some Prehistoric Populations. Current Anthropology 13(5):
            511-526.

PIGGOTT, S.

3135 1962 The West Kennett Long Barrow: Excavations 1955-56. Appendix II. Analysis of Cremations, Great Britain Ministry of Works, Archaeological Reports 4. London.

POWELL, B.W.

3136 1970 Aboriginal Trephination: Case from Southern New England? Science 170:732-734.

SANDISON, A.T.

3137 1963 The Study of Mummified and Dried Human Tissues. In D. Brothwell and E. Higgs, eds., Science in Archaeology:413-425. Thames and Hudson, London.

3138 1968 Pathological Changes in the Skeletons of Earlier Populations Due to Acquired Disease, and Difficulties in Their Interpretation. In D.R. Brothwell, ed., The Skeletal Biology of Earlier Human Populations. Pergamon Press, N.Y.

SAYLES, E.B.

3139 1937 Disposal of the Dead. Gila Pueblo, Medallion Papers 25: 91-100.

SMITH, M.

3140 1960 Blood Groups of the Ancient Dead. Science 131:699-702.

SNOW, C.E.

3141 1948 Indian Knoll Skeletons of Site Oh-2, Ohio County, Kentucky. Univ. of Kentucky, Reports in Anthropology 4(3): Part II.

STEWART, T.D.

3142 1970 Evaluation of Evidence from the Skeleton. In F.E. Camps, ed., Gradwohl's Legal Medicine:123-154. John Wright & Sons, Bristol.

STEWART, T.D., and M. TROTTER

3143 1954 Basic Readings on the Identification of Human Skeletons: Estimation of Age. Wenner-Gren Foundation, New York.

SWEDLUND, A.C., and W.D. WADE

3144 1972 Laboratory Methods in Physical Anthropology. Prescott College Press, Prescott, Ariz.

THIEME, F.P., and C.M. OTTEN

3145 1957 The Unreliability of Blood Typing Aged Bone. American Journal of Physical Anthropology 15:387-398.

THIEME, F.P., and W.J. SCHULL

3146 1957 Sex Determination from the Skeleton. Human Biology 29: 242-273.

TOULOUSE, J.H., Jr.

3147 1944 Cremation Among the Indians of New Mexico. American Antiquity 10:65-74.

von KOENIGSWALD, G.H.R.

3148 1965 Meeting Prehistoric Man. Harpers, New York.

WEINER, J.S.

3149 1954 Skeletons: Some Remarks on Their Value to the Human Biologist. Antiquity 112:197-200.

WELLS, C.

3150 1960 A Study of Cremation. Antiquity 34:29-37.

WELLS, L.H.

3151 1958 Burial Customs and Human Remains in Archaeology. South African Archaeological Bulletin 13(51):119-120.

WILKINSON, R.G.

3152 1975 Techniques of Ancient Skull Surgery. Natural History 84(8):94-101.

b. PALEOPATHOLOGY

ANGEL, J.L.

3153 1947 The Length of Life in Ancient Greece. Journal of Gerontology 2:18-24.

ARMELAGOS, G.J.

3154 1969 Disease in Ancient Nubia. Science 163:255-259.

ARMELAGOS, G.J., J.H. MIELKE, and J. WINTER

3155 1971 Bibliography of Human Paleopathology. Department of Anthropology, University of Massachusetts, Research Reports 8.

AYNESWORTH, K.H.

3156 1936 Flint Arrowhead Wounds of Bones as Shown in Skeletons in Central Texas. Bulletin, Central Texas Archaeological Society 2:74-80.

BARR, T.P.

3157 1968 Arrow Wounds. Kansas Anthropological Association Newsletter 13(9).

BOURKE, J.B.

3158 1967 A Review of the Paleopathology of the Arthritic Diseases.
            In D. Brothwell and A.T. Sandison, eds., Diseases in
            Antiquity. C.C. Thomas, Springfield, Ill.

BROTHWELL, D.

3159 1971 Forensic Aspects of the So-Called Neolithic Skeleton Q1
            from Maiden Castle, Dorset. World Archaeology 3(2):233-
            241.

BROTHWELL, D.R., and R. POWERS

3160 1968 Congenital Malformations of the Skeleton in Earlier Man.
            In D.R. Brothwell, ed., The Skeletal Biology of Earlier
            Human Populations:173-204. Pergamon Press, New York.

BROTHWELL, D., and A.T. SANDISON

3161 1967 Disease in Antiquity: A Survey of the Diseases, Injuries
            and Surgery of Early Populations. C.C. Thomas, Spring-
            field, Ill.

BROTHWELL, D., D. MORSE, and P.J. UCKO

3162 1964 Tuberculosis in Ancient Egypt. American Review of
            Respiratory Diseases 90(4).

COCKBURN, T.A.

3163 1971 Infectious Diseases in Ancient Populations. Current
            Anthropology 12(1):45-62.

COURVILLE, C.B.

3164 1950 Cranial Injuries in Prehistoric Man with Particular
            Reference to Neanderthals. Yearbook of Physical Anthro-
            pology 6:185-205.

CRAIN, J.B.

3165 1966 Population Dynamics, Disease, and Paleopathology. Cornell
            Journal of Social Relations 1:25-38.

3166 1971 Human Paleopathology: A Bibliographic List. Sacramento
            Anthropological Society Paper 12.

EMERY, G.T.

3167 1963 Dental Pathology and Archaeology. Antiquity 37(148):
            274-281.

GOLDSTEIN, M.S.

3168 1957 Skeletal Pathology of Early Indians in Texas. American
            Journal of Physical Anthropology 15:299-311.

3169 1970 The Paleopathology of Human Skeletal Remains. In D.
            Brothwell and E. Higgs, eds., Science in Archaeology:
            480-489. 2nd ed. Praeger, New York.

HANEY, P.

3170 1974 Atlatl Elbow in Central California Prehistoric Cultures.
     In R. Kautz, ed., Readings in Archaeological Method and
     Technique:30-34. Center for Archaeological Research at
     Davis, Publication 4. University of California, Davis.

HARRIS, J.E.

3171 1972 X-raying the Pharoahs. Scribner's, New York.

HARRISON, R.G., and A.B. ABDALLA

3172 1972 The Remains of Tutankhamun. Antiquity 46:8-15.

HOFFMAN, J.M., and L. BRUNKER

3173 1976 Studies in California Paleopathology. University of
     California, Contributions of the Archaeological Research
     Facility 30.

INSKEEP, R.R.

3174 1969 Health Hazards and Healing in Antiquity. South African
     Archaeological Bulletin 24:21-39.

JANSSENS, P.

3175 1970 Palaeopathology: Diseases and Injuries of Prehistoric
     Man. John Baker, London.

JARCHO, S.

3176 1964 Lead in the Bones of Prehistoric Lead-Glaze Potters.
     American Antiquity 30:94-96.

3177 1964 Some Observations on Disease in Prehistoric North America.
     Bulletin of the History of Medicine 38:1-19.

KROGMAN, W.M.

3178 1940 The Skeletal and Dental Pathology of an Early Iranian
     Site. Bulletin of the History of Medicine 8:28-48.

3179 1962 The Human Skeleton in Forensic Medicine. C.C. Thomas,
     Springfield, Ill.

KUNITZ, S.J., and R.C. EULER

3180 1972 Aspects of Paleoepidemiology in the Southwest. Prescott
     College Press, Prescott, Ariz.

LEIGH, R.W.

3181 1928 Dental Pathology of Aboriginal California. University of
     California, Publications in American Archaeology and
     Ethnology 23:399-440. Berkeley.

MOLNAR, S.

3182 1970 A Consideration of Some Cultural Factors Involved in the
     Production of Human Tooth Wear. Journal, Steward Anthro-
     pological Society 2(1):10-18.

MONTAGU, M.F.A.

3183 1960 Introduction to Physical Anthropology. C.C. Thomas,
            Springfield, Ill.

MOODIE, R.L.

3184 1923 Paleopathology: An Introduction to the Study of Ancient
            Evidence of Disease. University of Illinois Press,
            Urbana.

MORSE, D.

3185 1969 Ancient Disease in the Midwest. Illinois State Museum,
            Reports of Investigations 15.

NEUMANN, G.K.

3186 1940 Evidence for the Antiquity of Scalping from Central
            Illinois. American Antiquity 5:287-289.

PENN, W.S.

3187 1967 Possible Evidence from Springhead for the Great Plague
            of A.D. 166. Archaeologia Cantiana 82:263-271.

PIGGOTT, S.

3188 1940 A Trepanned Skull of the Beaker Period from Dorset and
            the Practice of Trepanning in Prehistoric Europe. Pro-
            ceedings, Prehistoric Society 6(1):112-132.

RONEY, J.G.

3189 1959 Paleopathology of a California Archeological Site.
            Bulletin of the History of Medicine 33:97-109.

SANDISON, A.T.

3190 1968 Pathological Changes in the Skeletons of Earlier Popula-
            tions Due to Acquired Disease, and Difficulties in Their
            Interpretation. In D.R. Brothwell, ed., The Skeletal
            Biology of Earlier Human Populations:205-244. Pergamon
            Press, New York.

SAUL, F.R.

3191 1972 The Human Skeleton Remains of Altar de Sacrificios: An
            Osteobiographic Analysis. Papers, Peabody Museum
            63(2). Cambridge, Mass.

SINGER, R.

3192 1961 Pathology in the Temporal Bone of the Boskop Skull.
            South African Archaeological Society Bulletin 16(63):103-
            104.

3193 1962 A Skeleton with Diaphyseal Aclasis. South African
            Archaeological Bulletin 17(65):14-19.

SNYDER, R.G.

3194 1960 Hyperodontia in Prehistoric Southwest Indians. Southwest
            Journal of Anthropology 16:492-502.

UBELAKER, D.H.

3195 1978 Human Skeletal Remains: Excavation, Analysis, Interpreta-
            tion. Aldine, Chicago.

WADE, W.D., ed.

3196 1967 Miscellaneous Papers in Paleopathology: I. Museum of
            Northern Arizona, Flagstaff.

WAKEFIELD, E.G., and S.C. DELLINGER

3197 1936 Diet of the Bluff Dwellers of the Ozark Mountains and Its
            Skeletal Effects. Annals of Internal Medicine 9:1412-1418.

WELLS, C.

3198 1964 Bones, Bodies and Disease. Thames and Hudson, London.

3199 1967 A New Approach to Paleopathology: Harris's Lines. In
            D. Brothwell and A.T. Sandison, eds., Diseases in
            Antiquity:390-404. C.C. Thomas, Springfield, Ill.

11. Rock Art and Ancient Writing Analysis

a. ROCK ART

i. Methodology

BORCHERS, P.E.

3200 1977 Photogrammetric Recording of Cultural Resources. National
            Park Service Publication 186, Office of Archeological
            Historic Preservation, U.S. Department of Interior,
            Washington, D.C.

BRECHWOLDT, G.H.

3201 1969 The Use of the International System of Heraldic Hatchings
            for the Transcription of Bushman Paintings. South African
            Archaeological Bulletin 19(76), Pt. 4:111-112.

CLEGG, J.K.

3202 1971 A Metaphysical Approach to the Study of Aboriginal Rock
            Painting. Mankind 8(1):37-41.

CLOUTEN, N.

3203 1974 The Application of Photogrammetry to Recording Rock Art.
            Newsletter 1, Australian Institute of Aboriginal Studies:
            33-39. Canberra.

3204 1976 Photogrammetry and the Measurement of Rock Form and

Aboriginal Art. Newsletter 6, Australian Institute of Aboriginal Studies:33-45. Canberra.

3205 1977 Further Photogrammetric Recordings of Early Man Shelters, Cape York. Newsletter 7, Australian Institute of Aboriginal Studies:54-59. Canberra.

COOK, C.K.

3206 1961 The Copying and Recording of Rock-Paintings. South African Archaeological Society Bulletin 16(62):61-65.

De GIECO, A.M.L.

3207 1965 Sobre la Aplicación de Métodos Estadísticos al Estudio del Arte Repestre. Anales de Arqueología y Etnología, Tomo XX, Mendoza, Argentina.

GOODWIN, A.J.H.

3208 1956 Prehistoric Paintings: Preservation and Perpetration. South African Archaeological Bulletin 11(43):73-76.

JOHNSON, T.

3209 1958 Facsimile Tracing and Redrawing of Rock-Paintings. South African Archaeological Bulletin 13(50):67-69.

JONES, T.E.H.

3210 1969 Problems in Recording Rock Paintings in the Pre-Cambrian Shield. Verhandlungen des XXXVIII. Internationalen Amerikanistenkongresses, Stuttgart-München 1:109-116. Kommissionsverlag Klaus Renner, München, Germany.

LORANDI de GIECO, A.M.

3211 1965 Sobre la Aplicación de Métodos Estadísticos al Estudio del Arte Repestre. Anales de Arquelogía y Etnología, Universidad Nacional de Cuyo, Mendoza, Argentina 20:7-26.

MAGGS, T.M. O'C.

3212 1967 A Quantitative Analysis of the Rock Art from a Sample Area in the Western Cape. South African Journal of Science 63(3):100-104.

NEWCOMB, W.W., Jr.

3213 1976 Pecos River Pictographs: The Development of an Art Form. In C.E. Cleland, ed., Cultural Change and Continuity: Essays in Honor of James Bennett Griffin. Academic Press, New York.

SCOGINGS, D.A.

3214 1975 Photogrammetric Recording of Petroglyphs. Wild Reporter 9:15-16. Heerbrugg, Switzerland.

TEN RAS, E.

3215 1971 Dead Art and Living Society: A Study of Rockpaintings in a Social Context. Mankind 8(1):42-58.

VINNICOMBE, P.

3216 1967 Rock-Painting Analysis. South African Archaeological Bulletin 22(88), Pt. 4:129-141.

WALKER, M.J.

3217 1970 An Analysis of British Petroglyphs. Science and Archaeology 3.

WILLCOX, A.R.

3218 1962 Prehistoric Art. In B.D. Malan and H.B.S. Cooke, eds., The Contribution of C. van Riet Lowe to Prehistory in Southern Africa. South African Archaeological Bulletin, Supplement to 17(65):57-63.

ii. General Surveys and Major Reports

ACKERMAN, R.E.

3219 1965 Art or Magic: The Incised Pebbles from Southern Alaska. Michigan Archaeologist 11(3-4):181-188.

ANATI, E.

3220 1955 Rock Engravings of the Central Negev. Archaeology 8(1): 31-42.

3221 1958 Rock Engravings in the Italian Alps. Archaeology 11(1): 30-39.

3222 1968 Rock-Art in Central Arabia: Tome 3(1). The Oval-Headed People of Arabia. Inst. Orientaliste, Univ. de Louvain, Belgium.

BARD, J.C., F. ASARO, and R.F. HEIZER

3223 1978 Perspectives on the Dating of Prehistoric Great Basin Petroglyphs by Neutron Activation Analysis. Archaeometry 20:85-88.

BÉGOUEN, C.

3224 1929 The Magic Origin of Prehistoric Art. Antiquity 3:5-19.

BERENGUER, M.

3225 1973 Prehistoric Man and His Art: The Caves of Ribadesella. Trans. by M. Heron. Souvenir Press, London.

3226 1974 Prehistoric Man and His Art. Noyes Press, Park Ridge, N.J.

BLANC, A.C.

3227 1953 The Finest Paleolithic Drawings of the Human Figure-- Revealed by the Demolition of Artillery Shells in a Sicilian Cave. Illustrated London News 223:187-189.

BRANDT, J.D., and R.A. WILLIAMSON

3228 1979 The 1054 Supernova and Native American Rock Art. Archaeo-
            astronomy 1. Science History Publications Ltd., Bucks,
            England.

BREUIL, A.H.

3229 1952 Four Hundred Centuries of Cave Art. Centre d'Études et
            de Documentation Préhistoriques, Montignac.

3230 1955 The Rock Paintings of Southern Africa. Trianon Press,
            London.

BURKITT, M.C.

3231 1928 South Africa's Past in Stone and Paint. University
            Press, Cambridge, England.

3232 1929 Rock Carvings in the Italian Alps. Antiquity 3:155-164.

BUSINK, T.A.

3233 1957- Darstellungen Altmesopo Amischer Bauworker. Jeol 15:
      1958   219-231.

BUTZER, K.W., et al.

3234 1979 Dating and Context of Rock Engravings in Southern Africa.
            Science 203:1201-1214.

CAMPBELL, R.G.

3235 1969 Dating Prehistoric Rock Art of Southeastern Colorado.
            Southwestern Lore 35(1):1-10.

CLARK, D.W.

3236 1970 Petroglyphs on Afognak Island, Kodiak Group, Alaska.
            Anthropological Papers of the University of Alaska 15(1):
            13-17.

CLARK, G.

3237 1937 Scandinavian Rock-Engravings. Antiquity 11(41):56-59.

COOKE, C.K.

3238 1963 The Painting Sequence in the Rock Art of Southern
            Rhodesia. South African Archaeological Bulletin 18(72),
            Pt. 4:172-175.

3239 1965 Handprints in Southern Rhodesian Rock Art. South African
            Archaeological Bulletin 20(1):46-47.

3240 1969 Rock Art of Southern Africa. Books of Africa, Cape Town.

3241 1970 Shelters for Late Stone Age Man Shown in the Paintings
            of Rhodesia. South African Archaeological Bulletin 25
            (98), Pt. 2:65-66.

COY, F.E., Jr., and T.C. FULLER

3242 1966 Petroglyphs of North Central Kentucky. Tennessee Archaeologist 22(2):53-67.

DANIEL, G.

3243 1958 The Minnesota Petroglyph. Antiquity 32(128):264-267.

DAVIS, J.V., and K.S. TONESS

3244 1974 A Rock Art Inventory at Hueco Tanks State Park, Texas. El Paso Archeological Society, Special Reports 12.

DELGADO, R.

3245 1976 Los Petroglifos Venezolanos. Monte Avila Editores, Caracas.

DEWDNEY, S.

3246 1970 Dating Rock Art in the Canadian Shield Region. Occasional Paper, Royal Ontario Museum Art and Archaeology 24.

FRASSETTO, M.F.

3247 1960 A Preliminary Report on Petroglyphs in Puerto Rico. American Antiquity 25:381-391.

GARCIA, L.P., and E.R. PERELLO, eds.

3248 1964 Prehistoric Art of the Western Mediterranean and the Sahara. Viking Fund Publication in Anthropology 39.

GEBHARD, D.

3249 1960 Prehistoric Paintings of the Diablo Region of Western Texas. Roswell Museum and Art Center, Publications in Art and Science 3. Roswell, N.M.

GOODALL, E.

3250 1946 Domestic Animals in Rock Art. Transactions, Rhodesian Science Association 41:57-62. Salisbury.

GOODALL, E., C.K. COOKE, and J.D. CLARK

3251 1959 Prehistoric Rock Art of the Federation of Rhodesia and Nyasaland. National Publication Trust, Rhodesia and Nyasaland.

GRANT, C.

3252 1965 The Rock Paintings of the Chumash. University of California Press, Berkeley.

3253 1967 Rock Art of the American Indian. Thomas Y. Crowell, New York.

3254 1978 Canyon de Chelly: Its People and Rock Art. University of Arizona Press, Tucson.

GRANT, C., J.W. BAIRD, and J.K. PRINGLE

3255 1968 Rock Drawings of the Coso Range, Inyo County, California.
            Maturango Museum, Publication 4. Maturango Press, China
            Lake, Cal.

GRAZIOSI, P.

3256 1960 Palaeolithic Art. McGraw-Hill, New York.

3257 1964 New Discoveries of Rock Paintings in Ethiopia. Antiquity
            38(150):91-98.

3258 1964 New Discoveries of Rock Paintings in Ethiopia. Antiquity
            38(151):187-190.

GRIEDER, T.

3259 1966 Periods in Pecos Style Pictographs. American Antiquity
            31:710-720.

HAGEN, A.

3260 1965 Rock Carvings in Norway. Oslo.

HARNER, M.J.

3261 1953 Gravel Pictographs of the Lower Colorado River Region.
            University of California Archaeological Survey Report
            20:1-32.

HEINE-GELDERN, R., and G. EKHOLM

3262 1951 Significant Parallels in the Symbolic Arts of Southern
            Asia and Middle America. In The Civilizations of Ancient
            America; Selected Papers of the XXIX International Congress
            of Americanists:299-309.

HEIZER, R.F., and M.A. BAUMHOFF

3263 1959 Great Basin Petroglyphs and Prehistoric Game Trails.
            Science 129:904-905.

3264 1962 Prehistoric Rock Art of Nevada and Eastern California.
            University of California Press, Berkeley.

HEIZER, R.F., and C.W. CLEWLOW

3265 1973 Prehistoric Rock Art of California. 2 vols. Ballena
            Press, Ramona, Cal.

HENSON, B.B.

3266 1976 A Southeastern Ceremonial Complex Petroglyph Site. Journal
            of the Alabama Archaeological Society 22(2):174-185.

HILL, B., and R. HILL

3267 1975 Indian Petroglyphs of the Pacific Northwest. University
            of Washington Press, Seattle.

HOLLIMAN, R.B.

3268 1967 Engraved Basalt Stones from the Great Salt Desert, Utah.
            Southwestern Lore 32(4):86-87.

3269 1969 Further Studies on Incised Stones from the Great Salt
            Lake Desert, Utah. Southwestern Lore 35(2):24-25.

JACKSON, A.T.

3270 1938 Picture-Writing of Texas Indians. Anthropological Papers
            2, University of Texas Publication 3809, Austin.

JOHNSON, T.

3271 1957 An Experiment with Cave-Painting Media. South African
            Archaeological Bulletin 47:98-101.

3272 1960 Rock-Painting of Ships. South African Archaeological
            Bulletin 15(59):111-113.

KEITHAHN, E.L.

3273 1940 The Petroglyphs of Southeastern Alaska. American Antiquity
            6:123-132.

KEYSER, J.D.

3274 1979 The Plains Indian War Complex and the Rock Art of Writing-
            on-Stone, Alberta, Canada. Journal of Field Archaeology
            6(1):41-48.

KOSOK, P., and M. REICHE

3275 1949 Ancient Drawings on the Desert of Peru. Archaeology 2:
            206-215.

KUHN, H.

3276 1956 The Rock Pictures of Europe. Sedgwick and Jackson, London.

LAMING, A.

3277 1959 Lascaux: Paintings and Engravings. Penguin Books A-419,
            Baltimore.

LAWTON, S.P.

3278 1962 Petroglyphs and Pictographs in Oklahoma: An Introduction.
            Plains Anthropologist 7(17):189-193.

LEASON, P.A.

3279 1939 A New View of the Western European Group of Quaternary
            Cave Art. Proceedings, Prehistoric Society 5(1):51-60.

LEE, D.N., and H.C. WOODHOUSE

3280 1966 An Interim Report on the Study of Dress Depicted in the
            Rock Paintings of Southern Africa. South African Journal
            of Science 62(4):114-118.

LOTHSON, G.A.

3281 1976 The Jeffers Petroglyphs Site: A Survey and Analysis.
            Minnesota Historical Society, The Minnesota Prehistoric
            Archaeology Series, St. Paul.

MacCURDY, G.G.

3282 1916 The Dawn of Art; Cave Paintings, Engravings and Sculptures.
            Art and Archaeology 4:71-90.

McKEE, E.H., and D.H. THOMAS

3283 1972 Petroglyph Slabs from Central Nevada. Plateau 44(3):85-
            104.

MADDOCK, K.

3284 1970 Imagery and Social Structure at Two Rock Art Sites.
            Anthropological Forum 2(4):444-463.

MALAN, B.D.

3285 1957 Old and New Rock Engravings in Natal, South Africa: A
            Zulu Game. Antiquity 123:153-154.

3286 1965 The Classification and Distribution of Rock Art in South
            Africa. South African Journal of Science 61(12):427-430.

MASSON, J.R.

3287 1961 Rock-Paintings in Swaziland. South African Archaeological
            Bulletin 16(64):130-135.

MEIGHAN, C.W.

3288 1965 The Painted Caves of Baja. Desert 28(7):16-20.

3289 1969 Indian Art and History; the Testimony of Prehispanic
            Rock Painting in Baja California. Baja California
            Travel Series 13. Dawson's Book Shop, Los Angeles.

MEIGHAN, C.W., and V.L. PONTONI, eds.

3290 1978 Seven Rock Art Sites in Baja California. Ballena Press
            Publications on North American Rock Art 2. Socorro, N.M.

MINOR, R.

3291 1975 The Pit-and-Groove Petroglyph Style in Southern California.
            Ballena Press, Ramona, Cal.

MORIN-JEAN, A.

3292 1911 Les Dessins des Animaux en Grèce d'après les Vases Peints.
            Laurens, Paris.

MOSTNY, G.

3293 1964 Los Petroglifos de Angostura, Chile. Zeitschrift für
            Ethnologie 89(1):51-70.

MURRAY, W.B.

3294 1979 Description and Analysis of a Petroglyphic Tally County
Stone at Presa de la Mula, Nuevo Leon, Mexico. Mexicon
(March).

NAVARRETE, C.

3295 1974 The Olmec Rock Carvings at Pijijiapan, Chiapas, Mexico.
Papers of the New World Archaeological Society 35.
Brigham Young University, Provo, Utah.

NESBITT, P.E.

3296 1968 Stylistic Locales and Ethnographic Groups: Petroglyphs
of the Lower Snake River. Idaho State University Museum,
Occasional Papers 23. Pocatello, Idaho.

NEWBOLD, D.

3297 1928 Rock-Pictures and Archaeology in the Libyan Desert.
Antiquity 2:261-291.

PAGER, H.

3298 1975 Stone Age Myth and Magic as Documented in the Rock
Paintings of South Africa. Akademische Druck und Verlags-
anstalt, Graz, Austria.

PARADISI, U.

3299 1965 Prehistoric Art in the Gebel el-Akhdar Cyrenaica.
Antiquity 39(154):95-101.

PARKINGTON, J.

3300 1969 Symbolism in Paleolithic Cave Art. South African
Archaeological Bulletin 24(93), Pt. 1:3-13.

PEEL, R.F.

3301 1939 Rock-Paintings from the Libyan Desert. Antiquity 13(52):
389-402.

POLLAK-ELTZ, A.

3302 1975 Venezuelan Petroglyphs. Akademische Druck und Verlags-
anstalt, Graz, Austria.

RAVINES, R.

3303 1967- Piedras Pintadas del Sur del Perú. Revista del Museo
1968 Nacional 35:312-319.

REICHE, M.

3304 1949 Los Dibujos Gigantescos en el Suelo de Las Pampas de
Nazca y Palpa. Editoria Medica Peruana, Lima.

3305 1969 Giant Ground-Drawings on the Peruvian Desert. Verhandlungen
des XXXVIII. Internationalen Amerikanistenkongresses,

Stuttgart-München 1:379-384. Kommissionsverlag Klaus
Renner, München, Germany.

RIDDELL, W.H.

3306 1942 Palaeolithic Paintings of the Magdalenian Period. Antiquity 16(62):134-150.

RIDE, W.D.L., R.M. BERNDT, et al.

3307 1964 Rock Art in Australia: Report on the Aboriginal Engravings
and Flora and Fauna of Depuch Island, Western Australia.
Western Australia Museum Special Publication 2.

RITCHIE, C.

3308 1979 Rock Art of Africa. A.S. Barnes, South Brunswick, N.J.

ROSENTHAL, E., and A.J.H. GOODWIN

3309 1953 Cave Artists of South Africa. A.A. Balkema, Cape Town,
S. Africa.

RUDNER, J., and I. RUDNER

3310 1970 The Hunter and His Art; a Survey of Rock Art in Southern
Africa. C. Struik, Cape Town.

SANGUINETTI de CATALDO, N.

3311 1968 Algunos Petroglifos de Piguchen. Valparaiso, Chile.
Museo de Historia Natural, Anales 1:249-259.

SCHAAFSMA, P.

3312 1965 Southwest Indian Pictographs and Petroglyphs. Museum of
New Mexico Press, Santa Fe.

3313 1971 The Rock Art of Utah. A Study from the Donald Scott
Collection, Peabody Museum, Harvard University, Cambridge,
Mass.

3314 1975 Rock Art and Ideology of the Mimbres and Jornada Mogollon.
The Artifact 13(3):1-14.

3315 1975 Rock Art in New Mexico. University of New Mexico Press,
Albuquerque.

SEDDON, J.D., and P. VINNICOMBE

3316 1967 Domestic Animals, Rock-Art and Dating. South African
Archaeological Bulletin 22(87), Pt. 3:112-113.

SIEGRIST, R., ed.

3317 1972 Prehistoric Petroglyphs and Pictographs in Utah. Utah
State Historical Society, Salt Lake City.

SIM, I.M.

3318 1969 A Gallery of Cave Art in the MacDonald River District, New
South Wales. Archaeology and Physical Anthropology in
Oceania 4(2):144-180.

SMITH, P.E.L.

3319   1968   Problems and Possibilities of the Prehistoric Rock Art
              of Northern Africa. African Historical Studies I(I).
              Boston.

STEWARD, J.H.

3320   1929   Petroglyphs of California and Adjoining States. University
              of California, Publications in American Archaeology and
              Ethnology 24(2). Berkeley.

SWAUGER, J.L.

3321   1962   Canadian Rock Drawings. Pennsylvania Archaeologist 32(2):
              84-88.

3322   1963   The East Liverpool Petroglyph Data: A Tribute. Pennsyl-
              vania Archaeologist 33(3):127-129.

3323   1974   Rock Art of the Upper Ohio Valley. American Rock Painting
              and Petroglyphs 2. Akademische Druck und Verlagsanstalt,
              Graz, Austria.

TATUM, R.M.

3324   1946   Distributions and Bibliography of the Petroglyphs of the
              United States. American Antiquity 12:122-125.

TUNNELL, C.

3325   1970   American Indian Pictographs in the Amistad Reservoir Area,
              Val Verde County, Texas. Office of the State Archeologist
              Special Reports I. Texas Historical Survey Committee and
              Texas Historical Foundation.

TURNER, C.G., II

3326   1963   Petrographs of the Glen Canyon Region. Museum of
              Northern Arizona, Bulletin 38 (Glen Canyon Series 4).

3327   1971   Revised Dating for Early Rock Art of the Glen Canyon
              Region. American Antiquity 36(4):469-471.

UCKO, P., and A. ROSENFELD

3328   1967   Paleolithic Cave Art. McGraw-Hill, New York.

Van NOTEN, F.

3329   1973   Rock Art of Jebel Uweinat (Lybian Sahara). With Con-
              tributions by X. Misonne and H. Rhotbert. Akademische
              Druck und Verlagsanstalt, Graz, Austria.

Van RIET LOWE, C.

3330   1945   Colour in Prehistoric Rock Paintings. South African
              Archaeological Bulletin 1(1):13-18.

van WERLHOF, J.C.

3331   1965   Rock Art of Owens Valley, California. University of
              California Archaeological Survey Report 65. Berkeley.

VINNICOMBE, P.

3332 1961 A Painting of a Fish-Trap on Bamboo Mountain, Underberg
             District, Southern Natal. South African Archaeological
             Bulletin 16(63):114-115.

WALKER, M.

3333 1971 Spanish Levantine Rock Art. Man 6(4):553-589.

WALTERS, E.

3334 1971 Further Studies of Rock Art in Pecos and Crockett
             Counties (Texas). Transactions, Sixth Regional Archeo-
             logical Symposium for Southeastern New Mexico and Western
             Texas:9-38.

WEISBROD, R.L.

3335 1978 Rock Art Dating Methods. Journal of New World Archeaeology
             2(4):1-8.

WELLMAN, K.F.

3336 1972 Polydactylism in North American Indian Rock Art. Journal
             of the American Medical Association 219(12):1609.

3337 1979 A Survey of North American Indian Rock Art. Akademische
             Druck und Verlagsanstalt, Graz, Austria.

WILLCOX, A.R.

3338 1961 Rock Engravings in Tarkastad District. South African
             Archaeological Society Bulletin 16(61):22-27.

3339 1965 Petroglyphs of Domestic Animals. South African Archaeo-
             logical Bulletin 20(80), Pt. 4:214.

3340 1968 A Survey of Our Present Knowledge of Rock-Paintings in
             South Africa. South African Archaeological Bulletin 23
             (89), Pt. 1:20-23.

WINDELS, F.

3341 1949 The Lascaux Cave Paintings. Faber and Faber, London.

WINKLER, H.A.

3342 1938- Rock Drawings of Southern Upper Egypt. 2 vols. Egypt
      1939 Exploration Society, Archaeological Survey of Egypt,
             London.

WOODHOUSE, H.C.

3343 1966 Prehistoric Hunting Methods as Depicted in the Rock
             Paintings of Southern Africa. South African Journal of
             Science 62(6):169-171.

WOOLSTON, F.P., and P.J. TREZISE

3344 1969 Petroglyphs of Cape York Peninsula. Mankind 7(2):120-
             127.

b. ANCIENT WRITING

BARBER, E.J.W.

3345 1974 Archaeological Decipherment: A Handbook. Princeton University Press, Princeton, N.J.

BENSON, E.P., ed.

3346 1971 Mesoamerican Writing Systems: A Symposium Held at Dumbarton Oaks, October 30-31, 1971. Dumbarton Oaks, Washington, D.C.

BOARDMAN, J., and L.R. PALMER

3347 1964 The Knossos Tablets. Antiquity 38(149):45-51.

CHADWICK, J.

3348 1959 Minoan Linear A. Antiquity 33(132):269-278.

3349 1959 A Prehistoric Bureaucracy. Diogenes 26:7-18.

3350 1964 The Prehistory of the Greek Language. The Cambridge Ancient History, rev. ed., Vol. 2, chapter 39. University Press, Cambridge, England.

3351 1967 The Decipherment of Linear B. 2nd ed. University Press, Cambridge, England.

3352 1972 Life in Mycenaean Greece. Scientific American 227(4):36-44.

CHADWICK, J., et al., eds.

3353 1971 Knossos Tablets: A Transliteration. 4th ed. University Press, Cambridge, England.

CHAMPOLLION, J.F.

3354 1971 The Secret of the Rosetta Stone. In R.F. Heizer, Man's Discovery of His Past; a Sourcebook of Original Articles: 183-192. Peek Publications, Palo Alto, Cal.

CLEATOR, P.E.

3355 1962 Lost Languages. Mentor Book No. MT427, New York.

DIBBLE, C.E.

3356 1971 Writing in Central Mexico. Handbook of Middle American Indians 10(1):322-332.

DOBLHOFER, E.

3357 1959 Le Déchiffrement des Écritures. Arthaud, Paris.

EVANS, A.

3358 1909 Scripta Minoa. Clarendon Press, Oxford.

FRANKFORT, H.

3359 1939 Cylinder Seals. Macmillan and Co., London.

FRIEDRICH, J.

3360   1957   Extinct Languages. Philosophical Library, New York.

GELB, I.J.

3361   1963   A Study of Writing. Phoenix Books P109, University of
              Chicago Press, Chicago.

GRAHAM, I., and E. von EUW

3362   1975- Corpus of Maya Hieroglyphic Inscriptions. 5 vols. Pea-
       1979   body Museum of Archaeology and Ethnology, Harvard
              University, Cambridge, Mass.

HIGGINS, C.G., and W.K. PRITCHETT

3363   1965   Engraving Techniques in Attic Epigraphy. American Journal
              of Archaeology 69(4):367-371.

HOOKE, S.H.

3364   1937   The Early History of Writing. Antiquity 11(43):261-277.

KELLEY, D.H.

3365   1962   A History of the Decipherment of Maya Script. Anthropo-
              logical Linguistics 4(8).

3366   1976   Deciphering the Maya Script. The University of Texas
              Press, Austin.

KNOROZOV, Y.V.

3367   1958   The Problem of the Study of the Maya Hieroglyphic Writing.
              American Antiquity 23:284-291.

LEON-PORTILLA, M.

3368   1971   Pre-Hispanic Literature. Handbook of Middle American
              Indians 10(1):452-458.

MORLEY, S.G.

3369   1915   An Introduction to the Study of the Maya Hieroglyphs.
              Bureau of American Ethnology, Bulletin 57. Washington,
              D.C.

PIGGOTT, S.

3370   1960   Prehistory and Evolutionary Theory. In S. Tax, ed., The
              Evolution of Man:85-97. University of Chicago Press,
              Chicago.

POPE, M.

3371   1966   The Origins of Writing in the Near East. Antiquity 40:
              17-23.

3372   1976   The Story of Decipherment: From Egyptian Hieroglyphic
              to Linear B. Thames and Hudson, London.

RAWLINSON, H.C.

3373 1971 The Decipherment of Cuneiform. In R.F. Heizer, Man's Discovery of His Past; a Sourcebook of Original Articles: 194-195. Peek Publications, Palo Alto, Cal.

3374 1971 The Inscriptions of Assyria and Babylonia. In R.F. Heizer, Man's Discovery of His Past; a Sourcebook of Original Articles:196-199. Peek Publications, Palo Alto, Cal.

REUBINSON, H.C.

3375 1850 Notes on the Inscriptions of Assyria and Babylonia. Journal, Royal Asiatic Society of Arts, Britain and Ireland 12, Art. X:402-410. London.

SMITH, M.E.

3376 1973 Picture Writing from Ancient Southern Mexico. University of Oklahoma Press, Norman.

THOMPSON, J.E.S.

3377 1950 Maya Hieroglyphic Writing: Introduction. Carnegie Institution of Washington, Publication 589.

3378 1962 A Catalogue of Maya Hieroglyphs. University of Oklahoma Press, Norman.

3379 1972 A Commentary on the Dresden Codex: A Maya Hieroglyphic Book. American Philosophical Society Memoirs 93. Philadelphia.

WRIGHT, G.E., and D.N. FREEDMAN

3380 1961 The Biblical Archaeologist Reader. Anchor Books A250, Doubleday and Co., Garden City, N.Y.

12. Dating Methods

a. GENERAL

ATKINSON, R.J.C.

3381 1957 Worms and Weathering. Antiquity 33:219-233.

3382 1966 Moonshine on Stonehenge. Antiquity 40:212-216.

BARD, J.C., F. ASARO, and R.F. HEIZER

3383 1978 Perspectives on the Dating of Prehistoric Great Basin Petroglyphs by Neutron Activation Analysis. Archaeometry 20:85-88.

BAUMHOFF, M.A., and D.L. OLMSTED

3384 1963 Palaihnihan: Radiocarbon Support for Glottochronology. American Anthropologist 65:278-284.

BENNYHOFF, J.A., and R.F. HEIZER

3385 1958 Cross-Dating Great Basin Sites by Californian Shell Beads.
            University of California Archaeological Survey, Report
            42:60-92.

BERGSLAND, K., and H. VOGT

3386 1962 On the Validity of Glottochronology. Current Anthropology
            3:115-153.

BINFORD, L.R.

3387 1961 A New Method of Calculating Dates from Kaolin Pipe Stem
            Samples. Southeastern Archaeological Conference News-
            letter 9(1):19-21.

BOWEN, R.N.C.

3388 1958 The Exploration of Time. George Newnes, London.

BRAINERD, G.W.

3389 1951 The Place of Chronological Ordering in Archaeological
            Analysis. American Antiquity 16:301-313.

BRIGGS, L.J., and K.F. WEAVER

3390 1958 How Old Is It? National Geographic Magazine CXIV:
            234-255.

BULLEN, R.P.

3391 1968 Pottery, Radiocarbon Dates and Sea Level Rises. Pro-
            ceedings, 8th International Congress of Anthropological
            and Ethnological Sciences 3:168-169.

BURTON, D., J.B. POOLE, and R. REED

3392 1959 A New Approach to the Dating of the Dead Sea Scrolls.
            Nature 184:533-534.

CLOSS, M.P.

3393 1977 The Nature of the Maya Chronological Count. American
            Antiquity 42(1):18-27.

du TOIT, A.P.

3394 1964 Glass Beads as a Medium of Dating Archaeological Sites.
            South African Journal of Science 60(4):98-99.

FLEISCHER, R.L.

3395 1975 Advances in Fission Track Dating. World Archaeology
            7(2):136-150.

FLEISCHER, R.L., and P.B. PRICE

3396 1964 Glass Dating by Fission Fragment Tracks. Journal of Geo-
            physical Research 69:331-339.

FLEISCHER, R.L., P.B. PRICE, and R.M. WALKER

3397 1965 Fission-Track Dating of Bed I, Olduvai Gorge. Science 148:72-74.

FLEMING, S.J.

3398 1976 Dating in Archaeology: A Guide to Scientific Techniques. St. Martin's Press, New York.

GIDDINGS, J.L.

3399 1966 Cross-Dating in Archaeology of Northwestern Alaska. Science 153:127-135.

GRIFFIN, J.B.

3400 1955 Chronology and Dating Processes. In Yearbook of Anthropology:133-148. Wenner-Gren Foundation, New York.

HAMMOND, P.C.

3401 1975 Archaeometry and Time: A Review. Journal of Field Archaeology 1(3-4):329-336.

HEIZER, R.F.

3402 1953 Long-Range Dating in Archeology. In A.L. Kroeber, ed., Anthropology Today, an Encyclopedic Inventory:3-42. University of Chicago Press, Chicago.

3403 1965 Problems in Dating Lake Mojave Artifacts. Southwest Museum Masterkey 39:125-134.

HESTER, T.R.

3404 1973 Chronological Ordering of Great Basin Prehistory. Contributions, University of California, Archaeological Research Facility 17. Berkeley.

HUANG, W.H., and R.M. WALKER

3405 1967 Fossil Alpha-Particle Recoil Tracks: A New Method of Age Determination. Science 155:1103-1106.

JELINEK, A.J.

3406 1962 Use of the Cumulative Graph in Temporal Ordering. American Antiquity 28(2):241-243.

KERBY, M.D.

3407 1970 Archeological Dating Methods. Quarterly Bulletin of the Archeological Society of Virginia 25(1):28-34.

KIGOSHI, K.

3408 1967 Ionium Dating of Igneous Rocks. Science 156:932-934.

KRIEGER, A.D.

3409 1947 The Eastward Extension of Puebloan Datings Toward Cultures of the Mississippi Valley. American Antiquity 12:141-148.

MAUGH, T.H., II

3410 1979 Any Horse Trader Could Have Told You. Science 205:574.

MICHAEL, H.N., and E.K. RALPH, eds.

3411 1971 Dating Techniques for the Archaeologist. MIT Press,
             Cambridge, Mass.

MICHELS, J.W.

3412 1973 Dating Methods in Archaeology. Seminar Press, New York.

MORLAN, R.E.

3413 1967 Chronometric Dating in Japan. Arctic Anthropology 4(2):
             180-211.

NELSON, N.C.

3414 1916 Chronology of the Tano Ruins, New Mexico. American Anthro-
             pologist 18:159-180.

PATTERSON, T.C.

3415 1963 Contemporaneity and Cross-Dating in Archaeological Inter-
             pretation. American Antiquity 28:389-392.

QUIMBY, G.I.

3416 1960 Rates of Culture Change in Archaeology. American An-
             tiquity 25:416-417.

ROWE, J.H.

3417 1945 Absolute Chronology in the Andean Area. American Antiquity
             10:265-284.

SCHOENWETTER, J.

3418 1965 How Old Is It? The Story of Dating in Archeology. Museum
             of New Mexico Press, Santa Fe.

TAYLOR, D., and I. ROUSE

3419 1955 Linguistic and Archaeological Time Depth in the West
             Indies. International Journal of American Linguistics
             21:105-115.

TAYLOR, R.E.

3420 1975 Fluorine Diffusion: A New Dating Method for Chipped Lithic
             Materials. World Archaeology 7(2):125-135.

TAYLOR, R.E., J.L. SWAIN, and R. BERGER

3421 1969 New Developments in the Dating of Ceramic Artifacts.
             Verhandlungen des XXXVIII. Internationalen Amerikanisten-
             kongresses, Stuttgart-München 1:55-60. Kommissionsverlag
             Klaus Renner, München, Germany.

TAYLOR, W.W.

3422 1961 Archaeology and Language in Western North America. American Antiquity 27:71-81.

Van DEMAN, E.B.

3423 1912 Methods of Determining the Date of Roman Concrete Monuments. American Journal of Archaeology, (2nd Ser.) 16: 230-343.

WENDORF, F., and A.D. KRIEGER

3424 1959 Uranium Isotope Dating. American Anthropologist 25:71-73.

WOODBURY, R.B.

3425 1960 Nels C. Nelson and Chronological Archaeology. American Antiquity 25:400-401.

ZEUNER, F.E.

3426 1960 Advances in Chronological Research. Viking Fund Publications in Anthropology 28:325-350.

b. RADIOCARBON (C-14) ANALYSIS

ANDERSON, E.C., and H. LEVI

3427 1952 Some Problems in Radiocarbon Dating. Det Kongelige Danske Videnskabernes Selskab 27(6). Copenhagen.

ARNOLD, J.R., and W.F. LIBBY

3428 1949 Age Determination by Radiocarbon Content: Checks with Samples of Known Age. Science 110:678-680.

ATKINSON, R.J.C.

3429 1975 British Prehistory and the Radiocarbon Revolution. Antiquity 49(195):173-177.

BARKER, H.

3430 1958 Radiocarbon Dating: Its Scope and Limitations. Antiquity 32:253-263.

3431 1970 Critical Assessment of Radiocarbon Dating. In T.E. Allibone, et al., The Impact of the Natural Sciences on Archaeology:37-46. Oxford University Press, London.

BARTLETT, H.H.

3432 1951 Radiocarbon Datability of Peat, Marl, Caliche and Archaeological Materials. Science 114:55-56.

BENDER, M.

3433 1968 Mass Spectrometric Studies of Carbon 13 Variations in Corn and Other Grasses. Radiocarbon 10(2):468-472.

BENNETT, C.L.

3434 1979 Radiocarbon Dating with Accelerators. American Scientist
            67(4):450–457.

BENNETT, C.L., et al.

3435 1978 Radiocarbon Dating with Electrostatic Accelerators:
            Dating of Milligram Samples. Science 201:345–347.

BERGER, R.

3436 1975 Advances and Results in Radiocarbon Dating: Early Man in
            America. World Archaeology 7(2):174–184.

BERGER, R., A.G. HORNEY, and W.F. LIBBY

3437 1964 Radiocarbon Dating of Bone and Shell from Their Organic
            Components. Science 144:999–1001.

BERGER, R., R.E. TAYLOR, and W. LIBBY

3438 1966 Radiocarbon Content of Marine Shells from the California
            and Mexican West Coast. Science 153:864–866.

BLISS, W.L.

3439 1952 Radiocarbon Contamination. American Antiquity 17:250–251.

BROECKER, W.

3440 1964 Radiocarbon Dating: A Case Against the Proposed Link
            Between River Mollusks and Soil Humus. Science 143:596–
            597.

BROECKER, W., and J.L. KULP

3441 1956 The Radiocarbon Method of Age Determination. American
            Antiquity 22:1–11.

BROECKER, W., and E. OLSON

3442 1960 Radiocarbon from Nuclear Tests. Science 132:712–721.

BURLEIGH, R.

3443 1973 The New Zealand Radiocarbon Conference. Antiquity 47
            (185):54–55.

3444 1974 Radiocarbon Dating: Some Practical Considerations for the
            Archaeologist. Journal of Archaeological Science 1(1):
            69–88.

CAMPBELL, J.M.

3445 1965 Radiocarbon Dating and Far Northern (Arctic) Archeology.
            Proceedings, Sixth International Conference on Radiocarbon
            and Tritium Dating:179–186. Pullman, Wash.

CATCH, J.R.

3446 1961 Carbon-14 Compounds. Butterworths, Washington, D.C.

CLARK, J.G.D.

3447 1965 Radiocarbon Dating and the Expansion of Farming Culture from the Near East over Europe. Proceedings, Prehistoric Society 31:34-57.

CLARK, R.M.

3448 1975 A Calibration Curve for Radiocarbon Dates. Antiquity 49(196):251-266.

COLES, J., and R.A. JONES

3449 1975 Timber and Radiocarbon Dates. Antiquity 49(194):123-124.

COLLINS, H.B.

3450 1953 Radiocarbon in the Arctic. American Antiquity 18:197-203.

CRANE, H.R.

3451 1951 Dating of Relics by Radiocarbon Analysis. Nucleonics 9: 16-23.

DAMON, P.E., C.W. FERGUSON, A. LONG, and E.I. WALLICK

3452 1974 Dendrochronologic Calibration of the Radiocarbon Time Scale. American Antiquity 39(2):350-366.

DART, R.A., and P.R. BEAUMONT

3453 1969 Iron Age Radiocarbon Dates from Western Swaziland. South African Archaeological Bulletin 24(94), Pt. 2:71.

DEEVEY, E.S., R.F. FLINT, and I. ROUSE

3454 1967 Radiocarbon Measurements: Comprehensive Index, 1950-1965. Yale University, New Haven, Conn.

DELIBRIAS, G., and P.R. GIOT

3455 1970 Inadéquation, Hétérogénéité, et Contamination des Echantillons Soumis pour les Datations Radiocarbons. Bulletin, Société Préhistorique Française, Comptes Rendus 67:135-137.

DYCK, W.

3456 1967 The Geological Survey of Canada Radiocarbon Dating Laboratory. Geological Survey of Canada, Department of Energy, Mines and Resources, Paper 66-45.

3457 1967 Recent Developments in Radiocarbon Dating: Their Implications for Geochronology and Archaeology. Current Anthropology 8:349-351.

EVANS, C., and B.J. MEGGERS

3458 1962 Use of Organic Temper for Carbon 14 Dating in Lowland South America. American Antiquity 28:243-244.

FERNALD, A.T.

3459 1962 Radiocarbon Dates Relating to a Widespread Volcanic Ash
            Deposit, Eastern Alaska. United States Geological Survey,
            Professional Paper 450B.

FLINT, R.F., and E.S. DEEVEY, Jr.

3460 1951 Radiocarbon Dating of Late-Pleistocene Events. American
            Journal of Science 249:257-300.

GODWIN, H.

3461 1961 Half-Life of Radiocarbon. Nature 195:984.

3462 1969 The Value of Plant Materials for Radiocarbon Dating.
            American Journal of Botany 56(7):723-731.

3463 1970 The Contribution of Radiocarbon Dating to Archaeology in
            Britain. In The Impact of the Natural Sciences on
            Archaeology:57-76. Oxford University Press.

GRIFFIN, J.B.

3464 1963 A Radiocarbon Date on Prehistoric Beans from Williams
            Island, Hamilton County, Tennessee. Tennessee Archae-
            ologist 19(2):43-46.

GROOTES, P.M.

3465 1978 Carbon-14 Time Scale Extended: Comparison of Chronologies.
            Science 200:11-15.

HALL, R.L.

3466 1967 Those Late Corn Dates: Isotopic Fractionation as a Source
            of Error in Carbon-14 Dates. Michigan Archaeologist
            13(4):171-180.

HARBOTTLE, G., E.V. SAYRE, and R.W. STOENNER

3467 1979 Carbon-14 Dating of Small Samples by Proportional Counting.
            Science 206:683-685.

HARING, A., A.E. de VRIES, and H. de VRIES

3468 1958 Radiocarbon Dating up to 70,000 Years by Isotopic
            Enrichment. Science 128:472-473.

HAYNES, C.V., Jr.

3469 1966 Radiocarbon Samples: Chemical Removal of Plant Contami-
            nants. Science 151:1391-1392.

HESTER, J.J.

3470 1960 Late Pleistocene Extinction and Radiocarbon Dating.
            American Antiquity 26:58-77.

HRANICKY, W.J.

3471 1974 The Collection of Samples for Radiocarbon Dating. Ohio
            Archaeologist 24(4):15-18.

JELINEK, A.J.

3472 1961 An Index of Radiocarbon Dates Associated with Cultural
Materials. Current Anthropology 3:451-480.

JELINEK, A.J., and J.E. FITTING

3473 1963 Some Studies of Natural Radioactivity in Paleontological
Materials. Papers of the Michigan Academy of Sciences,
Arts and Letters 48:531-540.

JELINEK, A.J., and J.E. FITTING, eds.

3474 1965 Studies in the Natural Radioactivity of Prehistoric
Materials. Museum of Anthropology, University of
Michigan, Anthropological Papers 25.

JOHNSON, F., F. RAINEY, D. COLLIER, and R.F. FLINT

3475 1951 Radiocarbon Dating, a Summary. American Antiquity 27(1),
Pt. 2:58-65.

KAMEN, M.D.

3476 1963 Early History of Carbon-14. Science 140:584-590.

KEISCH, B.

3477 1968 Dating Works of Art Through Their Natural Radioactivity:
Improvements and Applications. Science 160:413-415.

KEITH, M.L., and G.M. ANDERSON

3478 1963 Radiocarbon Dating: Fictitious Results with Mollusk
Shells. Science 141:634-636.

3479 1964 Radiocarbon Dating of Mollusk Shells: A Reply to Broecker,
1964. Science 144:890.

KOHLER, E.L., and E.K. RALPH

3480 1961 C-14 Dates for Sites in the Mediterranean Area. American
Journal of Archaeology 65(4):357-368.

KOVAR, A.J.

3481 1966 Problems in Radiocarbon Dating at Teotihuacan. American
Antiquity 31:427-430.

LIBBY, W.F.

3482 1955 Radiocarbon Dating. 2nd ed. University of Chicago Press,
Chicago.

3483 1961 Radiocarbon Dating. Science 133:621-629.

3484 1963 The Accuracy of Radiocarbon Dates. Antiquity 37:213-219.

3485 1963 Radiocarbon Dating. Science 140:278-280.

McBURNEY, C.B.M.

3486 1952 Radiocarbon Dating Results from the Old World. Antiquity
26(101):35-45.

MacCALMAN, H.R.

3487   1965   Carbon 14 Dates from South West Africa. South African
              Archaeological Bulletin 20(80), Pt. 4:215.

MAUGH, T.H., II

3488   1978   Radiodating: Direct Detection Extends Range of the Tech-
              nique. Science 200:635-637.

MEIGHAN, C.W.

3489   1956   Responsibilities of the Archeologist in Using the Radio-
              carbon Method. University of Utah Anthropological Papers
              26:48-53.

MERRILL, R.S.

3490   1948   A Progress Report on the Dating of Archaeological Sites
              by Means of Radioactive Elements. American Antiquity
              13:281-286.

MOVIUS, H.L.

3491   1960   Radiocarbon Dates and Upper Paleolithic Archaeology in
              Central and Western Europe. Current Anthropology 1:355-
              392.

MULLER, R.A.

3492   1977   Radioisotope Dating with a Cyclotron. Science 196(4289):
              489-494.

MULLER, R.A., E.J. STEPHENSON, and T.S. MAST

3493   1978   Radioisotope Dating with an Accelerator: A Blind Measure-
              ment. Science 201:347-348.

MULVANEY, D.J.

3494   1961   Australian Radio-Carbon Dates. Antiquity 35(137):37-39.

NEUSTUPNÝ, E.

3495   1970   A New Epoch in Radiocarbon Dating. Antiquity 44:38-45.

OAKLEY, K.P., and A.E. DIXON

3496   1958   The Radioactivity of Materials from the Scharbauer Site
              near Midland, Texas. American Antiquity 24:185-187.

OLSON, E.A., and W. BROECKER

3497   1958   Sample Contamination and Reliability of Radiocarbon Dates.
              Transactions, New York Academy of Sciences, (Ser. II) 20:
              593-604.

OLSSON, I.U., ed.

3498   1970   Radiocarbon Variations and Absolute Chronology. Wiley
              Interscience, New York.

OTTAWAY, B.

3499 1973 Dispersion Diagrams: A New Approach to the Display of
Carbon 14 Dates. Archaeometry 15(1):5-12.

RAFTER, T.A.

3500 1955 C-14 Variations in Nature and the Effect on Radiocarbon
Dating. New Zealand Journal of Science and Technology,
Sec. B. 37:20-38.

RALPH, E.K.

3501 1965 Review of Radiocarbon Dates from Tikal and the Maya Calendar Correlation Problem. American Antiquity 30:421-427.

3502 1967 Methodological Problems of C^{14} Dating. In M. Levey, ed.,
Archaeological Chemistry:253-265. University of Pennsylvania Press, Philadelphia.

RUBIN, M., and D.W. TAYLOR

3503 1963 Radiocarbon Activity of Shells from Living Clams and
Snails. Science 141:637.

RUBIN, M., R.C. LIKENS, and E.G. BERRY

3504 1963 On the Validity of Radiocarbon Dates from Snail Shells.
Journal of Geology 71:84-89.

SATTERTHWAITE, L., and E. RALPH

3505 1960 New Radiocarbon Dates and the Maya Correlation Problem.
American Antiquity 26:165-184.

SMITH, H.S.

3506 1964 Egypt and C14 Dating. Antiquity 38(149):32-37.

STERNBERG, H. O'R.

3507 1960 Radiocarbon Dating as Applied to a Problem of Amazonian
Morphology. Comptes Rendus du XVIII Congrès International
de Géographie, Rio de Janeiro 1956, 2:399-424.

STUCKENRATH, R., Jr.

3508 1965 On the Care and Feeding of Radiocarbon Dates. Archaeology
18(4):277-281.

STUIVER, M.

3509 1978 Carbon-14 Dating: A Comparison of Beta and Ion Counting.
Science 200:635-637.

STUIVER, M., and P.D. QUAY

3510 1980 Changes in Atmospheric Carbon-14 Attributed to a Variable
Sun. Science 207(4426):11-19.

SUESS, H.

3511 1965 Secular Variations of the Cosmic-Ray Produced Carbon-14
            in the Atmosphere and Their Interpretations. Journal of
            Geophysical Research 70:5937-5992.

SWAN, D.A.

3512 1971 Carbon 14 and the Prehistory of Europe: A Review of the
            Revised Data. Mankind Quarterly 12(3):138-143.

SWITSUR, V.R.

3513 1973 The Radiocarbon Calendar Recalibrated. Antiquity 47(186):
            132.

VINTON, K.W.

3514 1960 Carbon-Dated Ocean Level Changes Offer a New System of
            Correlating Archaeological Data. Akten den 34 Internation-
            alen Amerikanistenkongresses:390-395.

VOGEL, J.C.

3515 1969 The Radiocarbon Time-Scale. South African Archaeological
            Bulletin 24(95/96), Pt. 3-4:83-87.

WICKMAN, F.E.

3516 1951 Variations in the Relative Abundance of the Carbon Isotopes
            in Plants. Geochimica et Cosmochimica Acta 2:243-254.
            London.

WILKE, P.J., and R.E. TAYLOR

3517 1971 Comments on Isochronous Interpretations of Radiocarbon
            Dates. Plains Anthropologist 16(52):115-116.

WILLETT, F.

3518 1971 A Survey of Recent Results in the Radiocarbon Chronology
            of Western and Northern Africa. Journal of African History
            12(3):339-370.

WILLIS, E.H.

3519 1963 Radiocarbon Dating. In D. Brothwell and E. Higgs, eds.,
            Science in Archaeology:35-46. Thames and Hudson, London.

WRIGHT, G.A.

3520 1973 Bristlecone Pine Calibrations of Radiocarbon Dates: Some
            Examples from the Near East. American Journal of Archae-
            ology 77(2):197-202.

c. GEOLOGICAL, CLIMATIC, SOILS, STRATIGRAPHY (ENVIRONMENTAL ASPECTS)

ANTEVS, E.

3521 1948 Climatic Changes and Pre-White Man. University of Utah
            Bulletin 38:168-191.

3522 1952 Climatic History and the Antiquity of Man in California. University of California Archaeological Survey, Report 16:23-31.

3523 1952 Valley Filling and Cutting. Journal of Geology 60:375-385.

3524 1953 Geochronology of the Deglacial and Neothermal Ages. Journal of Geology 61:195-230.

3525 1954 Telecorrelation of Varves, Radiocarbon Chronology and Geology. Journal of Geology 62:516-521.

3526 1955 Geologic-Climatic Dating in the West. American Antiquity 20:317-335.

3527 1957 Geological Tests of the Varve and Radiocarbon Chronologies. Journal of Geology 65:129-148.

3528 1959 Geological Age of the Lehner Mammoth Site. American Antiquity 25:31-34.

3529 1962 Transatlantic Climatic Agreement Versus C14 Dates. Journal of Geology 70:194-205.

AXELROD, D.I.

3530 1967 Quaternary Extinctions of Large Mammals. University of California Publications in Geological Sciences 74.

BROECKER, W.S.

3531 1966 Absolute Dating and the Astronomical Theory of Glaciation. Science 151:299-304.

BRYAN, K., and C.C. ALBRITTON, Jr.

3532 1943 Soil Phenomena as Evidence of Climate Changes. American Journal of Science 241:469-490.

BUTZER, K.W.

3533 1964 Environment and Archeology: An Introduction to Pleistocene Geography. Aldine, Chicago.

CARPENTER, E.F.

3534 1955 Astronomical Aspects of Geochronology. In T.L. Smiley, ed., Geochronology. University of Arizona Physical Sciences Bulletin 2:29-74.

DAVIES, O.

3535 1967 The Dates of the Late Pleistocene Sea-Levels. South African Archaeological Bulletin 22(85), Pt. 1:31.

DEEVEY, E.S., Jr.

3536 1948 On the Date of the Last Rise of Sea Level in Southern New England with Remarks on the Grassy Island Site. American Journal of Science 246:329-352.

de GEER, G.

3537   1912   A Geochronology of the Last 12,000 Years. 11th Inter-
              national Geological Congress, Stockholm (1910), Comptes
              Rendus 1:241-253.

3538   1928   Geochronology. Antiquity 2:308-315.

3539   1940   Geochronologia Suecica Principles. Konig. Svensk. Vetersk.
              Akad. Handl., (Ser. 3)(18):6.

DONN, W., W. FARRAND, and M. EWING

3540   1962   Pleistocene Ice Volumes and Sea Level Lowering. Journal
              of Geology 70:206-214.

DORF, E.

3541   1960   Climatic Changes of the Past and Present. American
              Scientist 48:341-364.

DREIMANIS, A.

3542   1957   Depths of Leaching in Glacial Deposits. Science 126:
              403-404.

FAIRBRIDGE, R.W.

3543   1958   Dating the Latest Movements of the Quaternary Sea Level.
              Transactions, New York Academy of Sciences II, 20:471-482.

FLINT, R.F.

3544   1957   Glacial and Pleistocene Geology. John Wiley & Sons, New
              York.

FRYXELL, R.

3545   1965   Mazama and Glacier Peak Volcanic Ash Layers: Relative
              Ages. Science 147:1288-1290.

FRYXELL, R., and R.D. DAUGHERTY

3546   1963   Late Glacial and Post Glacial Geological and Archaeological
              Chronology of the Columbia Plateau, Washington. Laboratory
              of Anthropology, Washington State University, Report of
              Investigations 23.

GEYER, D.

3547   1923   Die Quartarmollusken und die Klimafage. Palaeontolo-
              gisches Zeitschrift 5:72-94. Berlin.

GREENMAN, E.F.

3548   1943   The Archaeology and Geology of Two Early Sites near
              Killarney, Ontario. Papers of the Michigan Academy of
              Science, Arts and Letters 28:505-530.

HAYNES, C.V., Jr.

3549   1966   Geochronology of Late Quaternary Alluvium. Interim Re-
              search Report 10, University of Arizona, Geochronology
              Laboratories, Tucson.

HOLMES, G.W.

3550 1951 The Regional Significance of the Pleistocene Deposits in the Eden Valley, Wyoming. Museum Monographs, University of Pennsylvania Museum:95-102.

HOPKINS, D.M.

3551 1959 Cenozoic History of the Bering Land Bridge. Science 129: 1519-1528.

HUME, J.D.

3552 1966 Sea Level Changes During the Last 2,000 Years at Point Barrow, Alaska. Science 150:1165-1166.

JOHNSTON, D.W.

3553 1944 Problems of Terrace Correlation. Bulletin of the Geological Society of America 55:793-818.

JUDSON, S.

3554 1949 Pleistocene Stratigraphy of Boston, Massachusetts, and Its Relation to Boylston Street Fishweir. In F. Johnson et al., eds., The Boylston Street Fishweir II:7-48. Papers of R.S. Peabody Foundation for Archaeology 4(1).

KELLEY, J.C., T.N. CAMPBELL, and D.J. LEHMER

3555 1940 The Association of Archaeological Materials with Geological Deposits in the Big Bend Region of Texas. Sul Ross State Teachers College Bulletin 21(3).

KULP, J.L.

3556 1961 Geologic Time Scale. Science 133(3459):1105-1107.

MASON, R.J.

3557 1958 Late Pleistocene Geochronology and the Paleo-Indian Penetration into the Lower Michigan Peninsula. Museum of Anthropology, University of Michigan, Anthropological Papers 11.

MORSE, E.S.

3558 1882 Changes in Mya and Lunatia Since the Deposition of the New England Shell-Heaps. Proceedings, American Association for the Advancement of Science 30:345.

MOSS, J.H.

3559 1951 Glaciation in the Wind River Mountains and Its Relation to Early Man in the Eden Valley, Wyoming. Museum Monographs, University of Pennsylvania Museum:9-94.

NIKIFOROFF, C.C.

3560 1953 Pedogenic Criteria of Climatic Changes. In H. Shapley, ed., Climatic Change:189-200. Harvard University Press, Cambridge, Mass.

OAKLEY, K.P., and W.W. HOWELLS

3561 1961 Age of the Skeleton from the Lagow Sand Pit, Texas.
            American Antiquity 26:543-545.

PEWE, T.L.

3562 1954 The Geological Approach to Dating Archaeological Sites.
            American Antiquity 20:51-61.

REDFIELD, A.D.

3563 1976 Postglacial Change in Sea Level in the Western North
            Atlantic Ocean. Science 157:687-692.

RUSSELL, R.J.

3564 1957 Instability of Sea Level. American Scientist 45:414-430.

SCHOENWETTER, J., and F.W. EDDY

3565 1964 Alluvial and Palynological Reconstruction of Environments.
            Museum of New Mexico, Papers in Anthropology 13. Santa Fe.

SCHULTZ, G.B., G.C. LUENINGHOENER, and W.D. FRANKFORTER

3566 1948 Preliminary Geomorphological Studies of the Lime Creek
            Area. Bulletin of the University of Nebraska State
            Museum 3:31-42.

SHAPLEY, H., ed.

3567 1953 Climatic Change: Evidence, Causes and Effects. Harvard
            University Press, Cambridge, Mass.

SHEPARD, F.P.

3568 1956 Rate of Postglacial Rise of Sea Level. Science 123:1082-
            1083.

3569 1961 Sea Level Rise During the Past 20,000 Years. Zeitschrift
            für Geomorphologie 3:30-35.

3570 1964 Sea Level Changes in the Past 6,000 Years: Possible
            Archaeological Significance. Science 143:574-576.

SINIAGUIN, J.J.

3571 1943 A Method for Determining the Absolute Age of Soils.
            Comptes Rendus de l'Acad. des Sciences de l'URSS 40:335-336.

SMILEY, T.L.

3572 1955 Varve Studies. University of Arizona, Bulletin Series
            26:135-150.

SMILEY, T.L., ed.

3573 1955 Geochronology. University of Arizona Press, Tucson.

SOERGEL, W.

3574 1939 Unter Welchen Klimatischen Verhaltnissen Lebten zur
Bildungzert der Altdiluvialen Kiese von Sussenborn,
Rangifer, Ovibus, und Elephas Trogontherii in Middel-
und Norddeutschland. Zeitschrift Deutsch. Geol.
Gesellschaft 91:829-835.

SOKOLOFF, V.P., and G.F. CARTER

3575 1952 Time and Trace Metals in Archaeological Sites. Science
116:1-5.

TILTON, G.R., and S.R. HART

3576 1963 Geochronology. Science 140:357-366.

WILCOX, R.E.

3577 1965 Volcanic Ash Chronology. In H.E. Wright and D.G. Frey,
eds., The Quaternary of the United States:809-816.
Princeton University Press, Princeton, N.J.

WRIGHT, H.E., Jr.

3578 1952 Geological Dating in Prehistory. Archaeology 11:19-25.

WRIGHT, H.E., Jr., and D.G. FREY, eds.

3579 1965 The Quaternary of the United States. Princeton University
Press, Princeton, N.J.

ZEUNER, F.E.

3580 1951 Pleistocene Shore Lines. Geologische Rundschau 40:39-50.

3581 1955 Loess and Paleolithic Chronology. Proceedings, Prehistoric
Society 21:51-64.

3582 1958 Dating the Past: An Introduction to Geochronology. 4th
ed., revised. Methuen, London.

3583 1959 The Pleistocene Period. Hutchinson, London.

d. OBSIDIAN HYDRATION DATING

BELL, R.E.

3584 1977 Obsidian Hydration Studies in Highland Ecuador. American
Antiquity 42(1):68-77.

BRILL, R.H.

3585 1961 The Record of Time in Weathered Glass. Antiquity 14:
18-22.

3586 1963 Ancient Glass. Scientific American 209:120-130.

CLARK, D.L.

3587 1961 The Obsidian Dating Method. Current Anthropology 2:111-
116.

3588   1964   Archaeological Chronology in California and the Obsidian
              Hydration Method: Part 1. University of California at
              Los Angeles, Archaeological Survey, Annual Report 1963-64:
              139-228.

DAVIS, L.B.

3589   1966   Cooperative Obsidian Dating Research in the Northwestern
              Plains: A Status Report. Archaeology in Montana 7(2):
              3-5.

DIXON, K.A.

3590   1966   Obsidian (Hydration) Dates from Temesco, Valley of Mexico.
              American Antiquity 31:640-643.

3591   1968   A Comparison of Radiocarbon and Obsidian Hydration Dating
              as Applied to Ceremonial Architecture at Temesco, Valley
              of Mexico. Proceedings, 8th International Congress of
              Anthropological and Ethnological Sciences 3:187-189.

ERICSON, J.E.

3592   1975   New Results in Obsidian Hydration Dating. World Archae-
              ology 7(2):151-159.

FRIEDMAN, I.

3593   1978   Obsidian: The Dating Stone. American Scientist 66(1):
              44-51.

FRIEDMAN, I., and R.L. SMITH

3594   1960   A New Dating Method Using Obsidian: Part I, The Develop-
              ment of the Method. American Antiquity 25:476-493.

FRIEDMAN, I., N.V. PETERSON, and E.A. GROH

3595   1972   Obsidian Hydration Dating Applied to Basaltic Volcanic
              Activity. Science 176:1259-1260.

FRIEDMAN, I., R.L. SMITH, and D. CLARK

3596   1963   Obsidian Dating. In D. Brothwell and E. Higgs, eds.,
              Science in Archaeology:47-58. Thames and Hudson, London.

KATSUI, Y., and J. KONDŌ

3597   1965   Dating of Stone Implements by Using Hydration Layer of
              Obsidian. Japanese Journal of Geology and Geography 36:
              45-60.

LANFORD, W.A.

3598   1977   Glass Hydration; a Method of Dating Glass Objects.
              Science 196:975-976.

LAYTON, T.N.

3599   1973   Temporal Ordering of Surface Collected Obsidian Artifacts
              by Hydration Measurement. Archaeometry 15(1):129-132.

MEIGHAN, C.W., L.J. FOTTE, and P.V. AIELLO

3600 1968 Obsidian Dating in West Mexican Archeology. Science 160: 1069-1075.

MEIGHAN, C.W., F.J. FINDLOW, and S.P. De ATLEY, eds.

3601 1974 Obsidian Dates I: A Compendium of the Obsidian Determination Made at the UCLA Obsidian Hydration Laboratory. Institute of Archaeology, Archaeological Survey, University of California, Los Angeles, Monograph 1.

SINGLETON, W.L.

3602 1973 The Mechanisms of Obsidian Hydration and Their Application to Determining a General Hydration Rate. California Anthropologist 3:41-46.

TSONG, I.S.T., et al.

3603 1978 Obsidian Hydration Profiles Measured by Sputter-Induced Optical Emission. Science 201:339-341.

e. DENDROCHRONOLOGY

BABBAGE, C.

3604 1838 On the Age of Strata, as Inferred from the Rings of Trees Embedded in Them. In The Ninth Bridgewater Treatise, a Fragment (Note M:256-264). John Murray, London.

BAILEY, W.C.

3605 1948 Tree-Rings and Droughts. American Antiquity 14:59-60.

BANNISTER, B.

3606 1963 Dendrochronology. In D. Brothwell and E. Higgs, eds., Science in Archaeology:162-176. Thames and Hudson, London.

BANNISTER, B., and W.J. ROBINSON

3607 1975 Tree-Ring Dating in Archaeology. World Archaeology 7(2): 210-225.

BANNISTER, B., J.S. DEAN, and E.A.M. GALL

3608 1966 Tree-Ring Dates from Arizona E: Chinle-de Chelley-Red Rock Area. Laboratory of Tree-Ring Research, University of Arizona, Tucson.

BANNISTER, B., J.W. HANNAH, and W.J. ROBINSON

3609 1966 Tree Ring Dates from Arizona K: Puerco-Wide Run-Ganado Area. Laboratory of Tree-Ring Research, University of Arizona, Tucson.

BELL, R.E.

3610 1943 Tree Ring Chronology. Chicago Naturalist 6(1):2-8.

BRETERNITZ, D.A.

3611   1966   An Appraisal of Tree Ring Dated Pottery in the Southwest.
              University of Arizona Press, Tucson.

BROWN, F.M.

3612   1937   Dendrochronology. Antiquity 11(44):409-426.

CLARK, R.M., and C. RENFREW

3613   1972   A Statistical Approach to the Calibration of Floating
              Tree-Ring Chronologies Using Radiocarbon Dates.
              Archaeometry 14(1):5-20.

DEAN, J.S.

3614   1969   Dendrochronology and Archaeological Analysis: A Possible
              Ute Example from Southwestern Colorado. Southwestern
              Lore 35:29-41.

FRITTS, H.C.

3615   1965   Dendrochronology. In H.E. Wright and D.G. Frey, eds., The
              Quaternary of the United States:871-879. Princeton
              University Press, Princeton, N.J.

GIDDINGS, J.L.

3616   1941   Dendrochronology in Northern Alaska. University of
              Arizona Bulletin 12(4). Tucson.

3617   1962   Development of Tree-Ring Dating as an Archeological
              Aid. In T.T. Kozlowski, ed., Tree Growth:119-132.
              Ronald Press, New York.

GLOCK, W.S.

3618   1937   Principles and Methods of Tree-Ring Analysis. Carnegie
              Institution of Washington, Publication 486.

HALL, E.T.

3619   1939   Dendrochronology. Society of American Archaeology,
              Notebook 1:32-41.

HAURY, E.W.

3620   1935   Tree Rings--the Archaeologist's Time-Piece. American
              Antiquity 1:98-108.

McGINNIES, W.G.

3621   1963   Dendrochronology. Journal of Forestry 61:5-11.

MARCUS, G.

3622   1963   The Potential of Dendrochronology as an Archaeological
              Dating Method in Pennsylvania. Pennsylvania Archaeologist
              33(3):130-134.

O'BRYAN, D.

3623 1949 Methods of Felling Trees and Tree-Ring Dating in the
            Southwest. American Antiquity 15:155-156.

ROBINSON, W.J.

3624 1971 Tree-Ring Dates from the New Mexico C-D: Northern Rio
            Grande Area. Laboratory of Tree-Ring Research, University
            of Arizona, Tucson.

RUSH, J.H.

3625 1952 Tree Rings and Sunspots. Scientific American 186(1):
            54-59.

SCHOVE, J., and A.W.G. LOWTHER

3626 1957 Tree-Rings and Medieval Archaeology. Medieval Archaeology
            1:78-96.

SCHULMAN, E.

3627 1940 A Bibliography of Tree-Ring Analysis. Tree-Ring Bulletin
            6:1-12. University of Arizona, Tucson.

3628 1941 Some Propositions in Tree-Ring Analysis. Ecology 22:193-
            195.

3629 1956 Dendroclimatic Changes in Semiarid America. University
            of Arizona Press, Tucson.

SCOTT, S.

3630 1964 Dendrochronology in Mexico. In 35th International Congress
            of Americanists (1962), Actas y Memorias 3:211-216.
            Mexico, D.F.

SMILEY, T.L.

3631 1951 A Summary of Tree-Ring Dates from Some Southwestern
            Archaeological Sites. University of Arizona Bulletin 22(5).
            Tucson.

STUDHALTER, R.A.

3632 1955 Tree Growth: Some Historical Chapters. The Botanical
            Review 21:1-72.

TWINING, A.C.

3633 1833 On the Growth of Timber. American Journal of Science and
            Arts 24:391-393.

WEAKLY, W.F.

3634 1971 Tree-Ring Dating and Archaeology in South Dakota. Plains
            Anthropologist 16(54), Pt. 2, Memoir 8.

f. THERMOLUMINESCENCE DATING

ADAMS, G., and A.J. MORTLOCK

3635 1974 Thermoluminescent Dating of Baked Sand from Fire Hearths
            at Lake Mungo, New South Wales. Archaeology and Physical
            Anthropology in Oceania 9(3):236-237.

AITKEN, M.J.

3636 1970 Dating by Archaeomagnetic and Thermoluminescent Methods.
            In T.E. Allibone, et al., The Impact of the Natural
            Sciences on Archaeology:77-88. Oxford University Press,
            London.

AITKEN, M.J., et al.

3637 1964 Thermoluminescent Dating of Ancient Ceramics. Nature
            202(4936):1032.

BITTMANN SIMONS, B., and V. MEJDAHL

3638 1969 Brazilian Pottery Dated by Thermoluminescence. Verhand-
            lungen des XXXVIII. Internationalen Amerikanistenkon-
            gresses, Stuttgart-München 1:61-72. Kommissionsverlag
            Klaus Renner, München, Germany.

CAIRNS, T.

3639 1976 Archaeological Dating by Thermoluminescence. Analytical
            Chemistry 48(3):266-278.

DORT, W., et al.

3640 1965 Paleotemperatures and Chronology at Archeological Cave
            Sites Revealed by Thermoluminescence. Science 150:480-482.

FLEMING, S.J.

3641 1973 The Pre-Dose Technique. A New Thermoluminescent Dating
            Method. Archaeometry 15(1):13-30.

3642 1978 Thermoluminescent Dating: MASCA Date-List I, Quotation of
            Results. MASCA Journal 1:12-14.

GÖKSU, H.Y., et al.

3643 1974 Age Determination of Burned Flint by a Thermoluminescent
            Method. Science 183:651-653.

GROGLER, N., et al.

3644 1960 Über die Datierung von Keramik und Ziegel Durch Thermo-
            lumineszenz. Helvetica Physica Acta 33:595-596.

HALL, E.T.

3645 1963 Dating Pottery by Thermoluminescence. In D. Brothwell
            and E. Higgs, eds., Science in Archaeology:90-92. Thames
            and Hudson, London.

HUXTABLE, J., and M.J. AITKEN

3646 1978 Thermoluminescence Dating of Sherds from Sham Wan. In W.
            Meacham, ed., Sham Wan, Lamma Island; an Archaeological
            Site Study:116-123. Journal Monograph III, Hong Kong
            Archaeological Society.

HUXTABLE, J., M.J. AITKEN, and J.C. WEBER

3647 1972 Thermoluminescent Dating of Baked and Clay Balls of the
            Poverty Point Culture. Archaeometry 14(2):269-276.

KENNEDY, G., and L. KNOPFF

3648 1960 Dating by Thermoluminescence. Archaeology 13:147-148.

MAZESS, R.G., and D.W. ZIMMERMAN

3649 1966 Pottery Dating by Thermoluminescence. Science 152:347-348.

RALPH, E.K., and M.C. HAN

3650 1966 Dating of Pottery by Thermoluminescence. Nature 210:245-
            247.

3651 1969 Potential of Thermoluminescence in Supplementing Radio-
            carbon Dating. World Archaeology 1:157-169.

3652 1971 Potential of Thermoluminescence Dating. In R.H. Brill,
            ed., Science and Archaeology:244-250. MIT Press, Cambridge,
            Mass.

ROWLETT, R.M., M.D. MANDEVILLE, and E.J. ZELLER

3653 1974 The Interpretation and Dating of Human Worked Siliceous
            Materials by Thermoluminescent Analysis. Proceedings,
            Prehistoric Society 40:37-44.

TITE, M.S., and J. WAINE

3654 1962 Thermoluminescent Dating: A Re-Appraisal. Archaeometry
            5:53-79.

ZIMMERMAN, D.W., and J. HUXTABLE

3655 1971 Thermoluminescent Dating of Upper Palaeolithic Fired Clay
            from Dolni Vestonice. Archaeometry 13(1):53-58.

g. DATING OF BONE

BADA, J.L.

3656 1972 Amino Acids and Their Use in Dating Fossil Bones. En-
            vironment Southwest 448:1-4. San Diego Museum of Natural
            History.

BADA, J.L, and P.M. HELFMAN

3657 1975 Amino Acid Racemization Dating of Fossil Bones. World
            Archaeology 7(2):160-173.

BADA, J.L., and R. PROTSCH

3658 1973 Racemization Reaction of Aspartic Acid and Its Use in
            Dating Fossil Bones. Proceedings, National Academy of
            Sciences 70:1331-1334.

BADA, J.L., R.A. SCHROEDER, and G.F. CARTER

3659 1974 New Evidence for the Antiquity of Man in North America
            Deduced from Aspartic Acid Racemization. Science 184:791-
            793.

BADA, J.L., R. SCHROEDER, R. PROTSCH, and R. BERGER

3660 1974 Concordance of Collagen-Based Radiocarbon and Aspartic-
            Acid Racemization Ages. Proceedings, National Academy of
            Sciences 71:914-917.

BAUD, C.A.

3661 1960 Dating of Prehistoric Bones by Radiological and Optical
            Methods. Viking Fund Publications in Anthropology 28:
            246-264.

COOK, S.F.

3662 1960 Dating Prehistoric Bone by Chemical Analysis. Viking
            Fund Publications in Anthropology 28:223-245.

COOK, S.F., and H.C. EZRA-COHN

3663 1959 An Evaluation of the Fluorine Dating Method. Southwestern
            Journal of Anthropology 15:276-290.

COOK, S.F., and R.F. HEIZER

3664 1953 Archaeological Dating by Chemical Analysis of Bone.
            Southwestern Journal of Anthropology 9:231-238.

3665 1953 The Present Status of Chemical Methods for Dating Pre-
            historic Bone. American Antiquity 18:354-358.

3666 1959 The Chemical Analysis of Fossil Bone: Individual Variation.
            American Journal of Physical Anthropology 17:109-115.

DOBERENZ, A.R., and P. MATTER

3667 1963 Nitrogen Analyses of Fossil Bones. Comp. Biochem. Physiol.
            16:253-258.

EZRA-COHN, H.C., and S.F. COOK

3668 1957 Amino Acids in Fossil Human Bone. Science 126:80-81.

HARE, P.E.

3669 1974 Amino Acid Dating--a History and an Evaluation. MASCA
            Newsletter 10(1):4-7.

HEIZER, R.F., and S.F. COOK

3670 1952 Fluorine and Other Chemical Tests of Some North American
            Human and Fossil Bones. American Journal of Physical
            Anthropology 10:289-304.

3671 1959 New Evidence of Antiquity of Tepexpan and Other Human Remains from the Valley of Mexico. Southwestern Journal of Anthropology 15:36-42.

McCONNELL, D.

3672 1962 Dating of Fossil Bones by the Fluorine Method. Science 136:241-244.

OAKLEY, K.P.

3673 1951 The Fluorine Dating Method. Yearbook of Physical Anthropology 5 (for 1949):44-54.

3674 1953 Dating Fossil Human Remains. In Anthropology Today:43-57. University of Chicago Press, Chicago.

3675 1955 Analytical Methods of Dating Bones. The Advancement of Science 6:343-344.

3676 1963 Analytical Methods of Dating Bones. In D. Brothwell and E. Higgs, eds., Science in Archaeology:25-34. Thames and Hudson, London.

3677 1963 Dating Skeletal Material. Science 140:480.

3678 1963 Fluorine, Uranium and Nitrogen Dating of Bone. In E. Pyddoke, ed., The Scientist and Archaeology:111-119. Phoenix House, London.

3679 1964 Frameworks for Dating Fossil Man. Aldine, Chicago.

ORTNER, D.J., D.W. Von ENDT, and M.S. ROBINSON

3680 1977 The Effect of Temperature on Protein Decay in Bone: Its Significance in Nitrogen Dating of Archeological Specimens. Experimental Archaeology. Columbia University Press, New York.

SINEX, F.M., and B. FARIS

3681 1959 Isolation of Gelatin from Ancient Bones. Science 129:969.

STORIE, R.E., and F. HARRADINE

3682 1950 An Age Estimate of the Burials Unearthed near Concord, California. Based on Pedologic Observations. University of California Archaeological Survey, Report 9:15-17.

SZABO, B.J., H.E. MALDE, and C. IRWIN-WILLIAMS

3683 1969 Dilemma Posed by Uranium-Series Dates on Archaeologically Significant Bones from Valsequillo, Puebla, Mexico. Earth and Planetary Science Letters 6:237-244.

TANABE, G., and N. WATANABE

3684 1968 Dating Fossil Bones from Japan by Means of X-ray Diffraction Pattern. Journal of the Faculty of Science, University of Tokyo 3:199-216.

WELL, C.

3685 1963 The Radiological Examination of Human Remains. In D.

Brothwell and E. Higgs, eds., Science in Archaeology:
400-412. Thames and Hudson, London.

h. DATING THROUGH SERIATION AND QUANTITATIVE METHODS

ASCHER, M., and R. ASCHER

3686   1963   Chronological Ordering by Computer. American Anthropologist 65:1045-1052.

COWGILL, G.L.

3687   1972   Models, Methods and Techniques for Seriation. In D.L.
Clarke, ed., Models in Archaeology:381-424. Methuen,
London.

FORD, J.A.

3688   1938   A Chronological Method Applicable to the Southeast.
American Antiquity 3:260-264.

3689   1962   A Quantitative Method for Deriving Cultural Chronology.
Pan American Union, Technical Manual 1, Washington, D.C.

GELFAND, A.E.

3690   1971   Seriation Methods for Archaeological Materials. American
Antiquity 36(3):263-274.

LIPE, W.D.

3691   1964   Comment on Dempsey and Baumhoff's, The Statistical Use of
Artifact Distributions to Establish Chronological Sequence.
American Antiquity 30:103-104.

MARQUARDT, W.H.

3692   1978   Advances in Archaeological Seriation. In M.B. Schiffer,
ed., Advances in Archaeological Method and Theory, Vol.
1:266-314. Academic Press, New York.

MEIGHAN, C.W.

3693   1959   A New Method for the Seriation of Archaeological Collections. American Antiquity 25:203-211.

3694   1977   Recognition of Short Time Periods Through Seriation.
American Antiquity 42(4):628-629.

PETRIE, W.M.

3695   1899   Sequences in Prehistoric Remains. Journal, Royal Anthropological Institute 29:295-301.

ROBINSON, W.S.

3696   1951   A Method for Chronologically Ordering Archaeological
Deposits. American Antiquity 16:293-301.

ROE, P.

3697 1974 Further Exploration of the Rowe Chavin Seriation and Its Implications for the North Central Coast. Dumbarton Oaks, Washington, D.C.

ROWE, J.H.

3698 1959 Archaeological Dating and Cultural Process. Southwestern Journal of Anthropology 15:314.

3699 1961 Stratigraphy and Seriation. American Antiquity 26:324-330.

3700 1962 Stages and Periods in Archaeological Interpretation. Southwestern Journal of Anthropology 18:40-54.

3701 1962 Worsaae's Law and the Use of Grave Lots for Archaeological Dating. American Antiquity 28:129-137.

TROIKE, R.C.

3702 1957 Times and Types in Archeological Analysis: The Brainerd-Robinson Technique. Bulletin, Texas Archeological Society 28:269-284.

i. DATING THROUGH MOLLUSCAN ANALYSIS

BAKER, F.C.

3703 1937 Pleistocene Land and Fresh-Water Mollusca as Indicators of Time and Ecological Conditions. In G.G. McCurdy, ed., Early Man:67-74. Lippincott, Philadelphia.

CUNNINGTON, M.E.

3704 1933 Evidence of Climate Derived from Snail Shells and Its Bearing on the Date of Stonehenge. Wiltshire Archaeological Magazine XLVI:350-355.

DOKI, N.

3705 1934 On the Relationship Between the Number of Radial Costae of Prehistoric Anadara Shells and the Stratigraphy of Shell Mounds in the Kanto District. Shizengaku Zasshi 6: 321-348. (In Japanese.)

LAIS, R.

3706 1938 Molluskenkunde und Vorgeschichte. Deutsches Archäol. Inst., Romisch-Germanisch Komm. Ber. 26(1936):5-23. Berlin.

PETRBOK, J.

3707 1931 Bedeutung der Mollusken für die Prähistorische Archäologie. Archiv für Molluskenkunde 63.

RICHARDS, H.G.

3708 1937 Marine Pleistocene Mollusks as Indicators of Time and Ecological Conditions. In G.G. McCurdy, ed., Early Man: 75-84. Lippincott, Philadelphia.

SCHOUTE-VANNECK, C.A.

3709   1960   A Chemical Aid for the Relative Dating of Coastal Shell
              Middens. South African Journal of Science 56:67-70.

SPARKS, B.W.

3710   1969   Non-Marine Mollusca and Archaeology. In D. Brothwell and
              E. Higgs, eds., Science in Archaeology:395-406. 2nd ed.
              Thames and Hudson, London.

SUZUKI, H.

3711   1935   Chronological Study of Prehistoric Shell-Mounds Around
              the Bay of Tokyo Based Upon the Changes in the Form of
              Clam Shells. Shizengaku Zasshi 7:51-94. (In Japanese.)

WEBER, J.N., and A. La ROCQUE

3712   1963   Isotope Ratios in Marine Mollusk Shells After Prolonged
              Contact with Flowing Fresh Water. Science 142:1666.

j. ARCHAEOMAGNETIC DATING

AITKEN, M.J.

3713   1970   Dating by Archaeomagnetic and Thermoluminescent Methods.
              In T.E. Allibone, et al., The Impact of the Natural
              Sciences on Archaeology:77-88. Oxford University Press,
              London.

BARBETTI, M.

3714   1976   Archaeomagnetic Analyses of Six Glozelian Ceramic Arti-
              facts. Journal of Archaeological Science 3(2):137-152.

BUCHA, V.

3715   1970   Evidence for Changes in the Earth's Magnetic Field Inten-
              sity. In T.E. Allibone, et al., The Impact of the Natural
              Sciences on Archaeology:47-53. Oxford University Press,
              London.

CLARKE, D.L., and G. CONNAH

3716   1962   Remanent Magnetism and Beaker Chronology. Antiquity 36:
              206-209.

COOK, R.M.

3717   1969   Archaeomagnetism. In D. Brothwell and E. Higgs, eds.,
              Science in Archaeology:76-87. 2nd ed. Thames and Hudson,
              London.

COOK, R.M., and J.C. BELSHE

3718   1958   Archaeomagnetism. Antiquity 32(127):167-178.

3719   1959   Dating by Archaeomagnetism. Archaeology 12(3):158-162.

COX, A., R.R. DOELL, and G.B. DALRYMPLE

3720 1965 Quaternary Paleomagnetic Stratigraphy. In H.E. Wright and D.G. Frey, eds., The Quaternary of the United States: 817-830. Princeton University Press, Princeton, N.J.

CREER, K.M., and J.S. KOPPER

3721 1974 Paleomagnetic Dating of Cave Paintings in Tito Bustillo Cave, Asturias, Spain. Science 186:348-350.

KOPPER, J.S., and K.M. CREER

3722 1973 Cova dets Alexandres: Paleomagnetic Dating and Archaeological Interpretation of Its Sediments. Caves and Karsts 15:13-20.

3723 1976 Paleomagnetic Dating and Stratigraphic Interpretation in Archaeology. MASCA Newsletter 12(1).

TARLING, D.H.

3724 1975 Archaeomagnetism: The Dating of Archaeological Materials by Their Magnetic Properties. World Archaeology 7(2): 185-197.

THELLIER, E., and O. THELLIER

3725 1959 Sur l'Intensité du Champ Magnétique Terrestre dans le Passé Historique et Géologique. Annales Géophysiques 15: 285-376.

WATANABE, H.

3726 1959 An Introduction to Geomagnetochronology; the Direction of Remanent Magnetism of Baked Earth and Its Application to Chronology for Anthropology and Archaeology in Japan. Journal of the Faculty of Science, University of Tokyo (Section 2) 2:1-188.

3727 1971 Magnetic Dating of the Beginning of Porcelain Manufacture in Japan. Journal of the Faculty of Science, University of Tokyo (Section 5) 4(1):81-102.

WEAVER, G.H.

3728 1977 Archaeomagnetic Measurements on the Second Boston Experimental Kiln. Experimental Archaeology. Columbia University Press, New York.

WEAVER, K.F.

3729 1967 Magnetic Clues Help Date the Past. National Geographic Magazine 131:696-701.

k. POTASSIUM-ARGON DATING

CURTIS, G.H.

3730 1961 A Clock for the Ages: Potassium-Argon. National Geographic Magazine 120:590-592.

3731   1975   Improvements in Potassium-Argon Dating, 1962-1975. World
              Archaeology 7(2):198-209.

DALRYMPLE, G.B., and M.A. LANPHERE

3732   1969   Potassium-Argon Dating, Principles, Techniques and Appli-
              cations to Geochronology. W.H. Freeman, San Francisco.

EVERNDEN, J.F., and G.H. CURTIS

3733   1965   The Potassium-Argon Dating of Late Cenozoic Rocks in East
              Africa and Italy. Current Anthropology 6:343-385.

EVERNDEN, J.F., G. CURTIS, and J. LIPSON

3734   1957   Potassium-Argon Dating of Igneous Rocks. American
              Association of Petroleum Geologists 41:2120-2127.

EVERNDEN, J.F., D.E. SAVAGE, G.H. CURTIS, and G.T. JAMES

3735   1964   Potassium-Argon Dates and Cenozoic Mammalian Chronology
              of North America. American Journal of Science 262:145-198.

GENTNER, W., and H.J. LIPPOLT

3736   1963   The Potassium-Argon Dating of Upper Tertiary and Pleisto-
              cene Deposits. In D. Brothwell and E. Higgs, eds.,
              Science in Archaeology:72-84. Thames and Hudson, London.

13. Site Constituent Analysis

COOK, S.F., and A.E. TREGANZA

3737   1947   The Quantitative Investigation of Aboriginal Sites:
              Comparative Physical and Chemical Analysis of Two Cali-
              fornia Indian Mounds. American Antiquity 13:135-141.

3738   1950   The Quantitative Investigation of Indian Mounds. Univer-
              sity of California Publications in American Archaeology
              and Ethnology 40(5).

GREENWOOD, R.S.

3739   1961   Quantitative Analysis of Shells from a Site in Goleta,
              California. American Antiquity 26:416-420.

HEIZER, R.F., and S.F. COOK

3740   1960   Physical Analysis of Habitation Residues. In R.F. Heizer
              and S.F. Cook, eds., The Application of Quantitative
              Methods in Archaeology. Viking Fund Publications in
              Anthropology 28:93-157.

SPEED, E.

3741   1967   The Analysis of the Shell Content of the Midden. Appendix
              to the Report on the Bonteberg Shelter. South African
              Archaeological Bulletin 22(87):90-92.

TREGANZA, A.E., and S.F. COOK

3742   1948   The Quantitative Investigation of Aboriginal Sites: Complete Excavation with Physical and Archaeological Analysis of a Single Mound. American Antiquity 13:287-297.

14. Use of Computers in Archaeological Analysis

ANONYMOUS

3743 1970 Prospecting at South Cadbury: An Exercise in Computer Archaeology. Science and Archaeology 1.

BORILLO, M.

3744 1971 Formal Procedures and the Use of Computers in Archaeology. Norwegian Archaeological Review 4:2-27.

CAMPBELL, J.D., and H.S. CARON

3745 1964 Data Processing by Optical Coincidence. Science 133: 1333-1338.

CHENHALL, R.G.

3746 1967 The Description of Archaeological Data in Computer Language. American Antiquity 32:161-167.

CHRISTOPHE, J., and J. DESHAYES

3747 1964 Index de l'Outillage; Outils en Métal de l'Âge du Bronze, des Balkans à l'Indus. Centre National de la Recherche Scientifique, Paris.

COWGILL, G.L.

3748 1967 Computer Applications in Archaeology. In E.A. Bowles, ed., Computers in Humanistic Research:2-28. Prentice-Hall, Englewood Cliffs, N.J.

3749 1967 Computers and Prehistoric Archaeology. In E.A. Bowles, ed., Computers in Humanistic Research:47-56. Prentice-Hall, Englewood Cliffs, N.J.

3750 1968 Archaeological Applications of Factor, Cluster, and Proximity Analyses. American Antiquity 33:367-375.

3751 1970 Some Sampling and Reliability Problems in Archaeology. In Archéologie et Calculateurs:161-175. Editions du Centre National de la Recherche Scientifique, Paris.

DAVIS, E.L.

3752 1965 Three Applications of Edge-Punched Cards for Recording and Analyzing Field Data. Society for American Archaeology, Memoir 19:216-226.

DORAN, J.E.

3753 1970 Systems Theory, Computer Simulations and Archaeology. World Archaeology 1:289-298.

DORAN, J.E., and F.R. HODSON

3754 1966 A Digital Computer Analysis of Paleolithic Flint Assemblages. Nature 210:688-689.

GRAHAM, I., P. GALLOWAY, and I. SCOLLAR

3755 1976 Model Studies in Computer Seriation. Journal of Archaeo-
            logical Science 3(1):1-30.

GRAMLY, R.M.

3756 1970 A Computer Program for Archaeological Data Retrieval.
            Bulletin, Texas Archeological Society 41:287-300.

GUNN, J.

3757 1970 The Use of Computer Programs for Mapping Archaeological
            Data. Plains Anthropologist 13(49):219-228.

HODSON, J.E., and F.R. DORAN

3758 1975 Mathematics and Computers in Archaeology. Harvard Univer-
            sity Press, Cambridge, Mass.

HOLE, F., and M. SHAW

3759 1967 Computer Analysis of Chronological Seriation. Rice
            University Studies 53(3). Houston.

HRANICKY, W.J.

3760 1972 Computers in Archaeology. The Chesopiean 10(4):100-102.

HYMES, D.

3761 1963 Conference on the Use of Computers in Anthropology.
            Current Anthropology 4:123-129.

HYMES, D., ed.

3762 1965 The Use of Computers in Anthropology. Mouton, Paris.

KORVGA, J.

3763 1971 An Approach to the Use of Computers in Classifying Lithic
            Artifacts. Washington Archaeologist 15(4):1-9.

KOWALSKI, B.R., T.F. SCHATZKI, and F.H. STROSS

3764 1972 Classification of Archaeological Artifacts by Applying
            Pattern Recognition to Trace Element Data. Analytical
            Chemistry 44:2176-2180.

KUZARA, R.S., G.R. MEAD, and K.A. DIXON

3765 1966 Seriation of Anthropological Data: A Computer Program for
            Matrix-Ordering. American Anthropologist 68:1442-1455.

LEVINSON, M.

3766 1973 Settlement of Polynesia: A Computer Simulation. University
            of Minnesota Press, Minneapolis.

MOSIMANN, J.E., and P.S. MARTIN

3767 1975 Giant Mammals Killed Off by Computer: Simulating Overkill
            by Paleoindians. American Scientist 63:304-313.

SCOLLAR, I., and F. KRUCKEBERG

3768 1966 Computer Treatment of Magnetic Measurements from Archaeo-
            logical Sites. Archaeometry 9:61-71.

SOUDSKY, B.

3769 1967 Principles of Automatic Data Treatment Applied on Neo-
            lithic Pottery. Czechoslovak Academy of Sciences, Prague.

STERN, E.M.

3770 1966 Using the IBM 7090 in the Classification of Ground Stone
            Tools. Michigan Archaeologist 12(4):229-234.

WILCOCK, J.D.

3771 1970 Petroglyphs by Computer. Science and Archaeology 2 and 3.

WRIGHT, A.J., Jr.

3772 1966 Projectile Point Classification and Electronic Computers.
            Journal, Alabama Archaeology 12(2):138-153.

15. Archaeometry / Chemical Archaeology

AITKEN, M.J.

3773 1974 Physics and Archaeology. 2nd ed. Clarendon Press, Oxford.

BASCH, A.

3774 1972 Analyses of Oil from Two Roman Glass Bottles. Israel
            Exploration Journal 22:27-32.

BECK, C.W.

3775 1974 Archaeological Chemistry. The American Chemical Society,
            Washington, D.C.

BECK, C.W., E. WILBUR, S. MERET, E. KOSSOVE, and K. KERMANT

3776 1965 The Infra-Red Spectra of Amber and the Identification of
            Baltic Amber. Archaeometry 8:96.

BRILL, R.H.

3777 1970 Lead and Oxygen Isotopes in Ancient Objects. In The Im-
            pact of the Natural Sciences on Archaeology:143-164.
            Oxford University Press, London.

BRILL, R.H., and J.M. WAMPLER

3778 1967 Isotope Studies of Ancient Lead. American Journal of
            Archaeology 71(1):63-78.

BROTHWELL, D., and E. HIGGS, eds.

3779 1969 Science in Archaeology. 2nd ed. Thames and Hudson,
            London.

CARTER, G.F.

3780 1978 Archaeological Chemistry II. American Chemical Society,
            Washington, D.C.

C.B.A. SCIENTIFIC RESEARCH COMMITTEE

3781 1970 Handbook of Scientific Aids and Evidence for Archaeolo-
            gists. Council for British Archaeology, London.

CESAREO, R., et al.

3782 1972 Non-Destructive Analysis of Chemical Elements in
            Paintings and Enamels. Archaeometry 14(1):65-78.

CONDAMIN, J., F. FORMENTI, M.O. METAIS, M. MICHEL, and P. BLOND

3783 1976 The Application of Gas Chromatography to the Tracing of
            Oil in Ancient Amphorae. Archaeometry 18(2):195-201.

COOK, S.F.

3784 1964 The Nature of Charcoal Excavated at Archaeological Sites.
            American Antiquity 29:514-517.

COOK, S.F., and R.F. HEIZER

3785 1965 Studies on the Chemical Analysis of Archaeological Sites.
            University of California Publications in Anthropology 2,
            Berkeley.

DAVISON, C.C., and J.D. CLARK

3786 1974 Trade Wind Beads: An Interim Report of Chemical Studies.
            Azania 9:75-86.

FLEMING, S.J.

3787 1971 Authenticity Testing of Ceramics Using the Thermolumines-
            cence Method. University of California, Contributions of
            the Archaeological Research Facility 12:23-32.

3788 1971 Thermoluminescent Authenticity Testing of Ancient Ceramics;
            the Effects of Sampling by Drilling. Archaeometry 13(1):
            59-70.

3789 1973 Thermoluminescence and Glaze Studies of a Group of T'ang
            Dynasty Ceramics. Archaeometry 15(1):31-52.

FOLDVARI-VOGL, M., and M. KRETZOI

3790 1961 Kritische Untersuchungen über die Anwendbarkeit des
            Fluorverfahrens. Acta Geologica 7.

GÖKSU, H.Y., and J.H. FREMLIN

3791 1972 Thermoluminescence from Unirradiated Flints: Regeneration
            Thermoluminescence. Archaeometry 14(1):127-132.

HALL, E.T.

3792 1960 X-ray Fluorescent Analysis Applied to Archaeology.
            Archaeometry 3:29-35.

3793 1970 Analytical Techniques Used in Archaeometry. In The Impact of the Natural Sciences on Archaeology:135-142. Oxford University Press, London.

3794 1971 Two Examples of the Use of Chemical Analysis in the Solution of Archaeological Problems. In R.H. Brill, ed., Science and Archaeology:156-164. MIT Press, Cambridge, Mass.

HALL, E.T, M.S. BANKS, and J.M. STERN

3795 1964 Uses of X-ray Fluorescent Analysis in Archaeology. Archaeometry 7:84-89.

HALL, E.T., F. SCHWEIZER, and P.A. TOLLER

3796 1973 X-ray Fluorescence Analysis of Museum Objects: A New Instrument. Archaeometry 15(1):53-78.

HAMMOND, P.C.

3797 1961 The X-ray Geiger-Counter Spectroscope as an Archaeological Instrument. American Journal of Archaeology 65(3):305-306.

HERZ, N., and D.B. WENNER

3797a 1978 Assembly of Greek Marble Inscriptions by Isotopic Methods. Science 199:1070-1072.

HORNBLOWER, A.P.

3798 1962 Archaeological Applications of the Electron Probe Microanalyser. Archaeometry 5:108-112.

LITTMANN, E.R.

3798a 1980 Maya Blue--a New Perspective. American Antiquity 45(1): 87-100.

MATSON, F.R.

3799 1971 A Study of Temperatures Used in Firing Ancient Mesopotamian Pottery. In R.H. Brill, ed., Science and Archaeology: 65-79. MIT Press, Cambridge, Mass.

MEJDAHL, V.

3800 1970 Measurement of Environmental Radiation at Archaeological Excavation Sites. Archaeometry 12:147-160.

MELCHER, C.L., and D.W. ZIMMERMAN

3801 1977 Thermoluminescent Determination of Prehistoric Heat Treatment of Chert Artifacts. Science 197:1359-1362.

MEYERS, P.

3802 1968 Some Applications of Non-Destructive Activation Analysis. Bronder-Offset, Rotterdam.

MORGAN, E.D., C. CORNFORD, D.R.J. POLLOCK, and P. ISAACSON

3803   1973   The Transformation of Fatty Material Buried in Soil.
              Science and Archaeology 10:9-10.

MOSS, A.A.

3804   1954   The Application of X-rays, Gamma Rays, Ultra-Violet and
              Infra-Red Rays to the Study of Antiquities. Museums
              Association, London.

MOSS, R.J.

3805   1910   Chemical Notes on a Stone Lamp from Ballyetagh and Other
              Similar Stone Vessels in the Royal Irish Academy Collec-
              tion. Proceedings, Royal Irish Academy 28:162-168.

OLSEN, E.J.

3806   1962   Copper Artifact Analysis with the X-ray Spectrometer.
              American Antiquity 28:234-238.

ORGAN, R.M.

3807   1971   The Value of Analyses of Archaeological Objects.
              Archaeometry 13(1):27-29.

ORTEGA, R.F., and B.K. LEE

3808   1970   Neutron Activation Study of Ancient Pigments from Murals
              on Cholula and Teotihuacan. Archaeometry 12:197-202.

PURDY, B.A., and H.K. BROOKS

3809   1971   Thermal Alteration of Silica Minerals: An Archeological
              Approach. Science 173:322-325.

RAINEY, F.G.

3810   1966   New Techniques in Archaeology. Proceedings, American
              Philosophical Society 110:146-152.

RAINEY, F.G., and E.K. RALPH

3811   1963   Archeology and Its New Technology. Science 153:1481-1491.

SELIMKHANOV, I.R.

3812   1962   Spectral Analysis of Metallic Articles from Archaeological
              Monuments of the Caucasus, U.S.S.R. Proceedings, Prehis-
              toric Society 28:68-79.

SHEPARD, A.O.

3813   1971   Ceramic Analysis: The Interrelations of Methods; the
              Relations of Analysts and Archaeologists. In R.H. Brill,
              ed., Science and Archaeology:55-63. MIT Press, Cambridge,
              Mass.

SMITH, M.A., and A.E. BLYN-STOYLE

3814   1959   A Sample Analysis of British Middle and Late Bronze Age

Materials Using Optical Spectrometry. Proceedings, Prehistoric Society 25:188-208.

STROSS, F.H.

3815 1960 Authentication of Antique Stone Objects by Physical and
Chemical Methods. Analytical Chemistry 32:17A-24A.

STROSS, F.H., R.F. HEIZER, and J.A. GRAHAM

3816 1970 Vestigios de Artifactos Mesoamericanos. Instituto
Nacional de Anthropología e Historia, Boletin 40:51-55.

THORNTON, M.D., E.D. MORGAN, and F. CELORIA

3816a 1970 The Composition of Bog Butter. Science and Archaeology
2-3:20-25.

WALKER, R., et al.

3817 1971 Applications of Solid-State Nuclear Tract Detectors to
Archaeology. In R.H. Brill, ed., Science and Archaeology:
279-284. MIT Press, Cambridge, Mass.

WARREN, S.E.

3818 1973 Geometrical Factors in the Neutron Activation Analysis of
Archaeological Specimens. Archaeometry 15(1):115-122.

YAO, T.C., and F.H. STROSS

3819 1965 The Use of Analysis by X-ray Fluorescence in the Study of
Coins. American Journal of Archaeology 69(2):154-155.

16. Mathematical Methods for Ordering Archaeological Data

ASCHER, M.

3820 1959 A Mathematical Rationale for Graphical Seriation. American
Antiquity 25:212-214.

BASSHAM, E.

3821 1971 Application of Probability Theory to Recurring Variables
in Some El Paso Phase Archeological Sites. Transactions,
Sixth Regional Archeological Symposium for Southeast New
Mexico and Western Texas:83-90.

BECKES, M.L.

3822 1978 An Application of Ordinal Matrix Analysis to Archaeological
Data. Plains Anthropologist 23(82):301-310.

BERRY, K.J., K.L. KVAMME, and P.W. MIELKE, Jr.

3823 1980 A Permutation Technique for the Spatial Analysis of the
Distribution of Artifacts into Classes. American Antiquity
45(1):55-59.

314   The Work of the Archaeologist

BOHMERS, A.

3824 1956 Statistics and Graphs in the Study of Flint Assemblages;
            II, A Preliminary Report on the Statistical Analysis of
            the Younger Palaeolithic in Northwestern Europe. Palaeo-
            historia 5:7-26.

3825 1963 A Statistical Analysis of Flint Artifacts. In D. Broth-
            well and E. Higgs, eds., Science in Archaeology:469-481.
            Thames and Hudson, London.

3826 1964 Statistics and Graphs in the Study of Prehistoric Indus-
            tries; VIII, A Method for the Study of Potsherds. Palaeo-
            historia 10:63-70.

BOHMERS, A., and A. WOUTERS

3827 1956 Statistics and Graphs in the Study of Flint Assemblages.
            Palaeohistoria 5:1-38.

CLARKE, D.L.

3828 1962 Matrix Analysis and Archaeology with Special Reference to
            British Beaker Pottery. Proceedings, Prehistoric Society
            28:371-382.

3829 1963 Matrix Analysis and Archaeology. Nature 199:790-792.

COWGILL, G.L.

3830 1968 Archaeological Applications of Factor, Cluster, and
            Proximity Analyses. American Antiquity 33:367-375.

CROES, D., J. DAVIS, and H.T. IRWIN

3831 1974 The Use of Computer Graphics in Archaeology: A Case Study
            from the Ozette Site, Washington. Washington State Univer-
            sity, Laboratory of Anthropology, Reports of Investigations
            52.

CULLBERG, C., et al.

3832 1969 Practical and Statistical Approach to Some Flake Measuring
            Problems. Norwegian Archaeological Review 2:33-51.

DANIELS, S.

3833 1967 Statistics, Typology and Cultural Dynamics in the Transvaal
            Middle Stone Age. South African Archaeological Bulletin
            22:114-125.

DANIELS, S.G.H.

3834 1966 An Operational Scheme for the Analysis of Large Assem-
            blages of Archaeological Material. Archaeometry 9:151-154.

DEETZ, J., and E. DETHLEFSEN

3835 1965 The Doppler Effect and Archaeology: A Consideration of
            the Spatial Aspects of Seriation. Southwestern Journal
            of Anthropology 21:196-206.

De GIECO, A.M.L.

3836 1965 Sobre la Aplicación de Métodos Estadísticos al Estudio del Arte Repestre. Anales de Arquelogía y Etnología, Tomo XX. Mendoza, Argentina.

DEMPSEY, P., and M. BAUMHOFF

3837 1963 The Statistical Use of Artifact Distributions to Establish Chronological Sequence. American Antiquity 28:496-509.

DORAN, J.E.

3838 1975 Mathematics and Computers in Archaeology. Edinburgh University Press, Edinburgh.

DORAN, J.E., and F.R. HODSON

3839 1966 A Digital Computer Analysis of Palaeolithic Flint Assemblages. Nature 210:688-689.

DOWNIE, N.M., and R.W. HEATH

3840 1965 Basic Statistical Methods. Harper and Row, New York.

DUNNELL, R.C.

3841 1970 Seriation Method and Its Evaluation. American Antiquity 35(3):305-319.

FITTING, J.E.

3842 1965 A Quantitative Examination of Virginia Fluted Points. American Antiquity 30:441-445.

FORD, J.A.

3843 1962 A Quantitative Method for Deriving Cultural Chronology. Pan American Union I. Washington, D.C.

GILMAN, A., P. OSSA, and M. POHL

3844 1974 Multidimensional Scaling of Aurignacian Assemblages. Miscelanea Arquelógica I:339-351. Barcelona.

HEINZELIN de BRAUCOURT, J. de

3845 1960 Principes de Diagnose Numérique en Typologie. Mémoires d'Academie Royal de Belgique 14(1703):72.

HODSON, F.R.

3846 1969 Searching for Structure Within Multivariate Archaeological Data. World Archaeology I:90-105.

3847 1970 Cluster Analysis and Archaeology: Some New Developments and Applications. World Archaeology I:299-320.

HODSON, F.R., P.H.H. SNEATH, and J.E. DORAN

3848 1966 Some Experiments in the Numerical Analysis of Archaeological Data. Biometrika 53(3-4):311-324.

JELINEK, A.J.

3849 1962 Use of the Cumulative Graph in Temporal Ordering. American
            Antiquity 28:241-243.

JOHNSON, L., Jr.

3850 1968 Item Seriation as an Aid for Elementary Scale and Cluster
            Analysis. Museum of Natural History, University of
            Oregon, Bulletin 15.

3851 1971 Interdependent Data, Cluster Analysis and Archaeology.
            Proceedings, Prehistoric Society 37(1):231-233.

KENDALL, D.G.

3852 1969 Incidence Matrices, Interval Graphs, and Seriation in
            Archaeology. Pacific Journal of Mathematics 28:565-570.

3853 1969 Some Problems and Methods in Statistical Archaeology.
            World Archaeology I:68-76.

3854 1970 A Mathematical Approach to Seriation. The Impact of the
            Natural Sciences on Archaeology:125-134. Oxford Univer-
            sity Press, London.

KENDALL, D.G., et al.

3855 1972 Mathematics in the Archaeological and Historical Sciences.
            Aldine, Chicago.

KERRICH, J.E., and D.L. CLARKE

3856 1967 Notes on the Possible Misuse and Errors of Cumulative
            Percentage Frequency Graphs for the Comparison of Prehis-
            toric Artefact Assemblages. Proceedings, Prehistoric
            Society 33:57-69.

KNOROZOV, Y.V.

3857 1963 Machine Decipherment of Maya Script. Soviet Anthropology
            and Archaeology I:43-50.

KOLSTOE, R.H.

3858 1969 Introduction to Statistics for the Behavioral Sciences.
            Dorsey Press, Homewood, Ill.

KUHN, E.

3859 1938 Zur Quantitativen Analyse der Hausfierwelt der Pfahlbaufen
            der Schweiz. Viertelgahrsschrift der Naturforschenden
            Gesellschaft Zurich 83:253-263.

LYNCH, B.M., and R. DONAHUE

3860 1980 A Statistical Analysis of Two Rock-Art Sites in Northwest
            Kenya. Journal of Field Archaeology 7(1):75-85.

McGHEE, R.

3861 1970 A Quantitative Comparison of Dorset Culture Microblade
            Samples. Arctic Anthropology 7(2):89-96.

McMICHAEL, E.V.

3862 1958 Statistical Analysis in Archaeology. Proceedings, Indiana Academy of Science 68:65-69.

MATHES, E.W.

3863 1970 An Empirical Trial of the Effectiveness of Statistical Methodology with Site Survey Data. Plains Anthropologist 15(50):297-301.

MATTHEWS, J.

3864 1963 Application of Matrix Analysis to Archaeological Problems. Nature 198:930-934.

MOBERG, C.A.

3865 1961 Mangder av Fornfund (with English Summary: Trends in the Present Development of Quantitative Methods in Archaeology). Acta Universitadis Gothoburgensis, Goteborgs Universitets Arsskrift 47(1). Goteborg.

MYERS, O.H.

3866 1950 Some Applications of Statistics to Archaeology. Service des Antiquités de l'Egypte. Government Press, Cairo.

NANCE, J.D.

3867 1971 The Methodological Basis of Archaeological Classification. Western Canadian Journal of Anthropology 2(2):83-91.

NEWCOMER, M.H.

3868 1971 Some Quantitative Experiments in Handaxe Manufacture. World Archaeology 3(1):85-93.

PARTRIDGE, T.C.

3869 1965 A Statistical Analysis of the Limeworks Lithic Assemblage. South African Archaeological Bulletin 20(79), Pt. 3:112-116.

PETERS, C.R.

3870 1970 Introductory Topics in Probability Sampling Theory for Archaeology. Anthropology UCLA 2(2):33-50.

RENFREW, C., and K.L. COOKE, eds.

3871 1979 Transformations: Mathematical Approaches to Culture Change. Academic Press, New York.

SACKETT, J.R.

3872 1966 Quantitative Analysis of Upper Paleolithic Stone Tools. American Anthropologist 69(2), Pt. 2:356-394.

SPAULDING, A.C.

3873 1960 Statistical Description and Comparison of Artifact Assemblages. In R.F. Heizer and S.F. Cook, eds., Viking Fund Publications in Anthropology 28:60-92.

THOMAS, D.H.

3874 1972 The Use and Abuse of Numerical Taxonomy in Archaeology.
            Archaeology and Physical Anthropology in Oceania 12:31-49.

3875 1975 Figuring Anthropology: First Principles of Probability
            and Statistics. Holt, Rinehart and Winston, New York.

3876 1978 The Awful Truth About Statistics in Archaeology. American
            Antiquity 43(2):231-244.

THORN, A.

3877 1966 Megaliths and Mathematics. Antiquity 40:121-128.

TUGBY, D.J.

3878 1964 On the Use of Scale Analysis in the Study of Cultures.
            Man 181:144-146.

3879 1965 Archaeological Objectives and Statistical Methods: A
            Frontier in Archaeology. American Antiquity 31:1-16.

TURPIN, S., and J.A. NEELY

3880 1977 An Automated Computer Technique for Vessel Form Analysis.
            Plains Anthropologist 22(78):313-319.

WISSLER, C.

3881 1916 The Application of Statistical Methods of the Data on the
            Trenton Argillite Culture. American Anthropologist 18:
            190-197.

WITHERSPOON, Y.T.

3882 1961 A Statistical Device for Comparing Trait Lists. American
            Antiquity 26:433-436.

ZASLOW, B., and A.E. DITTERT

3883 1977 Pattern Mathematics and Archaeology. Arizona State
            University, Anthropological Research Papers 2. Tempe.

F. INTERPRETATION

1. Ethnographic Analogy

AGOGINO, G., and B. FERGUSON

3884 1978 Two Instances of the Use of Ethnographic Analogy in the
            Study of the Paleo-Indian. Anthropological Journal of
            Canada 16(4):15-16.

ASCHER, R.

3885 1961 Analogy in Archaeological Interpretation. Southwestern
            Journal of Anthropology 17:317-325.

3886 1962 Ethnology for Archaeology: A Case from the Seri Indians.
Ethnology 1:360-369.

BAERREIS, D.A.

3887 1961 The Ethnohistoric Approach and Archeology. Ethnohistory
8:49-77.

BALFET, H.

3888 1965 Ethnographical Observations (on Pottery Making) in North
Africa and Archeological Interpretation. Viking Fund
Publications in Anthropology 41:161-177.

BINFORD, L.R.

3889 1967 Smudge Pots and Hide Smoking: The Use of Analogy in
Archaeological Reasoning. American Antiquity 32:1-12.

3890 1975 Methodological Considerations of the Archeological Use
of Ethnographic Data. In R.B. Lee and I. DeVore, eds.,
Man the Hunter:268-273. Aldine, Chicago.

BINFORD, S.R.

3891 1975 Ethnographic Data and Understanding the Pleistocene. In
R.B. Lee and I. DeVore, eds., Man the Hunter:274-275.
Aldine, Chicago.

BLINKENBERG, C.

3892 1911 The Thunder Weapon in Religion and Folklore: A Study in
Comparative Folklore. Cambridge University Press,
Cambridge.

BULMER, R.M.H.

3893 1971 The Role of Ethnography in Reconstructing the Prehistory
of Melanesia. In R. Green and M. Kelly, eds., Studies
in Oceanic Culture History 2. Pacific Anthropological
Records 12:36-44.

CAMPBELL, J.M.

3894 1968 Territoriality Among Ancient Hunters: Interpretations
from Ethnography and Nature. In Anthropological Archeology
in the Americas:1-21. Anthropological Society of Washington.

CARNEIRO, R.

3895 1956 Slash-and-Burn Agriculture: A Closer Look at Its Implications for Settlement Patterns. Selected Papers of the
Fifth International Congress of Anthropological and Ethnological Sciences:229-234. University of Pennsylvania
Press, Philadelphia.

3896 1961 Slash-and-Burn Cultivation Among the Kuikuru and Its
Implications for Cultural Development in the Amazon Basin.
Antropológica (Supplement 2):47-67. Caracas, Venezuela.

CARPENTER, E.S.

3897   1961   Ethnological Clues for the Interpretation of Archeological
              Data. Pennsylvania Archaeologist 31(3-4):148-150.

CHANG, K.

3898   1967   Major Aspects of the Interrelationship of Archeology and
              Ethnology. Current Anthropology 8:227-243.

CLARK, J.G.D.

3899   1951   Folk-Culture and the Study of European Prehistory.   In
              W. Grimes, ed., Aspects of Archaeology in Great Britain
              and Beyond:49-65. London.

DEUEL, T.

3900   1952   Hopewellian Dress in Illinois. In J.B. Griffin, ed.,
              Archeology of Eastern United States:165-175. University
              of Chicago Press, Chicago.

DOMERRECH, E.

3901   1860   Seven Years' Residence in the Great Deserts of North
              America. Vol. 2. Longman, Green, Longman and Roberts,
              London.

DONNAN, C.B.

3902   1971   Ancient Peruvian Potters' Marks and Their Interpretation
              Through Ethnographic Analogy. American Antiquity 36(4):
              460-465.

DRIVER, H.E., and W.C. MASSEY

3903   1957   Comparative Studies of North American Indians. Transac-
              tions, American Philosophical Society 47(2). Philadelphia.

DRUCKER, P.

3904   1951   The Northern and Central Nootkan Tribes. Bureau of
              American Ethnology, Bulletin 144.

3905   1961   The La Venta Olmec Support Area. Kroeber Anthropological
              Society Papers 25:59-72. Berkeley.

EGGAN, F.

3906   1952   The Ethnological Cultures of Eastern United States and
              Their Archaeological Backgrounds. In J.B. Griffin, ed.,
              Archaeology of Eastern United States:35-45. University
              of Chicago Press, Chicago.

EISENBERG, L.

3907   1971   Anthropological Archaeology: Ethnography or Ethnology?
              Plains Anthropologist 16(54):298-301.

FREUDENTHAL, P.

3908   1966   Archaeology and Ethnographic Field Research (Fourth Con-
              ference of Nordic Anthropologists). Ethnos Supplement 31:
              89-91.

FRIEDRICH, M.H.

3909 1970 Design, Structure and Social Interaction: Archaeological Implications of an Ethnographic Analysis. American Antiquity 35(3):332-343.

GJESSING, G.

3910 1963 Socio-Archaeology. Folk 5:103-112.

GREY, G.

3911 1841 Journals of Two Expeditions of Discovery in North-West and Western Australia, During the Years 1837, 38 and 39. 2 vols. Boone, London.

GRINSELL, L.V.

3912 1976 Folklore of Prehistoric Sites in Britain. David and Charles, Newton Abbot, England and North Pomfret, Vt.

HALSETH, O.S.

3913 1933 Archeology in the Making. Southwest Museum Masterkey 7: 37-41.

HEIDER, K.G.

3914 1967 Archaeological Assumptions and Ethnographic Facts: A Cautionary Tale from New Guinea. Southwestern Journal of Anthropology 23:52-64.

HESTER, T.R.

3915 1972 Ethnographic Evidence for the Thermal Alteration of Siliceous Stone. Tebiwa 15(2):63-65.

HIROA, TE RANGI (P.H. BUCK)

3916 1930 Samoan Material Culture. B.P. Bishop Museum, Bulletin 75. Honolulu.

HOLMES, W.H.

3917 1913 The Relation of Archeology to Ethnology. American Anthropologist 15:566-567.

HOUGH, W.

3918 1916 Experimental Work in American Archeology and Ethnology. Holmes Anniversary Volume:194-197. Smithsonian Institution, Washington, D.C.

3919 1918 The Hopi Indian Collection in the United States National Museum. U.S. National Museum, Proceedings 54:235-296.

KEHOE, T.F.

3920 1958 Tipi Rings: The Direct Ethnological Approach Applied to an Archaeological Problem. American Anthropologist 60: 861-873.

LEAHY, M.J., and M. CRAIN

3921 1937 The Land That Time Forgot; Adventures and Discoveries in
            New Guinea. Funk and Wagnalls, London.

LESHNIK, L.S.

3922 1967 Archaeological Interpretation of Burials in the Light of
            Central Indian Ethnography. Zeitschrift für Ethnologie
            92(1):23-32.

MACALISTER, R.A.S.

3923 1949 The Archaeology of Ireland. Methuen, London.

McGEE, W.J.

3924 1898 The Seri Indians. Bureau of American Ethnology, Annual
            Report 17(1):9-344.

MALKIN, B.

3925 1962 Seri Ethnozoology. Occasional Papers of the Idaho State
            College Museum 7. Pocatello.

MYERS, T.P.

3926 1972 A Seasonal Campsite in the Peruvian Montana: Ethnography
            and Ecology in Archaeological Interpretation. American
            Antiquity 37(4):540-545.

NEUSTUPNÝ, J.

3927 1968 Ethno-Prehistory of Central Europe. Proceedings, 8th
            International Congress of Anthropological and Ethnological
            Sciences 3:191-193.

NUNLEY, J.P.

3928 1971 Archaeological Interpretation and the Particularistic
            Model--the Coahuiltecan Case. Plains Anthropologist
            16(54):302-310.

OPLER, M.E.

3929 1941 The Apache Life-Way. University of Chicago Press,
            Chicago.

PARSONS, E.C.

3930 1940 Relations Between Ethnology and Archaeology in the
            Southwest. American Antiquity 5:214-220.

PAULME, D.

3931 1949 Utilisation Moderne d'Objets Préhistoriques à des Fins
            Rituelles en Pays Kissi. Notes Africaines 44:119.
            Bulletin d'Information et de Correspondance. Institute
            Français d'Afrique Noire.

PETERSON, N.

3932 1968 The Pestle and Mortar: An Ethnographic Analogy for
Archaeology in Arnhem Land. Mankind 6:567-570.

POSPOSIL, L.

3933 1963 The Kapauku Papuans of West New Guinea. Holt, Rinehart
and Winston, New York.

REED, E.K.

3934 1962 Cultural Continuity from Pre-Spanish Archaeological
Groups to Modern Indian Tribes in the Southwestern United
States. Akten des 34 Internationalen Amerikanisten-
kongresses:298-300.

REINA, R.E., and R.M. HILL II

3935 1980 Lowland Maya Subsistence: Notes from Ethnohistory and
Ethnography. American Antiquity 45(1):74-79.

RIESENFELD, A.

3936 1950 The Megalithic Culture of Melanesia. E.J. Brill, Leiden.

ROBBINS, M.C.

3937 1966 House Types and Settlement Patterns: An Application of
Ethnology to Archaeological Interpretations. Minnesota
Archaeologist 28(1):2-35.

ROUSE, I.

3938 1965 The Place of Peoples in Prehistoric Research. Journal,
Royal Anthropological Institute 95:1-15.

SALISBURY, R.

3939 1962 From Stone to Steel. Melbourne University Press.

SANDIN, B.

3940 1962 Gawai Batu: The Iban Whetstone Feast. Sarawak Museum
Journal 10:392-408.

SAYCE, R.U.

3941 1963 Primitive Arts and Crafts: An Introduction to the Study
of Material Culture. Biblo and Tannen, New York.

SCOTT, W.H.

3942 1958 Economic and Material Culture of the Kalingas of Madukayan.
Southwestern Journal of Anthropology 14:318-337.

SERVICE, E.R.

3943 1964 Archaeological Theory and Ethnological Fact. In R.A.
Manners, ed., Process and Pattern in Culture; Essays in
Honor of Julian H. Steward:364-375. Aldine, Chicago.

SMITH, M.A.

3944 1955 The Limitations of Inference in Archaeology. The
            Archaeological Newsletter 6:1-7.

SPECTOR, J.D.

3945 1977 Winnebago Indians and Lead Mining: A Case Study of the
            Ethnohistoric Approach in Archaeology. Midcontinental
            Journal of Archaeology 2(1):131-137.

SPENCER, R.F.

3946 1959 The North Alaskan Eskimo. Smithsonian Institution,
            Bureau of American Ethnology, Bulletin 171.

SPIER, L.

3947 1955 Mohave Culture Items. Museum of Northern Arizona,
            Bulletin 28. Flagstaff.

STEWARD, J.H.

3948 1938 Basin-Plateau Aboriginal Sociopolitical Groups. Bureau
            of American Ethnology Bulletin 120.

TAYLOR, W.W.

3949 1972 The Hunter-Gatherer Nomads of Northern Mexico: A Com-
            parison of the Archival and Archaeological Records.
            World Archaeology 4(2):167-178.

THOMPSON, J.E.S.

3950 1967 The Maya Central Area at the Spanish Conquest and Later:
            A Problem in Demography. Proceedings, Royal Anthropological
            Institute of Great Britain and Ireland for 1966:23-38.

THOMPSON, R.H.

3951 1956 The Subjective Element in Archaeological Inference.
            Southwestern Journal of Anthropology 12:327-332.

THOMSON, D.F.

3952 1939 The Seasonal Factor in Human Culture, Illustrated From
            the Life of a Contemporary Nomadic Group. Proceedings,
            Prehistoric Society 5(2):209-221.

Van der MERWE, N.J., and R.T.K. SCULLY

3953 1971 The Phalaborwa Story: Archaeological and Ethnographic
            Investigation of a South African Iron Age Group. World
            Archaeology 3(2):178-196.

WATSON, P.J.

3954 1966 Clues to Iranian Prehistory in Modern Village Life.
            Expedition 8:9-19.

WAUGH, F.W.

3955 1916 Iroquois Foods and Food Preparation. Canada Department of Mines, Geological Survey, Memoir 86, Anthropological Series 12. Ottawa.

WEBB, W.S., and R.S. BABY

3956 1957 The Adena People: 2. Ohio Historical Society, Ohio State University Press, Columbus, Ohio.

WHITE, T.E.

3957 1953 Observations on the Butchering Technique of Some Aboriginal Peoples: 2. American Antiquity 19:160-164.

3958 1954 Observations on the Butchering Technique of Some Aboriginal Peoples: 3, 4, 5, 6. American Antiquity 19:254-264.

3959 1955 Observations on the Butchering Technique of Some Aboriginal Peoples: 7, 8, 9. American Antiquity 21:170-178.

WILLIAMS, B.J.

3960 1968 Establishing Cultural Heterogeneities in Settlement Patterns: An Ethnographic Example. In S. Binford and L. Binford, eds., New Perspectives in Archeology:161-170. Aldine, Chicago.

WILSON, G.L.

3961 1917 Agriculture of the Hidatsa Indians: An Indian Interpretation. University of Minnesota, Studies in the Social Sciences 9. Minneapolis.

WOODWARD, A.

3962 1933 Ancient Houses of Modern Mexico. Bulletin of the Southern California Academy of Sciences 32:79 98. Los Angeles.

2. Experimentation and Replication

ABERG, F.A., and H.C. BOWEN

3963 1960 Ploughing Experiments with a Reconstructed Donneruplund Ard. Antiquity 34:144-147.

ARTHURS, D.

3964 1973 The Freshwater Bivalve: A Versatile Pottery Decorating Tool. Pennsylvania Archaeologist 43(1):15-19.

ASCHER, R.

3965 1961 Experimental Archaeology. American Anthropologist 63: 793-816.

3966 1970 Cues 1: Design and Construction of an Experimental Archaeological Structure. American Antiquity 35(2): 215-216.

BANKOFF, H.A., and F.A. WINTER

3967   1979   A House-Burning in Serbia.   Archaeology 32(5):8-14.

BIBBY, G.

3968   1970   An Experiment with Time.   Horizon 12(2):96-101.

BIBERSON, P., and E. AGUIRRE

3969   1965   Expériences de Taille d'Outils Préhistoriques dans des
              Os d'Éléphant.   Quaternaria 7:165-182.

BIMSON, M.

3970   1956   The Technique of Greek Black and Terra Sigillata Red.
              Antiquaries Journal 36:200-204.

BONNICHSEN, R.

3971   1973   Millie's Camp: An Experiment in Archaeology.   World
              Archaeology 4(3):277-291.

BORDES, F.

3972   1950   Principes d'une Méthode d'Étude des Techniques de Débitage
              et de la Typologie du Paléolithique Ancien et Moyen.
              L'Anthropologie 54:19-34.

BOWEN, H.C., and P.D. WOOD

3973   1968   Experimental Storage of Corn Underground and Its Im-
              plications for Iron Age Settlements.   Bulletin of the
              University of London Institute of Archaeology 7:1-14.

BOWEN, R.L.

3974   1959   Experimental Nautical Research: Third Millennium B.C.;
              Egyptian Sails.   The Mariner's Mirror 45:332-337.

BREASTED, J.H.

3975   1935   Ancient Times.   2nd ed.   Ginn, New York.

BRILL, R.H.

3976   1963   Ancient Glass.   Scientific American 209:120-130.

BUSBY, C.I.

3977   1974   The Manufacture of a Petroglyph: A Replicative Experiment
              (with J.C. Bard).   Contributions, University of California
              Archaeological Research Facility 20:83-102.

CALLAHAN, E., ed.

3978   1971   Experimental Archaeology 499-E.   Newsletter Publication,
              Virginia Commonwealth University, Richmond.

3979   1973   The Old Rag Report: A Practical Guide to Living Archae-
              ology.   Department of Sociology and Anthropology, Virginia
              Commonwealth University, Richmond.

3980 1974 The Ape: Experimental Archeology Papers, No. 3. Student
          Papers from Department of Sociology and Anthropology,
          Virginia Commonwealth University, Richmond.

CALLENDER, D.W., Jr.

3981 1976 Reliving the Past: Experimental Archaeology in Pennsyl-
          vania. Archaeology 29(3):173-177.

CHILDE, V.G., and W. THORNEYCROFT

3982 1938 The Experimental Production of the Phenomena Distinctive
          of Vitrified Forts. Proceedings, Society of Antiquaries
          of Scotland 72:44-55.

CLAUSEN, C.J., et al.

3983 1979 Little Salt Spring, Florida: A Unique Underwater Site.
          Science 203(4381):609-614.

COLES, J.M.

3984 1968 Experimental Archaeology. Proceedings, Society of
          Antiquaries of Scotland 99:1-21.

3985 1973 Archaeology by Experiment. Hutchinson, London.

CRABTREE, D.E.

3986 1966 A Stoneworker's Approach to Analyzing and Replicating the
          Lindenmeier Folsom. Tebiwa 9:3-39.

CRABTREE, D.E., and B.R. BUTLER

3987 1964 Notes on Experiments in Flint Knapping: I. Heat Treatment
          of Silica Minerals. Tebiwa 7:1-6.

CRABTREE, D.E., and E.L. DAVIS

3988 1968 Experimental Manufacture of Wooden Implements with Tools
          of Flaked Stone. Science 159:426-428.

CURWEN, E., and E.C. CURWEN

3989 1926 The Efficiency of the Scapula as a Shovel. Sussex
          Archaeological Collections 67:139-145.

CUSHING, F.H.

3990 1894 Primitive Copper Working: An Experimental Study. American
          Anthropologist 7:93-117.

DAGENHARDT, J.R.

3991 1972 Perforated Soapstone Discs: A Functional Test. Notebook,
          Institute of Archaeology and Anthropology IV(3):65-68.

DANIEL, G.

3992 1962 The Megalith Builders of Western Europe. Pelican Books,
          Baltimore, Md.

De PRADENNE, A.V.

3993   1937   The Use of Wood in Megalithic Structures. Antiquity 11
              (41):87-132.

DUNHAM, D.

3994   1956   Building an Egyptian Pyramid. Archaeology 9:159-165.

ELLIS, H.H.

3995   1940   Flint-Working Techniques of the American Indian; an
              Experimental Study. Ohio State Museum Lithic Laboratory,
              Columbus.

ENGLEBACH, R.

3996   1923   The Problem of the Obelisks. George H. Doran, New York.

ERASMUS, C.

3997   1965   Monument Building: Some Field Experiments. Southwestern
              Journal of Anthropology 21:277-301.

EVANS, J.G., and S. LIMBREY

3998   1974   The Experimental Earthwork on Morden Bog, Wareham, Dorset,
              England: 1963 to 1972. Proceedings, Prehistoric Society
              40:170-202.

FINNEY, B.R.

3999   1977   Voyaging Canoes and the Settlement of Polynesia. Science
              196:1277-1285.

GORDON, D.H.

4000   1953   Fire and the Sword: The Technique of Destruction. Antiquity
              27:149-153.

GREBINGER, P., ed.

4001   1978   Discovering Past Behavior: Experiments in the Archaeology
              of the American Southwest. Gordon and Breach, New York.

GRIFFIN, J., and C.W. ANGELL

4002   1935   An Experimental Study of the Techniques of Pottery Making.
              Papers of the Michigan Academy of Science, Arts and Letters
              20:1-6.

HANSEN, H.-O.

4003   1961   Ungdommelige Oldtidshuse. Kuml 1961:128-145.

4004   1962   I Built a Stone Age House. Phoenix, London.

4005   1964   Mand og Hus. Rhodos, Copenhagen.

HARNER, M.J.

4006   1956   Thermo-Facts vs. Artifacts: An Experimental Study of the
              Malpais Industry. University of California Archaeological
              Survey Report 33:39-43.

HARTENBERG, R.S., and J. SCHMIDT, Jr.

4007 1969 The Egyptian Drill and the Origin of the Crank. Technology and Culture 10:155–165.

HENNIG, E.

4008 1961 Untersuchungen über den Verwendungsweck Urgeschichtlicher Schuhleistenkeile. Alt-Thuringen 5, S. 189–222. Weimar.

4009 1965 Bericht über die Praktischen Versuche zur Funktionellen Deutung der Neolithischen Steingerate. Archeologicke Rozhledy 17, S. 682–690. Praha.

HESTER, T.R., and R.F. HEIZER

4010 1972 Problems in Functional Interpretations: The Scraper-Planes of Mitla, Oaxaca, Mexico. Contributions, University of California Archaeological Research Facility 14: 107–123.

4011 1973 Bibliography of Archaeology I: Experiments, Lithic Technology, and Petrography. Addison-Wesley Modules in Anthropology 29.

HESTER, T.R., M.P. MILDNER, and L. SPENCER

4012 1974 Great Basin Atlatl Studies. Ballena Press Publications in Archaeology, Ethnology and History 2.

HEYERDAHL, T.

4013 1950 Kon-Tiki: Across the Pacific by Raft. Rand-McNally, Chicago.

4014 1950 The Kon Tiki Expedition by Raft Across the South Seas. Translated by F.H. Lyon. Allen & Unwin, London.

4015 1978 Early Man and the Ocean: A Search for the Beginning of Navigation and Seaborne Civilizations. Doubleday and Co., New York.

HONEA, K.H.

4016 1965 The Bipolar Flaking Technique in Texas and New Mexico. Bulletin, Texas Archeological Society 36:259–267.

4017 1965 A Morphology of Scrapers and Their Methods of Production. Southwestern Lore 31(2).

HUCKELL, B.

4018 1979 Of Chipped Stone Tools, Elephants, and the Clovis Hunters: An Experiment. Plains Anthropologist 24(58):177–190.

INGERSOLL, D., J.E. YELLEN, and W. MacDONALD

4019 1977 Experimental Archeology. Columbia University Press, New York.

ISAAC, G.L.

4020 1957 Towards the Interpretation of Occupation Debris: Some
            Experiments and Observations. Kroeber Anthropological
            Society Papers 37:31-57.

IVERSEN, J.

4021 1956 Forest Clearance in the Stone Age. Scientific American
            194:36-41.

JENNINGS, J.D.

4022 1949 Table-Top Archaeology. Plains Archaeological Conference
            Newsletter 2(2-3):30-33; 44-45.

JEWELL, P.A., ed.

4023 1963 The Experimental Earthwork on Overton Down, Wiltshire,
            1960. British Association for the Advancement of Science,
            London.

JEWELL, P.A., and G.W. DIMBLEBY, eds.

4024 1966 The Experimental Earthwork on Overton Down, Wiltshire,
            England: The First Four Years. Proceedings, Prehistoric
            Society 32:313-342.

JOHNSON, T.

4025 1957 An Experiment in Cave-Painting Media. South African
            Archaeological Bulletin 47:98-101.

JOHNSTONE, P.

4026 1972 Bronze Age Sea Trial. Antiquity 46:269-274.

JORGENSEN, S.

4027 1953 Skovrydhing Med Flintokse (Forest Clearance with Flint
            Axes). Fra Nationalmuseets Arbejdsmark, 1953:36-43; 109-
            110.

KNOWLES, F.H.S.

4028 1944 The Manufacture of a Flint Arrowhead by a Quartzite
            Hammer Stone. Pitt Rivers Museum, Oxford University,
            Occasional Papers on Technology 1.

LAYARD, N.F.

4029 1922 Prehistoric Cooking Places in Norfolk. Proceedings,
            Prehistoric Society (East Anglia) 3(IV):483-498.

LEECHMAN, D.

4030 1950 Aboriginal Tree-Felling. National Museum of Canada,
            Bulletin 118. Ottawa.

LEEK, F.

4031 1969 The Problem of Brain Removal During Embalming by the An-
            cient Egyptians. Journal of Egyptian Archaeology 55:112-
            116.

LEHMANN, H.

4032 1957 Ma Plus Belle Découverte. Marco Polo 27:13-24.

McADAM, E., and T. WATKINS

4033 1974 Experimental Reconstruction of a Short Cist. Journal of Archaeological Science 1(4):383-386.

McEWEN, J.M.

4034 1946 An Experiment with Primitive Maori Carving Tools. Journal of the Polynesian Society 55:111-116.

McGUIRE, J.D.

4035 1891 The Stone Hammer and Its Various Uses. American Anthropologist 4:301-312.

4036 1892 Materials, Apparatus and Processes of the Aboriginal Lapidary. American Anthropologist 5:165-176.

MacIVER, R.

4037 1921 On the Manufacture of Etruscan and Other Ancient Black Wares. Man 21:86-88.

MALLOUF, R.J., and C. TUNNELL

4038 1977 An Experiment in Aboriginal Subsistence Technique. In R.J. Mallouf and C. Tunnell, An Archeological Reconnaissance of the Lower Canyons of the Rio Grande:59-62. Office of the State Archeologist, Texas Historical Commission, Archeological Survey Report 22.

MAYES, P., et al.

4039 1961 The Firing of a Pottery Kiln of Romano-British Type at Boston, Lincs. Archaeometry 4:4-30.

4040 1962 The Firing of a Second Pottery Kiln of Romano-British Type at Boston, Lincs. Archaeometry 5:80-107.

MEWHINNEY, H.

4041 1957 Manual for Neanderthals. University of Texas Press, Austin.

NEILL, W.T.

4042 1952 The Manufacture of Fluted Points. Florida Anthropologist 5:9-16.

NEWCOMER, M.H.

4043 1974 Study and Replication of Bone Tools from Ksar Akil (Lebanon). World Archaeology 6(2):138-153.

NIETSCH, H.

4044 1939 Wald und Siedlung im Vorgeschichtlichen Mitteleuropa. Mannus-Bucherei, Leipzig.

NOBLE, J.V.

4045 1960 The Technique of Attic Vase Painting. American Journal
            of Archaeology 64:307-318.

O'KELLY, M.J.

4046 1954 Excavation and Experiments in Ancient Irish Cooking-
            Places. Journal, Royal Society of Antiquaries of Ireland
            84:105-155.

OSBORNE, C.M.

4047 1965 The Preparation of Yucca Fibers: An Experimental Study.
            American Antiquity 31(2), Pt. 2:45-50.

OUTWATER, J.O.

4048 1957 Pre-Columbian Wood-Cutting Techniques. American
            Antiquity 22:410-411.

PARK, E.

4049 1978 The Ginsberg Caper: Hacking It as in Stone Age. Smith-
            sonian 9(4):85-96.

PEETS, O.H.

4050 1960 Experiments in the Use of Atlatl Weights. American
            Antiquity 26:108-110.

PLEINER, R.

4051 1963 Rediscovering the Techniques of Early European Black-
            smiths. Archaeology 16:234-242.

POND, A.W.

4052 1930 Primitive Methods of Working Stone Based on Experiments
            by Halvor L. Skavlem. Logan Museum Bulletin 2(1).
            Beloit College, Beloit, Wis.

POOLE, J.B., and R. REED

4053 1962 The Preparation of Leather and Parchment by the Dead Sea
            Scrolls Community. Technology and Culture 3:1-26.

PULESTON, D.E.

4054 1971 An Experimental Approach to the Function of Classic Maya
            Chultuns. American Antiquity 36(3):322-334.

RAU, C.

4055 1869 Drilling in Stone Without Metal. Annual Report of the
            Smithsonian Institution 1868:392-400.

4056 1881 Aboriginal Stone Drilling. American Naturalist 15:536-
            542.

REYNOLDS, P.J.

4057 1969 Experiment in Iron Age Agriculture. Transcripts, Bristol and Gloucester Archaeological Society 88:29-33.

4058 1972 Experimental Archaeology. Worcester Archaeological Newsletter, Special Edition.

4059 1974 Experimental Iron Age Storage Pits. An Interim Report. Proceedings, Prehistoric Society 40:118-131.

4060 1979 Iron Age Farm; the Butser Experiment. British Museum Publications Ltd., London.

RIETH, A.

4061 1950 Geschliffene Bandkeramische Steingerate zur Holzbearbeitung. Praehistorische Zeitschrift 34/35, S. 230-232. Berlin.

RYDER, M.L.

4062 1966 Can One Cook in a Skin? Antiquity 40:225-227.

SARAYDAR, S.C., and I. SHIMADA

4063 1973 Experimental Archaeology: A New Outlook. American Antiquity 38(3):344-350.

SEBORG, R.M., and R.B. INVERARITY

4064 1962 Conservation of 200-Year-Old Water Logged Boats with Polyethylene Glycol. Studies in Conservation 7:11-12.

4065 1962 Preservation of Old, Waterlogged Wood by Treatment with Polyethylene Glycol. Science 136:649-650. Washington, D.C.

SEMENOV, S.A.

4066 1959 Eksperimentalnyje Issledovanija Pervobytnoj Techniki. Sovetskaja Archeologija 2, S. 35-46. Moskva.

4067 1963 Izucenije Pervobytnoj Techniki Metodom Eksperimenta. Novyje Metody v Archeologiceskich Issledovanijach, S. 191-214. Moskva.

4068 1964 Prehistoric Technology. Translated by M.W. Thompson. Cory, Adams, and McKay, London.

SHANAN, L., M. EVANAU, and N.H. TADMOR

4069 1969 Ancient Technology and Modern Science Applied to Desert Agriculture. Endeavor 28:68-72.

SMITH, C.S.

4070 1953 Digging Up the Plains Indians' Past. University of Kansas Alumni Magazine 52:4-5.

SOLLBERGER, J.B.

4071 1968 A Partial Report on Research Work Concerning Lithic

Typology and Technology. Bulletin, Texas Archeological
Society 39:95-110.

4072 1969 The Basic Tool Kit Required to Make and Notch Arrow
            Shafts for Stone Points. Bulletin, Texas Archeological
            Society 40:232-240.

4073 1970 Preforms are Not Projectile Point Types. Bulletin,
            Oklahoma Anthropological Society 19:151-154.

4074 1971 A Technological Study of Beveled Knives. Plains Anthro-
            pologist 16(53):209-218.

SOLLBERGER, J.B., and T.R. HESTER

4075 1972 Some Additional Data on the Thermal Alteration of
            Siliceous Stone. Bulletin, Oklahoma Anthropological
            Society 21:181-185.

SPEARS, C.

4076 1975 Hammers, Nuts and Jolts, Cobbles, Cobbles, Cobbles: An
            Experiment in Cobble Technologies in Search of Correlates.
            In C.M. Baker, ed., Arkansas Eastman Archeological Project,
            Arkansas Archeological Survey, Research Report 6.

STANTON, W.R., and F. WILLETT

4077 1963 Archaeological Evidence for Changes in Maize Type in West
            Africa: An Experiment in Technique. Man 43:117-123.

STEELE, R.H.

4078 1930 Experiments in Kaitahu (Ngai-Tahu) Methods in Drilling.
            Journal of the Polynesian Society 39:181-188.

STEENSBERG, A.

4079 1943 Ancient Harvesting Implements: A Study in Archaeology and
            Human Geography. Nationalmuseets Skriffer, Arkeologisk-
            Historisk Raekke 1. Copenhagen.

4080 1957 Some Recent Danish Experiments in Neolithic Agriculture.
            The Agricultural History Review 5:66-73.

4081 1964 A Bronze Age Ard Type from Hama in Syria Intended for
            Rope Traction. Berytus 15:111-139. Copenhagen.

STEGGERDA, M.

4082 1941 Maya Indians of Yucatan. Carnegie Institution of Washington,
            Publication 531.

SWAUGER, J.L., and B.L. WALLACE

4083 1964 An Experiment in Skinning with Egyptian Paleolithic and
            Neolithic Stone Implements. Pennsylvania Archaeologist
            34:1-7.

THORNEYCROFT, W.

4084 1933 Observations on Hut Circles near the Eastern Border of

Perthshire, North of Blaigowrie. Proceedings, Society
of Antiquaries of Scotland 67:187-208.

TREGANZA, A.E., and L.L. VALDIVIA

4085   1955   The Manufacture of Pecked and Ground Stone Artifacts:
A Controlled Study. University of California Archaeological Survey Report 32:19-29.

UERPMANN, H.P.

4086   1973   Animal Bone Finds and Economic Archaeology: A Critical
Study of Osteo-Archaeological Method. World Archaeology
4(3):307-322.

VUKOVIC, S.

4087   1974   Experiments in Drilling Holes in Stones. Translated by
M. Markotic. Calgary Archaeologist 2:20-21.

WALKER, I.C.

4088   1975   Cooking in a Skin. Antiquity 49(195):216-217.

WARREN, S.H.

4089   1914   The Experimental Investigation of Flint Fracture and Its
Application to Problems of Human Implements. Journal
of the Royal Anthropological Institute 44:412-450.

WESLEY, W.H.

4090   1968   Report on Precursory Experimentation with Edge Alterations
of Small Flint Flakes. Tennessee Archaeologist 24(2):
92-99.

WILLIAMS, P.W.

4091   1973   Making Stone Celts. Newsletter of the Northwest Chapter
of the Iowa Archaeological Society 21(3):3.

WILLOUGHBY, C.C.

4092   1903   An Early Experiment. In J. McQuire, ed., Primitive Metal
Working, Discussion as to Copper from the Mounds:55-57.
American Anthropologist, Special Publication.

WYNNE, E.J., and R.F. TYLECOTE

4093   1958   An Experimental Investigation into Primitive Iron-
Smelting Technique. Journal of the Iron and Steel Institute 191:339-348.

ZNACZKO-JAWORSKI, I.L.

4094   1958   Experimental Research on Ancient Mortars and Binding
Materials. Quarterly of History of Science and Technology
3:377-407. Warsaw.

3. Subsistence

a. GENERAL

BENITEZ, A.M. de

4095 1974 Cocina Prehispanica; Prehispanic Cooking. Translated by
            M.W. de Varela. Ediciones Euroamericanas, Mexico.

CLARK, G.

4096 1942 Bees in Antiquity. Antiquity 16(63):208-215.

CLELAND, C.E.

4097 1974 Comparison of the Faunal Remains from French and English
            Refuse Pits at Fort Michilimackinac: A Study in Changing
            Subsistence Patterns. National Historic Sites Branch of
            Parks, Department of Indian and Northern Affairs, Occa-
            sional Papers in Archaeology and History 3. Ottawa,
            Canada.

DAVIS, J.T.

4098 1960 An Appraisal of Certain Speculations of Prehistoric
            Puebloan Subsistence. Southwestern Journal of Anthro-
            pology 16(1):15-21.

GREENFIELD, S.M.

4099 1965 More on the Study of Subsistence Activities. American
            Anthropologist 67:737-744.

HOPE, G.S., and P.J.F. COUTTS

4100 1971 Past and Present Aboriginal Food Resources at Wilson's
            Promontory, Victoria. Mankind 8(2):104-114.

JENSEN, L.B.

4101 1953 Man's Foods. Garrard Press, Champaign, Ill.

JOHNSTON, F., et al., eds.

4102 1942 The Boylston Street Fishweir. Papers of the Peabody
            Foundation for Archaeology 2. Andover, Mass.

LEONE, M.P.

4103 1968 Neolithic Economic Autonomy and Social Distance. Science
            162:1150-1151.

NENQUIN, J.A.E.

4104 1961 Salt. A Study in Economic Prehistory. Dissertationes
            Archaeologicae Gandenses, VI. De Tempel, Brugge (Belgium).

SIMOONS, F.J.

4105 1961 Eat Not This Flesh. University of Wisconsin Press,
            Madison.

SMITH, C.E., Jr., ed.

4106 1973 Man and His Foods; Studies in the Ethnobotany of Nutrition: Contemporary, Primitive, and Prehistoric Non-European Diets. University of Alabama Press, University.

Van MENSCH, P.J.A., and G.F. IJZEREEF

4107 1977 Smoke-Dried Meat in Prehistoric and Roman Netherlands. In B.L. van Beek, et al., eds., Ex Horreo:144-150. Albert Egges van Giffen Instituut, Amsterdam.

WATANABE, N.

4108 1968 Functional Significance of Pottery in Neolithic Mode of Subsistence: Its Biological Background. 8th International Congress of Anthropological and Ethnological Sciences 3: 172.

WATERBOLK, H.T.

4109 1968 Food Production in Prehistoric Europe. Science 162:1093-1102.

WATERS, J.H.

4110 1962 Some Animals Used as Food by Successive Cultural Groups in New England. Bulletin, Archaeological Society of Connecticut 31:32-45.

WATSON, V.

4111 1955 Archaeology and Proteins. American Antiquity 20:288.

YUDKIN, J.

4112 1969 Archaeology and the Nutritionist. In P.J. Ucko and G.W. Dimbleby, eds., The Domestication and Exploitation of Plants and Animals:547-552. Aldine, Chicago.

b. *HUNTING AND GATHERING*

AMBRO, R.

4113 1967 Dietary-Technological-Ecological Aspects of Lovelock Cave Coprolites. University of California Archaeological Survey, Report 70:37-48.

BAYHAM, F.E.

4114 1979 Factors Influencing the Archaic Pattern of Animal Exploitation. Kiva 44(2-3):219-236.

BELLWOOD, P.

4115 1971 Fortifications and Economy in Prehistoric New Zealand. Proceedings, Prehistoric Society 37(1):56-95.

BINFORD, L.R.

4116 1966 The Predatory Revolution: A Consideration of the Evidence for a New Subsistence Level. American Anthropologist 68 (2):508-512.

CALDWELL, J.R.

4117 1965 Primary Forest Efficiency. Bulletin, Southeastern
            Archaeological Conference 3:66-69.

CARTER, P.L.

4118 1970 Late Stone Age Exploitation Patterns in Southern Natal.
            South African Archaeological Bulletin 25(98), Pt. 2:55-58.

CHANEY, R.W.

4119 1935 The Food of Peking Man. Carnegie Institution of Washing-
            ton, News Service Bulletin 3:199-202.

CLARK, G.

4120 1947 Whales as an Economic Factor in Prehistoric Europe.
            Antiquity 21(81):84-104.

CLARK, G.A.

4121 1971 The Asturian of Cantabria: Subsistence Base and the
            Evidence for Post-Pleistocene Climatic Shifts. American
            Anthropologist 73(5):1244-1257.

CLARK, J.G.D.

4122 1938 Reindeer Hunting Tribes of Northern Europe. Antiquity
            12(46):154-171.

4123 1948 The Development of Fishing in Prehistoric Europe.
            Antiquaries Journal 28:45-85.

4124 1948 Fowling in Prehistoric Europe. Antiquity 21:116-130.

DAVIS, E.L.

4125 1963 The Desert Culture of the Western Great Basin: A Lifeway
            of Seasonal Transhumance. American Antiquity 29:202-212.

DORNSTREICH, M.D.

4126 1973 Food Habits of Early Man: Balance Between Hunting and
            Gathering. Science 179:306-307.

ELDER, W.H.

4127 1965 Primeval Deer Hunting Pressures Revealed from American
            Indian Middens. Journal of Wildlife Management 29(2):
            366-370.

FRISON, G.C.

4128 1971 Shoshonean Antelope Procurement in the Upper Green River
            Basin, Wyoming. Plains Anthropologist 16(54), Pt. 1:
            258-284.

GALDIKAS, B.

4129 1970 The Shift from Mammoth to Bison in Paleo-Indian Subsistence:
            A Reappraisal. Anthropology UCLA 2(1):1-18.

GOODWIN, A.J.H.

4130 1946 Prehistoric Fishing Methods in South Africa. Antiquity
             20(79):134-141.

GREGORY, H.F., Jr.

4131 1965 Maximum Forest Efficiency: Swamp and Upland Potentials.
             Bulletin, Southeastern Archaeological Conference 3:70-74.

GUNDA, B.

4132 1949 Plant Gathering in the Economic Life of Eurasia.
             Southwestern Journal of Anthropology 5:369-378.

GUNNERSON, D.A.

4133 1972 Man and Bison on the Plains in the Prehistoric Period.
             Plains Anthropologist 17(55):1-10.

GUTHE, A.K.

4134 1967 Economic Basis of Tennessee Valley Prehistory. Bulletin,
             Southeastern Archaeological Conference 5:34-35.

HEIZER, R.F.

4135 1976 Man, the Hunter-Gatherer; Food Availability vs. Biological
             Factors. In S. Margen, ed., Progress in Human Nutrition
             2. Avi Publishers, Westport, Conn.

HEIZER, R.F., and M.A. BAUMHOFF

4136 1970 Big Game Hunters in the Great Basin: A Critical Review of
             the Evidence. Contributions, University of California,
             Archaeological Research Facility 7:1-12.

HEIZER, R.F., and L.K. NAPTON

4137 1970 Archaeology and the Prehistoric Great Basin Lacustrine
             Subsistence Regime as Seen from Lovelock Cave, Nevada.
             Contributions, University of California, Archaeological
             Research Facility 10.

HIGGS, E.S., C. VITA-FINZI, D. HARRIS, and A. FAGG

4138 1967 The Climate, Environment, and Industries of Stone Age
             Greece. Proceedings, Prehistoric Society 33(1):1-29.

ISAAC, G.L.

4139 1971 The Diet of Early Man: Aspects of Archaeological Evidence
             from Lower and Middle Pleistocene Sites in Africa. World
             Archaeology 2:278-299.

JARMAN, M.E., C. VITA-FINZI, and E.S. HIGGS

4140 1972 Site Catchment Analysis in Archaeology. In P.J. Ucko,
             R. Tringham, and G.W. Dimbleby, eds., Man, Settlement and
             Urbanism:61-66. Schenkman, Cambridge, Mass.

JOCHIM, M.A.

4141   1976   Hunter-Gatherer Subsistence and Settlement. Academic
              Press, New York.

JOLLY, C.J.

4142   1970   The Seed-Eaters: A New Model of Hominid Differentiation
              Based on a Baboon Analogy. Man 5:5-26.

KEHOE, T.F., and A.B. KEHOE

4143   1960   Observations on the Butchering Technique at a Prehistoric
              Bison Kill in Montana. American Antiquity 25:420-423.

KLEIN, R.G.

4144   1974   Environment and Subsistence of Prehistoric Man in the
              Southern Cape Province, South Africa. World Archaeology
              5(3):249-284.

4145   1979   Stone Age Exploitation of Animals in Southern Africa.
              American Scientist 67(2):151-160.

KLIKS, M.

4146   1976   Paleodietetics: A Review of the Role of Dietary Fiber in
              Preagricultural Human Diets. In G.A. Spiller and R.J.
              Amens, eds., Fiber in Human Nutrition. C.C. Thomas,
              Springfield, Ill.

KROEBER, A.L., and S.A. BARRETT

4147   1960   Fishing Among the Indians of Northwestern California.
              University of California Anthropological Records 21(1).

KROGH, A., and M. KROGH

4148   1915   A Study of the Diet and Metabolism of Eskimo Undertaken
              in 1908 on an Expedition to Greenland. Meddelelser om
              Gronland 2:1-52.

LEACH, B.F.

4149   1969   The Concept of Similarity in Prehistoric New Zealand; a
              Consideration of the Implications of Seasonal and Regional
              Variability of Food Resources for the Study of Prehistoric
              Economies. Anthropology Department, University of Otago,
              Studies in Prehistoric Anthropology 2.

LEOPOLD, A.C., and R. ARDREY

4150   1972   Early Man's Food Habits. Science 177:833-835.

4151   1972   Toxic Substances in Plants and Food Habits of Early Man.
              Science 176:512.

McCARTHY, F.D., and M. McARTHUR

4152   1960   The Food Quest and the Time Factor in Aboriginal Economic
              Life. In Records of the American-Australian Scientific Ex-
              pedition 2:145-194. University of Melbourne Press, Victoria.

PARMALEE, P.W.

4153 1965 The Food Economy of Archaic and Woodland Peoples at the
Tick Creek Cave Site. Missouri Archaeologist 27(1).

PARMALEE, P., A. PALOUMPIS, and N. WILSON

4154 1972 Animals Utilized by Woodland Peoples Occupying the Apple
Creek Site, Illinois. Illinois State Museum Reports
of Investigations 23:13.

PERKINS, D., Jr., and P. DALY

4155 1968 A Hunters' Village in Neolithic Turkey. Scientific
American 219(5):96-106.

RIVERA, T.

4156 1949 Diet of a Food-Gathering People, with Chemical Analysis of
Salmon and Saskatoons. In M.W. Smith, ed., Indians of the
Northwest. Columbia University Contributions to Anthro-
pology 36:19-36.

ROBBINS, L.H.

4157 1974 The Lothagam Site: A Late Stone Age Fishing Settlement in
the Lake Rudolf Basin, Kenya. Publications, Museum of
Michigan State University 1(2).

ROSTLUND, E.

4158 1951 Freshwater Fish and Fishing in Native North America.
University of California Publications in Geography 9.

ROTH, W.E.

4159 1901 Food: Its Search, Capture and Preparation. North Queensland Ethnographic Bulletin 3:1-31. Brisbane.

ROZAIRE, C.E.

4160 1963 Lake-Side Cultural Specializations in the Great Basin.
Nevada State Museum, Anthropological Papers 9.

SAHLINS, M.

4161 1972 Stone Age Economics. Aldine, Chicago.

STARK, B.L., and B. VOORHIES, eds.

4162 1978 Prehistoric Coastal Adaptations: Economy and Ecology in
Maritime Middle America. Studies in Archeology. Academic
Press, New York.

STEFANNSON, V.

4163 1937 Food of the Ancient and Modern Stone Age Man. Journal of
the American Dietetic Association 13:102-119.

STRUEVER, S.

4164 1968 Woodland Subsistence-Settlement Systems in the Lower

Illinois Valley. In S. Binford and L. Binford, eds., New
Perspectives in Archeology:285-312. Aldine, Chicago.

SULLIVAN, R.J.

4165 1942 The Ten'a Food Quest. Catholic University of America,
            Anthropological Series 11.

SWEENEY, R.J.

4166 1947 Food Supplies of a Desert Tribe. Oceania 17:289-299.

VOLMAN, T.P.

4167 1978 Early Archeological Evidence for Shellfish Collecting.
            Science 201:911-913.

WENDORF, F., and J.J. HESTER

4168 1962 Early Man's Utilization of the Great Plains Environment.
            American Antiquity 26:159-171.

WHITE, T.E.

4169 1953 A Method for Calculating the Dietary Percentage of
            Various Food Animals Utilized by Aboriginal Peoples.
            American Antiquity 18:396-398.

WILKE, P.J., and H.J. HALL

4170 1975 Analysis of Ancient Feces: A Discussion and Annotated
            Bibliography. University of California, Archaeological
            Research Facility, Berkeley.

YELLEN, J., and H. HARPENDING

4171 1972 Hunter-Gatherer Populations and Archaeological Inference.
            World Archaeology 4(2):244-253.

c. DOMESTICATION OF PLANTS AND ANIMALS

AMMERMAN, A.J., and L.L. CAVALLI-SFORZA

4172 1971 Measuring the Rate of Spread of Early Farming in Europe.
            Man 6(4):674-688.

ANGRESS, S., and C.A. REED

4173 1961 An Annotated Bibliography on the Origin and Descent of
            Domestic Mammals 1900-1955. Fieldiana: Anthropology 54(1).

APPLEBAUM, S.

4174 1954 The Agriculture of the British Early Iron Age as Exempli-
            fied at Figheldean Down, Wiltshire. Proceedings, Prehis-
            toric Society 20(1):103-114.

ASCH, D.L., and N.B. ASCH

4175 1977 Chenopod as Cultigen: A Re-Evaluation of Some Prehistoric
            Collections from Eastern North America. Midcontinental
            Journal of Archaeology 2(1):3-46.

BENDER, B., and P. PHILLIPS

4176 1972 The Early Farmers of France. Antiquity 46:97–105.

BRADLEY, B.

4177 1972 Prehistorians and Pastoralists in Neolithic and Bronze
            Age New England. World Archaeology 4(2):192–204.

BROWN, J.K.

4178 1970 Subsistence Variables: A Comparison of Textor and Sauer.
            Ethnology 9(2):160–164.

CHANG, K.

4179 1970 The Beginnings of Agriculture in the Far East. Antiquity
            44:175–185.

CLARK, H.H.

4180 1967 The Origin and Early History of the Cultivated Barleys.
            The Agricultural History Review 15(1).

CLARK, J.D.

4181 1970 The Spread of Food Production in Sub-Saharan Africa.
            In J.D. Fage and R.A. Oliver, eds., Papers in African
            Prehistory:25–42. Cambridge University Press, Cambridge.

4182 1971 A Re-Examination of the Evidence for Agricultural Origins
            in the Nile Valley. Proceedings, Prehistoric Society
            37(2):34–79.

CLARK, J.G.D.

4183 1945 Farmers and Forests in Neolithic Europe. Antiquity 19(74):
            57–71.

4184 1947 Sheep and Swine in the Husbandry of Prehistoric Europe.
            Antiquity 21:122–136.

COHEN, M.N.

4185 1977 The Food Crisis in Prehistory: Overpopulations and the
            Origins of Agriculture. Yale University Press, New Haven.

COOK, S.F.

4186 1947 The Interrelation of Population, Food Supply and Building
            in Pre-Conquest Central Mexico. American Antiquity 13:
            45–52.

CUMBAA, S.L.

4187 1974 Subsistence Strategy at Venadillo, Sinaloa, Mexico. In
            S.D. Scott, ed., West Mexican Prehistory:35–44. State
            University of New York, Buffalo.

CURWEN, E.C.

4188 1927 Prehistoric Agriculture in Britain. Antiquity 1:261–289.

4189 1935 Agriculture and the Flint Sickle in Palestine. Antiquity
            9(33):62-66.

4190 1938 Early Agriculture in Denmark. Antiquity 12(46):135-153.

DELABARRE, E.B., and H.H. WILDER

4191 1920 Indian Corn Hills in Massachusetts. American Anthropolo-
            gist 22(3):203-225.

DEMBINSKA, M.

4192 1959 Les Méthodes de Recherches sur l'Alimentation en Pologne
            Médiévale. Archaeologia Polona II:141-154.

DIXON, D.M.

4193 1969 A Note on Cereals in Ancient Egypt. In P.J. Ucko and
            G.W. Dimbleby, eds., The Domestication and Exploitation
            of Plants and Animals:131-142. Aldine, Chicago.

DREW, C.D.

4194 1948 Open Arable Fields at Portland and Elsewhere. Antiquity
            22(86):79-81.

DRUCKER, P., and R.F. HEIZER

4195 1960 A Study of the Milpa System of La Venta Island and Its
            Archaeological Implications. Southwestern Journal of
            Anthropology 16:36-45.

DUMOND, D.E.

4196 1962 Swidden Agriculture and the Rise of Maya Civilization.
            Southwestern Journal of Anthropology 17:301-316.

FAGAN, B.M.

4197 1959 Cropmarks in Antiquity. Antiquity 33(132):279-281.

FAIRBANKS, C.H.

4198 1965 Gulf Complex Subsistence Economy. Bulletin, Southeastern
            Archaeological Conference 3:57-62.

FEACHEM, R.W.

4199 1973 Ancient Agriculture in the Highland of Britain. Pro-
            ceedings, Prehistoric Society 39:332-353.

FITZER, P.

4200 1962 Evidence for Horticulture During Early-Middle Woodland
            Times in the Eastern United States. Pennsylvania
            Archaeologist 32(1):14-19.

FLANNERY, K.V.

4201 1965 The Ecology of Early Food Production in Mesopotamia.
            Science 147:1247-1256.

FLEMING, A.

4202 1972 The Genesis of Pastoralism in European Prehistory. World
            Archaeology 4(2):179-191.

FOX, A.

4203 1954 Celtic Fields and Farms on Dartmoor, in the Light of
            Recent Excavations at Kestor. Proceedings, Prehistoric
            Society 20(1):87-102.

FUSSELL, G.E.

4204 1967 Farming Systems of the Classical Era. Technology and
            Culture 8:16-44.

GHIDINELLI, A.

4205 1971 The Alimentation of the Maya. Ethnos 1-4:23-32.

HAGEN, A.

4206 1962 Problems Concerning Neolithic Agricultural Groups in
            Norway. Palaeohistoria 12:253-258.

HARLAN, J.R.

4207 1971 Agricultural Origins: Centers and Non-Centers. Science
            174:468-474.

HARLAN, J.R., J.M.J. de WET, and A.B.L. STEMIER

4208 1976 Origins of African Plant Domestication. Aldine, Chicago.

HARRISON, P.D., and B.L. TURNER II, eds.

4209 1978 Pre-Hispanic Maya Agriculture. University of New Mexico
            Press, Santa Fe.

HAWLEY, F., M. PIJOAN, and C.A. ELKIN

4210 1943 An Inquiry into the Food Economy of Zia Pueblo. American
            Anthropologist 45:547-556.

HEIZER, R.F.

4211 1960 Agriculture and the Theocratic State in Lowland South-
            eastern Mexico. American Antiquity 25:215-222.

HELBAEK, H.

4212 1953 Early Crops in Southern England. Proceedings, Prehistoric
            Society 18(2):194-233.

4213 1959 How Farming Began in the Old World. Archaeology 12(3):
            183-189.

HIGGS, E.S.

4214 1967 Early Domesticated Animals in Libya. In J.D. Clark and
            F.C. Howell, eds., Background to Evolution in Africa:165-
            173. University of Chicago Press, Chicago.

HIGGS, E.S., and M. JARMAN

4215 1969 The Origins of Agriculture: A Reconsideration. Antiquity
            43:31-41.

HUNTINGFORD, G.W.B.

4216 1932 Ancient Agriculture. Antiquity 6:327-388.

JACOBSEN, T., and R.M. ADAMS

4217 1958 Salt and Silt in Mesopotamian Agriculture. Science 128
            (3334):1251-1258.

JARMAN, M.R.

4218 1968 The Fauna and Economy of Early Neolithic Knossos. Annual,
            British School of Archaeology at Athens 63:241-276.

JASHEMSKI, W.

4219 1972 A Vineyard at Pompeii; Part 1: The Discovery. Archaeology
            25(1):48-56.

JENSEN, P.M., and R.R. KAUTZ

4220 1974 An Archaeo-Economic Modeling of Food Producing Economies
            in Highland Peru. In R. Kautz, ed., Readings in Archaeo-
            logical Method and Technique:67-82. University of Cali-
            fornia, Center for Archaeological Research at Davis,
            Publication 4.

LESHNIK, L.S.

4221 1972 Pastoral Nomadism in the Archaeology of India and Pakistan.
            World Archaeology 4(2):150-166.

LEWIS, H.T.

4222 1972 The Role of Fire in the Domestication of Plants and
            Animals in Southwest Asia: A Hypothesis. Man 7(2):195-222.

MacNEISH, R.S.

4223 1965 The Origins of American Agriculture. Antiquity 39(154):
            87-94.

4224 1967 A Summary of the Subsistence. In D.S. Byers, ed., The
            Prehistory of the Tehuacan Valley: I, Environment and
            Subsistence:290-310. University of Texas Press, Austin.

MANGELSDORF, P.C.

4225 1974 Corn: Its Origin, Evolution, and Improvement. Harvard
            University Press, Cambridge, Mass.

MANGELSDORF, P.C., R.S. MacNEISH, and W.C. GALINAT

4226 1972 The Domestication of Corn. Science 143(3606):538-545.

MASSON, V.M.

4227 1961 The First Farmers in Turkemonia. Antiquity 35(139):203-213.

MATHENY, R.T., and D.L. GURR

4228 1979 Ancient Hydraulic Techniques in the Chiapas Highlands. American Scientist 67(4):441-449.

MOBERG, C.-A.

4229 1966 Spread of Agriculture in the North European Periphery. Science 152:315-319.

MUNSON, P.J.

4230 1973 The Origins and Antiquity of Maize-Beans-Squash Agriculture in Eastern North America: Some Linguistic Implications. In D. Lathrap and J. Douglas, eds., Variations in Anthropology: Essays in Honor of John C. McGregor:107-135. University of Illinois, Urbana.

PARKER, A.C.

4231 1910 Iroquois Uses of Maize and Other Food Plants. New York State Museum, Bulletin 144.

PARSONS, J.J., and W.M. DENEVAN

4232 1967 Pre-Columbian Ridged Fields. Scientific American 217(1):92-101.

PATTERSON, T.C.

4233 1971 Central Peru: Its Population and Economy. Archaeology 24(4):316-321.

PERKINS, D.

4234 1969 Fauna of Catal Huyuk: Evidence of Early Cattle Domesticates in Anatolia. Science 164:177-179.

PITCHER, J.R., A.G. SMITH, G.W. PEARSON, and A. CROWDER

4235 1971 Land Clearance in the Irish Neolithic--New Evidence and Interpretations. Science 172(3983):560-562.

PROTSCH, R., and R. BERGER

4236 1973 Earliest Radiocarbon Dates for Domesticated Animals. Science 179:235-239.

REED, C.A., ed.

4237 1977 Origins of Agriculture. Aldine, Chicago.

ROYS, R.L.

4238 1975 The Ethno-Botany of the Maya. (Reprinted version.) The Institute for the Study of Human Issues, Philadelphia.

SCHROEDER, A.H.

4239 1943 Prehistoric Canals in the Salt River Valley, Arizona.
            American Antiquity 8:380-386.

SEARS, W.H.

4240 1971 Food Production and Village Life in Prehistoric South-
            eastern United States. Archaeology 24(4):322-329.

SIEMENS, A.H., and D.E. PULESTON

4241 1972 Ridged Fields and Associated Features in Southern Campeche:
            New Perspectives on the Lowland Maya. American Antiquity
            37(2):228-239.

SIMMONS, D.R.

4242 1969 Economic Change in New Zealand Prehistory. Journal,
            Polynesian Society 78(1):83-111.

SMITH, P.E.L.

4243 1972 The Consequence of Food Production. Addison-Wesley
            Module in Anthropology 31.

SOLHEIM, W.G., II

4244 1972 An Earlier Agricultural Revolution. Scientific American
            226(4):34-41.

STRUEVER, S., ed.

4245 1971 Prehistoric Agriculture. Natural History Press, Garden
            City, N.Y.

UCKO, P.J., and G.W. DIMBLEBY, eds.

4246 1969 The Domestication and Exploitation of Plants and Animals.
            Aldine, Chicago.

VITA-FINZI, C., and E.S. HIGGS

4247 1970 Prehistoric Economy in the Mount Carmel Area of Palestine.
            Proceedings, Prehistoric Society 36:1-37.

WAGNER, H.O.

4248 1969 Subsistence Potential and Population Density of the Maya
            on the Yucatan Peninsula and Causes for the Decline in
            Population in the Fifteenth Century. Verhandlungen des
            XXXVIII. Internationalen Amerikanistenkongresses,
            Stuttgart-München I:281-287. Kommissionsverlag Klaus
            Renner, München, Germany.

WATKINS, A.E.

4249 1933 The Origin of Cultivated Plants. Antiquity 7:73-132.

WEDEL, W.R.

4250 1941 Environment and Native Subsistence Economies in the

Central Great Plains. Smithsonian Institution, Miscellaneous Collections 101(3).

WENDORF, F., et al.

4251 1979 Use of Barley in the Egyptian Late Paleolithic. Science 205:1342-1347.

WHITE, K.D.

4252 1963 Wheat-Farming in Roman Times. Antiquity 37(147):207-212.

4253 1965 The Productivity of Labour in Roman Agriculture. Antiquity 39(154):102-107.

WILKE, P.J., et al.

4254 1972 Harvest Selection and Domestication in Seed Plants. Antiquity 46(183):203-309.

WILKEN, G.C.

4255 1971 Food-Producing Systems Available to the Ancient Maya. American Antiquity 36(4):432-448.

WRIGHT, H.E., Jr.

4256 1968 Natural Environment of Early Food Production North of Mesopotamia. Science 161:334-339.

YARNELL, R.A.

4257 1976 Early Plant Husbandry in Eastern North America. In C.E. Cleland, ed., Cultural Change and Continuity: Essays in Honor of James Bennett Griffin. Academic Press, New York.

ZEUNER, F.E.

4258 1963 A History of Domesticated Animals. Harper and Row, New York.

ZIER, C.J.

4259 1980 A Classical-Period Maya Agricultural Field in Western El Salvador. Journal of Field Archaeology 7(1):65-74.

4. Settlement Patterns / Systems

ANDERSON, K.M.

4260 1973 Prehistoric Settlement of the Upper Neches River. Bulletin, Texas Archeological Society 43:121-197.

ANDREWS, G.F.

4261 1975 Maya Cities: Placemaking and Urbanization. University of Oklahoma Press, Norman.

BICKEL, P.W.

4262 1978 Changing Sea Levels and the California Coast: Anthropo-
            logical Implications. Journal of California Anthropology
            5(1):6-20.

BINFORD, L.R.

4263 1980 Willow Smoke and Dogs' Tails: Hunter-Gatherer Settlement
            Systems and Archaeological Site Formation. American
            Antiquity 45(1):4-20.

BLANTON, R.E.

4264 1978 Monte Alban: Settlement Patterns at the Ancient Zapotec
            Capital. Academic Press, New York.

BLUHM, E.

4265 1960 Mogollon Settlement Patterns in Pine Lawn Valley, New
            Mexico. American Antiquity 25:538-546.

BORHEGYI, S.F. de

4266 1965 Settlement Patterns of the Guatemalan Highlands. Handbook
            of Middle American Indians 2:59-75. The University of
            Texas Press, Austin.

BROOK, V.R.

4267 1971 Some Hypotheses About Prehistoric Settlement in the
            Tularosa Hueco Bolson Between A.D. 1250-1350. Transactions,
            Sixth Regional Archaeological Symposium for Southeast New
            Mexico and Western Texas:63-82.

BROSE, D.S.

4268 1970 The Archaeology of Summer Island: Changing Settlement
            Systems in Northern Lake Michigan. University of Michigan,
            Museum of Anthropology, Anthropological Papers 41.

BULLARD, W.R.

4269 1966 Maya Settlement Pattern in Northeastern Peten. American
            Antiquity 25:355-372.

CALNEK, E.E.

4270 1972 Settlement Pattern and Chinampa Agriculture at Tenochtitlan.
            American Antiquity 37(1):104-114.

CASSELS, R.

4271 1972 Locational Analysis of Prehistoric Settlement in New
            Zealand. Mankind 8(3):212-222.

CHANG, K.C.

4272 1962 A Typology of Settlement and Community Patterns in Some
            Circumpolar Societies. Arctic Anthropology 1:28-41.

4273 1972 Settlement Patterns in Archeology. Addison-Wesley Module in Anthropology 24.

CHANG, K.C., ed.

4274 1968 Settlement Archaeology. National Press Books, Palo Alto, Cal.

CHISHOLM, M.

4275 1968 Rural Settlement and Land Use. Hutchinson, London.

CLARK, J.G.D.

4276 1939 Seasonal Settlement in Upper Palaeolithic Times. Proceedings, Prehistoric Society 5:268.

COE, M.D.

4277 1957 The Khmer Settlement Pattern: A Possible Analogy with That of the Maya. American Antiquity 22:409-410.

CURWEN, E.C.

4278 1930 Neolithic Camps. Antiquity 4:22-54.

DAVIDSON, J.M.

4279 1969 Settlement Patterns in Samoa Before 1840. Journal, Polynesian Society 78(1):44-82.

DICKSON, D.B.

4280 1979 Deduction on the Duck River: A Test of Some Hypotheses About Settlement Distribution Using Surface Site Survey Data from Middle Tennessee. Midcontinental Journal of Archaeology 4(1):113-138.

DRIVER, H.E.

4281 1957 Estimation of Intensity of Land Use from Ethnobiology: Applied to the Yuma Indians. Ethnohistory 4:174-197.

EARLE, T.K.

4282 1972 Lurin Valley, Peru: Early Intermediate Period Settlement Development. American Antiquity 37(4):467-477.

FITTING, J.E.

4283 1965 Observations on Paleo-Indian Adaptive and Settlement Patterns. Michigan Archaeologist 11(3-4):103-109.

4284 1969 Settlement Analysis in the Great Lakes Region. Southwestern Journal of Anthropology 25:360-377.

FLEMING, A.

4285 1971 Territorial Patterns in Bronze Age Wessex. Proceedings, Prehistoric Society 37(1):138-166.

GREBINGER, P.

4286 1971 The Potrero Creek Site: Activity Structure. Kiva 37(1):
            30-52.

GREEN, R.C.

4287 1970 Settlement Pattern Archaeology in Polynesia. In R. Green
            and M. Kelly, eds., Studies in Oceanic Culture History I.
            Pacific Anthropological Records 11:13-32.

GUMERMAN, G.J., ed.

4288 1971 The Distribution of Prehistoric Population Aggregates.
            Prescott College Anthropological Reports 1.

GUMERMAN, G.J., and R.R. JOHNSON

4289 1971 Prehistoric Human Population Distribution in Biological
            Transition Zone. In G.J. Gumerman, ed., The Distribution
            of Prehistoric Population Aggregates. Prescott College
            Anthropological Reports 1:83-102.

HAGGETT, P.

4290 1965 Locational Analysis in Human Geography. Edward Arnold,
            London.

HAMMOND, N.D.C.

4291 1972 Locational Models and the Site of Lubaantun: A Classic
            Maya Centre. In D.L. Clarke, ed., Models in Archaeology:
            757-800. Methuen, London.

HENKE, R.A.

4292 1971 Antlered Deer Skull Remains in Archaeological Sites: A
            Useful Indicator of Settlement Pattern. The Bulletin,
            New York State Archaeological Association 51:8-11.

HIRTH, K.G.

4293 1978 Problems in Data Recovery and Measurement in Settlement
            Archaeology. Journal of Field Archaeology 5(2):125-132.

JOCHIM, M.A.

4294 1976 Hunter-Gatherer Subsistence and Settlement: A Predictive
            Model. Academic Press, New York.

JONES, G.

4295 1961 Settlement Patterns in Anglo-Saxon England. Antiquity
            35(139):221-232.

JUDGE, W.J.

4296 1971 An Interpretative Framework for Understanding Site
            Locations. In G.J. Gumerman, ed., The Distribution of
            Prehistoric Population Aggregates. Prescott College
            Anthropological Reports 1:38-44.

KILMA, B.

4297 1954 Paleolithic Huts at Dolní Věstonice, Czechoslovakia.
Antiquity 28:4-14.

KRAFT, H.C.

4298 1970 Prehistoric Indian Housepatterns in New Jersey. Bulletin,
Archaeological Society of New Jersey 26:1-11.

LANE, R.A., and A.J. SUBLETT

4299 1972 Osteology of Social Organization: Residence Pattern.
American Antiquity 37(2):186-201.

LINDSAY, A.J., Jr., and J.S. DEAN

4300 1971 Changing Patterns of Human Settlement in the Long House
Valley, Northeastern Arizona. In G.J. Gumerman, ed.,
The Distribution of Prehistoric Population Aggregates.
Prescott College Anthropological Reports 1:111-125.

LIPE, W.D., and R.G. MATSON

4301 1971 Human Settlement and Resources in the Cedar Mesa Area,
Southeast Utah. In G.J. Gumerman, ed., The Distribution
of Prehistoric Population Aggregates. Prescott College
Anthropological Reports 1:126-151.

LONGACRE, W.A., and J.J. REID

4302 1971 Research Strategy for Locational Analysis: An Outline.
In G.J. Gumerman, ed., The Distribution of Prehistoric
Population Aggregates. Prescott College Anthropological
Reports 1:103-110.

McGREGOR, J.C.

4303 1957 Prehistoric Village Distribution in the Illinois River
Valley. American Antiquity 22:272-279.

McINTIRE, W.G.

4304 1958 Prehistoric Indian Settlements of the Changing Mississippi
River Delta. L.S.U., Coastal Studies Series 1.

MARCUS, J.

4305 1976 Emblem and State in the Classic Maya Lowlands: An Epi-
graphic Approach to Territorial Organization. Dumbarton
Oaks, Trustees for Harvard University, Washington, D.C.

MARKS, A.E.

4306 1971 Settlement Patterns and Intrasite Variability in the Central Negev, Israel. American Anthropologist 73(5):1237-
1244.

MASON, R.J.

4307 1972 Locational Models of Transvaal Iron Age Settlements. In

D.L. Clarke, ed., Models in Archaeology:871-886. Methuen, London.

MILLON, R., ed.

4308 1973 Urbanization at Teotihuacan, Mexico. University of Texas Press, Austin.

MOSELEY, M.E., and C.J. MACKEY

4309 1972 Peruvian Settlement Pattern Studies and Small Site Methodology. American Antiquity 37(1):67-81.

NAROLL, R.

4310 1962 Floor Area and Settlement Pattern. American Antiquity 27:587-589.

O'BRIEN, P.J.

4311 1972 Urbanism, Cahokia and Middle Mississippian. Archaeology 25(3):188-197.

O'CONNELL, J., and J.E. ERICSON

4312 1974 Earth Lodges to Wickiups: A Long Sequence of Domestic Structures from the Northern Great Basin. Nevada Archaeological Survey, Research Paper 5.

PAGE, W.

4313 1927 Notes on the Types of English Villages and Their Distribution. Antiquity 1:447-460.

PARSONS, J.R.

4314 1971 Prehistoric Settlement Patterns in the Texcoco Region, Mexico. University of Michigan, Ann Arbor.

RAJEWSKI, Z.

4315 1960 On Research Methods Concerning Settlement Complexes. Archaeologia Polona III:146-154.

RITCHIE, W.A.

4316 1961 Iroquois Archeology and Settlement Patterns. In W.N. Fenton and J. Gulick, eds., Symposium on Cherokee and Iroquois Culture. Bureau of American Ethnology, Bulletin 180:27-38.

4317 1965 The Development of Aboriginal Settlement Patterns in the Northeast and Their Socio-Economic Correlates. Bulletin, Southeastern Archaeological Conference 3:25-29.

ROBBINS, M.C.

4318 1966 House Types and Settlement Patterns: An Application of Ethnology to Archaeological Interpretations. Minnesota Archaeologist 28(1):2-35.

ROUSE, I.

4319   1968   Prehistory, Typology, and the Study of Society.   In
               K.C. Chang, ed., Settlement Archaeology:10-30.   National
               Press, Palo Alto.

SANDERS, W.T.

4320   1960   Prehistoric Ceramics and Settlement Patterns in Quintana
               Roo, Mexico.   Carnegie Institution of Washington, Con-
               tributions to American Anthropology and History 12(60).

4321   1971   Cultural Ecology and Settlement Patterns of the Gulf
               Coast.   Handbook of Middle American Indians 10(II):543-
               557.

4322   1971   Settlement Patterns in Central Mexico.   Handbook of
               Middle American Indians 10(I):3-44.

SANDERS, W.T., J.R. PARSONS, and R.S. SANTLEY

4323   1979   The Basin of Mexico: Ecological Processes in the Evolution
               of a Civilization.   Academic Press, New York.

SARG, THE MEMBERS OF

4324   1975   SARG: A Co-Operative Approach Towards Understanding the
               Locations of Human Settlement.   World Archaeology 6(1):
               107-116.

SCHOENWETTER, J., and A.E. DITTERT, Jr.

4325   1968   An Ecological Interpretation of Anasazi Settlement Pat-
               terns.   Anthropological Archaeology in the Americas.   The
               Anthropological Society of Washington, Washington, D.C.

SHACKLETON, N.J.

4326   1973   Oxygen Isotope Analysis as a Means of Determining Season
               of Occupation of Prehistoric Midden Sites.   Archaeometry
               15(1):133-142.

SISSON, E.B.

4327   1970   Settlement Patterns and Land Use in the Northwestern
               Chontalpa, Tabasco, Mexico.   Ceramica de Cultura Maya:41-54.

SKINNER, S.A.

4328   1971   Prehistoric Settlement of the De Cordova Bend Reservoir.
               Bulletin, Texas Archeological Society 42:149-270.

SMITH, B.D.

4329   1978   Mississippian Settlement Patterns.   Academic Press, New
               York.

STRUEVER, S.

4330   1968   Woodland Subsistence-Settlement Systems in the Lower
               Illinois Valley.   In S. Binford and L. Binford, eds., New
               Perspectives in Archeology:285-312.   Aldine, Chicago.

TAGGART, D.W.

4331 1967   Seasonal Patterns in Settlement, Subsistence and Indus-
             tries in the Saginaw Late Archaic. Michigan Archaeologist
             13(4):153-170.

THOMSON, D.F.

4332 1939   The Seasonal Factor in Human Culture. Proceedings, Pre-
             historic Society 5:209-221.

TRIGGER, B.

4333 1967   Settlement Archaeology: Its Goals and Promise. American
             Antiquity 32:149-160.

TUCK, J.A.

4334 1971   Onondaga Iroquois Prehistory. A Study in Settlement
             Archaeology. Syracuse University Press, Syracuse.

UCKO, P.J., R. TRINGHAM, and G.W. DIMBLEBY, eds.

4335 1972   Man, Settlement and Urbanism: Proceedings of a Meeting of
             the Research Seminar in Archaeology and Related Subjects
             Held at the Institute of Archaeology, London University.
             G. Duckworth, London.

VOORHIES, B.

4336 1972   Settlement Patterns in Two Regions of the Southern Maya
             Lowlands. American Antiquity 37(1):115-125.

WENDORF, F.

4337 1956   Some Distributions of Settlement Patterns in the Pueblo
             Southwest. In G. Willey, ed., Prehistoric Settlement
             Patterns in the New World:18-25. Wenner-Gren, New
             York.

WHITE, M.E.

4338 1963   Settlement Pattern Change in the New York-Ontario Area.
             Pennsylvania Archaeologist 33(1-2):1-11.

WILLEY, G.R.

4339 1953   Prehistoric Settlement Patterns in the Viru Valley, Peru.
             Bureau of American Ethnology Bulletin 153.

WOOD, J.J.

4340 1971   Fitting Discrete Probability Distributions to Prehistoric
             Settlement Patterns. In G.J. Gumerman, ed., The
             Distribution of Prehistoric Population Aggregates.
             Prescott College Anthropological Reports 1:63-82.

5. Social / Religious Systems

ADAMS, R.E.W.

4341   1977   The Origins of Maya Civilization.   University of New
              Mexico Press, Albuquerque.

ADAMS, R. McC.

4342   1966   The Evolution of Urban Society: Early Mesopotamia and
              Prehistoric Mexico.   Aldine, Chicago.

4343   1968   The Natural History of Urbanism.   In The Fitness of Man's
              Environment:39-59.   Smithsonian Institution, Washington,
              D.C.

ALLEN, D.

4344   1958   Belgic Coins as Illustrations of Life in the Late Pre-
              Roman Iron Age in Britain.   Proceedings, Prehistoric
              Society 24:43-64.

ALLEN, W.L., and J.B. RICHARDSON III

4345   1971   The Reconstruction of Kinship from Archaeological Data:
              The Concepts, the Methods, and the Feasibility.   American
              Antiquity 36(1):41-53.

ALONSO del REAL, C.

4346   1963   Notas de Sociología Paleolítica.   Journal of World History
              7(3):675-700.

BERGOUIOUX, F.M., and J. GOETZ

4347   1958   Les Religions des Préhistoriques et des Primitifs.   Arthème
              Fayard, Paris.

BLACKWOOD, B.

4348   1935   Both Sides of Buka Passage: An Ethnographic Study of
              Social, Sexual, and Economic Questions in the North-
              Western Solomon Islands.   Clarendon Press, Oxford.

BREUIL, H.

4349   1951   Pratiques Religieuses Chez les Humanités Quaternaires.
              Scienza e Civiltà 1951:45-75.

BROHOLM, H.C., and M. HALD

4350   1940   Costumes of the Bronze Age in Denmark. Nyt Nordisk
              Forlag, Copenhagen.

CARRASCO, P.

4351   1971   Social Organization of Ancient Mexico.   Handbook of
              Middle American Indians 10(I):349-375.

CHADWICK, J.

4352   1959   A Prehistoric Bureaucracy.   Diogenes 26:7-18.

CHANG, K.

4353   1958   Study of the Neolithic Social Grouping: Examples from
              the New World.   American Anthropologist 60:298-334.

CHILDE, V.G.

4354   1941   War in Prehistoric Societies.   Sociological Review 33:
              126-138.

CLARK, G.

4355   1970   Archaeology and Society.   Barnes and Noble, New York.

CLARK, G., and S. PIGGOTT

4356   1970   Prehistoric Societies.   Pelican, New York.

CULBERT, T.P.

4357   1974   The Lost Civilization: The Story of the Classic Maya.
              Harper and Row, New York.

CULBERT, T.P., ed.

4358   1973   The Classic Maya Collapse.   University of New Mexico
              Press, Albuquerque.

Di PESO, C.C.

4359   1958   The Reeve Ruin of Southeastern Arizona.   Amerind Founda-
              tion, Publication 8.   Dragoon, Ariz.

DOZIER, E.P.

4360   1965   Southwestern Social Units and Archeology.   American An-
              tiquity 31:38-47.

ELSASSER, A.B.

4361   1961   Archaeological Evidence of Shamanism in California and
              Nevada.   Kroeber Anthropological Society Papers 24:
              38-48.   Berkeley.

FLANNERY, K.V., and M.D. COE

4362   1968   Social and Economic Systems in Formative Mesoamerica.
              In S. Binford and L. Binford, eds., New Perspectives in
              Archeology:267-284.   Aldine, Chicago

FOLAN, W.J., L.A. FLETCHER, and E.R. KINTZ

4363   1979   Fruit, Fiber, Bark and Resin: Social Organization of a
              Maya Urban Center.   Science 204:697-701.

GIBSON, C.

4364   1971   Structure of the Aztec Empire.   Handbook of Middle American
              Indians 10(I):376-394.

GJESSING, G.

4365   1955   Prehistoric Social Groups in North Norway.   Proceedings,
              Prehistoric Society 21:84-92.

GREBER, N.

4366   1979   Variations in Social Structure of Ohio Hopewell Peoples.
              Midcontinental Journal of Archaeology 4(1):35-78.

GREBINGER, P.

4367   1974   Prehistoric Social Organization in Chaco Canyon, New
              Mexico: An Alternative Reconstruction.   Kiva 39(1):3-24.

GUERRA, F.

4368   1971   The Pre-Columbian Mind: A Study into the Aberrant Nature
              of Sexual Drives, Drugs Affecting Behavior and the Atti-
              tude Towards Life and Death, with a Survey of Psycho-
              therapy in Pre-Columbian America.   Seminar Press Ltd.,
              New York.

HAMMOND, N.

4369   1972   Classic Maya Music: Part I: Maya Drums.   Archaeology
              25(2):124-131.

4370   1972   Classic Maya Music: Part II: Rattles, Shakers, Raspers,
              Wind and String Instruments.   Archaeology 25(3):222-228.

HAVILAND, W.A.

4371   1968   Ancient Lowland Maya Social Organization.   Middle
              American Research Institute Publication 26.   Tulane
              University, New Orleans.

4372   1975   The Ancient Maya and the Evolution of Urban Society.
              University of Northern Colorado, Greenley.

HAWKINS, G.

4373   1963   Stonehenge Decoded.   Nature 200:306-308.

4374   1965   Callanish, a Scottish Stonehenge.   Science 147:127-130.

4375   1965   Stonehenge Decoded.   Doubleday, New York.

4376   1965   Sun, Moon, Men and Stones.   American Scientist 53:391-408.

HEIZER, R.F.

4377   1951   A Prehistoric Yurok Ceremonial Site (Hum - 174).   Univer-
              sity of California Archaeological Survey, Report 11:1-4.

4378   1960   Agriculture and the Theocratic State in Lowland South-
              eastern Mexico.   American Antiquity 26:215-222.

4379   1961   Inferences on the Nature of Olmec Society Based on Data
              from the La Venta Site.   Kroeber Anthropological Society
              Papers 25:43-57.   Berkeley.

4380   1962   The Possible Sociopolitical Structure of the La Venta
              Olmecs.   Akten des 34. Internationalen Amerikanisten-
              kongresses:310-317.

HEIZER, R.F., and J.A. GRAHAM, eds.

4381 1971 Observations on the Emergence of Civilizations in Meso-
            america. University of California, Contributions of the
            Archaeological Research Facility 11.

HEIZER, R.F., and G.W. HEWES

4382 1940 Animal Ceremonialism in Central California in the Light
            of Archaeology. American Anthropologist 42:587-603.

HILL, J.N.

4383 1966 A Prehistoric Community in Eastern Arizona. Southwestern
            Journal of Anthropology 22:9-30.

HOGBEN, L.

4384 1935 Mathematics in Antiquity. Antiquity 9(34):190-193.

HOWARD, J.H.

4385 1968 The Southeastern Ceremonial Complex and Its Interpreta-
            tion. Missouri Archaeological Society Memoir 6.

JAMES, E.O.

4386 1957 Prehistoric Religion: A Study in Prehistoric Archaeology.
            Praeger, New York.

JORALEMON, P.D.

4387 1971 A Study of Olmec Iconography. Studies in Pre-Columbian
            Art and Archaeology 7. Dumbarton Oaks, Washington, D.C.

KING, L.

4388 1969 The Medea Creek Cemetery (LAN-243): An Investigation of
            Social Organization from Mortuary Practices. UCLA
            Archaeological Survey Annual Report 11:23-68.

KIRCHNER, H.

4389 1952 Ein Archaeologischer Beitrag zur Urgeschichte des
            Schamanismus. Anthropos 47:244-286.

KROEBER, A.L.

4390 1927 Disposal of the Dead. American Anthropologist 29:308-315.

KRYZWICKI, L.

4391 1934 Primitive Society and Its Vital Statistics. Macmillan,
            London.

LEON-PORTILLA, M.

4392 1971 Philosophy in Ancient Mexico. Handbook of Middle American
            Indians 10(I):447-451.

LEROI-GOURHAN, L.

4393 1964 Les Religions de la Préhistoire (Paléolithique). Presses Universitaires de France, Paris.

LEVY, J.E.

4394 1979 Evidence of Social Stratification in Bronze Age Denmark. Journal of Field Archaeology 6(1):49-56.

LONGACRE, W.A.

4395 1964 Archeology as Anthropology: A Case Study. Science 144: 1454-1455.

4396 1966 Changing Patterns of Social Integration: A Prehistoric Example from the American Southwest. American Anthropologist 68:94-102.

LONGACRE, W.A., ed.

4397 1970 Reconstructing Prehistoric Pueblo Societies. School of American Research, University of New Mexico Press, Albuquerque.

LOTHROP, S.K.

4398 1937 Cocle, an Archaeological Study of Central Panama, I. Memoirs of the Peabody Museum 7(1). Harvard University, Cambridge, Mass.

MARINGER, J.

4399 1960 The Gods of Prehistoric Man. Alfred A. Knopf, New York.

MARSHACK, A.

4400 1964 Lunar Notation on Upper Paleolithic Remains. Science 146: 743-745.

MARTIN, M.

4401 1936 Comment Vivait l'Homme de La Qunia à l'Époque Moustérienne. Préhistoire 5:7-23.

MOORE, C.B.

4402 1974 Reconstructing Complex Societies: An Archaeological Colloquium. American Schools of Oriental Research, Cambridge, Mass.

MORGAN, L.H.

4403 1878 Ancient Society. Holt, New York.

NARR, K.J.

4404 1962 Approaches to the Social Life of Earliest Man. Anthropos 57:604-620.

NICHOLSON, H.B.

4405 1971 Religion in Prehispanic Central Mexico. Handbook of
            Middle American Indians 10(I):394-446.

O'CONNOR, D.

4406 1974 Political Systems and Archaeological Data in Egypt: 2600-
            1780 B.C. World Archaeology 6(1):15-38.

PERICOT, L.

4407 1961 The Social Life of Spanish Paleolithic Hunters as Shown
            in Levantine Art. Viking Fund Publications in Anthro-
            pology 31:194-213.

RANDSBORG, K.

4408 1975 Social Dimensions of Early Neolithic Denmark. Proceedings,
            Prehistoric Society 41:105-118.

REDMAN, C.L., ed.

4409 1978 Social Archeology: Beyond Subsistence and Dating.
            Studies in Archeology. Academic Press, New York.

RICARD, R.

4410 1933 La Conquête Spirituelle du Mexique. Mem. Inst. d'Ethnol.
            20:196-199. Paris.

SCHAEDEL, R.P.

4411 1966 Incipient Urbanization and Secularization in Tiahuanacoid
            Peru. American Antiquity 31:338-341.

SEARS, W.H.

4412 1954 The Sociopolitical Organization of Pre-Columbian Cultures
            on the Gulf Coastal Plain. American Anthropologist 56:
            339-346.

4413 1961 The Study of Social and Religious Systems in North
            American Archaeology. Current Anthropology 2:223-231.

TANZER, H.H.

4414 1939 The Common People of Pompeii. Johns Hopkins University,
            Studies in Archaeology 29.

THOMPSON, J.E.S.

4415 1954 The Character of the Maya. Proceedings of the 30th
            International Congress of Americanists, 1952:36-40.
            Cambridge, England.

THORVILDSEN, E.

4416 1952 Menneskeofringer i Oldtiden (Human Offerings in Antiquity).
            Kuml 1952:32-48. Aarhus.

TOYNBEE, J.M.C.

4417 1971 Death and Burial in the Roman World. Cornell University
            Press, Ithaca, N.Y.

VALLOIS, H.V.

4418 1961 The Social Life of Early Man: The Evidence of Skeletons.
            Viking Fund Publications in Anthropology 31:214-235.

VERTES, L.

4419 1965 Lunar Calendar from the Hungarian Upper Paleolithic.
            Science 149:855-856.

WACE, A.J.B.

4420 1960 Mycenaean Religion. Archaeology 13(1):33-39.

WALLACE, W., and D. LATHRAP

4421 1959 Ceremonial Bird Burials in San Francisco Bay Shellmounds.
            American Antiquity 25:262-264.

WARING, A.J., Jr., and P. HOLDER

4422 1945 A Prehistoric Ceremonial Complex in the Southeastern
            United States. American Anthropologist 47(1):1-34.

WASHBURN, S.L.

4423 1961 Social Life of Early Man. Viking Fund Publications in
            Anthropology 31.

WATSON, K.A.

4424 1970 Neanderthal and Upper Paleolithic Burial Patterns: A
            Re-Examination. Mankind 7(4):302-306.

WHALLON, R., Jr.

4425 1968 Investigations of Late Prehistoric Social Organization in
            New York State. In S. Binford and L. Binford, eds., New
            Perspectives in Archeology:223-224. Aldine, Chicago.

WINLOCK, H.E.

4426 1955 Models of Daily Life in Ancient Egypt from the Tomb of
            Meket-Rē at Thebes. Harvard University Press, Cambridge,
            Mass.

6. Trade, Commerce, and Communication

ADAMS, R. McC.

4426a 1974 Anthropological Perspectives in Ancient Trade. Current
            Anthropology 15:239-258.

AMMERMAN, A.J.

4427 1979 A Study of Obsidian Exchange Networks in Calabria. World
            Archaeology 11(1):95-110.

BARNETT, R.D.

4428 1956 Phoenicia and the Ivory Trade. Archaeology 9(2):87-97.

BECK, C.W.

4429 1970 Amber in Archaeology. Archaeology 23(1):7-11.

BELL, R.E.

4430 1947 Trade Materials at Spiro Mound as Indicated by Artifacts.
            American Antiquity 12:181-189.

BERNDT, R.M.

4431 1951 Ceremonial Exchange in Western Arnhem Land. Southwestern
            Journal of Anthropology 7:156-176.

BESSAIGNET, P.

4432 1956 An Alleged Case of Primitive Money (New Caledonian Beads).
            Southwestern Journal of Anthropology 12:333-345.

BLINDHEIM, C.

4433 1960 New Light on Viking Trade in Norway. Archaeology 13(4):
            275-278.

BOOMERT, A., and S.B. KROONENBERG

4434 1977 Manufacture and Trade of Stone Artifacts in Prehistoric
            Surinam. In B.L. van Beek, et al., eds., Ex Horreo:9-46.
            Albert Egges van Giffen Instituut, Amsterdam.

BRADLEY, R.

4435 1971 Trade Competition and Artefact Distribution. World
            Archaeology 2:347-352.

BRAND, D.D.

4436 1938 Aboriginal Trade Routes for Sea Shells in the Southwest.
            Association of Pacific Coast Geographers 4:3-10.

BRANIGAN, K.

4437 1967 Further Light on Prehistoric Relations Between Crete and
            Bylos. American Journal of Archaeology 71(2):117-123.

BROWMAN, D.L.

4438 1975 Trade Patterns in the Central Highlands of Peru in the
            First Millennium B.C. World Archaeology 6(3):322-338.

BUTLER, J.J.

4439 1960 A Bronze Age Concentration at Bargeroosterveld. With

Some Notes on the Axe Trade Across Northern Europe. Palaeohistoria 8:101-126.

4440 1963 Bronze Age Connections Across the North Sea; a Study in Prehistoric Trade and Industrial Relations Between the British Isles, the Netherlands, North Germany and Scandinavia c. 1700-700 BC. Palaeohistoria 9.

CALLMER, J.

4441 1977 Trade Beads and Bead Trade in Scandinavia, ca. 800-1000 A.D. Acta Archaeologica Lundensia 11.

CARDOS de M., A.

4442 1959 El Comercio de los Mayas Antiquos. Acta Anthropologia Epoca 2, 2(1). Mexico City.

CARNEIRO, R.L.

4443 1958 An Instance of the Transport of Artifacts by Migratory Animals in South America. American Antiquity 24:192-193.

CARPENTER, R.

4444 1956 A Trans-Saharan Caravan Route in Herodotus. American Journal of Archaeology 60(3):231-242.

CASSON, L.

4445 1954 Trade in the Ancient World. Scientific American 191(5): 98-104.

CASSON, S.

4446 1938 The Modern Pottery Trade in the Aegean. Antiquity 12(48): 464-473.

4447 1951 The Modern Pottery Trade in the Aegean: Further Notes. Antiquity 25(100):187-190.

CHAPMAN, A.M.

4448 1959 Puertos de Intercambio en Mesoamerica Prehispanica. Instituto Nacional de Antropología e Historia, Serie Historia 3. Mexico.

CHARLTON, T.H., D.C. GROVE, and P.H. HOPKE

4449 1978 The Paredon, Mexico, Obsidian Source and Early Formative Exchange. Science 201:807-809.

CLARK, J.G.D.

4450 1948 Objects of South Scandinavian Flint in the Northernmost Provinces of Norway, Sweden and Finland. Proceedings, Prehistoric Society 14:219-232.

COLTON, H.S.

4451 1941 Prehistoric Trade in the Southwest. Scientific Monthly 52:308-319.

DAVIS, J.T.

4452   1974   Trade Routes and Economic Exchange Among the Indians of
              California. Ballena Press, Ramona, Cal.

DIXON, J.E., J.R. CANN, and C. RENFREW

4453   1968   Obsidian and the Origins of Trade. Scientific American
              218(3):38-55.

FAGAN, B.M.

4454   1972   Ingombe Ilede: Early Trade in South Central Africa.
              Addison-Wesley Module in Anthropology 19.

FRY, R.E., and S.C. COX

4455   1974   The Structure of Ceramic Exchange at Tikal, Guatemala.
              World Archaeology 6(2):209-225.

HEIZER, R.F.

4456   1941   Aboriginal Trade Between the Southwest and California.
              Southwest Museum Masterkey 15:185-188.

HESTER, J.J., P.M. HOBLER, and J. RUSSELL

4457   1970   New Evidence of Early Roads in Nubia. American Journal
              of Archaeology 74:385-389.

HESTER, T.R., R.F. HEIZER, and R.N. JACK

4458   1971   Technology and Geologic Sources of Obsidian from Cerro de
              las Mesas, Veracruz, Mexico, with Observations of Olmec
              Trade. Contributions, University of California Archaeo-
              logical Research Facility 13:65-131.

HILL, W.W.

4459   1948   Navaho Trading and Trading Ritual: A Study of Cultural
              Dynamics. Southwestern Journal of Anthropology 4:371-396.

HIRTH, K.G.

4460   1978   Interregional Trade and the Formation of Gateway Com-
              munities. American Antiquity 43(1):35-45.

HORNELL, J.

4461   1941   Sea-Trade in Early Times. Antiquity 15(59):233-256.

HUGHES, R.E.

4462   1978   Aspects of Prehistoric Wiyot Exchange and Social Ranking.
              Journal of California Anthropology 5(1):53-66.

HUTTON, J.H.

4463   1951   Less Familiar Aspects of Primitive Trade. Proceedings,
              Prehistoric Society 17(2):171-176.

IMMERWAHR, S.A.

4464 1960 Mycenaean Trade and Colonization. Archaeology 13(1):4-13.

JOHNSTON, F.J.

4465 1957 An Indian Trail Complex of the Central Colorado Desert.
University of California Archaeological Survey, Report
37:22-39.

LATHRAP, D.W.

4466 1973 The Antiquity and Importance of Long-Distance Trade Relationships in the Moist Tropics of Pre-Columbian South
America. World Archaeology 5(2):170-186.

LAUER, P.K.

4467 1971 Changing Patterns of Pottery Trade to the Trobriand
Islands. World Archaeology 3(2):197-209.

LEE, T.A., Jr., and C. NAVARRETE

4468 1978 Mesoamerican Communication Routes and Cultural Contacts.
Papers, New World Archaeological Foundation 40. Provo,
Utah.

LOEB, E.M.

4469 1936 The Distribution and Function of Money in Early Societies.
In Essays in Anthropology:153-168. University of
California Press, Berkeley.

MALLOWAN, M.E.L.

4470 1965 The Mechanisms of Trade in Western Asia. Iran 3:1-7.

MALOUF, C.

4471 1940 Prehistoric Exchange in the Northern Periphery of the
Southwest. American Antiquity 6:115-122.

MERRILLEES, R.S.

4472 1962 Opium Trade in the Bronze Age Levant. Antiquity 36(144):
287-292.

MORIARTY, J.R.

4473 1968 The Socio-Political and Economic Influences Related to
the Production and Distribution of Salt. Anthropological
Journal of Canada 6(1):2-15.

MUHLY, J.D.

4474 1973 Copper and Tin: The Distribution of Mineral Resources and
the Nature of the Metals Trade in the Bronze Age. Shoe
String Press, Hamden, Conn.

MUHLY, J.D., T.S. WHEELER, and R. MADDIN

4475 1977 The Cape Gelidonya Shipwreck and the Bronze Age Metals
            Trade in the Eastern Mediterranean. Journal of Field
            Archaeology 4(3):353-362.

NAVARRO, J.M.

4476 1925 Prehistoric Routes Between Northern Europe and Italy
            Defined by the Amber Trade. Geographical Journal 66:481.

NELSON, C.E.

4477 1966 Prehistoric Pottery Trails of Colorado. Southwestern
            Lore 31(4):84-85.

ÖZGÜÇ, T.

4478 1963 An Assyrian Trading Outpost. Scientific American 208:
            96-106.

PARSONS, L.A., and B.J. PRICE

4479 1971 Mesoamerican Trade and Its Role in the Emergence of
            Civilization. University of California, Contributions
            of the Archaeological Research Facility 11:189-194.

PIGGOTT, S.

4480 1968 The Beginnings of Wheeled Transport. Scientific
            American 219(1):82-93.

PORTER, J.W.

4481 1969 The Mitchell Site and Prehistoric Exchange Systems at
            Cahokia, A.D. 1000±300. Illinois Archaeological Survey
            Bulletin 7:137-164.

PRATT, P.P.

4482 1961 Oneida Iroquois Glass Trade Bead Sequence 1585-1745.
            Indian Glass Trade Beads Color Guide Series 1. Onondaga
            Printing Co., Syracuse, N.Y.

RANDS, R.L.

4483 1969 Mayan Ecology and Trade: 1967-1968. Mesoamerican
            Studies, Research Records, Series 69M(2)A. Southern
            Illinois University, Carbondale.

RATHJE, W.L., and J.A. SABLOFF

4484 1973 Ancient Maya Commercial Systems: A Research Design for
            the Island of Cozumel, Mexico. World Archaeology 5(2):
            221-231.

RENFREW, C.

4485 1969 Trade and Culture Process in European Prehistory. Current
            Anthropology 10(2-3):151-169.

RENFREW, C., J.E. DIXON, and J.R. CANN

4486 1966 Obsidian and Early Cultural Contact in the Near East.
            Proceedings, Prehistoric Society 32:30-72.

SABLOFF, J.A., and C.C. LAMBERG-KARLOVSKY

4487 1975 Ancient Civilization and Trade. University of New
            Mexico Press, Albuquerque.

SABLOFF, J.A., and W.L. RATHJE, eds.

4488 1975 A Study of Changing Pre-Columbian Commercial Systems:
            Cozumel, Mexico. Peabody Museum, Monograph 3. Cambridge,
            Mass.

SAHLINS, M.D.

4489 1965 On the Sociology of Primitive Exchange. American Socio-
            logical Association, Monograph 1:139-236.

SAINT-PERIER, R. de

4490 1913 Gravure à Contours Découpés en Os et Coquilles Perforées
            de l'Époque Magdalénienne. Bull. et Mem. Soc. d'Anthrop.
            Paris, Ser. 6, 4:47-52.

SARIANIDI, V.I.

4491 1971 The Lapis Lazuli Route in the Ancient East. Archaeology
            24(1):12-15.

STJERNQUIST, B.

4492 1967 Models of Commercial Distribution in Prehistoric Times.
            Scripta Minora Regiae Societatis Humaniorum Litterarum
            Lundensis:65-66. Gleerup, Lund.

STONE, J.F.S., and L.C. THOMAS

4493 1956 The Use and Distribution of Faience in the Ancient East
            and Prehistoric Europe. Proceedings, Prehistoric Society
            22:37-85.

THOMPSON, J.E.S.

4494 1949 Canoes and Navigation of the Maya and Their Neighbours.
            Journal, Royal Anthropological Institute of Great Britain
            and Ireland 79(1-2):69-78.

TORTELLOT, G., and J.A. SABLOFF

4495 1972 Exchange Systems Among the Ancient Maya. American
            Antiquity 37(1):126-134.

TOWER, D.B.

4496 1945 The Use of Marine Mollusca and Their Value in Reconstruct-
            ing Prehistoric Trade Routes in the American Southwest.
            Papers of the Excavators' Club 2(3). Cambridge, Mass.

Van LOON, M.N.

4497   1977   Archaeological Evidence of Trade in Western Asia: Problems
              and Prospects. In B.L. van Beek, et al., eds., Ex Horreo:
              1-8. Albert Egges van Giffen Instituut, Amsterdam.

WARD-PERKINS, J.B., and P. THROCKMORTON

4498   1965   New Light on the Roman Marble Trade: The San Piertro
              Wreck. Archaeology 18(3):201-209.

WINTERS, H.

4499   1968   Value Systems and Trade Cycles of the Late Archaic in the
              Midwest. In S. Binford and L. Binford, eds., New Perspec-
              tives in Archeology:175-222. Aldine, Chicago.

WOODWARD, A.

4500   1965   Indian Trade Goods. Oregon Archaeological Society,
              Publication 2. Portland.

WRIGHT, G.A.

4501   1969   Obsidian Analyses and Prehistoric Near Eastern Trade:
              7500 to 3500 B.C. Museum of Anthropology, University of
              Michigan, Anthropological Papers 37. Ann Arbor.

4502   1974   Archaeology and Trade. Addison-Wesley Module in Anthro-
              pology 49.

WRIGLEY, C.

4503   1970   Speculations on the Economic Prehistory of Africa. In
              J.D. Fage and R.A. Oliver, eds., Papers in African Pre-
              history:59-74. Cambridge University Press, Cambridge.

7. Demography

AMMERMAN, A.J., L. CAVALLI-SFORZA, and D.K. WAGENER

4503a 1976   Toward the Estimation of Population Growth in Old World
              Prehistory. In E. Zubrow, ed., Demographic Anthropology:
              Quantitative Approaches:27-61. University of New Mexico
              Press, Albuquerque.

ANGEL, J.L.

4504   1947   The Length of Life in Ancient Greece. Journal of Geron-
              tology 2(1):18-24.

4505   1951   Population Size and Microevaluation in Greece. Cold
              Spring Harbor Symposium on Quantitative Biology 15:343-351.

4506   1968   Ecological Aspects of Palaeodemography. In D.R. Broth-
              well, ed., The Skeletal Biology of Earlier Human Popula-
              tions VIII:263-270. Pergamon Press, New York.

4507   1969   The Bases of Paleodemography. American Journal of
              Physical Anthropology 30(3):427-438.

4508 1969 Paleodemography and Evolution. American Journal of Physical Anthropology 31(3):343-354.

4509 1971 Early Neolithic Skeletons from Catal Hüyük: Demography and Pathology. Anatolian Studies 21:77-98.

4510 1972 Ecology and Population in the Eastern Mediterranean. World Archaeology 4(1):88-105.

ASCHER, R.

4511 1959 A Prehistoric Population Estimate Using Midden Analysis and Two Population Models. Southwestern Journal of Anthropology 15:168-178.

ATKINSON, R.J.C.

4512 1968 Odd Mortality: Some Aspects of Burial and Population in Neolithic England. In J.M. Coles and D.D.A. Simpson, eds., Studies in Ancient Europe:83-93. Leicester University Press, Leicester, England.

BIRDSELL, J.B.

4513 1957 Some Population Problems Involving Pleistocene Man. Cold Spring Harbor Symposia on Quantitative Biology 22: 47-69. Cold Spring Harbor, N.Y.

BROTHWELL, D.

4514 1972 Palaeodemography and Earlier British Populations. World Archaeology 4(1):75-87.

CARNEIRO, R.L.

4515 1967 On the Relationship Between Size and Complexity of Social Organization. Southwestern Journal of Anthropology 23(3):234-243.

CARNEIRO, R.L., and D.R. HILSE

4516 1966 On Determining the Probable Rate of Population Growth During the Neolithic. American Anthropologist 68(1):176-181.

CASSELBERRY, S.E.

4517 1974 Further Refinement of Formulae for Determining Population from Floor Area. World Archaeology 6(1):117-122.

CASTEEL, R.W.

4518 1972 Two Static Maximum Population-Density Models for Hunter-Gatherers: A First Approximation. World Archaeology 4(1): 19-40.

CHARLTON, T.H.

4519 1972 Population Trends in the Teotihuacan Valley, A.D. 1400-1969. World Archaeology 4(1):106-123.

CLARK, P., and F. EVANS

4520   1954   Distance to Nearest Neighbor as a Measure of Spatial
              Relationships in Populations. Ecology 35:445-453.

CLARKE, S.S.

4521   1974   A Method for the Estimation of Prehistoric Pueblo Popu-
              lations. Kiva 39(3-4):283-289.

COHEN, M.N.

4521a 1975   Archaeological Evidence for Population Pressure in Pre-
              agricultural Societies. American Antiquity 40:471-475.

COLTON, H.S.

4522   1936   The Rise and Fall of the Prehistoric Population of
              Northern Arizona. Science 84:337-343.

COOK, S.F.

4523   1946   Human Sacrifice and Warfare as Factors in the Demography
              of Pre-Colonial Mexico. Human Biology 18(2):81-102.

4524   1947   The Interrelation of Population, Food Supply and Building
              in Pre-Conquest Central Mexico. American Antiquity 13:
              45-52.

4525   1949   The Historical Demography and Ecology of the Teotlalpan.
              Ecology of the Teotlalpan. Ibero-Americana 33. Berkeley.

4526   1949   Soil Erosion and Population in Central Mexico. Ibero-
              Americana 34. Berkeley.

4527   1972   Prehistoric Demography. Addison-Wesley Module in
              Anthropology 16.

COOK, S.F., and W. BORAH

4528   1971   Essays in Population History: Mexico and the Caribbean.
              University of California Press, Berkeley.

DITTERT, A.E., Jr.

4529   1968   Some Factors Affecting Southwestern Populations During
              the Period A.D. 900-1540. Eastern New Mexico University,
              Contributions to Anthropology 1(1):14-16.

DIVALE, W.T.

4530   1972   Systemic Population Control in the Middle and Upper
              Palaeolithic: Inferences Based on Contemporary Hunter-
              Gatherers. World Archaeology 4(2):222-243.

DUMOND, D.E.

4531   1972   Demographic Aspects of the Classic Period in Puebla-
              Tlaxcala. Southwestern Journal of Anthropology 28(2):
              101-130.

DURAND, J.D.

4532 1960 Mortality Estimates from Roman Tombstone Inscriptions.
            American Journal of Sociology 65:365-373.

GOLDSTEIN, M.S.

4533 1953 Some Vital Statistics Based on Skeletal Material. Human
            Biology 25:3-10.

HAVILAND, W.A.

4534 1972 Estimates of Maya Population: Comments on Thompson's
            Comments. American Antiquity 37(2):261-262.

4535 1972 Family Size, Prehistoric Population Estimates, and the
            Ancient Maya. American Antiquity 37(1):135-139.

HAYDEN, B.

4536 1972 Population Control Among Hunter-Gatherers. World Archae-
            ology 4(2):205-221.

HOLLINGSWORTH, T.H.

4537 1971 Historical Demography. Cornell University Press, Ithaca,
            N.Y.

HOWELLS, W.W.

4538 1960 Estimating Population Numbers Through Archaeological and
            Skeletal Remains. Viking Fund Publications in Anthro-
            pology 28:158-180.

KUNITZ, S.J.

4539 1970 Disease and Death Among the Anasazi. Some Notes on South-
            western Paleoepidemiology. El Palacio 76(3):17-23.

4540 1972 Aspects of Southwestern Paleoepidemiology. Prescott
            College Press, Prescott, Ariz.

LEE, R.B.

4541 1963 The Population Ecology of Man in the Early Upper Pleisto-
            cene of Southern Africa. Proceedings, Prehistoric
            Society 29:235-257.

LOVEJOY, C.O.

4542 1971 Methods for the Detection of Census Error in Palaeodemog-
            raphy. American Anthropologist 73(1):101-109.

McARTHUR, N.

4543 1970 The Demography of Primitive Populations. Science 167:
            1097-1101.

MacDONNELL, W.R.

4544 1913 On the Expectation of Life in Ancient Rome and in the
            Provinces of Hispania and Lusitania. Biometrika 9:366-380.

McMICHAEL, E.V.

4545 1960 Towards the Estimation of Prehistoric Populations. Pro-
            ceedings of the Indiana Academy of Science for 1959, 69:
            78-81.

NOVGIER, L.R.

4546 1949 Densité Humaine et Population au Néolithique. Bulletin,
            Société Préhistorique Française 46:126-127.

PHILLIPS, P.

4547 1972 Population, Economy and Society in the Chassey-Cortaillod-
            Lagozza Cultures. World Archaeology 4(1):41-56.

RANDALL, H.J.

4548 1930 Population and Agriculture in Roman Britain: A Reply.
            Antiquity 4:80-90.

RAY, D.J.

4549 1964 Nineteenth Century Settlement and Subsistence Patterns
            in Bering Strait. Arctic Anthropology 2(2):61-94.

SCHROEDER, A.H.

4550 1965 Tentative Ecological and Cultural Factors and Their
            Effects on Southwestern Farmers. Eastern New Mexico
            University, Contributions to Anthropology 1(1):17-20.

SHAWCROSS, W.

4551 1970 Ethnographic Economics and the Study of Population in
            Prehistoric New Zealand Viewed Through Archaeology.
            Mankind 7(4):271-291.

SMITH, P.E.L.

4552 1972 Changes in Population Pressure in Archaeological Explana-
            tion. World Archaeology 4(1):5-18.

SWEDLUND, A.C., ed.

4553 1975 Population Studies in Archaeology and Biological Anthro-
            pology: A Symposium. Society for American Archaeology,
            Memoir 30.

TURNER, C.G., and L. LOFGREN

4554 1966 Household Size of Prehistoric Western Pueblo Indians.
            Southwestern Journal of Anthropology 22:117-132.

VALLOIS, H.V.

4555 1960 Vital Statistics in Prehistoric Populations as Determined
            from Archaeological Data. Viking Fund Publications in
            Anthropology 28:181-222.

WEISS, K.M.

4556 1973 Demographic Models for Anthropology. Society for American
            Archaeology, Memoir 27.

ZUBROW, E.B.W.

4557 1971 Carrying Capacity and Dynamic Equilibrium in the Prehis-
            toric Southwest. American Antiquity 36(2):127-138.

4558 1976 Demographic Anthropology: Quantitative Approaches.
            School of American Research Book. University of New
            Mexico Press, Albuquerque.

8. Population Movements

ANTEVS, E.

4559 1935 The Spread of Aboriginal Man to North America. Geo-
            graphical Review 25(2):302-309.

BIRD, J.

4560 1938 Antiquity and Migrations of Early Inhabitants of Pata-
            gonia. Geographical Review 28:250-275.

BORDEN, C.E.

4561 1969 Early Population Movements from Asia into Western North
            America. Syesis 2(1-2):1-14.

BOSCH-GIMPERA, P.

4562 1969 Some New Aspects of the Eurasian Paleolithic in Relation
            with the Origin of American Hunters. Anales de Antro-
            pología 5:163-179.

BRYAN, A.L.

4563 1968 Some Problems and Hypotheses Relative to the Early Entry
            of Man into America. Anthropologica 10(2).

BUSHNELL, G., and C. McBURNEY

4564 1959 New World Origins Seen from the Old World. Antiquity
            33(130):93-101.

CHARD, C.

4565 1959 New World Origins: A Reappraisal. Antiquity 33(129):44-49.

COLTON, H.S.

4566 1932 Sunset Crater: The Effect of a Volcanic Eruption on an
            Ancient People. Geographical Review 22:582-590.

CURRY, J.C.

4567 1928 Climate and Migrations. Antiquity 2:292-307.

DAVIS, E.L.

4568 1965 Small Pressures and Cultural Drift as Explanation for
            Abandonment of the San Juan Area, New Mexico and Arizona.
            American Antiquity 30:353-355.

FOWLER, W.S.

4569 1961 Movement of Prehistoric Peoples in the Northeast. Bul-
            letin, Massachusetts Archaeological Society 22(3-4):62-65.

FOX, J.W.

4570 1980 Lowland to Highland Mexicanization Processes in Southern
            Mesoamerica. American Antiquity 45(1):43-54.

GATHORNE-HARDY, G.M.

4571 1932 Alleged Norse Remains in America. Antiquity 6:420-433.

GIDDINGS, J.L.

4572 1960 The Archeology of Bering Strait. Current Anthropology 1:
            121-130.

GILBERT, B.M.

4573 1972 An Evaluation of Hypotheses Concerning the Earliest
            Peopling of the New World. Newsletter, Missouri Archaeo-
            logical Society 259.

GOSS, J.R.

4574 1965 Ute Linguistics and Anasazi Abandonment of the Four
            Corners Area. American Antiquity 31:73-81.

GREENMAN, E.F.

4575 1963 The Upper Paleolithic in the New World. Current Anthro-
            pology 4:41-91.

GRIGOR'EV, G.P.

4576 1965 Migrations, Indigenous Development and Diffusion in the
            Upper Palaeolithic. Arctic Anthropology 3:116-121.

HAAG, W.G.

4577 1962 The Bering Strait Land Bridge. Scientific American 206:
            112-123.

HAMMOND, N.G.L.

4578 1976 Migrations and Invasions in Greece and Adjacent Areas.
            Noyes Press, Park Ridge, N.J.

HEDRICK, J.D., and K. GOODRICH-HEDRICK

4579 1972 The Problem of Polynesian Origin. Expedition 14(4):33-
            39.

HESTER, J.J.

4580 1962 Early Navajo Migrations and Acculturation in the South-
          west. Museum of New Mexico Papers in Anthropology 6.
          Santa Fe.

HEYERDAHL, T.

4581 1952 American Indians in the Pacific: The Theory Behind the
          Kon-Tiki Expedition. Allen & Unwin, London.

4582 1958 Aku-Aku, the Secret of Easter Island. Rand McNally,
          Chicago.

4583 1963 Feasible Ocean Routes to and from the Americas in Pre-
          Columbian Times. American Antiquity 28:482-488.

IVES, R.L.

4584 1956 An Early Speculation Concerning the Asiatic Origin of
          the American Indian. American Antiquity 21:420-421.

JEFFREYS, M.D.W.

4585 1967 Polynesian Origins and the Kon Tiki Expedition. South
          African Journal of Science 63(3):73-76.

JELINEK, A.J.

4586 1965 The Upper Paleolithic Revolution and the Peopling of the
          New World. Michigan Archaeologist 11(3-4):85-88.

JETT, S.C.

4587 1964 Pueblo Indian Migrations: An Evaluation of the Possible
          Physical and Cultural Determinants. American Antiquity
          29:281-300.

KAELAS, L.

4588 1966 The Megalithic Tombs in South-Scandinavia--Migration or
          Cultural Influence. Paleohistoria 12:287-322.

KELLEY, J.C.

4589 1952 Factors Involved in the Abandonment of Certain Peripheral
          Southwestern Settlements. American Anthropologist 54:
          356-387.

LAUGHLIN, W.S.

4590 1967 Human Migration and Permanent Occupation in the Bering
          Sea Area. In D.M. Hopkins, ed., The Bering Land Bridge:
          409-450. Stanford University Press, Stanford.

LINNÉ, L.

4591 1955 The Bering Isthmus--Bridge Between Asia and America.
          Ethnos 1955:210-215.

MATHER, J.R.

4592 1954 The Effect of Climate on the New World Migration of
            Primitive Man. Southwestern Journal of Anthropology 10:
            304-321.

MULLER-BECK, H.

4593 1966 Paleohunters in America: Origins and Diffusion. Science
            152(3726):1191-1210.

4594 1967 Migrations of Hunters on the Land Bridge in the Upper
            Pleistocene. In D.M. Hopkins, ed., The Bering Land
            Bridge:373-408. Stanford University Press, Stanford.

RANDALL, E.O.

4595 1908 The Mound Builders and the Lost Tribes: The Holy Stones
            of Newark. Ohio Archaeological and Historical Society
            Publication 17:208-218.

ROUSE, I.

4596 1958 The Inference of Migrations from Anthropological Evidence.
            University of Arizona, Social Science Bulletin 27:63-68.

SHUTLER, M.E.

4597 1967 Origins of the Melanesians. Archaeology and Physical
            Anthropology in Oceania 2(2):91-99.

SMITH, G.E.

4598 1929 The Migration of Early Cultures. University of Manchester
            Press, Manchester.

SOLECKI, R.

4599 1951 How Man Came to North America. Scientific American
            184(1):11-15.

STEWART, T.D.

4600 1960 A Physical Anthropologist's View of the Peopling of the
            New World. Southwestern Journal of Anthropology 16:259-
            273.

THOMPSON, R.H., ed.

4601 1958 Migrations in New World Culture History. Social Science
            Bulletin 27, University of Arizona, Tucson.

WAUCHOPE, R.

4602 1962 Lost Tribes and Sunken Continents. University of Chicago
            Press, Chicago.

WENDORF, F.

4603 1966 Early Man in the New World: Problems of Migration.
            American Naturalist 100(912):253-270.

WRIGHT, G.A.

4604   1978   The Shoshonean Migration Problem. Plains Anthropologist
              23(80):113-137.

9. Diffusion and Trans-Oceanic Contacts

BANDELIER, A.

4605   1905   Traditions of Pre-Columbian Landings on the West Coast
              of South America. American Anthropologist 7(2):250-270.

BORDEN, C.E.

4606   1968   New Evidence of Early Cultural Relations Between Eurasia
              and Western North America. Proceedings, 8th International
              Congress of Anthropological and Ethnological Sciences 3:
              331-337.

CAMPBELL, J.M.

4607   1962   Ancient Alaska and Paleolithic Europe. Anthropological
              Papers of the University of Alaska 10:35-49.

CASO, A.

4608   1965   Semejanzas de Diseño que no Indican Contactos Culturales.
              Cuadernos Americanos 6:147-152.

CHARD, C.S.

4609   1961   Invention versus Diffusion: The Burial Mound Complex of
              the Eastern United States. Southwestern Journal of
              Anthropology 17:21-25.

DRAGOO, D.M.

4610   1964   Relationship of the Eastern North American Burial Cult to
              Central America and the Old World. Actas y Memorias.
              XXXV Congreso Internacional des Americanistas 1:101-111.
              Mexico.

EDMONSON, M.S.

4611   1961   Neolithic Diffusion Rates. Current Anthropology 2:71-102.

EDWARDS, C.R.

4612   1969   Possibilities of Pre-Columbian Maritime Contacts Among
              New World Civilizations. Mesoamerican Studies 4:3-10.

EKHOLM, G.

4613   1953   A Possible Focus of Asiatic Influence in the Late Classic
              Cultures of Mesoamerica. Society for American Archaeology,
              Memoir 9:72-89.

4614   1964   Transpacific Contacts. In J.D. Jennings and E. Norbeck,
              eds., Prehistoric Man in the New World:489-510. University
              of Chicago Press, Chicago.

ESTRADAM, E., B.J. MEGGERS, and C. EVANS

4615 1962 Possible Transpacific Contact on the Coast of Ecuador.
             Science 135:371-372.

FORD, J.A.

4616 1969 A Comparison of Formative Cultures in the Americas:
             Diffusion or the Psychic Unity of Man. Smithsonian
             Institution Press, Washington, D.C.

GENOVÉS, S.

4617 1973 Papyrus Rafts Across the Atlantic. Current Anthropology
             14(3):266-267.

GLADWIN, H.S.

4618 1947 Men out of Asia. McGraw-Hill, New York.

GORDON, C.H.

4619 1971 Before Columbus. Crown Publishers, New York.

GRIFFIN, J.B.

4620 1960 Some Prehistoric Connections Between Siberia and America.
             Science 131(3403):801-812.

IKAWA, F.

4621 1968 The Japanese Paleolithic in the Context of Prehistoric
             Cultural Relationships Between Northern Eurasia and the
             New World. Proceedings, 8th International Congress of
             Anthropological and Ethnological Sciences 3:197-199.

JAIRAZBHOY, R.A.

4622 1974 Ancient Egyptians and Chinese in America. Rowman and
             Littlefield, Totowa, N.J.

KROEBER, A.L.

4623 1940 Stimulus Diffusion. American Anthropologist 42:1-20.

LEAR, J.

4624 1970 Ancient Landings in America. Saturday Review, July 18:
             18-34.

O'BRIEN, P.

4625 1968 Doctrinaire Diffusion and Acts of Faith. American
             Antiquity 33:386-388.

O'CONNOR, D.

4626 1971 Ancient Egypt and Black Africa--Early Contact. Expedition
             14(1):2-9.

PICKERSGILL, B.

4627 1972 Cultivated Plants as Evidence for Cultural Contacts. American Antiquity 37(1):97-103.

RANDS, R.L.

4628 1953 The Water Lily in Maya Art: A Complex of Alleged Asiatic Origin. Bureau of American Ethnology, Bulletin 151:79-153.

ROWE, J.H.

4629 1966 Diffusionism and Archaeology. American Antiquity 31: 334-337.

TOLSTOY, P.

4630 1966 Method in Long Range Comparison. Actas de XXXVI Congreso Internacional de Americanistas, Madrid 1964, 1:69-89. Seville.

VERHOOG, P.

4631 1959 De Ontdekking Van Amerika Voor Columbus. C. de Boer, Jr., Hilversum, Netherlands.

WILLEY, G.R.

4632 1956 An Archaeological Classification of Culture Contact Situations. Society for American Archaeology, Memoir 11:1-30.

WUTHENAU, A. von

4633 1975 Unexpected Faces in Ancient America: 1500 B.C.-A.D. 1500, the Historical Testimony of Pre-Columbian Artists. Crown Publishers, New York.

10. Language

ABERLE, D.

4634 1960 The Influence of Linguistics on Early Culture and Personality Theory. In G. Dole and R. Carneiro, eds., Essays in the Science of Culture in Honor of Leslie A. White: 1-29. Thomas Y. Crowell, New York.

BURTON, H.

4635 1979 The Arrival of the Celts in Ireland. Expedition 21(3): 16-22.

CLEATOR, P.E.

4636 1962 Lost Languages. Mentor Books, New York.

CROSSLAND, R.A.

4637 1957 Indo-European Origins: The Linguistic Evidence. Past and Present 12:16-46.

EHRET, C.

4638   1976   Linguistic Evidence and Its Correlation with Archaeology.
                World Archaeology 8(1):5-18.

FRIEDRICH, J.

4639   1957   Extinct Languages.   Philosophical Library, New York.

GUTHRIE, M.

4640   1970   Some Developments in the Prehistory of the Bantu Languages.
                In J.D. Fage and R.A. Oliver, eds., Papers in African
                Prehistory:131-140.   Cambridge University Press, Cambridge.

HASS, M.R.

4641   1969   The Prehistory of Languages.   Janua Linguarum, Series
                Minor 57.   Mouton, The Hague.

HENCKEN, H.C.

4642   1955   Indo-European Languages and Archaeology.   American Anthro-
                pological Association, Memoir 84.

HOCKETT, C.R.

4643   1953   Linguistic Time-Perspective and Its Anthropological Uses.
                International Journal of Anthropological Linguistics 19:
                146-151.

4644   1958   A Course in Modern Linguistics.   Macmillan, New York.

HOIJER, H.

4645   1956   The Chronology of the Athapaskan Languages.   International
                Journal of Linguistics 22:219-232.

4646   1956   Lexicostatistics: A Critique.   Language 32:49-60.

HOPKINS, N.A.

4647   1965   Great Basin Prehistory and Uto-Aztecan.   American
                Antiquity 31:48-60.

HYMES, D.H.

4648   1960   Lexicostatistics So Far.   Current Anthropology 1:3-44.

JOSSERAND, J.K.

4649   1975   Archaeological and Linguistic Correlations for Mayan Pre-
                History.   Actas, XLI Congreso Internacional de Americanis-
                tas I:501-510.

KAUFMAN, T.

4650   1976   Archaeological and Linguistic Correlations in Mayaland
                and Associated Areas of Meso-America.   World Archaeology
                8(1):101-118.

KINKADE, M.D., and J.V. POWELL

4651 1976 Language and the Prehistory of North America. World
Archaeology 8(1):83-100.

KROEBER, A.L.

4652 1955 Linguistic Time Depth Results So Far and Their Meaning.
International Journal of Anthropological Linguistics
21:91-104.

LEES, R.B.

4653 1953 The Basis of Glottochronology. Language 29:113-127.
(See also Language 23:344-375, 1947.)

PULGRAM, E.

4654 1959 Proto-Indo-European Reality and Reconstruction. Language
35(3):421-426.

RHEA, J.A.

4655 1958 Concerning the Validity of Lexico-Statistics. International Journal of Anthropological Linguistics 24:145-
150.

SWADESH, M.

4656 1952 Lexico-Statistic Dating of Prehistoric Ethnic Contacts.
Proceedings, American Philosophical Society 96:452-463.

4657 1959 Linguistics as an Instrument of Prehistory. Southwest
Journal of Anthropology 15(1):20-35.

4658 1960 Estudios Sobre Lengua y Cultura. Acta Anthropologica,
2a Epoca 2(2). Mexico City.

4659 1962 Linguistic Relations Across Bering Strait. American
Anthropologist 64:1262-1291.

TOVAR, A.

4660 1954 Linguistics and Prehistory. Word 10:333-350.

TRAGER, G.L.

4661 1955 Linguistics and the Reconstruction of Culture History.
In New Interpretations of Aboriginal American Culture
History:110-115. Anthropological Society of Washington,
Washington, D.C.

11. Astronomy (Archaeoastronomy)

AVENI, A.F.

4662 1972 Astronomical Tables Intended for Use in Astro-Archaeological
Studies. American Antiquity 37(4):531-539.

4663 1974 Archaeoastronomy in Pre-Columbian America. University of
Texas Press, Austin.

4664   1979   Venus and the Maya. American Scientist 67(3):274–285.

4665   1980   Skywatchers of Ancient Mexico. University of Texas
              Press, Austin.

       AVENI, A.F., and R.M. LINSLEY

4666   1972   Mound J, Monte Alban: Possible Astronomical Orientation.
              American Antiquity 37(4):528–530.

       BAITY, E.C.

4667   1969   Some Implications of Astro-Archaeology for Americanists.
              Verhandlungen des XXXVIII. Internationalen Amerikanisten-
              kongresses Stuttgart-München 1:85–94. Kommissionsverlag
              Klaus Renner, München, Germany.

       BRANDT, J., and R.A. WILLIAMSON

4668   1979   The 1054 Supernova and Native American Rock Art. Archaeo-
              astronomy 1. Science History Publications Ltd., Bucks,
              England.

       BROWN, P.L.

4669   1976   Megaliths, Myths and Men: An Introduction to Astroarchae-
              ology. Taplinger, New York.

       COLLER, B.R., and A.F. AVENI

4670   1978   A Selected Bibliography on Native American Astronomy.
              Colgate University, Hamilton, N.Y.

       EDDY, J.A.

4671   1974   Astronomical Alignment of the Bog Horn Medicine Wheel.
              Science 184:1035–1043.

       FREEMAN, P.R., and W. ELMORE

4672   1979   A Test for the Significance of Astronomical Alignments.
              Archaeoastronomy 1. Science History Publications Ltd.,
              Bucks, England.

       HATCH, M.P.

4673   1971   An Hypothesis on Olmec Astronomy, with Special Reference
              to the La Venta Site. University of California, Contribu-
              tions of the Archaeological Research Facility 13:1–64.

       HAWKINS, G.S.

4674   1965   Stonehenge Decoded. Doubleday and Co., Garden City, N.Y.

4675   1973   Beyond Stonehenge. Harper and Row, New York.

4676   1974   Celestial Clues to Egyptian Riddles. Natural History
              83(4):54–63.

       HEGGIE, D.C.

4677   1972   Megalithic Lunar Observations: An Astronomer's View.
              Antiquity 46(181):43–48.

HUDSON, T., and E. UNDERHAY

4678 1978 Crystals in the Sky: An Intellectual Odyssey Involving
            Chumash Astronomy, Cosmology and Rock Art. Ballena Press
            Anthropological Papers 10. Socorro, N.M.

KRUPP, E.C., ed.

4679 1977 In Search of Ancient Astronomies. Doubleday and Co.,
            Garden City, N.Y.

LaCOMBE, C.H., and S.S. BLOCK

4680 1977 The Maya Astronomical Computer. National Security Agency
            Technical Journal, June:43-66.

LAMB, W.

4681 1980 The Sun, Moon and Venus at Uxmal. American Antiquity
            45(1):79-86.

LYNCH, B.M., and L.H. ROBBINS

4682 1978 Namoratunga: The First Archaeoastronomical Evidence in
            Sub-Saharan Africa. Science 200:766-769.

MacGOWAN, K.

4683 1945 The Orientation of Middle American Sites. American
            Antiquity 11:118-121.

MARSHACK, A.

4684 1964 Lunar Notations on Upper Paleolithic Remains. Science
            146:743-745.

G. WRITING OF REPORTS

ADAMS, W.H.

4685 1974 Preparation of Line Drawings from Photographs. Historical
            Archaeology 6:112-114.

BRODRIBB, C.

4686 1970 Drawing Archaeological Finds for Publication. John
            Baker, London.

BRYANT, V.M., and R.K. HOLTZ

4687 1965 A Guide to the Drafting of Archeological Maps. Bulletin,
            Texas Archeological Society 36:269-285.

COMBES, J.D.

4688 1964 A Graphic Method for Recording and Illustrating Burials.
            American Antiquity 30:216-219.

GRINSELL, L., P. RAHTZ, and A. WARHUST

4689   1966   The Preparation of Archaeological Reports.   John Baker,
              London.

4690   1974   The Preparation of Archaeological Reports.   St. Martin's
              Press, New York.

HARRISON, M.W.

4691   1945   The Writing of American Archaeology.   American Antiquity
              10:331-339.

ISHAM, L.B.

4692   1965   Preparation of Drawings for Paleontologic Publication.
              In B. Kummel and D. Raup, eds., Handbook of Paleonto-
              logical Techniques:459-468.   W.H. Freeman, San Francisco.

IVES, R.L.

4693   1948   Line Drawings from Unsatisfactory Photographs.   American
              Antiquity 13:323.

KENRICK, P.

4694   1971   Aids to the Drawing of Finds.   Antiquity 45:205-209.

KOBAYASHI, T., and P. BLEED

4695   1971   Recording and Illustrating Ceramic Surfaces with Takuhon
              Rubbings.   Plains Anthropologist 16(53):219.

LESTER, J.D.

4696   1967   Writing Research Papers, a Complete Guide.   Scott,
              Foresman, and Co., Glenview, Ill.

PIGGOTT, S., and B. HOPE-TAYLOR

4697   1965   Archaeological Draughtsmanship: Principles and Practice.
              Antiquity 39:165-176.

PLATZ, K.A.

4698   1971   Drawing Artifacts for Identification Purposes.   Missouri
              Archaeological Society Newsletter 250:5-8.

RIDGWAY, J.L.

4699   1938   Scientific Illustration.   Stanford University Press, Palo
              Alto, Cal.

RIVARD, S.J.

4700   1964   Technical Illustrations Applied to Archaeology.   Bulletin,
              Massachusetts Archaeological Society 25(2):44-45.

STANILAND, L.N.

4701   1953   The Principles of Line Illustration with Emphasis on the
              Requirements of Biological and Other Scientific Workers.
              Harvard University Press, Cambridge, Mass.

van RIET LOWE, C.

4702 1954 Notes on the Drawing of Stone Implements. South African
            Archaeological Bulletin 9(33):30-33.

VINNICOMBE, P.

4703 1963 Proposed Scheme for Standard Representation of Colour in
            Black-and-White Illustrations for Publication. South
            African Archaeological Bulletin 18(70):49-51.

WATLINGTON, A.G., and D.R. JACKSON

4704 1979 Simple Methods and Materials for Preparing Drawings for
            Publication. Historical Archaeology 11:119-121.

WEBER, T.J.

4705 1966 A Three-Dimensional Method for Rapid Reproduction of
            Small Artifacts. American Antiquity 31:437-438.

YOUNG, K.S.

4706 1970 A Technique for Illustrating Pottery Designs. American
            Antiquity 35:488-491.

IV. ARCHAEOLOGY AS A PROFESSION

A. GENERAL

LEAKEY, L.S.B., and H. van LAWICK

4707 1963 Adventures in the Search for Man. National Geographic
             Magazine 123:132-152. Washington, D.C.

MANDELBAUM, D.G.

4708 1964 Anthropology as Study and as Career. In J.S. Childers,
             ed., Listen to Leaders in Science:177-192. Holt, Rinehart,
             and Winston, New York.

MEIGHAN, C.W.

4709 1961 The Archaeologist's Notebook. Chandler, San Francisco.

ROWE, J.H.

4710 1954 Archaeology as a Career. Archaeology 7:229-236.

STUART, G.

4711 1977 Your Career in Archaeology. Society for American Archae-
             ology, Washington, D.C.

STURTEVANT, W.C.

4712 1958 Anthropology as a Career. Smithsonian Institution of
             Washington, Publication 4343.

B. TEACHING OF ARCHAEOLOGY

ASCH, T.

4713 1975 Using Film in Teaching Anthropology: One Pedagogical
             Approach. In P. Hockings, ed., Principles of Visual
             Anthropology. Mouton, The Hague.

ASCHER, R.

4714 1968 Teaching Archaeology in the University. Archaeology 21(4):
             282-287.

CHILCOTT, J.H., and J.J. DEETZ

4715 1964 The Construction and Use of a Laboratory Archaeological
            Site. American Antiquity 29:328-337.

CLARK, G.

4716 1943 Education and the Study of Man. Antiquity 17(67):113-121.

DANIEL, G.E.

4717 1954 Archaeology and Television. Antiquity 28(112):201-205.

FAGAN, B.M.

4718 1977 Genesis I:1; or, Teaching Archaeology to the Great
            Archaeology-Loving Public. American Antiquity 42(1):
            119-125.

FOX, A.

4719 1944 The Place of Archaeology in British Education. Antiquity
            18(71):153-157.

FRANTZ, C.

4720 1972 The Student Anthropologist's Handbook, a Guide to Re-
            search, Training and Career. Schenkman, Cambridge, Mass.

HORPEL, R.J.

4721 1966 Archaeology in the Social Studies Curricula. Journal,
            Archaeology Society of Maryland 2(1):76-79.

LOGAN, P.A.

4722 1968 Anthropology in the Elementary School. Kansas Anthro-
            pological Association Newsletter 13(1).

McDONALD, W.A.

4723 1975 Archaeology in the Graduate School. Journal of Field
            Archaeology 1(3/4):371-374.

McHUGH, W.P., ed.

4724 1977 Teaching and Training in American Archaeology. Southern
            Illinois University, Museum Studies 10.

MEAD, M.

4725 1975 Visual Anthropology in a Discipline of Words. In P.
            Hockings, ed., Principles of Visual Anthropology.
            Mouton, The Hague.

PETERSON, A.Y.

4726 1975 Some Methods of Ethnographic Filming. In P. Hockings, ed.,
            Principles of Visual Anthropology. Mouton, The Hague.

SPIER, R.F.G., D.R. HENNING, and J.R. VINCENT

4727 1971 Graphic Teaching Aids in Basic Anthropometry. University of Missouri-Columbia, Museum of Anthropology, Publication 6.

STEFFY, D.M.

4728 1975 Toward a Personalized System of Instruction for Introductory Anthropology. Council on Anthropology and Education Quarterly 6:30-34.

STRONG, W.D.

4729 1952 The Value of Archeology in the Training of Professional Anthropologists. American Anthropologist 54:318-321.

WALLACE, W.S.

4730 1949 An Experiment in Archaeology in the Secondary School. Southwestern Lore 15:21-24.

WEIANT, C.W.

4731 1952 An Inductive Approach in the Teaching of Archaeology. American Antiquity 17:251-253.

V. SOURCES OF PRIMARY DATA

A. BIBLIOGRAPHIES

ALCINA, J.

4732 1960 Bibliografía Basica de Arqueología Americana. Publica-
            ciones del Seminario de Antropología America 1. Sevilla.

ALEXANDER, H.L.

4733 1975 Archaeological Laboratory Techniques, an Annotated
            Bibliography. Simon Fraser University, Department of
            Archaeology, Publication 2.

ANDERSEN, R.R.

4734 1966 North Dakota Archaeology 1966: A Bibliography of General
            Sources. Plains Anthropologist 11(33).

ANGELES ROMERO FRIZZI, M. de los

4735 1974 Bibliografía Antropológica del Estado de Oaxaca, Cuadernos
            de los Centros 5. Centro Regional de Oaxaca, Instituto
            Nacional de Antropología e Historia.

ANGRESS, S., and C.A. REED

4736 1962 An Annotated Bibliography on the Origin and Descent of
            Domestic Mammals 1900-1955. Fieldiana, Anthropology
            54(1).

ANONYMOUS

4737 1962 Bibliography of Geochronology. Geochron Laboratories,
            Cambridge, Mass.

ANONYMOUS

4738 1970 An Experimental Bibliography on Science and Archaeology.
            Science and Archaeology 1.

ARMELAGOS, G.I., J.H. MIELKE, and J. WINTER

4739 1971 Bibliography of Human Paleopathology. Research Reports,
            Department of Anthropology, University of Massachusetts 8.

ASTROM, P.

4740 1971 Who's Who in Cypriote Archaeology: Biographical and Biblio-
            graphical Notes. Studies in Mediterranean Archaeology 23.

BACHATLY, C.

4741 1942 Bibliographie de la Préhistoire Egyptienne 1869-1938.
            Le Caire.

BAILEY, E.R.

4742 1971 From Adze to Vermillion: A Guide to the Hardware of
            History, and the Literature of Historic Sites Archaeology.
            Socio-Technical Books, Pasadena.

BEFU, H., C.S. CHARD, and A. OKADA

4742a 1964 An Annotated Bibliography of the Preceramic Archaeology
            of Japan. Arctic Anthropology 2(1):1-83.

BELL, R.E.

4743 1969 Oklahoma Archaeology: An Annotated Bibliography. Stovall
            Museum Publication, University of Oklahoma Press, Norman.

BERGHE, L.V., and H.F. MUSSCHE

4744 1956 Bibliographie Analytique de l'Assyriologie et de
            l'Archéologie du Proche-Orient. Leiden.

BLAKESLEE, D.J.

4745 1971 A Bibliography of Nebraska Archeology. Nebraska Anthro-
            pologist 1.

BLECK, R.D.

4746 1966 Bibliographie der Archäologisch-Chemischen Literatur.
            Alt-Thüringen, Weimar.

4747 1968 Bibliographie der Archäologisch-Chemischen Literatur.
            Beiheft. Alt-Thüringen, Weimar.

BOSS, E.C.

4748 1964 Bibliography of Archaeological Periodicals of the United
            States, Adjacent Canada and Mexico. McMurray, Pa.

BOWMAN, M.L.

4749 1973 A Bibliography of Kentucky Archaeology. Kentucky Archaeo-
            logical Association, Bulletin 2. Bowling Green.

BREW, J.O.

4750 1943 A Selected Bibliography of American Indian Archaeology
            East of the Rocky Mountains. Papers of the Excavator's
            Club 2(1). Cambridge, Mass.

BROYLES, B.J., ed.

4751 1967 Bibliography of Pottery Type Descriptions from the
            Eastern United States. Southeastern Archaeological
            Conference, Bulletin 4.

CAMPBELL, T.N.

4752 1958 Texas Archeology: A Guide to the Literature. Bulletin, Texas Archeological Society 29:177-254.

COLLER, B.R., and A.F. AVENI

4753 1978 A Selected Bibliography on Native American Astronomy. Colgate University, Hamilton, N.Y.

COOKE, C.K.

4754 1970 An Archeological Bibliography of Rhodesia from 1874. Historical Monuments Commission of Rhodesia, Bulawayo.

COTTER, J.L., ed.

4755 1980 Bibliography of Historical Sites Archaeology. Society for Historical Archaeology (in press).

COULSON, W.D.E.

4756 1975 An Annotated Bibliography of Greek and Roman Art, Architecture, and Archaeology. Garland, New York.

DeJARNETTE, D.L., and V. SCARRITT, eds.

4757 1970 A Selected Bibliography of Alabama Archaeology. Journal of Alabama Archaeology 16(1).

DEKIN, A.A., Jr.

4758 1977 Arctic Archaeology: A Bibliography and History. Garland, New York.

DOCKSTADER, F.J.

4759 1957 The American Indian in Graduate Studies. Museum of the American Indian, Heye Foundation.

EVERITT, C.

4760 1975 Paleo-Indian Bison Kill Sites in North America: A Bibliography. El Paso Archaeological Society, The Artifact 13(3):39-49.

FAY, G.E.

4761 1964 A Bibliography of Fossil Man. Appendix to Part I. 1845-1955. Museum of Anthropology, Colorado State College, Greeley.

FIELD, H.

4762 1967 Bibliography of Soviet Archaeology and Physical Anthropology, 1936-1967. Coconut Grove, Florida.

FOWLER, C.S.

4763 1970 Great Basin Anthropology--a Bibliography. Desert Research Institute, Technical Report Series S-H: Social Sciences and Humanities Publication 5. University of Nevada, Reno.

GRAYSON, D.K.

4764   1975   A Bibliography of the Literature on North American
              Climates of the Past 13,000 Years. Garland, New York.

HANTZSCHEL, W., F. EL-BAX, and G.C. AMSTUTZ

4765   1968   Coprolites: An Annotated Bibliography. Geological Society
              of America, Memoirs 108.

HARRISON, W.J.

4766   1901   Bibliography of Stonehenge and Avebury. Wiltshire Archaeo-
              logical and Natural History Magazine 32:1-169.

HAYNES, R.E., and K.T. PRIBANIC

4767   1977   A Bibliography of Historic Preservation: Selected Publica-
              tions of the Office of Archaeology and Historic Preserva-
              tion. U.S. Department of the Interior, National Park
              Service, Washington, D.C.

HEIZER, R.F., and A.B. ELSASSER

4768   1977   A Bibliography of California Indians: Archaeology,
              Ethnography, and Indian History. Garland, New York.

HEIZER, R.F., A.B. ELSASSER, and C.W. CLEWLOW, Jr.

4769   1970   A Bibliography of California Archaeology. University
              of California, Contributions of the Archaeological Re-
              search Facility 6.

HESTER, T.R., and R.F. HEIZER

4770   1973   Bibliography of Archaeology I: Experiments, Lithic Tech-
              nology and Petrography. Addison-Wesley Module in Anthro-
              pology 29.

HULAN, R., and S.S. LAWRENCE

4771   1970   A Guide to the Reading and Study of Historic Site Archae-
              ology. University of Missouri-Columbia, Museum of
              Anthropology, Publication 5.

KAPITAN, G.

4772   1966   A Bibliography of Underwater Archaeology. Argonaut,
              Chicago.

KARKLINS, K., and R. SPRAGUE

4773   1972   Glass Trade Beads in North America: An Annotated Bib-
              liography. Historical Archaeology 6:87-101.

KENDALL, A.

4774   1973   The Art of Pre-Columbian Mexico: An Annotated Bibliography
              of Works in English. Institute of Latin American Studies,
              University of Texas, Austin.

4775 1977 The Art and Archaeology of Pre-Columbian Middle America: An Annotated Bibliography of Works in English. G.K. Hall, Boston.

KENYON, W.A.

4776 1966 A Bibliography of Ontario Archaeology. Ontario Archaeology 9:35-62.

KNEZ, E.I., and C.-S. SWANSON

4777 1978 A Selected and Annotated Bibliography of Korean Anthropology. National Technical Information Service, U.S. Department of Commerce, Washington, D.C. (Contains entries on archaeology, archaeological map.)

LAIRD, W.D.

4778 1977 Hopi Bibliography: Comprehensive and Annotated. University of Arizona Press, Tucson.

LYMAN, R.L.

4779 1979 Archaeological Faunal Analysis: A Bibliography. Idaho State Museum, Occasional Paper 31. Pocatello.

MELODY, M.E.

4780 1977 The Apaches: A Critical Bibliography. Indiana University Press, Bloomington, for the Newberry Library.

MICHAEL, R.L.

4781 1969 Bibliography of Literature on Indiana Archaeology. B.K. Swartz, Jr., ed. Department of Sociology and Anthropology, Ball State University, Archaeological Reports 5. Muncie, Ind.

MOELLER, R.W., and J. REID, compilers

4782 1978 Archaeological Bibliography for Eastern North America. Eastern States Archaeological Federation and American Indian Archaeological Institute, Attleboro, Mass.

MONTANDON, R.

4783 1917- Bibliographie Générale des Travaux Paléoethnologiques et
     1938 Archéologiques (Époques Préhistorique, Protohistorique, Celtique, Romaine, et Gall-Romaine). Five volumes with supplement. Ernest Leroux, Paris.

MORATTO, M.J.

4784 1973 Theoretical and Applied Archaeology: A Bibliography. Type Ink Press, Berkeley.

MURDOCK, G.P., and T. O'LEARY

4785 1975 Ethnographic Bibliography of North America. 5 vols. Human Relations Area Files Press, New Haven.

NEUMAN, R.W.

4786   1962   An Archaeological Bibliography: The Central and Northern
              Plains Prior to 1950. Plains Anthropologist 7(15).

NEUMAN, R.W., and L.A. SIMMONS

4787   1969   A Bibliography Relative to Indians of the State of
              Louisiana. Louisiana Department of Conservation, Anthro-
              pological Study 4. Louisiana Geological Survey, Baton
              Rouge.

OKADA, A., H. OKADA, and C.S. CHARD

4788   1967   An Annotated Bibliography of the Archaeology of Hokkaido.
              Arctic Anthropology 4(1):1-163.

OLSEN, S.J.

4789   1961   A Basic Annotated Bibliography to Facilitate the Identifi-
              cation of Vertebrate Remains from Archaeological Sites.
              Bulletin, Texas Archeological Society 30:219-222.

PAVESIC, M.G., M.G. PLEW, and R. SPRAGUE

4790   1979   A Bibliography of Idaho Archaeology, 1889-1976. Northwest
              Anthropological Research Notes, Memoir 5. Moscow, Idaho.

PETSCHE, J.E.

4791   1968   Bibliography of Salvage Archeology in the United States.
              Smithsonian Institution, River Basin Surveys, Publications
              in Salvage Archeology 10.

PHILLIPS, J.M.

4792   1977   Archaeology of the Collective East: Greece, Asia Minor,
              Egypt, Lebanon, Mesopotamia, Syria, Palestine: An Annotated
              Bibliography. Gordon Press, New York.

PORTER, B., and R.L.B. MOSS

4793   1960   Topographical Bibliography of Ancient Egyptian Hiero-
              glyphic Texts, Reliefs and Paintings. 2nd ed. Clarendon
              Press, Oxford.

SALWEN, B., and G.M. GYRISCO

4794   1978   An Annotated Bibliography, Archeology of Black American
              Culture. 11593 Supplement 3(1):1-4. Heritage Conservation
              and Recreation Service, Washington, D.C.

SCHAEFFER, C.E., and L.J. ROLAND, eds.

4795   1941   A Partial Bibliography of the Archaeology of Pennsylvania
              and Adjacent States. Pennsylvania Historical Commission,
              Harrisburg.

SCURLOCK, D.

4796   1973   Spain in North America: Selected Sources on Spanish
              Colonial History, Archeology, Architecture and Art, and

Material Culture. Texas Historical Commission, Office of the State Archeologist, Special Report 8. Austin.

4797 1978 Selected Sources on the Spanish Borderlands, 1492–1850. Acoma Books, Ramona, Cal.

SHAW, T., and J. VANDERBURG

4798 1969 Bibliography of Nigerian Archaeology. Ibadan University Press, Ibadan, Nigeria.

SMITH, D.L.

4799 1973 Indians of the United States and Canada: A Bibliography. American Bibliographical Center, Clio Press, Santa Barbara, Cal.

SPRAGUE, R.

4800 1967 A Preliminary Bibliography of Washington Archaeology. Washington State University, Laboratory of Anthropology, Report of Investigations 43. Pullman.

STURTEVANT, W.C.

4801 1965 Preliminary Annotated Bibliography of Eastern North American Indian Agriculture. Bulletin, Southeastern Archaeological Conference 3:1–24.

SWARTZ, B.K., Jr.

4802 1967 A Bibliography of Klamath Basin Anthropology with Excerpts and Annotations. Rev. ed. Northwest Anthropological Research Notes 2(2).

TATUM, R.M.

4803 1946 Distribution and Bibliography of the Petroglyphs of the United States. American Antiquity 1?:122–125.

WELLMAN, K.F.

4804 1978 A Bibliography of North American Indian Rock Art. The Artifact 16(1). El Paso Archaeological Society, El Paso, Texas.

WORKMAN, K.W.

4805 1972 Alaskan Archaeology: A Bibliography. Alaska Division of Parks, History and Archaeology Series 1. Anchorage.

B. DICTIONARIES AND ATLASES

AVI-YONAH, M., ed.

4806 1976 Encyclopedia of Archaeological Excavations in the Holy Land. Prentice-Hall, Englewood Cliffs, N.J.

BRAY, W., and D. TRUMP

4807   1970   A Dictionary of Archaeology. Allen Lane, The Penguin
              Press, London.

BRÉZILLON, M.N.

4808   1969   Dictionnaire de la Préhistoire. Librairie Larousse, Paris.

CHARLES-PICARD, G., ed.

4809   1972   Larousse Encyclopedia of Archaeology. Putnam, New York.

COTTRELL, L.

4810   1971   The Concise Encyclopedia of Archaeology. 2nd ed. Haw-
              thorn, New York.

COZENS, W., and R.H. GOODSELL

4811   1967   Short Dictionary of Archaeology. Philosophical Library,
              New York.

DAVAMBEZ, P., ed.

4812   1967   The Praeger Encyclopedia of Ancient Greek Civilization.
              Praeger, New York.

DAVIES, D.

4813   1973   A Dictionary of Anthropology. Crane Russak, New York.

HAWKES, J.

4814   1974   Atlas of Ancient Archaeology. McGraw-Hill, New York.

PALMER, G., and N. LLOYD

4815   1968   Archaeology A-Z, a Simplified Guide and Dictionary.
              F. Warne and Co., Ltd.

STEWART, J.S.

4816   1960   An Archaeological Guide and Glossary. 2nd ed. Phoenix
              House, London.

VILLA, G.

4817   1968   Dictionnaire de l'Archéologie. Librairie Larousse, Paris
              (pp. 10-18).

WHITEHOUSE, D., and R. WHITEHOUSE

4818   1976   Archaeological Atlas of the World. Thames and Hudson,
              London.

INDEX